Women and Domestic Violence Law in India

This book critically examines domestic violence law in India. It focuses on women's experiences and perspectives as victims and litigants with regard to accessibility to law and justice. It also reflects on the manner in which the legal process reproduces gender hierarchies.

This volume:

- Analyzes the legal framework from a gender perspective to pinpoint the inherent stereotypes, prejudices and discriminatory practices that come into play while interpreting the law;
- Includes in-depth interviews and case studies, and explores critical themes such as marriage, rights, family, violence, property and the state;
- Presents alternatives beyond the domain of law, such as qualitative medical care and legal aid facilities, shelter homes, short-stay homes, childcare facilities, and economic and social security provisions to survivors and their children.

Drawing on extensive testimonies and ethnographic studies situated in a theoretical framework of law, this book will be of great interest to scholars and researchers of law, gender, human rights, women's studies, sociology and social anthropology and South Asian studies.

Shalu Nigam is an advocate, researcher and activist working at the intersection of gender, law, governance and human rights issues. She is currently practicing at the courts in Delhi and is associated with the People's Union for Civil Liberties, Delhi, India. She has previously worked with the Indian Social Institute, New Delhi, as well as the Centre for Women's Development Studies, New Delhi. She was awarded a Senior Fellowship by the Indian Council for Social Science Research, New Delhi. She is the co-author of *The Founding Mothers: 15 Women Architects of the Indian Constitution* and has published several other books. She has been a regular contributor to countercurrents.org and has published her essays in journals such as the *South Asia Journal*, *Social Action*, *International Journal of Gender and Women's Studies* and *Legal News and Views*.

Women and Domestic Violence Law in India

A Quest for Justice

Shalu Nigam

Routledge
Taylor & Francis Group
LONDON AND NEW YORK

First published 2020
by Routledge
2 Park Square, Milton Park, Abingdon, Oxon OX14 4RN

and by Routledge
605 Third Avenue, New York, NY 10017

First issued in paperback 2021

Routledge is an imprint of the Taylor & Francis Group, an informa business

British Library Cataloguing-in-Publication Data
A catalogue record for this book is available from the British Library

Library of Congress Cataloging-in-Publication Data
Names: Nigam, Shalu, author.
Title: Women and domestic violence law in India : a quest for justice / Shalu Nigam.
Identifiers: LCCN 2019030526 (print) | LCCN 2019030527 (ebook)
Subjects: LCSH: Women—Crimes against—India. | Marital violence—Law and legislation—India.
Classification: LCC KNS4049.5.W65 N54 2020 (print) | LCC KNS4049.5.W65 (ebook) | DDC 345.54/025553—dc23
LC record available at https://lccn.loc.gov/2019030526
LC ebook record available at https://lccn.loc.gov/2019030527

Typeset in Sabon
by Apex CoVantage, LLC

ISBN 13: 978-0-367-77771-5 (pbk)
ISBN 13: 978-1-138-36614-5 (hbk)

This work is dedicated to all women who are fighting their lonely battles, often with or without support or resources in any form be they legal, emotional, social, financial or otherwise. These women are the warriors who confronted violence and challenged patriarchy in the domain of law and society. I salute the courage which they exhibit amidst all the vulnerabilities that they face. This work celebrates the strong will and determination of these women who stood up against all odds in search of justice and fought a valiant struggle to assert their rights.

Contents

Acknowledgements

This book would not have been possible without the help and support of research participants who spent hours sharing their saga of intense pain, vulnerabilities, hopes, defiance and courage with me as a stranger and a researcher in the courts in Delhi. There is a mix of hurt, anguish, helplessness, betrayal and distress, as these are the narratives of sufferings at the hands of those who are expected to provide love and security. There is an element of repeated assaults, continuous horror and hurtful reactions, as well as action and inaction on the part of varied institutions. These are the experiences of rebellions, of raising voices against injustice and challenging the oppression. This exchange among two ordinary people is extraordinary. It is intensely agonizing, yet, at the same time, it is about bonding where the truth of intimate experiences has been shared despite variables of class, caste or age that transcends kinship or familial arrangements to alliances that are forged to build new hopes, new solidarities and possibly a new world. These enriching encounters signaled optimism in the midst of the network of a deeply embedded brutal patriarchy which reinforces the alienation, exclusion and subordination of women.

These discussions may have aided survivors to share their anxieties, fears and tears, which at times they could not share with their known relations. In opening up with a complete stranger, these women may have experienced a cathartic effect, and I, as a captivated listener, immersed myself in their journey to discover facets of human subjectivities. I established a deep connection with them while relating to their realities, and at times, I couldn't stop myself from shedding tears, expressing anger or being astonished at the capabilities of women when they negotiated for 'personal' and yet made deep political interventions. My professional skills facilitated me to draw linkages between the social and legal aspects of violence while filtering the emotions. These women are 'warriors', or 'sheros', I would prefer to call them because of their fearlessness to fight battles against all odds, at times with little or no support.

Working through the material gathered aided me to reflect about the institution of family and enabled me to delve into my own encounter with these complex units. I am deeply indebted to informants who shares their personal narratives, struggles and journeys towards justice in the patriarchal world order. This has helped me by providing a glimpse into the manner in which law operates within the given hierarchical social structure. My training in an interdisciplinary perspective enabled me to draw a multi-dimensional framework while connecting the dots and collating the richness of different elements together to weave the stories of survivors. The contradictory approach of being an outsider, a researcher and yet at the same time an insider, an advocate, enabled me to absorb the realities around violence while at the same time grasp the complexities of the legal mechanism.

While there are too many credits to document, I mention here a short list of those people and institutions that I cannot ignore. Over a decade, I barged unapologetically into all kinds of official and non-official spaces, including courtrooms, police stations, counseling centers and formal and non-formal organizations, meeting different people. Listening to varied opinions helped me understand the subject from its different dimensions. I would like to thank them for their generosity in responding to inexplicable enquiries. I acknowledge the support provided by colleagues in various organizations who facilitated this work by sharing not only umpteen cups of tea but also by providing their valuable insights and inputs. Interacting with activists has been a vital source of learning. I am grateful to the generosity of friends for their thoughtful views and wealth of professional knowledge.

At the Centre for Women's Development Studies (CWDS), New Delhi, I got the opportunity to be mentored by the eminent luminaries Prof. Lotika Sarkar and Prof. Veena Mazumdar. As a young researcher, it was a golden moment for me to learn and see the world from a different perspective. Interacting with faculty across disciplines has enabled me to grasp various facets through inspiring and enriching discussions on a range of issues. I express my gratitude to the institute for once again providing me the space to take up the study.

I am indebted to Indu Agnihotri for her insightful, thought-provoking discussions around the issue patiently while giving her precious time to this project. A series of discussions with her has helped me to provide a discerning understanding of the manner in which the women's movement has struggled over years and battled to protect hard-won rights. I am also grateful to Indrani Mazumdar for enriching discussions and offering her valuable insights and inputs.

I would specifically like to thank the Indian Council for Social Science Research, New Delhi, for awarding the fellowship while acknowledging my ability to take up this study and for providing institutional support and funding the research. My special thanks go to Dr. Sanchita Dutta, as well as Dr. S. M. Verma and the dynamic team at ICSSR.

I would also like to convey my heartfelt appreciation for the staff of the libraries of CWDS, the district courts and the High Court of Delhi for providing me space where I could immerse myself in the ocean of the numerous legal texts and judicial pronouncements to grasp the legal technicalities.

I also thank lawyers with whom I discussed not only technical aspects and operational nuances of law but also legal culture and the fine nuances of the working of the courts. This list of professionals is exhaustive, but I am specifically thankful to Fr. P. D. Mathew, Advocate Mr. N. D. Pancholi and Advocate Mr. Ravinder Kumar. I also express my gratitude to Prof. Shamsul Islam and Prof. Arun Kumar, who helped me to acquire insights into the issue in its varied dimensions.

I am deeply indebted to anonymous reviewers who have patiently reviewed this work and provided valuable suggestions and useful insights, encouraging me to see the pitfalls and imagine different ways to look at the available material. I express my gratitude to Taylor & Francis for agreeing to publish this work. More specifically, I am thankful to Mr. Akash Chakraborty and Ms. Brinda Sen for their patience and time while going through the multitude of pages several times and providing their insightful inputs, which helped me to put this material in the form it is presented here.

'The personal is political' – I experienced this truth through analyzing the situations and circumstances in my own life. I owe the existence of this book to my parents and my daughter, who supported me and handled my eccentricity and let me be me. I missed the support provided to me by my late father, who nurtured his daughters in an environment of freedom despite all limitations. I am deeply obliged to my mother with whom I have had never-ending arguments about conflicting traditions, ideologies and kinship norms; nevertheless, she remained my continuous supporter. Also, this research would not have been possible without the unconditional love and sacrifices made by my adorable daughter, Jigyasa. With her, I got the opportunity to grow up once again and could learn and re-learn about life in numerous possible ways. At times, this loving togetherness acted to heal pains and to deal with uncertainties and to re-live and re-imagine a meaningful life. I am enlightened by her courageous, positive spirit, which inspires me as a delightful guide, a wise ally and a prudent companion.

Author's note

The names of women I met have been changed to protect the identity of the victims and survivors. The chapters written are based on first-hand information provided by the survivors. The author has conducted an extensive research study in Delhi. Other geographical territories have not been covered due to monetary limitations and time constraints. The material gathered consists of interview notes, referral to legal documents including First Information Reports, court records, multiple case records, judgements, paper clippings, research articles, books and other material available on the subject.

Abbreviations

ADR	Alternative Dispute Resolution
AIDS	Acquired Immune Deficiency Syndrome
AIR	All India Reporter
CAW	Crime Against Women's Cells
CEDAW	Convention on Elimination of Discrimination Against Women
CPC	Civil Procedure Code of India
CrPC	Criminal Procedure Code
DCW	Delhi Commission for Women
DIR	Domestic Incident Report
DV	Domestic Violence
DVCM	Dahej Virodhi Chetna Manch
DWCD	Department of Women and Child Development
FIR	First Information Report
GOI	Government of India
HC	High Court
HIV	Human Immunodeficiency Virus
HMA	Hindu Marriage Act
HAMA	Hindu Adoption and Maintenance Act
HUF	Hindu Undivided Family
ICRW	International Center for Research on Women
IO	Investigation Officer
IPC	Indian Penal Code
IPV	Intimate Partner Violence
JSC	Joint Select Committee
LC	Lawyers' Collective
MP	Member of Parliament
MHRD	Ministry of Human Resource Development
MWCD	Ministry of Women and Child Development
NCRB	National Crime Record Bureau
NCW	National Commission of Women
NDA	National Democratic Alliance
NFHS	National Family Health Survey
OCD	Obsessive-Compulsive Disorders

PIL	Public Interest Litigation
PO	Protection Officer
PS	Police Station
PTSD	Post-traumatic Stress Disorder
PWDVA	Protection of Women Against Domestic Violence Act, 2005
SC	Supreme Court
SCC	Supreme Court Cases
SP	Service Provider
STD	Sexually Transmitted Diseases
STI	Sexually Transmitted Infections
UDHR	Universal Declaration of Human Rights
UN	United Nations
UNICEF	United Nations Children's Fund
UPA	United Progressive Alliance
VAW	Violence Against Women
WHO	World Health Organization

Introduction

Family holds a significant place in Indian society and is being romanticized in literature, movies, television serials and folklore by religion, the market and the media. However, glorification of the family undermines the violence women face every day. Statistics show that one in every three women face domestic abuse. The NCRB report shows that in 2016, 7,621 cases were registered for dowry deaths. This book investigates the issue of domestic violence and the manner in which it is being dealt by the law and society.

Based on my readings, while building my arguments, I borrowed extensively from multiple fields of studies, such as medical sciences, psychology, law, human rights, economics, history, sociology, anthropology, social work and gender studies, as well as the narratives of the women complainants whom I met in the courts in Delhi. The task is significant yet arduous, and I may have faltered at many places. I humbly accept the responsibility for this.

The 1980s witnessed a process of legal reforms. These stemmed from the contradictions in the law and its failure to remedy a situation of persistent legal and social inequality within the existing patriarchal structures that resulted in the abuse of women within the confines of the home. In order to stop the escalating incidences of dowry deaths, the women's movement demanded stringent legal actions. After much delay and persistence, the state responded, and the Criminal Law Amendment Act 1983 added Section 304B, IPC that deals with the death of a woman within seven years of marriage in suspicious circumstances, while Section 498A criminalized cruelty within a marriage. Later, lawyer-free family courts were created in 1984 with a view to provide a single-window system to cater to the concerns affecting families.

However, earlier while conducting field research in 2002 to 2005 and interacting with women facing domestic violence who came to seek justice within courts, I observed a huge gap between on-the-ground reality and the theoretical understanding among different actors – those who frame the law, those who implement it and those who are using it.[1] As survivors, women approached the courts with the hope of seeking justice. However, courts frequently ended up offering them compulsory counseling, which entails undesired results and narrow options. Laws could neither address the immediate needs of victims nor could offer practical remedies in terms of medical aid, short-stay homes, creche facilities, psychological support, shelter homes or economic or material assistance to the women which they need the most. No other alternative or support is being offered by the state beyond the network of family. Those women who persist in staying away from the violent relationship are compelled to either negotiate their survival with their natal families or to remarry and face the risk of re-entering another violent relationship. For those who wish to stay away from the familial network, they are left on their own and are forced to sink deep into poverty in cases where they could not manage to survive on their own.

While I was conducting the research then, concerns had already been raised about bringing a new civil law on domestic violence. It was a period of great excitement. Drafts of the proposed law were being discussed, and many activists and organizations zealously discussed its provisions. There was much resentment too. The Malimath Committee Report,[2] the Shinghal's Committee report[3] and others suggested that the provisions of Section 498A be diluted because of their potential to be misused by women. There also emerged a deep anguish when the then-NDA government induced changes that were deemed anti-women in the bill in March 2002. Colossal efforts were made to fervently prevent such dilution and to ensure that women-friendly provisions could be retained. Finally, the Protection of Women Against Domestic Violence Act (PWDVA) was enacted in 2005, which offered civil remedies to the victims of domestic violence.

PWDVA upheld the rights of women to reside in a shared household, with custody of children, maintenance and compensation, among others. It defines the term domestic violence comprehensively and broadens the scope to cover varied 'domestic relationships'. Under this law, civil remedies could be sought in criminal courts and the respondent could be penalized for the breach of orders. An aggrieved woman may approach the police station, Protection Officer, Service Provider or the court directly to obtain relief and may file a complaint against the accused under Section 498A, IPC.

Despite using a multifaceted legal matrix to address the situation of domestic abuse, currently the magnitude of violence is increasing. This implies that there are limitations. This work begins by framing the concept of violence within conjugality and questions the manner in which this is dealt under the given framework. Drawing from ethnographic research, this book collates the experiences of litigants who faced domestic abuse and approached the courts with the expectation that they receive justice. This work also investigates the working of law and examines difficulties women face during litigation.

Though much has been done in this field from different dimensions, a gap still exists because most of the research is based on the top-down approach. Also, though a substantial body of feminist critique is available that looks at the gendered nature and has illuminated the inadequacies in the laws, there has not been much focus on the voices of survivors. This book emphasizes a bubble-up approach and looks at the contextual definition of domestic violence as interpreted within the legal realm and its ability to provide justice. It looks into the manner in which rights provided under the law are being interpreted and implemented at the ground level. It analyzes case law from a gender perspective to highlight the manner in which the courts have been reinforcing inherent stereotypes, prejudices and discriminatory practices against women while interpreting the law.

I conducted informal interviews with the survivors of violence within the court premises in Delhi in the period between 2013 and 2015 and later translated and analyzed these conversations. In addition to the views of lawyers, those of Protection Officers, police officials, Service Providers and women's organizations have been obtained in order to get a comprehensive picture. One of the limitations of this work is that it is based in the geographical territory of Delhi and therefore is partial. It therefore suggests that studies could be replicated across the country that may consider views of a range of survivors to provide a more complete picture.

In this book, I argue that gaps exist while implementing this law, because the state could not consider the comprehensive situation and the law could provide only a temporary relief to the victims until the so-called 'matrimonial dispute' is resolved under the provisions relating to personal laws. In the process, the law cannot fix the accountability of violent men or penalize them for their criminal act. This book concludes that the lofty goals in law remain unaccompanied by the will or the obligation of the state to provide for material, economic, political or social interventions. Domestic violence law, though, is supposed to address the rights of women within a marriage, yet in its implementation, it could not imagine the possibilities of women's existence outside the family. In no manner could the law challenge the unequal marital relationship or the structural inequalities that exist to make women's situation vulnerable within the marriage.

I contend that irony lies in the fact that when women approach the court to seek relief from violence, these institutions compulsorily counsel survivors to go back to the very same violent homes, with no assurance of safety or security. The state utilizes this law to push for 'reconciliation', 'compromise', 'adjustment' and 'settlement' while mixing up women's rights to bargain for material and economic support, rather than actually delivering rights-based justice to the complainants. What is prioritized by the state is the goal to 'preserve the family', even if this is done at the cost of life and limb of women. Pushing women back into a violent situation is considered an 'optimal' solution for redressing their woes, without realizing that women cross the boundaries of the homes only in extreme situations and that the purpose of the law is not to 'break' or to 'save' the family, but to deter violence and to provide relief to the complainants. A 'law-centric' as well as 'family-centric' approach is prioritized over a 'women-centric' or 'survivors-centric' approach by the state.

Frequently, what is ignored is the fact that women are not helpless victims of their circumstances. Rather, they are challenging and defying the patriarchy and in the process are negotiating their rights with the family, the state and the society. Their journey is for survival with dignity. As change makers, they are contesting their claims against the regressive patriarchal social norms. Provided with material and economic support, they may act as trendsetters to reform the age-old patriarchal structure.

Also, what is overlooked by the state is that women's vulnerable situation in a marriage cannot be transformed without questioning and critiquing the institution of conjugality per se. When discourse on the issues relating to the 'Triple Talaq' is being highlighted and the Supreme Court has pronounced significant decisions relating to the applicability of Section 377 IPC, a large number of women were facing abuse within their homes are being neglected. Ironically, when they knock on the doors of the court to access justice, they are frequently turned away as 'liars, gold diggers or disgruntled women' who are falsely accusing their husbands and in-laws.

Contradictions lie in the fact that, on one hand, the concept of marriage and family is glorified, whereas on the other, the rights of women within the domain of conjugality are not appreciated. The discrepancies between the constitutional rights and the limitations within the personal laws become more glaring when a married woman asserts her right to lead a violence-free life within her family. A married woman is not seen as an independent entity apart from her existence as a wife, a daughter-in-law or a mother. Women who are approaching the courts with complaints of domestic violence are not seen as neutral citizens who are claiming their rights. Rather, a patriarchal lens is used to filter their complaints. The state hesitates to intervene within the sacred domain of families, whereas these women assert that the 'personal is political' and the state should protect their rights.

Further, the rights of women in terms of matrimonial property are still not available. Amendments made to the Hindu Succession Act in 2005 provide relief to women as daughters; however, women as wives still have no right to the matrimonial property, in case they separate from their husbands or dare to approach the court the obtain a divorce against violent husbands. Personal law provisions offer maintenance, but the focus is not on protecting the right to property of the married women. The concept of *streedhan*, or maintenance, as recognized under the law does not consider women's paid and unpaid contributions to the household.

Added to this is the backlash that emerged lately wherein the state and other stakeholders wrongly assumed that this law is being misused by women. Apathy by those who implement the law and the lackadaisical approach of policymakers created further problems where gender-sensitive laws gained negative publicity over the period when not only vocal male groups but also the police, judiciary and lawyers began to assert that the law was being abused. In fact, today, the situation is that the law against domestic violence is looked upon as a weapon misused by the educated and elite women to harass their husbands. The law created to stop violence is viewed as an instrument to 'break marriages' and 'destroy families'. This could not have been envisaged by those who demanded legal reforms.[4] Yet, currently, the situation is that neither the civil nor the criminal law can deter or reduce violence.

This book examines the fault lines between the legislative reforms and the everyday lives of survivors of violence, besides understanding their vulnerabilities and agency in the face of the prevailing patriarchal socio-legal discourse. Through persuasive ethnographic vignettes, as well as looking at the theoretical framework of law relating to marriage, rights, family, violence, property and the state, and through a practical re-examination, this research reflects on the manner in which the legal reform process reproduces gender hierarchies in an intensely patriarchal society.

This book is divided into seven chapters. Chapter 1 introduces the concept of domestic violence and its impact on the health and life of women, the prevalence and extent of the domestic violence and human rights, as well as the legal framework being put in place to deal with this issue. Chapter 2 focuses on the making of the law relating to domestic violence, its provisions and the gaps. It also examines the developments that preceded the enactment of the law and highlights the need the present study, including its rationale and objective.

Chapter 3 weaves the narratives of women who attempt to seek justice in the domain of law. While providing background as to who these women are who are challenging social norms and defying patriarchy, it looks at the forms of violence women have faced. Through qualitative analysis, this chapter examines the problems that women confront once they file a complaint and suggests that survivors are not passive sufferers but are active agents who take steps to transform their lives. Such litigants require a space and support that may enable them to translate their right to lead a violence-free, dignified life into a reality and not a handout from the law makers or policy framers.

Chapter 4 examines the operation of the law through the experiences of women litigants. It explores the manner in which the courts deal with cases, the problems women face and the gaps in the legal framework. It observes that while the law tries to bring order in the family, the law itself has been mediated by and enmeshed in a complex cultural framework of saving families rather than protecting the rights and dignity of women within the families.

Chapter 5 analyzes the economic aspects of conjugality. While examining several case studies, it argues that when considering the changing economic scenario, a social protection mechanism is required in addition to a comprehensive legal framework, which may also include women's right to property in their matrimonial relationships. It argues that the solutions lie within the legal domain as well as in socio-political realm beyond the law to provide a comprehensive socio-economic apparatus to address the situation of domestic violence, which may include providing basic services such as shelter homes, short stay homes, medical aid, legal aid, support for children in domestic violence situations, priority in employment and similar such measures to include *rozi-roti aur maakan* (employment and housing) with *sammaan* or dignity to survivors and victims of domestic violence.

Chapter 6 scrutinizes the operation of law and highlights that though domestic violence was criminalized in India in 1983, the legal system continues to treat wife beating as an offense different from other cases of assault and battery. Also, the authorities intervene only sporadically in cases of marital violence. Men who beat their wives are offered formal and informal immunities, while the courts uphold the concept of 'family harmony' and endorse the prerogative of the husband to 'chastise' his wife. The legal system treats the family as a private space where a public law could not be applied. It concludes that the law uses gendered notions of citizenship while adjudicating the cases of violence against women.

Chapter 7 is the concluding chapter and points out the problems and prospects of the domestic violence law. It observes that though the law provides a platform for women to raise their concerns, yet there is a dire need to strengthen this law. Constitutional provisions relating to a life with dignity, equality and social justice need to be accorded to women facing violence within homes while lifting the veils of family privacy. As per the principles of restorative and distributive justice, the system may be made effective and sensitive to the concerns of women while fixing the accountability of violent men. It suggests that there is a need to explore solutions beyond the domain of law, such as qualitative medical care and legal aid facilities, shelter homes, short-stay homes, childcare facilities and economic and social security provisions to the victims and survivors of domestic violence in order to ensure a life with dignity. It is necessary that the backlash against this law be countered, and it is recommended that the challenges that exist at a broader level, such as inequalities, discrimination and the hierarchical power imbalance within the institution of marriage and society, may be re-examined. A patriarchal approach and mind-set must be dealt with.

Notes

1 Nigam Shalu (2005) *Understanding Justice Delivery System from the Perspective of Women Litigants as Victims of Domestic Violence*, Occasional Paper No. 35, CWDS, New Delhi
2 Government of India (2003) *Report of the Committee on Reforms of Criminal Justice System, Ministry of Home Affairs*, This Report Is Referred as Malimath Committee Report
3 Shinghal NK (undated) *Study Report on Crime Against Women – Role of Section 498-A IPC in the State of Delhi and Haryana, Sponsored by Bureau of Police Research and Development*, Ministry of Home Affairs, GOI, New Delhi
4 Nigam S (2017) *Is Domestic Violence A Lesser Crime? Countering the Backlash Against Section 498A, IPC*, Occasional Paper No. 61, CWDS, New Delhi

1 Conceptualizing domestic violence

> *"In this silent war (domestic violence and dowry violence) waged by society against women more lives have been lost than in any war on the frontiers of independent India".*[1]

"NIA ends Kerala probe, says there's love but no *jihad*", reads one of the news items published in the *Hindustan Times* on 18 October 2018. In this famous case, a young woman, Hadiya (alias Akhila Asokan), converted to Islam and got married to Shafin Jahan. This marriage was annulled by the Kerala High Court on the basis of a petition filed by Hadiya's father. At the insistence of the Supreme Court, the National Investigation Agency (NIA) was assigned the task of determining if inter-faith marriages are taking place because of a larger political conspiracy where Hindu women are coerced into converting and marrying Muslim men through a false expression of love. The NIA examined 11 out of the list of 89 cases of the so-called 'love-jihad' cases where parents have complained that their children have been forcefully converted. The investigation revealed that in 4 of 11 cases, Hindu men have embraced Islam, and in the rest Hindu women married Muslim men of their own will. The Supreme Court later set aside the order of the High Court in Hadiya's matter.[2]

This incident shows the manner in which the imaginary concept of 'love jihad' has been evoked by the state as well as Hindu fundamentalists.[3] A patriarchal propaganda similar to this was evoked in 1920, 2009[4] and 2014 in Uttar Pradesh, where an aggressive systematic campaign was planned by right-wing organizations to orchestrate inflammatory appeals while polarizing social boundaries around the bodies of women.[5] Hindu women have been projected as innocent victims at the hands of inscrutable Muslims while ignoring the concept of agency or choice, including women's legitimate right to love someone. Love between two people hailing from different religious communities has been declared 'anti-national' and against the idea of Hindu *rashtra*. In Hadiya's case, the paternalist state, including the courts as well as the NIA, zealously invaded the personal space of two individuals while interfering and intruding in the 'private', legally valid relationship between two consenting adults.[6]

In contradiction to Hadiya's matter,[7] Seema,[8] a 26-year-old from Sultanpuri, Delhi, whom I met in the Karkardooma Court in July 2014, complained:

> My drunkard husband used to beat me black and blue regularly and demanded one lakh rupees from my parents. He broke my legs and my jaw got fractured. He tried to burn me alive. And now he has started living with another woman. I ran around for several months to get the case registered but police has not kept him even for one day in jail. The court has ordered for maintenance, but for past 4 years, he has not given anything. My six-year-old child is suffering from crippling disease since her birth. My father has been paying for her treatment but he expired three months back. My brother is refusing to take care of us. I don't know now what to do?[9]
>
> (2014)

Seema's case shows that the state agencies have failed to protect the rights of a battered wife and her child. These two cases, that of Hadiya and Seema, show the manner in which the state selectively chooses to intervene in 'family-related' 'private' issues. Both matters relate to the dignity of women, yet the state made an extensive intervention in Hadiya's case but not in Seema's case, even when the latter made a request as per the existing legal provisions. The state assumed that Hadiya's case has linkages to a grand conspiracy. However, in Seema's case, the despicable violence committed by her husband, although it negates her rights and dignity, is not seen with the lens of suspicion; perhaps, from the state's perspective, it does not have larger implications. This case reflects the fact that battered women as wives or citizens do not receive adequate protection by the state when they complain against their abusive husbands. Why is the state reluctant to intervene in domestic abuse matters? The state's role is as a neutral arbiter remains questionable; because, without looking at the larger repercussions in Seema's case, it acted arbitrarily in addressing her claim.

There are many women in similar circumstances to that of Seema who are facing violence within the home and also running from pillars to post to seek justice. In fact, in 2016, under Section 498A IPC,[10] 1,10,378 cases have been reported, or almost 12 crimes have been registered per hour.[11] Also, in the same year, 7,621 cases were registered under Section 304B IPC, the law pertaining to dowry deaths. The conviction rate is 9.5 percent in cases pertaining to Section 498A and 39.1 percent in cases of dowry deaths. Thus, the lived experiences of women and the available data indicate that neither the courts nor any investigation agency is keen to provide justice to women in domestic violence cases despite the existence of favorable laws. Perhaps women's rights in situations of domestic abuse are least prioritized by the state.

As I worked on the drafts of this book, an interesting phenomenon took place in the larger socio-political context. On the one hand, the number of incidents relating to crimes against women is rising and brutal incidents of violence are being reported in Kathua, Unnao, Mandsaur and other places;[12] at the same time, the Supreme Court has pronounced significant decisions relating to 'Triple Talaq',[13] decriminalizing homosexuality[14] and declaring Section 497 IPC relating to adultery as violating constitutional provisions.[15] The court, while pronouncing the latter two decisions, has extensively focused on the concept of individual autonomy and the sexual independence of consenting adults. Meanwhile, the verdict pronounced in the *Sabrimala* case upheld that devotion cannot be subjected to discrimination,[16] though the entry of women in the age group of 10 to 50 years is being violently resisted by several right-wing protestors.[17] During the same period, the debate pertaining to the MeToo movement gained momentum and a union minister was forced to resign when several journalists accused him of sexual harassment,[18] and a dismissed employee filed an affidavit against the chief justice of India, alleging harassment.[19] The situation therefore is tempestuous. On the one hand, the courts in several cases are liberally interpreting the rights framework, and on the other hand, there are forces which are insisting conservative traditions be preserved. Yet, on another extreme, several women are courageously resisting the power structures by sharing their experiences of workplace harassment while naming and shaming the perpetrators, and others are trying to enter the temple – despite resistance – asserting their lawful claims.

Among all these incongruities and contradictions, there are abused women who are fighting their painful battles as wives and citizens against their violent husbands. These women undergo tough struggles while resisting violence and challenging their abusive partners within the social domain before they reach the courts. Their journey to justice is not easy.[20] The courts, which are liberally interpreting rights in all other cases, are turning litigating wives away as 'liars' or 'gold diggers' who are 'falsely accusing their husbands and in-laws'. For instance, the Supreme Court in *Arnesh Kumar vs State of Bihar*[21] in 2014 issued guidelines relating to arrests in cases pertaining to Section 498A on the presumption that the law is being misused by 'disgruntled women'. On 27 July 2017, the two-judges bench of the apex court in *Rajesh Kumar vs State of UP*,[22] while noting the misuse of Section 498A, recommended setting up family welfare committees comprised of paralegal volunteers, retired persons and wives of officers, among others, who could scrutinize complaints made under this law, after which arrests could be made. Later, after a protest by women's organizations, these directions were modified by a three-judge bench on 14 September 2018, in *Social Action Forum for Manav Adhikar vs Union of India*[23] where it ordered the formation of committees be done away with while retaining the provision relating to arrest and bail for the accused persons. Thus, the courts upheld the prerogative of violent husbands to chastise their wives and refused to apply the common law provisions in cases tried under 498A.

Even earlier, in a spate of decisions, the courts have declined to apply the common law provisions while adjudicating the claims of married women. For example, the Delhi High Court in *Harvinder Kaur vs Harmander Singh Choudhary*[24] held that the

> [i]ntroduction of constitutional law in the home is most inappropriate. It is like introducing a bull in a china shop. It will prove to be a ruthless destroyer of the marriage institution and all that it stands for. In the privacy of the home and the married life neither Article 21 nor Article 14 have any place. In a sensitive sphere, which is at once most intimate and delicate the introduction of the cold principles of constitutional law will have the effect of weakening the marriage bond.

This view was reaffirmed in several other decisions pronounced by the Supreme Court.[25] The sanctity attached to marriage is linked to the unwillingness to intrude therein.

Such a situation gives rise to several questions. Why are the laws made to protect the rights of women within marriage not facilitating them to seek remedies? Are the existing laws against domestic abuse sufficient enough to eradicate or prevent this crime and to provide justice to women facing violence? Is wife battering considered a serious issue by the state? Are the courts holding men accountable under the law for assaulting their wives? Why is the state reluctant to intervene in matters relating to wife abuse or is apathetic to the concerns of litigating wives? When the courts are liberally interpreting other rights, why are battered wives seen with suspicion? Why is the state, as a neutral arbiter, not addressing the claims of wives as citizens in a fair manner? Are these wives misusing the law or is it underutilized? Why are the procedures of law relating to wife beating being bent, twisted and turned to cater to the demands of the patriarchy?

The women's movement in India has laid heavy emphasis on the law to deal with the concern of domestic abuse. Both civil and criminal remedies pertaining to domestic violence have been obtained after a long struggle. The number of cases reported under these laws are increasing over the years, while at the same time, the conviction rate remains low. This implies that remedies provided under the law are not adequate or enough of a deterrent to prevent the occurrence of crime, or contradictions exist in the manner in which these laws are applied. This book examines the manner in which the law is framed to support victims of domestic abuse and is being implemented. It is about gendered notions of violence, the legacy of reforms around the issue of wife abuse and women's experiences and perspectives as survivors of violence and as users of the legal platform to access justice. It seeks to inspect the manner in which the police, courts and other stakeholders, including those appointed under the PWDVA such as Protection

Officers and Service Providers, are protecting the rights of women within the private familial sphere. The book also analyzes the case law to examine the manner in which the courts have been protecting the rights of women while holding violent husbands accountable.

Examining the nuances of domestic violence

"Husband, in-laws try to cremate woman alive for 'being childless' ",[26] reads a newspaper clipping in January 2019. Another reads, "Gurugram: Man killed wife for refusing sex, shoved her corpse in bed box, arrested"[27] (February 2019). Others read "Ex-Army doctor held for chopping wife's body into 300 pieces and saving them in iron box"[28] (June 2013), "Woman burnt alive for dowry"[29] (October 2018), "Woman burnt alive by husband and in-laws in Bengal due to her 'dark complexion' "[30] (May 2018), "Delhi Engineer, his brother chopped wife's body in 7 pieces, says cops"[31] (June 2018). Similar stories appear routinely in newspapers, yet no one pays attention. Perhaps society has become immune to the screams of women who are brutally being tortured, murdered or abused day in and day out within homes.

The violence women face in homes frequently remains hidden behind the veils of family privacy and is shielded in secrecy. Females within the household are aborted;[32] killed as infants; discriminated against in terms of food, education, health and other resources; neglected; forcefully married off at an early age; denied sexual and reproductive autonomy; denied choices to select one's partner or to decide when to marry; coerced to uphold patriarchal traditions;[33] tortured; raped; forced to undergo abortions; sold; trafficked; killed for honor; hunted as witches; thrown out of the house; denied property rights; burned alive; murdered; and abused in numerous ways.[34] Violence may also involve economic subordination, coercion, intimidation, isolation and other control tactics. However, not all kinds of brutalities are acknowledged, recognized or highlighted. Much of these varied forms of violence remain outside the purview of law.

In fact, violence against women within the confines of the home is an age-old, ubiquitous phenomenon, where within the institution of the family, a male adult may abuse his power to control a woman by instilling fear through physical or sexual assault; psychological, mental or emotional abuse; or financial violence. And this is done in the guise of love and discipline. The frequency of violence could be episodic, occasional or continuous, from which there is no escape. It is pervasive and exists beyond territorial, socio-economic, class, caste, religious or ethnic boundaries. Such behavior has an adverse impact on the health of women and the well-being of children and entails an enormous cost to communities.[35]

Due to its private, intimate nature, domestic violence remains mostly unaccounted for. Its prevalence can only be estimated.[36] A report released by the UN in 2015 pointed out that around one-third of women worldwide have experienced physical and/or sexual violence by an intimate partner at some point in their lives.[37] In South Asia, the regional prevalence of partner violence with increased levels of physical and sexual abuse are highest in India, and this does not occur once, but multiple times.[38]

Domestic abuse, in legal and social parlance, is frequently recognized as abuse of a married woman by her husband or in-laws, but in fact, this is an embedded, hidden form of violence which is affecting a large number of women, yet is least understood. It is invisible because it remains buried behind the complex, stratified and complicated layers of the intricate relationship "between a husband and a wife with the overtones of romanticism, sexuality and patriarchy".[39] Elsewhere, domestic violence is also known as intimate partner violence, inter-couple violence, wife battering or 'cross-bedroom terrorism' as compared to cross-border terrorism.[40] Many of these terms focus on the dyadic relationship between the victim and perpetrator, yet these highlight the significant aspect of 'violence' rather than erasing the seriousness of the situation by labelling it as a 'dispute', 'quarrel' or 'discord'.

However, within the North Indian context, it is ironic that though the term 'domestic violence' has specific connotations as it takes place within an explicit patriarchal, socio-cultural context, the term 'dispute' is often used to dissipate the intensity of the situation. Frequently, the violence within a marriage is referred as '*miya-biwi ke jhagde*' (duel between a husband and a wife) or *parivarik kalah* (family disputes). The term '*mar-peet*' (physical battering) is seldom used. The use of such vocabulary does neither convey the deeper connotations of abuse nor focus on multiple dimensions such as emotional, mental, sexual or economic violence. Often, the gravity of the situation is undermined while treating it as the dispute between two parties when they are not on equal footing and where no outsider is allowed to intervene. The term '*Gharelu Hinsa*'[41] used in legal terminology is a phrase that is not commonly deployed in local usage, even though it has deep connotations.

Different dimensions of domestic violence

Domestic violence is basically centered on three key elements: violence, domesticity and structural inequality, where domesticity contextualizes both spatial location and the relationship between the abused and the victim, and structural inequalities work through the paradigm of power and control.[42] However, in a patriarchal society, what I construe is that domestic violence is distinguished from all other forms of violence against women because of 'seven dimensions of powerlessness in the relationship'. Briefly these are:

First, domestic violence takes place within the confines of 'home', a place which assumingly provides safety, security, comfort and escape from the outside world;

Second, the perpetrator of the violence is the man, who assumingly is considered as the 'protector and the provider' in the general parlance;
Third, an inegalitarian relationship exists between the perpetrator and the victim because of the emotional, material and economic dependence of a woman on her abuser;
Fourth, the relationship in which violence takes place is not dyadic – other family members also get involved;
Fifth, the volatility of the situation is enhanced because the relationship is adorned with notions of intimacy, sexuality and romanticism, so any hurt in the 'realm of emotions' has a much more drastic impact than may be seen in a situation of custodial violence, where power and authority augment the gravity of the abuse;
Sixth, patrilineal and patrilocal arrangements exist in North India, where a woman is transferred spatially from her parental home to her matrimonial house upon marriage, and this adds to her disadvantage because the shift to a new location enhances her vulnerability while isolating her and putting her in the lowest position within the family hierarchy in her marital household; and
Seventh, the culture of patriarchy and culture of violence co-exist and operate in a manner to deny women their rightful entitlements while upholding the male prerogative to control and chastise women.[43] Contextualizing violence within these 'dimensions of powerlessness', I see domestic violence as a '*daman chakra*' implying a 'spiral of oppression'[44] or oppression intensified due to situation of powerlessness.

Johnson[45] rightly suggested that domestic violence is embedded in a general pattern of controlling behavior by the abuser that is rooted in patriarchal traditions and may take extreme forms.[46] Other theorists have described the continuous pattern of power and control behavior as depicted by the Power and Wheel theory,[47] which includes the use of non-violent control techniques such as emotional abuse, isolation, using children, using male privilege, economic abuse, threat, blaming and other tactics, besides the extreme depiction of violent behavior. Thus, wife battering has broader connotations beyond the physical, mental or emotional violence to the denial of basic human rights.

Theorizing domestic violence

In the familial domain, a man has long been considered a 'king of his castle' or the master of the household, where he enjoys specific privileges. He is adorned with the right to discipline women and children and could subject his wife to corporal punishment, or 'chastisement'.[48] He is seen as the preserver of the sanctity of a household, irrespective of whether he himself is orderly or not or whether he is a tyrant, ruthless or despicable. Also, in the given context, a poor man belonging to a marginalized community may be oppressed by privileged men, yet back in his home, this subjugated man is entitled to rule. In the context of conjugality, a man is adorned with power and authority to control his wife, whereas for a woman, love implies sacrifice and selfless devotion. The concept of marriage, therefore, is inegalitarian. Like chattel, a wife 'belongs' to her husband, and any act of oppression is considered a private matter. Centuries ago, marriage was conceptualized as an instrument to enslave women, and it continues to do so today. Frequently, restrictions are placed on married women. They are not allowed to manage property or enter into contracts. This makes them economically, emotionally and legally dependent on their husbands. John Stuart Mill, in 1869 in his thesis on the *Subjection of Women*,[49] while questioning women's subordinate status, argued that "man as a master not only wants a woman's labor but also her sentiments so he conspires to exploit her to accomplish this desire for a submissive docile slave over whom he could have an absolute control". Therefore, for ages, men have mistreated, abused and battered their wives, yet the legal system began responding only towards the end of the twentieth century. Slavery in general has been abolished, yet the slavery of women within marriage has not been touched upon. Rather, marriage is overvalued and protected by the law. Laws are coded to protect a man from oppression by another man, but little enthusiasm is shown to protect a woman being abused within home.

Blackstone[50] theorized that through marriage, the existence of a woman is suspended, incorporated and consolidated into that of her husband. Through this doctrine of marital unity, a wife's legal identity is merged into her husband's upon marriage, as both become one person in the law. Based on this Victorian notion of marriage, then, Blackstone propounded the theory of the 'rule of the thumb' whereby it is assumed that a man may use a stick of the size of the thickness of the thumb to moderately discipline his wife. In the United States, during the nineteenth century, "the authorities denied that a husband has a right to beat his wife yet they intervened only intermittently in the cases of marital violence in order to protect the privacy of the family and to promote 'domestic harmony' ".[51] Domestic abuse is not recognized as a 'problem which requires any intervention', based on the assumption that a family is a private institution. It was when the feminist movement in the West challenged the concept of family privacy that shielded abuse that reforms were designed to protect women from marital violence.

Today, the world over, domestic violence is being recognized as a major social, legal and health issue which involves considerable adverse impact and high costs. Wife battering has been studied abroad in its multi-dimensional perspective. Different theories have been propounded to understand the cause and effect of such abuse.[52] Biological theories focus on the aggressive behavior of the perpetrator and highlight genetic or congenital reasons. Scholars have examined neurological reasons, brain infections, alcohol use and other aspects besides psychological factors such as personality disorders, social learning,[53] psychopathological reasons, low self-esteem, impulse control, attitudes regarding the acceptability of violence and the role of emotional attachment within the relationship, as reasons for inflicting violence. However, emphasis on the biological or psychological factors ascertain that the problem lies with an individual. These theories could not visualize the issue of domestic abuse in a larger context of power relationships or structural inequalities. Sociological theories[54] see violence as a reaction to stress, frustrations and blocked goals. Lower income, lack of job opportunities or unfavorable conditions are ascribed as reasons for violence. However, what is ignored in this conceptualization is that educated or elite men do commit abuse. In fact, a study by the WHO[55] confirmed that domestic violence exists across socio-economic, cultural and ethnic boundaries.

Walker[56] argued that violence is a learned behavior which is reinforced and repeated because it produces desirable consequences. Other scholars identify the role of sex stereotyping[57] to suggest that males identify themselves as those occupying the dominant position and thus are licensed to display aggression, while women understand themselves primarily through their relations with their abusers, which make them dependent, non-individualistic and accepting of violence. The 'resource' and the 'exchange' theory[58] argues that power plays a critical role in violence.[59] Heise[60] proposed a broad ecological framework suggesting that violence arises from the interplay of personal, situational and socio-cultural factors, while Levinson[61] suggested that domestic abuse occurs because of male authority, divorce restrictions for women and societal acceptance of the use of violence for conflict resolution. 'Evolutionary' theory holds that the need of men to control the sexuality of women is a fundamental aspect of gender relations. The roots of domestic violence are deeply entrenched and began with the emergence of a pattern of monogamous pairing relationships which were devised in a manner such that a man is supposed to control and protect the woman and enjoys privileges such as authority over her and the children in return.[62] Engels contended that this arrangement serves as a tool to perpetuate patriarchal relations through control of labor, reproduction and property. A woman's job is restricted to 'procreation and child rearing', 'looking after' the needs of her husband and children and taking care of the household. Such heterosexual arrangements are almost ubiquitously celebrated and legitimized in societies where state regulations reward such arrangements while stigmatizing and criminalizing all other forms of relationships by enforcing coercive rules.

The feminist explanation of violence focuses on the relationship between the cultural ideology of male dominance and structural discrimination that limit women's access to resources.[63] It has been held that in an asymmetric, gendered society, heterosexual marriage enhances women's vulnerability and causes economic subordination under the guise of moral protection.[64] Friedan[65] saw housewives trapped in the "chains of mistaken ideas and misinterpreted facts of incomplete truths and unreal choices". In fact, violence is slyly entwined with the notion of romantic love in literary and popular texts so that abused women subjected to torture may position themselves within the layered construction of love to 'make sense' of their situation.[66] Often, the idea of a public-private dichotomy is used as "an ideological curtain that conceals the reality of women's systematic oppression".[67] Thus, domestic assault is not a personal issue. Rather, it is a larger social and political question.[68] Wife abuse is a manifestation of unequal power relations between men and women within a conjugal tie and also reflects on a widespread discrimination against women in a hierarchical society.

Attempts have been made to comprehensively understand the situation of a battered wife and to find out the reason why she continues to stay in a violent relationship. The term 'battered woman syndrome', coined by Lenore Walker,[69] has been used to describe the psychological condition of a woman who is assaulted multiple times for a prolonged period. Such a woman depicts distinct psychological and behavioral symptoms, specifically in situations when multiple episodes of violence are combined with patterns of intimidation, mental abuse and control. Consequently, she suffers from 'learned helplessness'[70] when she begins to believe that there is no escape from the terror situation. Threat of further violence and intimidation prevents her from sharing her concerns, thus ensuring isolation. A woman assaulted for years may develop irrational beliefs and blame herself.[71] She becomes hypervigilant, has disrupted interpersonal relationships and may develop fear for her life or the lives of loved ones.[72] This fear and threat of violence compel her to indulge in destructive behavior. Battered woman syndrome, thus, is a deeply layered multiple victimization, where a woman can think of no other option but to attack her perpetrator. However, this theory is criticized for being victim-centric even though the term battered woman syndrome is now accepted legally across America, Europe and many other countries and refers to severe psychological trauma caused by domestic abuse.

Another theory holds that a woman continues to stay in a violent relationship because she develops a traumatic bond with her abuser. This is termed as Stockholm syndrome.[73] Coined in 1973, this term was used to describe the response of four employees who were held hostage during a bank robbery in Stockholm, Sweden, yet they expressed sympathy towards their captors. This is considered as a highly irrational behavior, because their life was in danger, yet they construed their captors as kind. Essentially, it is seen as a survival strategy. Scholars have used this paradox to define male–female relations in a violent situation where a female hostage refuses to leave because she develops a bond with the male perpetrator. Based on these well-informed research studies, the women's movement elsewhere has developed legal and other strategic action plans to deal with cases of domestic violence.

The battered women's movement outside India

During the 1970s, the women's movement abroad formed consciousness-raising groups and realized that there exists a systemic discrimination in the manner in which society treats women; hence emerged the slogan the 'personal is political'.[74] Prior to the 1970s, the phenomenon of domestic violence was not prioritized either by the state or by society.[75] The dominant discourse considered the four walls of the home as a benevolent unit providing safety and security to all its members. Regulating violence inside the home was a distant thought.[76] From the 1970s onwards, activists reframed wife battering as a mechanism of male domination and control. They saw domestic abuse as an expression of patriarchy[77] and came out with the slogan "We will not be beaten". The battered women's movement in the West began with the demand for shelter or refuge. Initially, shelter groups arose out of demands by the consciousness-raising groups.[78]

In Britain, the Chiswick Women's Aid initiated a campaign where 500 women and children marched throughout the town. In the United States, the battered women's movement began a few years later, in 1973 and 1974, with the opening of women's advocates homes in Minnesota and a transition house in Boston. The movement focused on battering in a wider context in terms of power relations between the sexes. It focused on three major goals: assisting victims, challenging violence and changing the position of women in society. The movement saw 'refuge' as a physical space to provide respite to an abused woman, where she can momentarily escape her oppressive environment and could find space to make decisions about her life. Contact with other women helps her to overcome isolation. Refuge is seen as a link between women's autonomy and economic independence.[79] It is considered a crucial means of responding to and rejecting men's control over women. For the movement, the 'refuge' provides a location that could be used to organize and to serve as a base for feminist politics. The movement further includes the goal of securing legal protections besides focusing on housing for women, while considering the fact that violence-free homes are essential to live a violence-free life. It advocated for laws to eliminate the state's discretion by mandating the arrest and prosecution of batterers.[80] As a result, domestic abuse was not only criminalized but civil protection orders could be obtained while the coordinated community response dedicated to domestic abuse was developed. Today, several countries have developed an elaborate set of laws to protect battered wives.

Legislating domestic violence: laws across different countries

As many as 119 countries have passed laws against domestic violence, and 52 have laws against marital rape.[81] Seven countries – Belgium, Canada,

Estonia, Iceland, Morocco, the Netherlands and Tunisia – have no explicit laws on domestic abuse but have addressed the issue by intensifying penalties when criminal offenses are committed against spouses or within the family.

In the United States, the Violence Against Women Act was enacted in 1994, which recognized wife abuse as a crime. The law pushes for 'zero tolerance' of abuse and mandated civil remedies.[82] Marital rape is recognized as serious a crime as rape by a stranger.[83] It is mandatory that the courts order restitution and damages to the victim. Losses include costs of medical and psychological care, transportation, temporary housing, childcare expenses, loss of income, attorney's fees, costs incurred in obtaining a protection order and other expenditures. An offender is penalized depending on the extent of bodily injury to the victim and if a weapon is used. Terms of imprisonment range from 5 years when there is no injury to the victim, to 10 years in cases of serious bodily harm, to 20 years if there is permanent disfigurement or life-threatening bodily injury, to life imprisonment if the crime resulted in her death. Some states have made specific provisions which consider violence as a 'marital fault' and a factor in the division of matrimonial property. Mediation is avoided in cases where domestic violence is a pattern.[84] Mandatory arrest policies are being followed, and many jurisdictions follow a no-drop policy, according to which the prosecutor must continue, regardless of the wishes of a victim, though the prosecutor cannot force the victim to participate in the prosecution.[85]

In UK, the Domestic Violence, Crime and Victims Act of 2004 amended the earlier Family Law Act of 1996 and has provisions relating to homicide, made common assault an arrestable offense and ensures that surcharges be paid by the offender.[86] Provisions exist to obtain protection orders, non-molestation orders and occupation orders. In situations where an abuser controls the victim via social media or spying online, he faces a five-year imprisonment.[87] After the Istanbul Convention, new measures have been announced to ensure that if abusive behavior involves a child, a court can impose the sentence accordingly.[88] A multi-agency approach has been adopted to provide remedies to victims.

The Family Law Act of 1975 in Australia defines domestic violence as "violent, threatening or other behaviour by a person that coerces or controls a member of the person's family or causes the family member to be fearful". In several cases, victims have been awarded compensation for physical and mental trauma. In New Zealand and the territories of Australia, the prosecutorial policy instructs the police and prosecutors to proceed in domestic violence cases, as these are similar to cases of violence against strangers, even if the victim indicates that she would prefer not to proceed. Theoretically, this situation helps the victim and relieves her from the pressure to withdraw the charges. Some jurisdictions have made the wife a compellable witness in trials where her husband is an accused. In February 2019, the Australian government conducted an enquiry into dowry abuse among migrants and on the basis of the Senate Report directed that no visa to be granted to men convicted of violence.[89]

Bangladesh has enacted the Domestic Violence Act of 2010 which provides civil remedies in such cases. In the Philippines, the Anti-Violence Against Women and Their Children Act covers violence in intimate relationships and provides for a range of penalties beside civil remedies. It sets out mechanisms for inter-agency coordination and provision of services for victims. The Spanish law on gender-based violence defines violence broadly to include psychological abuse, sexual aggression, threat, compulsion, coercion and deprivation of free will. Other than criminal and civil provisions, this law focuses on preventive and educational measures. In Canada, the schemes in a few provinces award compensation to the victims who have been assaulted. Jurisdictions in Great Britain and North Ireland have established state-funded compensation schemes for victims to pay for medical and other expenses, besides compensation for mental pain or injury incurred as a result of the crime.

At the international level, the idea of violence against women as a violation of human rights gained legitimacy around 1993, when at the World Conference on Human Rights in Vienna, women from different continents testified about distinct forms of violence they experienced within their homes. At the global level, too, the international women's movement struggled for years to highlight the issue of domestic violence. Although recognized as a priority issue, it took four decades to bring violence onto the international agenda.[90] Today, it is seen as a universal problem and not just a phenomenon associated with any specific culture, community or class.[91]

International framework on violence against women within homes

Domestic violence is recognized as the violation of human rights, and it was raised at the UN world conference in Mexico in 1975. Under the Convention on the Elimination of All Forms of Discrimination against Women (CEDAW), adopted in 1979, states are required to take legislative measures, both civil and criminal, to address the issue. In Nairobi, in 1985, the issue of gender-based violence was construed as a hindrance to attaining the goal of human rights and peace. In 1991, the Commission on the Status of Women recommended the development of an international instrument on violence against women, and an expert group subsequently prepared a draft declaration. The following year, the CEDAW treaty committee issued the General Recommendation 19, which recognized gender-based violence as a form of discrimination and identified a range of measures to eradicate it. In 1993, the UN General Assembly unanimously adopted the Declaration on the Elimination of Violence against Women. In 1994, the establishment of the Special Rapporteur on Violence against Women established four key focus areas, one of which was domestic violence, and this has been reinforced by the Vienna Accord. At the UN's Fourth World Conference in Beijing in 1995, 180 governments agreed that violence against women is a critical issue.[92]

In 1996, the UN Special Rapporteur on Violence Against Women recommended A Framework for Model Legislation on Domestic Violence. This framework calls on countries to comply with the international standards, prescribing domestic violence as gender-specific violence.[93] Since then, these guidelines have formed a base and a source for demanding and developing legislation in numerous countries.[94] It defines essential components for legislation such as complaint mechanisms, duties of judicial officers, criminal and civil proceedings and provisions for various services. It calls for speedy remedies and effective enforcement to provide relief and prevent further abuse. Other non-legal measures incumbent on the state include capacity building for law implementers and service providers, raising awareness, education and actions towards a comprehensive response.

With regard to the legal provisions in India, theoretically, it may be said that even on paper, Indian laws are ambivalent on issues such as those pertaining to the arrest of the accused, punishment in relation to the bodily injury or harm, providing compensation and damages to victims, mandatory counselling in cases where there is a pattern of extreme violence, division of matrimonial property, inter-agency coordination and many other aspects. This is despite the fact that India is a signatory to the CEDAW,[95] as well as the Beijing Declaration. India has also endorsed the 2030 Sustainable Development Goals that focus on gender equity. The constitution of India binds the state to take affirmative action in favor of the women and the marginalized, and under Article 51(c), the state is bound to respect international treaties and obligations. It is in light of these international frameworks that the country needs to formulate strategies, laws and actions to support women's emancipation. In the landmark judgement in *Vishakha vs State of Rajasthan*,[96] the Supreme Court, while relying on CEDAW, filled in gaps in the then-existing framework on sexual harassment. However, in the realm of domestic violence, the state adopts a different stance. Therefore, before critically examining the fact as to why the government has failed to meet the international obligations as well as the constitutional commitments within the domain of the family, it is essential to consider the historical context of women's position within families.

Inegalitarian relationships and the situation of women in India

The constitution of India adopted in 1949 promised equality on the basis of sex and guaranteed a just and democratic society. While framing the constitution, the makers recognized the existence of institutionalized inequalities in society and provided mandatory instruments for affirmative actions, while radically moving away from inherited social values. Laws have been formulated to ensure that protections could be availed of by citizens, irrespective of their background. The state acts as a locus to frame, construe and operationalize these basic rights. From a citizen's perspective, it involves 'living with the state' and actively engaging with the bureaucratic regulations.[97] However, given the patriarchal structure, women are excluded within this framework, as citizenship is exclusively viewed as the domain of men.[98] This notion of gendered citizenship existed during the colonial rule, and it continues to exist today, where women are seen not only as a category that is different from men but also women are further "categorized' within laws and policies on the basis of their religious identities, as working and non-working, 'good' and 'bad' (housewives and prostitutes), 'normal' and 'deviant' (where deviant consists of the destitute, insane, mentally retarded and criminal populations), child and adult".[99] This 'construction of women' primarily by the state in its function and formulation of 'women's issues' as merely an item on the development agenda indirectly repudiates the rights of women. During the colonial regime, the 'status of women' served as a crucial signifier whereby Britishers utilized it as an indicator to legitimize their rule, while at the same time left the large part of it untouched as a 'private' domain. This trend continued in post-colonial India, where 'social reforms' have failed to address reality.

The CSWI[100] Report in 1974, a document solely devoted to the 'question of women' in independent India, observed that 'large masses' of women could not realize their rights and charged the state with not fulfilling its constitutional mandates of sex-based equality. The committee noted,

> All indicators of participation, attitudes and impact come up with the same result – the resolution in social and political status of women for which constitutional equality was to be the only instrument, still remains a distant objective. While there is no doubt that the positions of some groups of women have changed for better by opening to them positions of power and dignity, the large masses of women continue to lack spokesmen who understand their special problems and be committed for their removal, in the representative bodies of the State. . . . From this point of view, though women do not numerically constitute a minority, they are beginning to acquire the features of minority community by the three recognized dimensions of inequality: Inequality of class (economic situation), status (social position) and political power.
> (p 300–1)

Pro-women policies that have been framed later could not ensure that women received their due share of economic or other benefits emanating from 'development'.[101] Sharma and Sujaya[102] noted that many policies and programs for improving the situation of women could not work because,

> 'Women' were positioned – *marginally* and *precariously* – within the confines of narrowly conceived *social welfare* sector. Marginally because women had to jostle for space and resources within this

> poorly endowed sector with many other groups of citizens; precariously because the entirety of social context and situation of women, the issues thrown up and the successes achieved during the social reform and freedom movement, the unfinished tasks and an overall follow-up – all were missing in the social welfare lens, the cognitive map of policy makers. Even more serious, the social welfare sector did not concern itself with legal rights and entitlements.
>
> (p xxv)

Therefore, more than seven decades after the country attained freedom, women are struggling hard to claim their legal and social entitlements. The state does not an enabling mechanism as per the constitutional provisions, and society has not created space to ensure that women receive their due entitlements. Rather, the state and society reiterate patriarchal values that marginalize women and interfere with the desired outcomes of gender progressive policies.[103] The logic of the state constrains the freedom of women.[104] Factors range from subjectivities and biases of those who implement the law and policies to the 'crime–politics–governance nexus' and lack of legal literacy among the population.

Today, the crisis has deepened with the effects of globalization that coexist with regressive feudal ideologies and make the situation worse.[105] Despite a spate of laws, violence against women is increasing. A controversial survey[106] in 2018 ranked India as the most dangerous country for women due to a high risk of sexual violence. The government denied these findings, yet the situation on the ground remains disastrous.[107] More specifically, in matters relating to marriage and family, the law in itself has neither succeeded in transforming the regressive ideologies that promote violence nor could it help to synchronize the mandate of equality or justice within the given stratified arrangements. In fact, the constitutional standards are hollow and are fraught with contradictions – so much so that the law is considered a 'subversive site'.[108] The situation that exists today is that women are marginalized within public spaces, including the courtrooms, as well as in workspaces, within government schemes and within homes.

Marriage, family and patriarchy in North India

Conjugal relationships frequently are not based on companionship or partnership. The patriarchy creates an institution consisting of an uninterrupted hierarchical system of shaping and defining identities; it organizes kinship, division of labor and property rights while controlling women's sexualities and subjectivities within the boundaries of strict censures and rigid norms. Families socialize individuals to accept gender subordination and assist in establishing male control over women's sexuality, mobility and labor. In such hierarchical arrangements, a husband is perceived as a 'provider' and can compel a wife to be obedient and submissive. The state and society sanction authority to a man to deprive his wife of her liberty. Femininity implies that women have to be docile, submissive, obedient, malleable, self-sacrificing and tolerant, whereas masculinity values manliness, toughness, dominance and similar such traits.[109] Commonly, men are conditioned to be aggressive, whereas women are expected to be the silent recipients.

In a patriarchal setup that exists in North India, joint families operate with the ideology of shared production and mutual consumption of common resources.[110] Often, marriage and kinship are intertwined, and therefore the joint family as a unit has its own structured set of rules and behaviors.[111] Family is considered an autonomous unit and immune to state interference, having its own social and emotional sanctity, or, in other words, a government of its own. Any attempt to scrutinize the family is not permissible because of its ideological glorification legitimized by the elements of unconditional love, altruism and care, making it non-political. These notions hide any form of discrimination, violence or exploitation women face in asymmetrical arrangements. The irony is that in the guise of discipline and love, women are not allowed to exercise choice in terms of marriage or[112] reproductive autonomy and are deprived of the freedom to get educated or step outside to work.[113]

The right to inheritance is recognized through the male lineage. The *Mitakshara* school of law recognizes the joint family as a group of coparceners, where patrilineally related males have a joint right to property. Similarly, the *Dayabagha* school of law, as well as the Muslims and other communities, follow a pattern where couples related through patrilineal bonds – fathers, sons and brothers with their wives and children – are recognized as having a common blood line. The law recognizes the Hindu Undivided Family (HUF) as a separate independent legal entity with a unique position. In fact, the HUF enjoy several distinct rights and privileges.[114] The head of HUF is the male patriarch, or *karta*, though this position changed after the amendments made in the Hindu Succession Act in 2005.

Usually, male progeny is considered a father's natural apprentice and successor, who is expected to look after his parents in their old age, whereas a daughter is considered to have only residual, contingent rights, and upon marriage she is expected to shift spatially to her husband's house. Frequently within this system, an individual's identity and needs are disregarded for the benefit of the larger group. The family becomes a smaller unit that reproduces patriarchy while catering to the needs of the larger hierarchical society. However, older women are in a position to assert power in covert form over younger ones.[115] Further, hierarchical relationships are preferred over horizontal relationships. Thus, a father–son or a mother–son tie is favored over the relationship between a son and his wife.

Moreover, marriage is seen as a union of two souls and is deemed to be an insoluble, irrevocable and preordained bond. Walking out of such relationship is not easy. Any adult woman is expected to marry and remain in the marriage, despite the fact that it is oppressive.[116] The larger socio-cultural machinery surrounding marriage works impeccably in favor of men and reinforces the entrenched stereotypes while reiterating the traditional power relations. The patriarchy slyly uses a system of reward and punishment to control and manage relationships within private spaces. Therefore, it is not love that governs family; rather, it is the male authority that rules. In such an authoritarian society, the vital rationale of existence as a female lies in procreation (i.e. fulfilling the role of a being a wife and a mother). The media, market and religious and social institutions reinforce an image of the 'perfect marriage' which is sacrosanct and reiterates the role of a 'good wife' as sacrificing, caring, loving, docile, subservient, obedient and a perfect woman. Privileges are granted to those who fit into this role. If a woman dares to defy these norms, violence is used to show her, her place.[117]

The patriarchal arrangement of the Hindu family alienates and dispossesses daughters

A girl is considered a temporary member in the natal family who needs to be 'safeguarded and protected' until she is transferred to the marital house with a big feast and a large dowry.[118] The natal family controls a girl's sexuality until she reaches her husband's house. Marriage implies that an uneven relationship is created between the two families. '*Betiyan parayi hain*' (Daughters are aliens in the natal home) is a common saying whereby upon marriage, a daughter is not only spatially transferred to her matrimonial household, or *sasural*, but also is dispossessed from her natal home, or *maika*. Since her childhood, a girl is conditioned to believe that she belongs to her husband's house, and after her marriage, her belongingness to her *maika* is taken away. The patrilineal kinship system practices virilocality, which denies women their right to stay in the natal home after their marriage. A woman is also not entitled to claim her property rights in her *sasural*.[119] An adult woman is considered socially and economically dependent on a man – her father before her marriage – and her identity is merged with that of her husband upon marriage – who may be a complete stranger in the case of an arranged marriage. It is socially expected that a woman after her marriage will adopt the surname of her husband,[120] and the children born out of the wedlock acquire the surname of their biological father.[121] Any existence apart from this arrangement is deemed undesirable.[122]

Marriage is considered a rigid institution that involves a load of expectations and many responsibilities for women. Being a new entry in the marital home, a woman is powerless and vulnerable. She is expected to be controlled by and is dependent on other adults in the household.[123] She occupies the lowest rung in the hierarchy of relationships; therefore, the prerogative of chastisement rests with those who hold seniority in a graded arrangement. As a young adult, a woman has no control over her body or her assets, including the dowry she receives. Along with her identity, her wealth is merged with that of her husband and she is left with nothing to call her own. Rights to the value of a woman's paid or unpaid labor and any wages she earns are acquired by her husband. She is obliged to obey and serve selflessly, and he gets the right to chastise her. This authority is not questioned even if the husband is a drunkard, gambler or criminal. Rather, the patriarchal culture celebrates the subjugation of women through practices such as *kanyadaan* and *karvachauth*.

In this context, the major reasons for inflicting violence on women within the home are men's sense of their right and authority to punish women for perceived wrongdoing; men's sense of control; expectations from women as wives, as mothers and as daughters-in-law; men's possessiveness and jealousy; and their urge to assert power, among others. For women, a sense of shame, stigma and guilt, along with the fear of reprisal, prevents them from speaking up against violence. Many keep silent for years. The internal dynamics of traditional families play a significant role while constricting the bonds of affection and isolating women at a time of crisis.[124] Any deviation from this norm is considered an anomaly. Divorce has its own implications[125] even in the post-colonial modern nation. A wide gap continues to exist today between the constitutional norms and the manner in which the laws, customs and rituals relating to marriage and family have been implemented in independent India.

Women within families: construing conjugality through a socio-legal lens

Pre-colonial India was pluralistic and heterogeneous, where multiple tribes, sects, castes and groups co-existed following their own customary practices, with no monolithic authority or the corresponding notion of legality.[126] Later, those practices were codified, and the vast ancient traditions were captured in several works of literature, such as *Dharamshastras, smritis* and, most importantly, the Laws of Manu as detailed in *Manusmriti*. All such texts were composed by elderly upper-caste *Brahmin* males and therefore biases crept in.[127] Division of society on the basis of caste hierarchy and the influence of the Brahmanical patriarchy made a strong dent on the situation of women,[128] where even the upper-caste women were sexually controlled in order to preserve the caste-based purity.[129] Customs and practices that were used to adjudicate matters within the segregated communities changed significantly during the colonial era.

The drastic impact of colonialism was observed in the manner in which women's position and status were conceptualized during the nineteenth and twentieth centuries. The indigenous patriarchy and upper-caste hegemony were reactivated by the imperial rulers. Colonial influences were characterized by the unsteady alliances and interests between the British men and Indian native elite men which infused patriarchal and colonial values without the understanding of diverse history or culture. Therefore, most of the reforms that were sought in law served the interest of Britishers while frustrating the claims of women. This insight indicated the manner in which multiple patriarchies colluded and competed in a layered hierarchical society. Kolsky[130] demonstrated that while codifying the laws, Britishers created a culture of impunity and placed a heavy burden on women seeking a judicial remedy in the colonial courts. The notion of women complainants being untrustworthy and incredible was imported, which was further grouped with colonial views of the Indian culture to position the victim as dubious, thus in a way putting the victim on trial. The compromised legal system proposed by Thomas Babington Macaulay accommodated the colonial hierarchy and was grounded on regressive patriarchal understanding. What is imposed is the rule of men rather than the rule of law.

Also, during the late nineteenth century, the nationalist Hindu orthodox, mostly elderly men, while resisting any colonial intervention in the domestic sphere, construed womanhood through the prism of love and pain.[131] These nationalists in the domain of conjugality "reimagined family as a contrast and critique of alien rule"[132] with two different versions of subjection: the colonized Hindu man and subordinate Hindu wife, where the household was seen as a last independent space left to the colonized Hindu male. Patriarchal absolutism was not challenged in the context of the Hindu family, where collective rights were prioritized and individual rights were submerged – and therefore remained shielded from the invasion of colonial rules. This nationalist discourse guided the colonial law where laws governing intimate areas of life such as property, inheritance or family relationships have been seen as 'personal'.

Attempts to change the rigid structure met with extreme resistance. For instance, when Dr Ambedkar, the first law minister of independent India, prepared the draft of the Hindu Code Bill that sought to codify the diverse systems and property practices; alter the order of succession; and design new laws on maintenance, marriage, divorce, adoption or guardianship, it was bitterly opposed by the members of the Congress and the Hindu *Mahasabha* because it challenged the very basis of Brahmanical patriarchy. Ambedkar imagined a casteless, gender-just society and advocated for the abolition of birthright to property, half-share to daughters, conversion of women's limited estate, abolition of caste in matters of marriage and adoption and principles of monogamy, among others.[133] But because of resistance, the Bill was shelved. It was only after re-working in several stages that amendments have been sought in the Hindu laws during the 1950s.

The Brahmanical patriarchy that forms the basis of Hindutva ideology has been propagated for years by the right-wing forces in independent India, in contradiction to the constitutional values that have further intensified the patriarchy in its virulent form. Sarkar and Bhutalia[134] relate in their work the participation and involvement of women in communal conflict during the destruction of *Babri Masjid* in Ayodhaya in 1992 and the subsequent riots. This shows that feminist scholarship has failed to address critical factors that explain women's involvement in Hindutva politics. The fact that fundamentalists could mobilize women is well depicted in the *Roop Kanwar Sati* incident[135] and later in Shahbano's case.[136] Even recently, the release of the movie *Padmavati* and the discourse relating to the *Sabrimala* temple[137] entry issue demonstrate that women could be mobilized for violent actions. In fact, the right wing has appropriated the ideas and symbols of the liberal movement and has pilfered the language of law and rights.[138] The progressive women's movement has not countered the regressive right-wing agenda that has made an adverse impact not only on the situation of women in post-colonial India but also on the manner in which the laws and rights relating to women are construed.

In fact, after going through the many feminist writings available on the history of the women's movement in India, I understand that most of these distinguish between the pre-colonial and post-colonial period, possibly because colonial rule has made a profound impact on the interpretation of customs, local laws, traditions and cultural interpretations related to women's rights. However, while deviating from the established practice, I choose to focus on the ideological divisions because of the significant impact on women's status and position within families that has captured the imagination of the law framers and implementers while envisaging and applying the domestic violence law. Also, in the current socio-political context, understanding ideological nuances has gained importance when the constitutional ideals of liberalism and social justice are under threat.[139]

More specifically, in the context of family law, which exists in contrast to the constitutional provisions, *shastras* and similar texts have been evoked as rigid laws to construe a woman's body as loyal, subservient and chaste, bound by an indissoluble bond to her husband and his family. Love, here, demands a sacrifice from women, but for men no such requirements are being imposed. Similarly, rules of monogamy are imposed on women, but for men, no guidelines have been made. The notion of consent finds no place in such a matrix where *sati* and child marriages are being celebrated and where sacramental aspects of marriage, as well as the high form of love, is valorized. The pride and glory of a chaste women are highlighted through religious as well as cultural practices and rituals. Marital rape is not being criminalized while harsh miseries have been imposed on women. This trend continues today.

For instance, in one of the booklets[140] being sold by Gita Press[141] titled *Gribastha Mein Kaise Rahen*[142] (How to Stay Within Matrimony), while preaching on how to live the marital life in a Hindu way, advised that wives, if being beaten by their husbands, should bear it silently while believing that it is a sin for one's past life or a debt which one has to repay in this life and that one is getting purified this way and may achieve salvation. It explains,

> If a husband physically abuses his wife what should she do?[143]
>
> (Translation mine)

The author says in answer:

> The wife should understand it is because of her sins in the past life that she is repaying and she may achieve salvation. In case, her natal family came to know that she is being physically violated, they can take her back because they have not arranged her marriage so that she could be abused.

The next question is

> If her natal family refused to take her, in such situation what should she do?

It is answered that

> She should bear the violence thinking that she is repaying for her sins because being vulnerable she can't do much. She must bear the violence silently and patiently because this way it is possible that her husband may shower his affection one day. In case she is unable to bear violence than she should take permission from her husband to stay separately and must spent her life praying while also earning for self.[144]

This misogynist literature read by millions of readers, men and women, across the country, reiterates the regressive patriarchy and erroneously suggests that bearing violence is a destiny of a woman. This form of literature is seen as more sanctified than the constitutional values that endorse the vision of equality, liberty and justice. This conflict between modern values and traditions was visible at the time of the drafting of the constitution, as well as during the making of the Hindu Code Bill, and it continues to exist today in the 'New', 'Shining' and 'Incredible' India.

An example of such a conflict is evident in the working of the *Rashtra Sevika Samiti*, a Hindu nationalist organization, parallel to the *Rashtriya Swayamsevak Sangh* (RSS), and is known as the women's wing of RSS.[145] It unapologetically promotes the idea of Hindu *Rashtra*[146] and provides young girls with lessons rooted in patriarchy. According to this notion,

> A woman within the understanding of RSS, has no individual identity; her only identity is associated with the various roles she plays within a family unit. She isn't supposed to work and be independent or do anything that varies from her associated gender roles. The organization subtly indicates that families break because of women stepping out of the house through their teachings to young girls about how to keep family united: by being a good wife and a good mother and letting the men deal with the task of earning money.[147]

This chauvinist ideology is not supported by theoretical studies or documentation, yet it finds a practical appeal with its members.[148] What is promoted is the concept of 'family-ism and not feminism' as it prefers '*dampatya*', or conjugal life, while upholding the patriarchal notion of honor. These ideas are perhaps guided by Gowalkar, who in his writings titled *Bunch of Thoughts*[149] in a chapter 'Call to Motherhood' implores women to be ideal mothers, to teach their sons the idea of Hindu nationalism and to desist from being modern or Western. It endorses the view that women play a crucial role in nation building, and for that they need to make sacrifices as mother and wives. It sees domesticity as the sole purpose of women's existence and "never empowers women and alter[s] gender relations in the household".[150] Similar to ideas propagated during the Nazi regime,[151] this ideology sees women as the nurturers who impart patriotism to their children.[152]

To address the issues of wife beating, the Samiti clarifies, "Don't parents admonish their children for misbehaviour? Just as a child must adjust to his/her parents, so must a wife act keeping in mind her husband's moods and must avoid irritating him. Only this can keep the family together."[153] Chastisement is being pushed as a norm where the husband is considered superior to the wife. Similarly, divorce is not an option that is made available to women, as one of the members explained, "Our task is to keep the family together, not break it. We tell the women to adjust".[154] The Samiti believes in 'low priority, non-innovative, routine-bound existence and it is that passivity and unquestioning attitude', and this is being indoctrinated in young girls. Girls are being brainwashed with the idea of Hindu nationalism that seeks legitimacy in the notion of female selflessness, sacrifice and martyrdom. The image of a sustaining, nurturing community is used to undercut attacks by the left on social and political hierarchies, including the demands for greater autonomy for women or emphasis on equal rights.[155] This ideology is hence promoting misogynistic notions where wife beating is justified on the principle of discipline and control of women, in contradiction with the existing laws that criminalize domestic violence. In contrast to the constitutional values of equality and justice, this idea constrains women through patriarchal domination and cannot be seen as an alternative to feminism.[156]

In sharp contrast this, other organizations working at the ground level include the women's wing affiliated with political parties or trade unions, such as the All India Women's Conference, or AIWC, that was founded in 1927; the National Federation of Indian Women, or NFIW, established in 1954; and similar such organizations which emerged later and advocate for women's rights and justice. The left-oriented organization, All India Democratic Women's Association,[157] AIDWA claims to have a membership of 10 million and is committed to achieving democracy, equality and women's emancipation.[158] Also, several groups alongside the liberal or autonomous women's organizations are claiming to work with the progressive ideology while advocating for the cause of Muslim, Christian, tribal or Dalit women, all working with different labels, making a complex and complicated network of various ideologies, thoughts and understandings. There are straddled silos of corporate women groups, those related to media, law or similar institutions and those associated with universities, departments, women's studies centers and national and international organizations. These are working across the length and breadth of the country with no connections with others, and the work of the majority remains undocumented. Roy succinctly put it that the women's movement is 'inordinately NGO-ised' where funds determine what constitute women's issues.[159] Not all are geared to embrace the demand for women's emancipation. These varied positions affect the construction of women's situation and status. Kumar[160] has brilliantly suggested that perhaps the middle-class and upper-caste bias exists in documenting the details and not much has been recorded about the nature, tactics or strategies of the campaigns of many who are working silently yet successfully.

In contradiction to this complex ideological network, there are number of women whom I met as a researcher who are fighting independent, lonely battles – sometimes with little or scant support. They are challenging the patriarchy, defying norms, resisting cultural boundaries and striving for justice with their own resilience and grit. With little knowledge about the law or legal rights, minimal resources and lack of material or economic support, these women have developed their own imagination pertaining to justice within the relationship and are attempting to grapple with the patriarchy in their own way, despite the fact that they have been conditioned to accept and believe that marriage is a compulsion, whether violent or not, or that marriage is an undisputed institution that could not be challenged, or that existence of the women apart from marriage is stigmatized and is unacceptable.

The magnitude, prevalence, extent and impact of domestic violence in India

Available data from across the globe indicate that one in every three women have experienced physical or sexual violence at one point in their life, and two in three victims of intimate partner violence related to homicide are women.[161] A study by the WHO concluded that at an international level, as much as 38 percent murders of women are committed by male partners.[162] In India, the report titled 'Crimes in India' 2016[163] indicates that as many as 39 crimes against women are reported every hour. Over 2.24 million cases of crime against women have been reported over the past decade – one complaint is reported every two minutes. The data depict that the situation is volatile. Whether at home or in public spaces, women are facing different forms of grave violence.

The NCRB data as put together in Table 1.1 indicate that almost 10,75,175 cases have been registered from 2006 to 2016 under Section 498A, IPC and 89,301 cases of dowry deaths have been reported over the same period. Statistics indicate that the culture of violence predominates where women are subjected to outright abuse. These are the reported cases and show only the tip of the iceberg. Many cases are not even reported for various reasons. Thus, in a country where women deities are being worshipped as goddesses, on one hand, it is a situation of complete embarrassment that, on the other hand, the safety of women in homes is compromised. The notion of protection in marriage seems to be contrary, as well as fictitious, from this very observation.

Further, the NFHS-4[164] (2015–16) shows that 76 percent of women who face violence never sought help. Forty-nine percent accept and approve violence as the normal wear and tear of married life. Seventy-five percent blamed the husband's drinking problem, which made them aggressive. Instead, the patriarchy is so deeply internalized that, shockingly, a large number of married women accept and justify beatings by their husband as natural consequences when they ignore their wifely duties, such as disrespecting parents, neglecting housework or refusing sex. The NFHS-3[165] (2005–06) also reveals that 54 percent of women and 51 percent of men agree that it is justifiable for a husband to beat his wife. This shows that violence is pervasive and normalized. To explain a similar phenomenon of oppression in another context, Freire[166] used the term 'culture of silence' to indicate the existence of unequal social relations that instill a negative, passive and suppressed self-image onto the oppressed. Similarly, in the current

Table 1.1 Total number of domestic violence cases reported in India in the past ten years

Year	*498A*	*Dowry Deaths*	*Dowry Prohibition Act*	*PWDVA*	*Abetment to Suicide*
2006	63,128	7,618	4,504	–	–
2007	75,930	8,093	5,623	–	–
2008	81,344	8,172	5,555	–	–
2009	89,546	8,383	5,650	–	–
2010	94,041	8,391	5,182	–	–
2011	99,135	8,618	6,619	–	–
2012	106,527	8,233	9,038	–	–
2013	118,866	8,083	10,709	–	–
2014	122,877	8,455	10,050	426	3,734
2015	113,403	7,634	9,894	461	4,060
2016	110,378	7,621	9,683	437	4,485

Source: Adapted from Crimes in India published by NCRB, government of India. Data from 2006 to 2016 have been presented pertaining to these specific legal provisions

context, oppression has been internalized to the extent that women think they deserve battering if they refuse to conform to the norms.

Several other studies also estimated the high incidences of violence women faced in their homes. For instance, the ICRW in 2000 shows that half of the respondents in a sample of 10,000 across urban slum, non-slum and rural populations in seven cities stated that they had faced violence,[167] and almost 66 percent women responded that their husbands had physically forced them to have sexual intercourse against their will.[168] Nearly 66 percent of women in abusive relationships remain silent about their mistreatment.[169] In 2014, the ICRW,[170] in another research study, found that about 52 percent of women testified to facing violence and 60 percent of men reported acting violently toward their partners.

Studies indicate that demographic factors such as age, number of male living children and type of family arrangement all determine individual and household risk associated with domestic violence.[171] Child marriage,[172] low income, illiteracy, caste and alcoholism place women at a greater risk of experiencing battering.[173] Son preference is a cultural practice that not only results in female feticide, sex-selective abortions or abandonment of the girl child[174] but also a mother may be abandoned, beaten or tortured if she fails to give birth to a male child.[175] It is also a common reason for separation and divorce.[176] Deep-rooted patriarchal norms operate to create the culture of violence. Higher socio-economic status and social support act as buffers against violence.[177] Other protective factors include women's economic independence, quality of the marital relationship[178] and women's education.[179]

The crime of domestic violence is not only confined to geographical limits, but as Indians are migrating, increasing incidences of dowry abuse are being reported from other countries too. The culture of violence travels along with the cultural baggage across political boundaries. Data[180] show that in 2017, 1,186 women married to NRI spouses have reported dowry-related complaints, harassment and ill treatment by their husbands. These complaints have been made to ministry and overseas missions/posts. In 2016, 1,510 such complaints were reported. This number was 796 in 2015. Hence, over the years, an increasing number of cases of violence have been reported by women who marry NRI men and shows the manner in which the patriarchy works in an ugly way to torment women. Also, in many cases grooms marry multiple times, desert or abandon their wives and children and ran away crossing the political boundaries. Estimates reveal that 30,000 deserted women are from Punjab alone.[181]

Dowry deaths and bride murders

Incidents relating to dowry deaths are reported in a few newspapers. It is generally assumed that since the 1980s after the vociferous protest by the women's movement, not many women are being murdered for not fulfilling dowry demands. However, the NCRB data estimate that one woman dies every hour because dowry demands remain unfulfilled. In 2015 alone, 7,634 women were killed for their dowry, and this rate was recorded as 7,621 in 2016. Despite the fact that dowry violence is a cognizable offense, women are being murdered brazenly and with impunity. These alarming figures indicate that the society has become deaf and the legal system has become immune to the screams of women who are being burned alive. Perhaps the greed and the consumeristic attitude have made them apathetic or, possibly, indifference has become a norm. Gramsci[182] defined the concept of cultural hegemony similarly in this situation – the dominant ideology shapes the social norms while the reality is ignored because those in power do not want that these voices should be heard.

Statistics indicate that more Indian women aged between 15 and 50 are more prone to fire-related deaths as compared to women in any other country. The WHO reported that India is the only country where, in 1998, fire was reported among the 15 leading causes of death of women.[183] This is further substantiated by the National Burns Programme, which estimated that out of 7 million burn injuries in the country annually, 140,000 are fatal, and out of these 91,000 resulted in deaths of women; a figure higher than that for maternal mortality.[184] Women of child-bearing age, on average, are three times more likely than men to die of burn injuries. The ratio is 18 times more than Pakistan women and 38 times more than Chinese women.[185] Young women are targeted because their natal families could not fulfill dowry demands. Probably the compulsion to stay in the marriage because of economic and social reasons prevent women from walking away from a violent relationship, resulting in their murders.

Several women's organizations, as well as those working in health issues, have conducted independent research studies and have reached the similar conclusion – that young women are dying unnatural deaths – but these reports are hardly making any difference because both the state and society have closed their eyes and ears to the issue of dowry deaths. A study in Bangalore observed that 70 percent of young brides died unnatural deaths.[186] These claims are further substantiated in another hospital-based study,[187] which observed that out of 163,000 fire-related deaths in 2001, which is six times higher than that reported by the police, 106,000 were women in the age group of 15 to 34 years. The ratio of fire-related deaths of young women was three times higher than that of men in the same age group.

Similarly, Kumar and Tripathi[188] observed that when dowry expectations were not met, the young brides were murdered, frequently by burning. In a cohort of 152 burned wives, it was observed that 31 percent were homicidal burns, and most women were from extended families. The murders occurred within the initial phase of marriage. Seventy-seven percent victims were of 16 to 25 years of age and sustained more than 70 percent total body surface area burns because they were doused with kerosene and set alight. Most died immediately or within the subsequent 24 hours. Tragically, MKCG Medical College[189] also obtained similar results. From a total of 58 burned wives, 32 were homicidal burns. Ninety percent of those affected were of 18 to 26 years of age. Death occurred within the initial years of marriage. Most of them had no children, and all were Hindus. Eighty-three percent hailed from joint families. Seventy-two percent occurred in rural areas, 62.5 percent occurred during the daytime. Kerosene was the accelerant used, and offenders include husbands and their relatives. In 69 percent of cases, the total body surface area involved was more than 80 percent. Most victims died within 24 hours due to hypovolemic shock. In fact, bride burning is no longer limited to North India. Mohanty et al[190] observed a similar pattern in the south. The majority of victims were young, and two-thirds were childless. Eighty percent were illiterate. Sixty-three percent were from a rural background. Seventy-seven percent died within four years of marriage. The place of occurrence was the in-laws' house, where the husband alone or along with the in-laws committed the crime. Agency of the in-laws is depicted through a range of actions, from incitement to actual participation in the violent act. Yet the misplaced priorities emphasize cow shelters as an issue[191] while ignoring the plight of women murdered for dowry.

Most of the burn injuries were deliberately reported as accidents in order to avoid investigation, though the interviews with the survivors and their families indicate that victims experienced abuse prior to burning.[192] CEHAT[193] observed a difference in 62 percent of cases about the cause of burns as mentioned in the medical records in comparison to those of counsellors' records. While the medical records stated the reason for burns as "accidental" or "no information", counsellors mentioned the causes as suicidal, homicidal and abuse. Reasons for poor documentation by health providers include no enquiry into a history of violence and fear of police investigation. Classification of the manner of death of women dying of burns by the hospital depends on multiple factors, including the attitude of the staff, the woman herself, her natal family, her spouse and his family, as well as that of police.[194] Hence, biases and injustice against the victim prevail even in documenting the incident.

Thus, various independent studies indicate that the heinous crime of bride burning remains highly under-reported and is increasingly underestimated, but it is consuming women's lives. Yet the policymakers and law makers are ignoring the gravity of the situation. The state has not invested in concerted research on violence. Women's commissions, human rights commissions, WCD departments or similar such institutions have seldom taken steps to intervene in situations where, despite laws, the dowry is glorified and celebrated. The patriarchal mind-set operates to make violence invisible. Regardless of its high prevalence, wife battering is being normalized and trivialized. The media shies away from reporting such issues and instead indulges in negative propaganda.[195] The gravity of the issue is overlooked and its impact on not only individuals and families but also on the community, economy and society as a whole.

The impact of domestic violence

Domestic abuse harms women in multiple ways. It not only results in broken hearts, battered bodies or scarred souls but its impacts are much intense. Domestic abuse affects a woman's physical and mental health and makes her prone to chronic health conditions. Women who experience constant abuse may suffer from depression, post-traumatic stress disorder, anxiety and trauma. In terms of health, the consequences of domestic violence range from wounds, cuts, bruises, broken bones and internal bleeding to organ damage, mental ailments, suicidal tendencies and death.

As per an estimate, non-injurious assaults such as pushes, shoves, grabs and kicks constitute 95 to 99 percent of violence, which are part of a larger coercive and intimidatory behavior and have a cumulative impact on the victim.[196] Domestic abuse has also found linkages with increased risk of anemia[197] and chronic fatigue among the victims. Researchers from the Harvard School of Public Health found that victims of wife abuse have a 37 percent increased risk of suffering from common respiratory conditions, including asthma.[198] Escalating violence is also linked to an increased risk of developing heart and blood vessel related diseases, including stroke.[199] Continuous exposure to abuse affects the immune system and may cause inflammation.[200]

Wife abuse results in an increased risk of unwanted pregnancy,[201] primarily through its restrictive effect upon women's ability to practice contraception.[202] During pregnancy, violence may lead to physical trauma to the fetus, maternal anemia and high mortality.[203] Evidence shows a strong association between violence resulting in low-birth-weight babies and premature deliveries and[204] risks of peri-natal, neo-natal[205] and childhood mortality.[206] About one in ten child deaths under the age of one is attributed to abuse against the mother.[207] Violence experienced by mothers severely affects the well-being of children, including reduced breastfeeding[208] and less attention being paid to immunizations.[209] A strong relationship exists between domestic abuse and death during pregnancy.[210] Domestic abuse is also linked with an increased risk of sexually transmitted diseases and infections[211] and HIV.[212]

Domestic abuse has an adverse impact on the mental health of women and children.[213] Women who experienced battering reported attempting to harm themselves[214] and exhibited suicidal tendencies.[215] Perhaps inequalities in the marriage where women are subjugated place enormous stress on their mental health.[216] The traditional monotonous role of a female is restricting and prevents her from expressing her emotions, leading to depression. However, while framing or implementing laws and policies, such significant aspects are being ignored. The situation that exists today is that neither the law nor the policies respond to the health aspects of violence or address its consequences on the lives of women and children. In terms of resources, no funds are being allocated for the purpose. Similarly, while enacting PWDVA or the Family Court Act 1984, stress has not been laid on providing emergency care or health facilities to the victims or survivors. Though PWDVA mentioned medical facilities, this provision is being nonchalantly ignored by those who enforce the law.

Survivors require medical and psycho-social support, yet none of the available institutions provide for health care or rehabilitation. Available data show that India is facing a shortage of 600,000 doctors and 2 million nurses.[217] In his reply to the question in Lok Sabha on 17 March 2017, the Ministry of Health and Family Welfare stated that as per the estimates, "there are 3827 Psychiatrists, 898 Clinical Psychologists, 850 Psychiatric Social Workers, and 1500 Psychiatric Nurses in the country".[218] With this acute shortage of professionals, to expect that victims will receive proper care is a distant dream in a country where health has received a low priority in general.[219]

The Ministry of Health and Family Welfare emphasize the prevention of diseases; however, the health of women and children facing violence within families is ignored. Similarly, the WCD Ministry or similar departments could not connect to the reality or could determine the cause of violence. Domestic violence can be prevented and ended, yet no effort has been made by the state to connect different dimensions with policy or legal interventions. In fact, the state or the society, while glorifying family, undermines the impact of domestic violence on women and children.

Cost of domestic abuse and its implications

Domestic assault not only harms the individual woman or her family, it also incurs an expenditure for households, communities and economies. It entails costs not only in terms of obtaining medical treatment but also in terms of getting psychological support and legal aid.[220] At a micro level, violence shatters the life of a woman and has a devastating impact on children. Besides, violence seriously affects overall educational attainments, creativity, mobility, innovative potential and skill development of a woman. She is compelled to undergo a vicious cycle of violence which may affect her participation in the labor market and may further escalate her chances to experience more violence. It also costs a woman in terms of her productivity, irrevocable emotional damages and economic expenditure in terms of job loss, lost work days, cost of legal assistance, disruption in life, moving and changing jobs, instability and cost in terms of safety and security.[221] Trauma inflicted by violence may lead to employment instability and results in high job turnover, fewer opportunities for career advancements and a range of other adversities. For survivors in jobs, it is difficult to continue with the work pressure after facing years of abuse. Of those working, many are struggling to cope with managing children, earning a wage and attending court proceedings. Importantly, women's freedom and autonomy are at stake and affect their ability to actualize citizenship.[222]

Overall, it may be said that wife abuse contradicts with the goal of social and economic development and involves a huge cost for families, communities and nations. Forbes[223] reported that domestic abuse costs $8.3 billion annually, which includes a combination of medical costs ($5.8 billion) and lost productivity ($2.5 billion). Violence has negative consequences for economies. It drains resources and leads to increased inequalities, corroded social and human capital and enhanced expenditures. Violence impoverishes society. It hinders the participation of citizens in public life. Apart from human costs, what is affected is the social stability through the intergenerational transmission of violence. Thus, the longer the issue of domestic violence is being dismissed as a private matter, the more damage that is done.[224]

Summary

This chapter conceptualizes the framework and various dimensions of domestic violence and its magnitude and prevalence in India and elsewhere. It explores domestic violence as a human rights issues and looks at the laws that exist across countries and argues that domestic violence violates the basic right to dignity. Domestic violence adversely affects women and children and entails a huge cost to nations, societies and economies.

Notes

1 As quoted by Agnihotri I (2001) *Rereading Histories, Seminar 505*, www.in.undp.org/content/dam/india/docs/re_reading_histories.pdf accessed on 13.03.16
2 Shafin Jahan vs Asokan KM Criminal Appeal 366 of 2018 decided by the Supreme Court on 9 April 2018
3 The Citizen (2014) Women Real Targets of 'Love Jihad' Jihadists, October 14, www.thecitizen.in/index.php/en/NewsDetail/index/2/936/Women-Real-Targets-of-Love-Jihad-Jihadists
4 Gupta Charu (2009) Hindu Women: Muslim Men, Love Jihad and Conversions, *Economic and Political Weekly*, 44 (51) 13–15
5 Gupta Charu (2014) The Myth of Love Jihad, *The Indian Express*, August 28, https://indianexpress.com/article/opinion/columns/the-myth-of-love-jihad/
6 The Special Marriage Act 1954 legalizes marriage, irrespective of the religion and faith followed by either party.
7 Hadiya's case gained attention by the media, Seema's did not. Many other women in similar situations have filed cases under the domestic violence law against their abusive partners, but the media does not highlight those cases.
8 All names and locations have been changed to protect the identity of the interviewees.
9 Seema filed a complaint under Section 498A, on the basis of which her husband was arrested but was released on bail the same day. She opined that had the police kept him for a week in jail, he would have realized his wrongs. According to her, her lawyer has not opposed his bail. The court has fixed the maintenance of Rs 3000/ for the child and 3000/ for her under the PWDVA. In court her husband claimed that he has no job and therefore could not pay. The day this interview was conducted, the magistrate strictly ordered her husband to pay Rs 20,000 within a week.

10 A criminal law pertaining to cruelty against married women by their husbands and in-laws.
11 National Crime Record Bureau (2016) *Crimes in India*, Government of India
12 Joshua A (2018) Trolls Milk the Identity of Child Rapists, *The Telegraph*, July 1 p. 10
13 Shayra Bano vs Union of India (2017) 9 SCC 1
14 Navtej Singh Johar vs Union of India WP Cri 76 of 2016
15 Joseph Shine vs Union of India, WP Cri 194 of 2017
16 Indian Young Women Lawyers Association vs State of Kerala, WPC 373 of 2006
17 *The Hindustan Times* (2018) Sabrimala Row Live Updates: 38-year-old Woman at Base Camp Won't be Taken to Hill-top, say Police, October 20, https://www.hindustantimes.com/india-news/sabarimala-row-live-updates-never-before-break-in-puja-at-temple-triggers-protests-in-kerala/story-L9wSK8tpUg0GwLXRiSA5lK.html
18 *Livemint* (2018) Big Win for India's #MeToo Movement as MJ Akbar Resigns, October 18, https://www.livemint.com/Politics/HRXhfbNbE95F7KXywrwMII/MJ-Akbar-resigns-as-minister.html
19 Rajagopal K (2019) CJI Appears Before A Panel Probing Sexual Harassment Charges, *The Hindu*, May 2, https://www.thehindu.com/news/national/justice-bobde-panel-hears-cji-on-sexual-harassment-allegations/article27005563.ece
20 Nigam S (2005) *Understanding Justice Delivery Mechanism from the Perspective of Women Litigants*, Occasional Paper No. 35 CWDS, Delhi
21 (2014) 8 SCC 273
22 Criminal Appeal No. 1265 of 2017
23 WPC 73 of 2015 decided by the SC on 14.9.2018
24 AIR 1984 Delhi 66; p. 33
25 Krishna Singh vs Mathura Ahir AIR 1980 SC707 and in State of Bombay vs Narasu Appa Mali AIR 1952 Bom 84
26 Ranjan P (2019) Husband, In-laws Try to Cremate Woman Alive for Being Childless, *The Hindustan Times*, January 23, https://www.pressreader.com/india/hindustan-times-delhi/20190123/textview
27 *Mirror Now* (2019) Gurugram: Man Killed Wife for Refusing Sex, Shoved Her Corpse in Bed Box Arrested, February 5, https://www.timesnownews.com/mirror-now/crime/article/gurugram-man-killed-wife-for-refusing-sex-shoved-her-corpse-in-bed-box-arrested/360075
28 Dixit Rakesh (2013) Ex-Army Doctor Held for Chopping Wife's Body into 300 Pieces and Saving Them in Iron Box, *India Today*, Bhubaneshwar, June 22, https://www.indiatoday.in/india/east/story/odisha-army-doctor-chops-wife-body-into-300-pieces-167642-2013-06-22
29 Sharma Pankul (2018) Woman Burnt Alive for Dowry, *The Times of India*, October 24, https://timesofindia.indiatimes.com/city/bareilly/woman-burnt-alive-for-dowry/articleshow/66338008.cms
30 Nath Sujit (2018) Woman Burnt Alive by Husband and In-Laws in Bengal Due to Her Dark Complexion, *News 18*, May 29, https://www.news18.com/news/india/woman-burnt-alive-by-husband-and-in-laws-in-bengal-due-to-her-dark-complexion-1763251.html
31 Tiwari Vaibhav (2018) Delhi Engineer, His Brother Chopped Wife's Body in 7 Pieces, Says Cops, *NDTV*, June 27, https://www.ndtv.com/delhi-news/delhi-how-delhi-police-used-a-cardboard-box-to-find-womans-murderers-1873521
32 Sex ratio in 1901 was 972 females per 1000 males. It went down to 943 in 2011. Source: Census of India 2011
33 Babu R (2019) Woman Who Entered the Shrine Turned Away By her Family, *The Hindustan Times*, January 23, https://www.pressreader.com/india/hindustan-times-delhi/20190123/textview

34 Sharma S (2016) Return their Names, Dignity, *The Tribune*, September 11, https://www.tribuneindia.com/news/sunday-special/perspective/return-their-names-dignity/293373.html. It reports that thousands of women are sold and resold in Mewat for sexual gratification and are forced to live a worse life than that of animals.

35 Kaur R and Garg S (2008) Addressing Domestic Violence Against Women: An Unfinished Agenda, *Indian Journal of Community Medicine*, 33 (2) 73–76

36 UNICEF (2000) *Domestic Violence Against Women and Girls*, Innocenti Digest, Italy

37 United Nations Statistics Division (2015) *The World's Women 2015* chapter 6 UN New York

38 Solotaroff JL and Pande RP (2014) *Violence Against Women and Girls: Lessons from South Asia*, World Bank, Washington pp. 34–36

39 Gandhi N and Shah N (1992) *Issues and Stake: Theory and Practice in Contemporary Women's Movement in India*, Kali for Women, New Delhi, p. 61

40 The available literature from fields such as medicine, feminism, social sciences and law has utilized different terms to express the phenomenon of domestic abuse

41 The word '*hinsa*' was used by MK Gandhi during the colonial rule to describe political violence, and to counter it, he gave the philosophy of '*Ahinsa*', or 'non-violence'. In the context of domestic violence, it may be said that men who may have been seeking freedom from imperial rule acted as oppressors within their own home because the concept of *Ahinsa* remained confined to a larger political struggle but could not liberate women in families until today.

42 Dempsey MM (2006) What Counts as Domestic Violence? A Conceptual Analysis, *William and Mary Journal of Women and Law*, 12 (2) 301–33

43 Hindu marriage recognizes *Saptapadi* or *saat phere*, or seven steps around the sacred fire, with *saat vachan*, or seven promises, taken in every step, yet it underscores the serious abuse women face in marriage

44 Gupte M and More A (2010) *Chakrabedh*: Coil of Domestic Violence and Safety Measures (Hindi) MASUM, Pune have used the term 'chakrabedh', or coils of violence, to explain the situation.

45 Johnson MP (1995) Patriarchal Terrorism and Common Couple Violence: Two Forms of Violence Against Women, *Journal of Marriage and Family*, 57, 283–94

46 Johnson MP and Leone JM (2005) Differential Effects of Intimate Terrorism and Situational Couple Violence: Findings from National Violence Against Women Survey, *Journal of Family Issues*, 26 (3) 322–49

47 Pence E and Paymar M (1993) *Education Groups for Men who Batter: The Duluth Model*, Springer, New York

48 Seigel RB (1996) The Rule of Love: Wife Beating as Prerogative and Privacy, *Yale Law Journal*, 105, 2117–207

49 Mill John Stuart (1869) What Good Reform Would Do? Subjection of Women, www.earlymoderntexts.com/assets/pdfs/mill1869.pdf

50 Blackstone W (1765) *Commentaries on the Laws of England*, University of Chicago Press republished in 1979

51 Seigel (1996) supra p. 2118

52 Nigam S (2008) *Domestic Violence in India: What One Should Know? A Resource Book*, We the People Trust, New Delhi

53 Dutton DG (1999) Limitations of Social Learning Model in Explaining Intimate Aggression, In *Violence in Intimate Relationship*, edited by XB Arriaga and S Oskamp, Sage, Thousand Oaks, CA

54 Lawson J (2012) Sociological Theories of Intimate Partner Violence, *Journal of Human Behaviour in Social Environment*, 22 (5) 572–90

55 WHO (2007) *Multi-Country Study on Women's Health and Domestic Violence Against Women*, WHO, Geneva
56 Walker LE (1979) *The Battered Women*, Harper and Row, New York
57 Gerber GL (1991) Gender Stereotypes and Power: Perception of the Roles in Violent Marriage, *Sex Roles*, 24 (7–8) 439–58
58 Foa EB and Foa UG (1976) Resource Theory of Social Exchange, In *Contemporary Topics in Social Psychology*, edited by JW Thibaut, JT Spence and RC Carson, General Learning Press, Morristown, NJ
59 Gelles RJ (1983) An Exchange and Social Control Theory, In *The Dark Side of Families: Current Family Violence Research*, edited by D Finkelhor, RJ Gelles, GT Hotaling and MA Straus, Sage, Thousand Oaks pp. 151–65
60 Heise E Gottemoeller (1999) Ending Violence Against Women, *Population Reports*, 27 (11) L 8–38, *School of Public Health*, John Hopkins University, Baltimore
61 Levinson D (1989) *Violence in Cross Cultural Perspective*, Sage, Newbury Park
62 Martin Del (1976) *Battered Wives*, Glide, San Francisco
63 Yllo K (1993) Through A Feminist Lens: Gender, Power and Violence, In *Current Controversies on Family Violence*, edited by RJ Gelles and DR Loseke, Sage, New York pp. 47–62
64 Susan Miller Okin (1989) *Justice, Gender and Family*, Basic Books, New York
65 Betty Friedan (1963) *The Feminist Mystique*, WW Norton and Company Inc, New York p. 20
66 Seuffert Nan (1999) Domestic Violence, Discourses of Romantic Love, and Complex Personhood in Law, *Melbourne University Law Review*, 8, 211
67 MacKinnon Catherine (1989) *Towards a Feminist Theory of the State*, Harvard University Press, USA pp. 193–94
68 Fraser Nancy (1990) Struggle Over Needs: Outline of Socialist Feminist Critical Theory, In *Women State and the Welfare*, edited by Linda Gordon, University of Wisconsin Press, Madison pp. 213–15
69 Lenore E Walker (1984) *The Battered Woman Syndrome*, Springer Publishing Company, New York
70 MEP Seligman (1972) Learned Helplessness, *Annual Review of Medicine*, 23 (1) 407–12
71 Lenore E Walker (1979) *The Battered Women*, Harper and Row, New York
72 The movie *Provoked* (2006), based on a real-life incident, depicts Kiranjit Ahluwalia, an Indian woman who moved to the UK after her marriage, who was convicted for the murder of her husband. She was sentenced to life imprisonment. This was later overturned and replaced by voluntary manslaughter on the grounds of diminished responsibility. This case of *R vs Ahluwalia* changed the legal discourse abroad. Nigam S (2016) Battered Women Syndrome: Applying this Legal Doctrine in the Indian Context, *Countercurrents.org*, August 6
73 Graham DL, Rawlings E and Rimini N (1988) Survivors of Terror: Battered Women, Hostages, and the Stockholm Syndrome, In *Feminist Perspectives on Wife Abuse*, edited by K Yllo and M Bograd, Sage, Thousand Oaks, CA pp. 217–33
74 Gavison Ruth (1992) Feminism and the Public/Private Distinction, *Stanford Law Review*, 45 (1) 29
75 Hague G and Wilson C (2000) The Silenced Pain: Domestic Violence 1945–1970, *Journal of Gender Studies*, 9
76 Dobash RE and Dobash RP (1979) *Violence Against Wives*, Free Press, New York
77 Liddle AM (1989) Feminist Contributions to An Understanding of Violence Against Women-Three Steps Forward, Two Steps Back, *Canadian Review Sociology and Anthropology*, 26, 759–76

78 Dobash RE and Dobash RP (1992) *Women, Violence and Social Change*, Routledge, London
79 Kurz D (1998) Women, Welfare, and Domestic Violence, *Social Justice*, 25, 105–21
80 Epstein Deborah (1999) Effective Intervention in Domestic Violence Cases: Rethinking the Roles of Prosecutors, Judges, and the Court System, *Yale Journal of Law and Feminism*, 11 (3)
81 United Nations (2015) *The World's Women 2015: Trends and Statistics*, Department of Economic and Social Affairs, New York p. 160
82 Violence Against Women Act 1994 And Violence Against Women Reauthorisation Act Of 2013
83 Ressler Tara-Culp (2014) How the Country Has Changed Under The Violence Against Women Act, *Think Progress*, September 12, https://Thinkprogress.Org/How-The-Country-Has-Changed-Under-The-Violence-Against-Women-Act-2348c358dbda/
84 Snyder ES and Morgan LW (2005) Domestic Violence Ten Years Later, Law Trends and News, *Newsletter*, American Bar Association 1:4
85 Sack EJ (2004) Battered Women and the State: The Struggle for the Future of Domestic Violence Policy, *Wisconsin Law Review*, 1657, 1669–70
86 Herring J (2007) *Family Law*, 3rd Edition, Pearson Longman, Cambridge, UK
87 *BBC News* (2015) New Domestic Abuse Law Comes into Force, December 29, https://www.bbc.com/news/uk-35192256
88 Johnston Chris (2017) New Measures on Violence Against Women to Be Put in Domestic Abuse Bill, *The Guardian*, June 28
89 *Mail Online* (2019) No Visas for Domestic Violence Convictions, March 2, www.dailymail.co.uk/wires/aap/article-6764541/No-visas-domestic-violence-convictions.html
90 Weldon SL (2006) Inclusion, Solidarity, and Social Movements: The Global Movement Against Gender Violence, *Perspectives on Politics*, 4, 55–74
91 Joachim J (1999) *Shaping the Human Rights Agenda: The Case of Violence Against Women*, Rowman And Littlefield, Lanham
92 Weldon SL and Htun M (2013) Feminist Mobilisation and Progressive Policy Change: Why Governments Take Action to Combat Violence Against Women, *Gender & Development*, 21, 231–47
93 Coomaraswamy R (1996) *Report of the Special Rapporteur on Violence Against Women*, Its Causes and Consequences: A Framework for Model Legislation on Domestic Violence UN
94 UN Women (2013) *Domestic Violence Legislation and Its Implementation: An Analysis for ASEAN Countries Based on International Standards and Good Practices*, UN Office for Asia and the Pacific, 5 ed. Thailand, Bangkok
95 Ratified on 25-6-1993
96 AIR 1997 SC 3011
97 Yuval Davis N and Werbner P (1999) *Women, Citizenship and Difference*, Zed Books, London
98 Rajan RS (2003) *The Scandals of the State: Women, Law and Citizenship in Post-Colonial India*, Permanent Black, New Delhi
99 Ibid
100 CSWI (1974) *Towards Equality: Report on the Committee on the Status of Women in India*, Government of India
101 Mazumdar V (2000) *Political Ideology of Women's Movement Engagement with the Law*, Occasional Paper No. 34, CWDS, New Delhi p. 7
102 Sharma K and Sujaya CP (2012) Introducing Towards Equality: Report of the Committee on the Status of Women in India, In *Women's Equality and the Republic: Landmarks in Indian Story*, edited by V Mazumdar, CWDS and Pearson, New Delhi

103 Kabeer N and Subrahmanian R (1996) *Institutions, Relations and Outcomes: Framework and Tools for Gender Aware Planning*, IDS Discussion Paper, UK
104 Rajan (2003) supra
105 Mohan D (2018) Rising Number of Crime Against Women Reflects Decay in India's Institutions, *The Wire*, April 18
106 Thomson Reuter Foundation 2018, http://poll2018.trust.org/
107 History repeated itself. Even earlier in 1927, Katherine Mayo, in her work titled 'Mother India', or later L. Udwin, through her movie *India's Daughter*, highlighted the adverse situation, and these were strongly resisted without making any efforts to improve the existing conditions.
108 Kapur R and Cossman B (1996) *Subversive Sites: Feminists Engagement with the Law in India*, Sage, New Delhi
109 Sarkar L, Ramanathan U and Mehra M (1994) *Gender Bias in Law: Dowry, A Report*, Karmika, New Delhi
110 Visaria Leela (2000) Violence Against Women: A Field Study, *Economic and Political Weekly*, 13, 1745
111 Patel Tulsi (2005) *The Family in India: Structure and Practices*, Sage Publications, New Delhi
112 The Times of India (2018) Honour Killing: More than 300 cases in last Three Years, September 22
113 National Commission for Protection of Child Rights (2017) National Colloquium Report: Vocational and Life Skill training of Out of School Adolescent Girls in the Age Group of 15 to 18 years Held on 27th October at Delhi
114 Gupta CD (2013) The Tenacity of Hindu Undivided Family: Gender, Religion and Tax Concessions, *Economic and Political Weekly* (40) 73–75
115 Mies M (1980) *Indian Women and Patriarchy*, Concept Publishing Company, New Delhi
116 Sahoo P (2015) 10 Things Indian Parents Say to Blackmail You into Marriage, *The Hindustan Times*, June 28, https://www.hindustantimes.com/sex-and-relationships/10-things-indian-parents-say-to-blackmail-you-into-marriage/story-maZkLPueVurFUGVyQiBpuK.html
117 Agnes Flavia (1990) Wife Beating: Changes in Social Structure Crucial to Combat the Problem, In *Violence Against Women*, edited by S Sood, Arihant Publications, Meerut, UP pp. 57–70
118 Dube L (1988) On the construction of Gender: Hindu girls in patrilineal India, *Economic and Political Weekly*, 23 (18) WS11–WS19
119 Even after amendments were made to the Hindu succession law, not many women have claimed their right to property owned by the natal family. Landesa (2013) Report on Formal and Informal Barriers in Implementation of Hindu Succession Act 2005, UN Women, www.landesa.org/wp-content/uploads/hsaa-study-report.pdf
120 Mantri G (2016) What It's Like to Be an Indian Woman Who Hasn't Changed Her Surname After Her Marriage? *The News Minute*, September 22, www.thenewsminute.com/article/whats-it-be-indian-woman-who-hasnt-changed-her-surname-after-marriage-50272
121 Section 6(a) of the Hindu Minority and Guardianship Act 1956 reads that the natural guardian of a Hindu minor with respect to her person and property is the father and, 'after' him, the mother. This was challenged in *Gita Hariharan vs Reserve Bank of India* 1999 AIR SC 1149 where the Supreme Court held that the word 'after' does not imply only after the death of the father. The mother may be considered a natural guardian, but it shall be interpreted while keeping in mind the welfare of the minor.
122 In my own case, I fought the legal battle as a single mother to claim the rights and identity of my daughter as a neutral citizen because the surname she adopted is different from that of her biological father. WPC 155 of 2016 Delhi HC

123 Jejeebhoy S and Sathar ZA (2001) Women's Autonomy in India and Pakistan: The Influence of Religion and Region, *Population and Development Review*, 27 (4) 687–712

124 Agnihotri I and Parliwala R (Undated) Tradition, the Family and the State: Politics of Women's Movement in Eighties p. 3

125 Amato PR (1994) The Impact of Divorce on Men and Women In India and the United States, *Journal of Comparative Family Studies*, 25 (2) 207–21 Also, Rathi P and Pachauri JP (2018) Problems Faced by Divorced Women in Their Pre and Post-Divorce Period: A Sociological Study With Reference to District Meerut, *Journal of Pharmacognosy and Phytochemistry*, 7 (1) 207–12

126 Chitnis V and Wright D (2007) The Legacy of Colonialism: Law and Women's Rights in India, *Washington and Lee Law Review*, 64, 1315–48

127 Sinha Kanad (2014) Be It Manu, Be It Macaulay: Indian Law and the 'Problem' of the Female Body, *Journal of Indian Law Society*, 5, 61–94

128 Rege S (2013) *Against the Madness of Manu: BR Ambedkar's Writing on Brahmanical Patriarchy*, Navanya, New Delhi

129 Chakravarti U (1993) Conceptualizing Brahmanical Patriarchy in Early India, Gender, Caste, Class and State, *Economic and Political Weekly*, 28 (14) 579–85

130 Kolsky Elizabeth (2010) The Rule of Colonial Indifference: Rape on Trial in Early Colonial India, 1805–57, *The Journal of Asian Studies*, 69 (4) 1093–117

131 Sarkar Tanika (2001) *Conjugality and Hindu Nationalism, In Hindu Wife: Hindu Nation: Community Religion and Cultural Nationalism*, Permanent Black, New Delhi pp. 119–225

132 Ibid p. 198

133 See Rege (2013) supra

134 Bhutalia U (1995) Muslims and Hindus, Men and Women: Communal Stereotypes and Partition of India, In *Women and Right-Wing Movements: Indian Experience*, edited by Tanika Sarkar and Urvashi Bhutalia, Zed Books, London

135 Kumar R (1993) *History of Doing: An Illustrated Account of Movements for Women's Rights and Feminism in India 1800–1900*, Zubaan, New Delhi

136 Kalpagam U (2000) Review: The Women's Movement in India today – New Agendas and Old Problems, *Feminist Studies*, 26 (3) 645–60, 656

137 Jitheesh MP (2018) Appropriation of Ayyappa Cult: The History and Hinduisation of Sabarimala Temple, *The Wire*, October 12

138 Turner Elen (2012) Empowering Women? Feminist Response to Hindutva, Intersections: Gender and Sexuality in Asia and the Pacific, 28, http://intersections.anu.edu.au/issue28/turner.htm

139 Naryanan SV (2017) How Far Have We Deviated from the Ideology of Our Constitution? *The Wire*, December 4

140 This is highlighted by Prof Shamsul Islam in one of the discussions organized by Delhi PUCL in 2017. I am grateful to him for an enriching discussion.

141 Gita Press, Gorakhpur, Uttar Pradesh is a largest publisher of Hindu religious text. It promotes the principles of *Sanatan Dharma*.

142 Author Swami Ramsukh Das in the 37th edition. It is claimed that this book sold more than 1 million copies

143 Das Swami Ramsukh (undated) *Gristha Mein Kaise Rahen*, Gita Press, Gorakhpur p. 70

144 Translated from page 70 of the booklet

145 Founded by Laxmi Bai Kelkar in 1936, it claimed that it has more than 5,000 active Shakhas and estimated membership of around a million women.

146 Bacchetta P (1996) Hindu Nationalist Women as Ideologues: The "Sangh" the "Samiti" and their Differential Concepts of Hindu Nation, In *Embodied Violence: Communalizing Women's Security in South Asia*, edited by K Jayawardena and M de Alwis, Zed Books, London pp. 108–47

147 Gupta Shagun (2017) RSS Women's Wing Camp Teaches Girls to be Good Mothers, *Feminism in India*, June 16, https://feminisminindia.com/2017/06/16/rss-womens-wing-camp-motherhood/ accessed on 20.07.17
148 Sharma P (2016) At Home and Work, RSS has a Model for the New Age Women, *The Hindustan Times*, December 8
149 Gowalkar MS (1980) *Bunch of Thoughts*, Jagrana Prakashna, Bangalore
150 Dixit Neha (2013) Holier Than Cow: Wisdom on Women from Rashtra Sevika Sangh Camp, *The Outlook*, January 28
151 Mosse L George (1996) *The Image of a Man: The Creation of Modern Masculinity*, Oxford University Press, New York p. 167
152 Venugopal Vasudha (2016) Celebrating 80 Years, Women's Wing of RSS Offering Self Defence Training, Lessons on Nationalism, *The Economic Times*, August 6, https://economictimes.indiatimes.com/news/politics-and-nation/celebrating-80-years-womens-wing-of-rss-offering-self-defence-training-lessons-on-nationalism/articleshow/53565167.cms
153 Dixit supra n 150
154 Dixit supra n 150
155 Dixit supra n 150
156 Sen A (2007) *Shiv Sena Women: Violence and Communalism in a Bombay Slum*, Hurst and Company, London
157 The Democratic Women's Association was set up in Tamil Nadu in 1973 to work on issues relating to employment, education, status, casteism and child rights. In affiliation with the other states-based organizations, the unified AIDWA came into existence in 1981. Formulated as a mass organization, it focuses on an anti-imperialist and pro–working-class actions while challenging and resisting cultural practices demeaning to women.
158 Website of AIDWA accessed on 20.02.14
159 Roy Arundhati (2012) Capitalism: A Ghost Story, *Outlook*, March 26
160 Kumar Radha (1993) *History of Doing: An Illustrated Account of Movements for Women's Rights and Feminism in India 1800–1900*, Zubaan, New Delhi
161 World Health Organization (2013) *Global and Regional Estimates of Violence Against Women: Prevalence and Health Effects of Intimate Partner Violence and Non-Partner Sexual Violence*, Report No. 1, Geneva
162 World Health Organization (2017) Fact Sheet: Violence Against Women, Intimate Partner and Sexual Violence Against Women, November, Http://Www.Who.Int/Mediacentre/Factsheets/Fs239/En/
163 National Crime Record Bureau (2016) *Crimes in India, 2016: Statistics, NCRB*, Ministry of Home Affairs, New Delhi
164 Ministry of Health and Family Welfare (2015–2016) National Family Health Survey – 4, Government of India, http://rchiips.org/NFHS/nfhs4.shtml
165 Ministry of Health and Family Welfare (2017) National Family Health Survey, Government of India, http://rchiips.org/nfhs/factsheet.shtm.l
166 Freire P (1972) *Cultural Action for Freedom*, Penguin Books, Harmondsworth
167 ICRW and Center for Development and Population Activities (2000) *Domestic Violence in India: A Summary Report of a Multi-Site Household Survey*, ICRW and Center for Development and Population Activities, Washington, DC
168 Rukmini S (2014) Marital and Other Rapes Grossly Under-Reported, *The Hindu*, October 22
169 No Private Matter: Confronting Domestic Violence in India, 14, www.dasra.org/research/flip/index.php?report=38#features/63 accessed 30.10.14
170 Nanda P, Gautam A, Verma R et al (2014) *Study on Masculinity, Intimate Partner Violence and Son Preference in India*, ICRW, New Delhi
171 Rao V (1997) Wife-beating in Rural South India: A Qualitative and Econometric Analysis, *Social Science Medicine*, 44, 1169–80

172 Raj A, Saggurti N, Lawrence D, Balaiah D et al. (2010) Association Between Adolescent Marriage and Marital Violence Among Young Women in India, *Indian Journal of Gynecology and Obstetrics*, 110 (1) 35–39
173 Mahapatro M, Gupta RN and Gupta V (2012) The Risk Factor of Domestic Violence in India, *Indian Journal of Community Medicine*, 37 (3) 153–57
174 Gundappa A and Rathod PB (2012) Violence Against Women in India: Preventive Measures, *Indian Streams Research Journal*, 2 (4) 1–4
175 Mahapatro M, Gupta RN, Gupta V et al. (2011) Domestic Violence During Pregnancy in India, *Journal of Interpersonal Violence*, 26 (15) 2973–90
176 Bose Sunita and South SJ (2003) Sex Composition of Children and Marital Disruption in India, *Journal of Marriage and Family*, 65 (4) 996–1006
177 Jeyseelan L, Kumar S, Neelkantan N et al. (2007) Physical Spousal Violence Against Women in India: Some Risk Factors, *Journal of Biosocial Science*, 39 (5) 657–70
178 Visaria L (2000) Violence Against Women: A Field Study, *Economic and Political Weekly*, 35, 1742–51
179 Jejeebhoy SJ and Cook RJ (1997) State Accountability for Wife-Beating: The Indian Challenge, *Lancet*, 349 Suppl 1, sI10–12
180 Ministry of External Affairs (2018) Complaints from NRI Women, Lok Sabha Unstarred Question No. 3139 Answered on 14.3.2018, Government of India
181 Khanna M (2018) Chandigarh RPO Comes to Aid of Women Deserted by NRI Grooms, *The Tribune India*, Chandigarh, June 7
182 Bates TR (1975) Gramsci and Theory of Hegemony, *Journal of the History of Ideas*, 36 (2) 351–66
183 World Health Organization (2002) *World Report on Violence and Health*, edited by EG Krug, LL Dalhberg, JA Mercy et al., World Health Organization, Geneva
184 Gupta JL, Makhija LK and Bajaj SP (2010) National Programme for Prevention of Burn Injuries, *Indian Journal of Plastic Surgery*, 43, S6–10
185 Saha D (2017) Indian Women Most Prone to Death by Fire, *IndiaSpend*, January 28, www.indiaspend.com/special-reports/indian-women-most-prone-to-death-by-fire-61951 accessed on 10.10.17
186 Fernandes D (2011) Investigating Kitchen Accidents. In *Daughters of Fire: Speaking Pain: Seeking Justice, Sustaining Resistance*, Streelekha Publications, Vimochana
187 Sanghavi P (2009) Fire-Related Deaths in India in 2001: A Retrospective Analysis of Data, *Lancet*, 373 (9671) 1282–88
188 Kumar V and Tripathi CB (2004) Burnt Wives: A Study of Homicides, *Science and Law*, 44 (1) 55–60
189 Shaha KK and Mohanty S (2006) Alleged Dowry Death: A Study of Homicidal Burns, *Medical Science and Law*, 46 (2) 105–10
190 Mohanty S, Sen M and Sahu G (2013) Analysis of Risk Factors of Dowry Deaths – A South Indian Study, *Journal of Forensic and Legal Medicine*, 20 (4) 316–20
191 *The Times of India* (2019) Haryana Spends 40 Paisa on Each Cow in Shelter, Delhi Rs 40: Arvind Kejriwal, January 14 Chandigarh Edition
192 Bhate-Deostahli P (2016) Busting the Kitchen Accident Myth: Case of Burn Injuries in India, *International Journal of Applied and Innovative Studies*, 17 (2) 388–93
193 Belur J, Tilley N and Daruwalla N (2014) The Social Construction of 'Dowry Deaths', *Social Science & Medicine*, 119, 1–9
194 Bhate-Deosthali P, Ravindran S and Vindhya U (2012) Addressing Domestic Violence Within Health Settings: The Dilaasa Model, *Economic and Political Weekly*, 47, 66–75

195 Cacophony about issues such as '*looteri dulhan*' (robber brides) is used to hide the actual cases of brutal violence. *The Times of India* (2018) Man cheated by 'Looteri dulhan' March 12 Ahmedabad edition, https://timesofindia.indiatimes.com/city/ahmedabad/man-cheated-by-looteri-dulhan/articleshow/63261007.cms
196 Stark E (2007) *Coercive Control: How Men Entrap Women in Personal Lives*, Oxford University Press, New York
197 Ackerson LK and Subramanian SV (2008) Domestic Violence and Chronic Malnutrition Among Women and Children in India, *American Journal of Epidemiology*, 167 (10) 1188–96
198 Sinha K (2007) Domestic Violence Raises Risk of Asthma: Study, *The Times of India*, May 11, https://timesofindia.indiatimes.com/india/Domestic-violence-raises-risk-of-asthma-Study/articleshow/2030533.cms
199 Reported by Bahuguna Karnika (2016) Study Links Violence to Early Signs of Heart, Blood Vessel Diseases in Women, *Down to Earth*, March 4, https://www.downtoearth.org.in/news/health/study-links-violence-to-early-signs-of-heart-blood-vessel-diseases-in-women-53089
200 Subramanian SV, Ackerson LK, Subramanyam MA et al. (2007) Domestic Violence Is Associated with Adult and Childhood Asthma Prevalence in India, *Indian Journal of Epidemiology*, 36 (3) 569–79
201 Raj Anita and Lotus McDougal (2015) Associations of Intimate Partner Violence with Unintended Pregnancy and Pre-Pregnancy Contraceptive Use in South Asia, *Contraception*, 91 (6) 456–63
202 Krug, Dalhberg, Mercy et al. (2002) supra pp. 149–81
203 Ackerson, LK and Subramanian SV (2008) Domestic Violence and Chronic Malnutrition among Women and Children in India, *American Journal of Epidemiology*, 167 (10) 1188–96. Also, Ahmed Saifuddin, Michael A Koenig et al. (2006) Effects of Domestic Violence on Perinatal and Early-Childhood Mortality: Evidence from North India, *American Journal of Public Health*, 96 (8) 1423–28
204 Murphy Claire C, Berit S, Myher TL et al. (2001) Abuse: A Risk Factor for Low Birth Weight? A Systematic Review and Meta-Analysis. *Canadian Medical Association Journal*, 164 (11) 1567–72
205 Menon Seetha (2015) *Unfinished lives: The Effect of Domestic Violence on Neonatal and Infant Mortality*, University of Essex, Colchester
206 Jejeebhoy SJ (1998) Associations Between Wife-Beating and Fetal and Infant Death: Impressions from a Survey in Rural India, *Studies in Family Planning*, 29 (3) 300–8
207 Menon S (2016) Domestic Violence and Child Mortality Rates, *The Independent*, UK, November 8, https://www.independent.co.uk/news/world/asia/india-domestic-violence-and-child-mortality-rates-a7399321.html
208 Shroff ML, Griffith PL et al (2011) Does Maternal Autonomy Influence Feeding Practices and Infant Growth in Rural India, *Social Science Medicine*, 73 (3) 447–55
209 Sabarwal S, Mccormick MC, Silverman JG et al. (2012) Association Between Maternal IPV, Victimization and Childhood Immunization in India, *Journal of Tropical Pediatrics*, 58 (2) 107–13
210 Ganatra BR, Coyaji KJ and Rao VN (1998) Too Far, Too Little, Too Late: A Community-Based Case – Control Study of Maternal Mortality in Rural West Maharashtra, India, *WHO Bulletin*, 76, 591–98
211 Weiss HH, Patel V, West B et al. (2008) Spousal Sexual Violence and Poverty Are the Risk Factors for Sexually Transmitted Infection in Women: A Longitudinal Study of Women in Goa, *Sexually Transmitted Infection*, 84 (2) 133–39
212 Silverman JG, Decker MR, Saggurti N et al. (2008) Intimate partner Violence and HIV Infection Among Indian Women, *JAMA*, 300 (6) 703–10

213 Kumar S, Jeyaseelan L, Suresh S et al. (2005) Domestic Violence and Its Mental Health Correlates in Indian Women, *The British Journal of Psychiatry: The Journal of Mental Science*, 187, 62–67

214 Choudhwry AN, Brahma A, Banerjee S et al. (2009) Pattern of Domestic Violence Amongst Non-fatal Deliberate Self Harm Attempters: A Study From primary Care of West Bengal, *Indian Journal of Psychiatry*, 51 (2) 96–100

215 Vaccher AS and Sharma AS (2010) Domestic Violence Against Women and Their Mental Health Status in a Colony in Delhi, *Indian Journal of Community Medicine*, 35 (3) 403–5. Also, Maselko J and Patel V (2008) Why Women Attempted Suicide: The Role of Mental Illness and Social Disadvantage in A Community Cohort Study in India, *Journal of Epidemiology and Community Health*, 62 (9) 817–22

216 Thara R (1998) *A Study of Mentally Disabled Women, Sponsored by NCW*, SCARF Publication, New Delhi

217 *The Economic Times* (2019) India Facing Shortage of 600,000 Doctors and 2 Million Nurses: Study, April 14, https://economictimes.indiatimes.com/industry/healthcare/biotech/healthcare/india-facing-shortage-of-600000-doctors-2-million-nurses-study/articleshow/68875822.cms?from=mdr

218 Government of India (2017) Unstarred Lok Sabha Question Number 2709 Answered on 17.3.2017 on Shortage of Mental Health Care Professionals, http://164.100.47.194/Loksabha/Questions/QResult15.aspx?qref=48992&lsno=16

219 Prabhakar A and Dubois K (2013) Finally, a National Survey on Mental Health Disorders in India, *DNA*, June 16, https://www.dnaindia.com/health/report-finally-a-national-survey-on-mental-health-disorders-in-india-1848694

220 Jejeebhoy, S, Santhya KG and Acharya R (2010) *Health and Social Consequences of Marital Violence: A Synthesis of Evidence from India*, United Nations Population Council, New Delhi

221 Duvvury N, Callan A, Carney P and Srinivas R (2013) *Intimate Partner Violence: Economic Costs and Implications for Growth and Development.* In Women's Voice, Agency, and Participation Research Series No. 3, World Bank, Washington DC

222 Stark E (2007) *Coercive Control: How Men Entrap Women in Personal Life*, Oxford University Press, New York

223 Robert Pearl (2013) Domestic Violence: The Secret Killer that Cost $ 8.3 Billion Annually, *Forbes*, December 5

224 Raghvendra Srinivas (2017) Dismissing Domestic Violence As a 'Private Matter' Ignore Adverse Impact on Economy, *The Wire*, August 22, https://thewire.in/gender/domestic-violence-women-private-matter-economy

2 Legislating the laws relating to domestic violence

"Patriarchy requires violence or the subliminal threat of violence in order to maintain itself. . . . The most dangerous situation for a woman is not an unknown man in the street, or even an enemy in the wartime, but a husband or lover in the isolation of their own home".[1]

The 'rule of law' has evolved gradually over time while responding to social changes. However, in the context of regulation of conjugality or kinship, the rule of law could not alter the rigid and biased family norms or the authority vested with patriarchs in the family. In other words, the rule of patriarchy continued despite interventions continuously being sought by the women's movement to make interventions through the law. The legal system frequently reiterates the patriarchy and reinforces the subordinated status of women. Legal reforms made rhetorical changes but failed to alter subjugated position of women in marriage. The male prerogative to discipline women has been reinforced by the law, which upholds the notion of preserving 'domestic harmony' and non-interference in marital privacy while clandestinely supporting violence within homes. It could only provide symptomatic relief or could fix the problem superficially rather than imagining the possibility of liberating women or erasing the inherent structural inequalities within the institution of the family. This chapter examines the process of legal reform in the context of domestic violence in India. It focuses on the nuances of the process by which laws to prevent domestic abuse have been made. Further, it examines the rationale and defines the methodology taken up to conduct this work.

Domestic violence and legal reforms in the Indian context

In India, the debate on domestic violence law draws a linkage to the issue of dowry abuse. Domestic abuse did not appear as an issue affecting women until the 1980s, when Section 498A IPC was introduced along with Section 304B IPC relating to dowry death. In post-colonial India, over time, the concept of dowry has evolved as a compulsive, coercive, non-voluntary and oppressive practice[2] to such an extent that today it has become a burden.[3] Today, the dowry has taken the form of gold, clothes, cash, car, expensive gifts and lavish weddings. Often, marriages are decided on the amount of the dowry the girl's parents are willing to pay. A marital relationship therefore becomes a commercial transaction where the bride is accepted only when she is accompanied by material wealth. Transactions do not end with marriage; later demands often follow in the form of festivals, birth of children or whenever the in-laws wish. Yet women face violence not only because dowry demands remain unfulfilled but also for many other (non) reasons, such as not serving hot food, talking to a stranger, disobedience, using contraceptives without permission, not being able to produce babies[4] and many more – most of which relate to devaluing the status of women within families. This barbaric practice of coercion, control and chastisement in the guise of love and discipline could not be challenged successfully by the women's movement or the state and that has cemented the regressive family ideology with its traditional authority structure. Attempts to lift the veil of family sanctity to question the gender hierarchy which puts women on a lower pedestal could not be made.

Examining dowry abuse

Dowry is a hegemonic, upper-caste, Brahmanical practice that replaced the custom of 'bride price' with the giving of gifts by the parents and relatives of the bride at the time of the marriage or before or after it.[5] Dowry has become more pervasive with the sanskritization and emergence of a consumerist culture in a feudal society. Marketization has fueled materialistic attitudes, and the concept of dowry became further entrenched with globalization, wherein the greed to acquire wealth made it more virulent.[6] As a daughter-in-law, a woman is viewed as a vector for status preservation and potential upward mobility for her marital family, and therefore her status is devalued.[7]

Some scholars viewed dowry as *streedhan*, or a woman's property, to be used by her, as a form of inheritance in land-dominated agriculture economies. In fact, women's status and share in property are both linked to marriage.[8] This is a problematic construct. A glimpse into the practice shows that a woman is neither in a position to determine its quantity nor does she have the right to control the dowry. The amount of the dowry is negotiated by the patriarchs within the two families. Thus, dowry, in practice, is less of a form of social security to a woman; rather, it is a means to coercively and forcefully pressure her to submit to demands made by the husband and in-laws.

Even earlier, imperial rulers drew erroneous linkages between dowry and infanticide as a 'moral mission of civilizing Indians' and 'preventing them from killing their own women'. This is characterized by Spivak's[9] famous phrase "White men saving brown women from brown men". The colonial rulers connected dowry to expensive marriage, greed, hypergamy, female infanticide and caste practices while ignoring factors such as the commodification of women or denial of their property rights. Oldenburg argued that the pre-colonial communal land-sharing model in Punjab was changed entirely during the colonial rule based on the British model of private property, which was masculine.[10] The crux of this argument is that dowry is not a customary practice; rather, it was an evolving institution and has linkages with violence because of the restructuring of property rights that occurred under the colonial rulers. The idea of private ownership was alien to Indian soil, and it was during the colonial regime that men in North India became the sole managers of the family property while women's right to land was completely eroded. Britishers, in their zeal to collect revenue, expanded the system of privatization of property and made the situation worse for women by intensifying a harsher form of a patriarchal system that completely curtailed women's autonomy, even in peasant communities where women used to contribute economically.

In the patriarchal North Indian society, even before property was privatized, male progeny was in high demand because additional sons apparently enhance 'power' as well as the capacity to defend land and water rights in an agrarian economy.[11] Chowdhry[12] pointed out that in the economically depressed region of Haryana, because of dependence on the family-run farm labor, male progeny was preferred, leading to the practice of female infanticide. Daughters have been viewed as burdens and marginal members and therefore are denied rights in the parental family.[13] In fact, linkages exist between dowry and sex-selective abortions, as well as other forms of discrimination and subordination, including son preference, indebtedness among poor families and devaluation of women.[14] The worth of a woman is reduced to a commodity, while prerogatives are given to men to chastise and exploit women.

This connection between dowry, greed and the burden of a girl child lasted throughout the nineteenth and twentieth centuries and remained a major area of concern for the women's movements after independence. It led to the formulation of the Dowry Prohibition Act of 1961. Though many women actively took part in the freedom movement and played a dynamic role in the framing of the constitution, the question relating to dowry and violence in marriage could not receive sufficient attention. Basu, while pointing to the Parliamentary debate in 1959, observed that "Most legislators objected virulently to the 1959 joint committee's suggestion to ban all the gifts . . . revealing an understanding of dowry as an indubitable element of Hindu marriage and a protective gesture toward women".[15] A few members advocated banning all forms of gifts; however, "the prevailing discourse was one of retaining traditions and conveying a symbolic disapproval over extravagance and extortion in the form of legislation".[16] Dowry could not be construed as an exploitative practice; rather, the legislators deem it as a traditional, harmless voluntary gift exchange. This view has a negative repercussion where preserving traditions, practices and customs is prioritized over protecting women from violence. Given the limited scope of the Dowry Prohibition Act, not many cases were filed in the period from 1961 to 1984, and even those which were filed resulted in few convictions.

Legal reforms to address violence in marriage

The 1980s witnessed a process of legal reforms. These stemmed from the contradictions in the law and its failure to remedy the situation of persistent inequalities within the patriarchal society that resulted in murders or 'stove-deaths' of women. The ruthless killing of 21-year-old Shashibala in March 1979[17] within a year of her marriage while she was pregnant acted as a stimulus. Soon 'dowry violence' became a metaphor for describing cases of killings of young women in their matrimonial homes, while unmasking the internal dynamics and daily trauma of 'traditional family life'.[18] Women's organizations highlighted the fact that the deaths were not accidents but murders due to dowry abuse. On 17 May 1979, Tarvinder Kaur, a 24-year-old Sikh bride from Model Town, Delhi, was burned alive, but her death was registered as a suicide by police even though in her dying statement, she clearly stated that her in-laws had set her on fire. Similarly, Kanchan Chopra, a stenographer in Delhi, was burned by her husband after she was forced to swallow acid. Police again registered this case as a suicide. This callousness and corruption on the part of police created outrage and resulted in demonstrations.

In fact, in 1979, 358 deaths were reported in Delhi, where fewer than 50 were reported as suicides, 23 were labeled as bride burning and the remaining were classified as accidental. These increased to 466 in 1981 and 537 by 1982.[19] Also, in response to a question in Parliament, the then Minister of Home Affairs Mr. Chidambaram noted that registered cases of dowry deaths nationwide numbered 999 in 1985, 1,319 in 1986 and 1,786 in 1987. The real number remains much higher, as many cases were not reported or registered inaccurately by the police. Experiences reveal that in cases relating to dowry murders, police showed apathy in investigating, or the courts acquitted the accused for frivolous reasons. An increasing number of women have been burned alive, yet the consciousness to save women could not emerge among the law implementers or policy framers.

Public protests against police apathy grew vehemently when women were murdered ruthlessly and yet police refused to act.[20] An anti-dowry campaign was held around shaming the families and a social boycott of those who demanded a dowry. Raising consciousness about dowry violence and insisting that the police take strict action in such cases were a few of the steps taken. Conducting *dharna* outside the husband's house who allegedly tortured a bride was seen as a swift means of redressal. The major object of the campaign was to condemn the dowry as a social evil.[21] It focused on the inadequacy in laws and procedures. Domestic abuse, in itself, was not raised as an issue. The patriarchy was so deeply internalized that no concerns were raised even when women were compelled to adjust to brutal torture or harassment within their marital home. Neither the chastisement prerogative of husbands nor their violent behavior toward wives were questioned.

Meanwhile, a private member's[22] bill was introduced to amend the Dowry Prohibition Act 1961, and the matter was subsequently referred to a Joint Select Committee (JSC) of both the Houses of Parliament. By August 1982, the JSC[23] presented its report and identified several deficiencies, such as the narrow definition of dowry, procedural lapses in filing cases and lack of deterrent punishment. The notorious murder of Sudha Goel[24] became a point to rally round when the High Court overturned the conviction of the husband, mother-in-law and brother-in-law. Several women's organizations came together under the banner of *Dahej Virodhi Chetna Manch*[25] (DVCM). Members of DVCM

> viewed legal changes as an instrument of social change, aware of inadequacies in laws and the collusion and connivance of the police and local administration. Its efforts were directed at changing public consciousness, in order to build the necessary social and political will to ensure action that would be effective in eradicating both the practice of dowry and increasing brutalities against brides.[26]

The recommendations of the JSC became a point of mobilization for the movement and provided the basis for evolving a demand charter. The memorandum issued by the DVCM in 1982 stated that "dowry was not an isolated phenomenon" but an aspect of "inferior female condition" and "the erosion of women's status and devaluation of female life". It called for a transformation of family relations and mandated for "legal, administrative and social measures". Demands were made for the registration of marriages, legal aid, use of mass media and changes in school curricula. The DVCM took up signature and postcard campaigns; held public meetings; and organized street plays, seminars, rallies, marches and demonstrations to mobilize public opinion while lobbying with the MPs.[27] Mass pledges were organized against the dowry system.

Confronting, educating and pushing the disinterested government to fulfill its responsibilities emerged as major challenges before the movement. Yet the movement succeeded in shaping the public response and breaking the culture of silence around violence. These efforts played a significant role in influencing the laws, persuading the government's response and shaping public consciousness while signaling the entry of domestic violence, a 'private matter', into the public discourse as a social problem worthy of moral condemnation and legal sanctions.[28] One of the major hurdles was that the 'Indian family and its traditions' had been cast as the bedrock of the social fabric by several government 'representatives' of society, the judiciary and academics. The view of dowry as the degeneration of moral, social and familial values and demands made by the movement had been thwarted in the name of 'custom', 'family' and 'religion'. The movement thus had to find ways to negotiate within two separate domains – the state and the community, which are interlinked in complicated ways; therefore, the articulation of many issues became challenging.[29] Also, the organizations involved in the DVCM had different perspectives of women's oppression; therefore, working out a concrete set of demands was crucial in order to work under a common umbrella. However, several scholars argued that the anti-dowry movement played a significant role in bringing the issue of violence to public fora, while at the same time condemning it and therefore has reshaped the domestic violence discourse.[30] Nonetheless, the campaign could not be sustained for long once the law was amended.

Efforts made by the movement could not alter the situation, probably because the protests of the 1980s began in the face of police refusal to register cases against families accused of burning wives because either they were bribed by the grooms' families or police ignored the evidence and filed the case as a suicide and not as a dowry death despite the contradictory dying statements, yet the focus was laid on strengthening the state.[31] Ironically, the movement relied on the state's (in)ability to protect women when the state itself appeared as a culprit of not addressing women's concerns. Police hesitated to interfere and advised women to use social pressure rather than taking the recourse of the law.[32] Yet the misplaced strategy focused on police action which empowered the police rather than consolidated gains for women. Further, dowry violence has been projected as a social evil rather than as a serious crime, which diluted the impact of the interventions. The movement has extensively focused on legal reforms, despite of the fact that the law does not ensures gender justice. The structures of gendered inequality in which the dowry is embedded remain untouched while a range of socio-economic inequalities that devalue women could not be addressed.[33] Also, for abandoned or single women, no remedy is being made available.[34] Agnihotri and Mazumdar[35] noted a sense of defeat in the women's movement with regard to the agitation initiated in the 1980s as it ended up perpetuating a 'women as victim syndrome'.

Additionally, establishing links between dowry violence and domestic abuse has weakened the campaign. Agnes stated that perhaps "it was easier to focus on 'dowry' as an external element and project the mother-in-law as the main culprit, than address the issue of sexual control, lack of property rights in the natal home and stigma of divorce".[36] Patrilocal and patrilineal families where the mother-in-law and daughter-in-law are often at odds for the control of power, status and finances has not been raised as an issue. Discriminatory practices such as *kanyadaan* which objectify a woman could not be confronted. Further, marriage is not construed as a relationship based on companionship. Finally, neither hierarchy in the conjugality could be challenged nor could conjugal contracts could be reworked to push democratic norms.

Anti-arrack movements and alcohol ban protests have been held at various places where the agitating wives continuously have drawn attention to links between wife beating and their husbands' drinking habits and that drunk men as husbands are vile and deviant who destroy the 'sanctity of the family'. However, the discourse on domestic violence could not demonstrate the fact that these men are 'incompetent' to rule within their homes. Similarly, greedy men and their families who were burning brides or abandoning women to remarry to recollect dowry from other women could not be held accountable for their rapacious criminal acts. Rather, the authority of violent husbands could neither be questioned nor they were held accountable; instead, gruesome reports of wife battering have been suppressed under the garb of 'protection' and 'privacy'. Domestic violence is not visualized as a 'law and order' issue by the state. Rather, the state promoted dowry and exploitation of girls in the guise of several schemes, such as Sumangli in Tamil Nadu,[37] Arundhati in Assam,[38] Laadli Scheme in Goa[39] or Rupashree in West Bengal.[40] Marriage is an institution that reinforces patriarchy and subordination with regard to property, sexual oppression, division of labor and reproduction – this construction has not been challenged.[41] Kapur[42] has rightly stated that the movement has pushed for equal rights without "disrupting the dominant, culture, familial and sexual norms that define Indian womanhood:.

In the cases of Tarvinder Kaur, Sudha Goel, Shashibala, Kanchan Chopra and many others, the secondary status of women in marriage came to light. Despite repeated complaints of torture, these women were compelled to 'adjust' within the marriage until finally they were murdered. Yet, no efforts have been made to tackle this tremendous pressure on women to stay in a violent relationship. The discourse on violence has not questioned the vulnerable position of a bride in her matrimonial household. Perhaps marriage is imagined as the only way to control women's sexuality. Domestic violence is seen as an effect of the devaluation of the status of women, yet not much is done to eliminate the power imbalance with the hierarchical family arrangements. Demands have been made to strengthen laws, but no interventions have been sought to create shelter homes, short-stay homes or creches, or to provide medical facilities or legal aid to support victims of violence. Neither recommendations could be made to create conditions to facilitate women's economic independence, nor material or emotional support could be imagined by the state or society. The independent existence of a single women as citizens could not be conceptualized, while the idea of inequality within marriage has been upheld as divine above the rule of law. This nourished the right-wing ideology that co-opted the women's movement agenda.

The creation of criminal law against domestic violence

It was only after women's groups took to the streets to protest dowry-related murders that the Criminal Law (Second) Amendment Act 1983 was introduced by the state as a package to curb violence. The then Minister of Home Affairs Venkatasubbaiah introduced the bill to "cover cases of cruelty on account of dowry or otherwise" in recognition of the ineffectiveness of the Dowry Prohibition Act 1961. In its statement of objects and reasons it says that "Cases of cruelty by husband and relatives of husbands which culminates in suicide by, or murder of the helpless women concerned, constitute only a small fraction of the cases involving such cruelty". During the debates, Parliament members argued that the legal provisions were inadequate and not punitive enough. For instance, Geeta Mukherjee[43] suggested,

> In our experience, it is not necessary that this phenomenon (of Marital cruelty) is only connected with dowry, but with certain other things which are equally cruel leading to death. Secondly, I think that it is not only a question of husband and wife. . . . Take, for example, the wife of a brother. If the brother dies, the widow still remains within the family . . . this woman is harassed, sometimes so much that very often death takes place because of that harassment also. This should be included in 498A.[44]

Others opposed it while raising the plea of the 'sacred family'. There were those who perceived women as agents challenging the domestic hierarchy, while others saw them as helpless victims.[45] Some viewed domestic violence as a male-versus-female issue,[46] while others added a 'salacious tinge' to the debate where the use of female sexuality was depicted as a tool while negating the issue of women's vulnerability within marriage.[47] For instance, Shri Moil Chand Dada stated, "You women influence men at night, you can persuade them to do anything".[48] Also, a few projected traditional stereotypical images of women as wives and mothers rather than seeing women as citizens claiming rights. Yet others reinforced the misogynistic position that 'women are women's worst enemies' while pitting mothers-in-law against daughters-in-law. One of the members argued,

> Can I put one straight question? Who is the mother-in-law? Is she also a male member? . . . The mother-in-law not only insists, but also compels the husband of the poor girl to live separately. . . . So why do you look at the problem as male or female?[49]

Another member also raised a similar argument: "where women are beaten and even killed, aren't women also responsible? Mother-in-law and sister-in-law are women. Don't women provoke and encourage men, so that men are forced to commit crime?"[50] Thus, in all such positions, the issue of domestic violence was trivialized, normalized and reduced to a man-versus-woman issue rather than as a larger question relating to patriarchy. Legislative debates ignored the specificity of wife beating. The concept of setting up shelter homes was not taken up, and the existence of women apart from the family was considered an anomaly.[51]

Nonetheless, a consensus finally emerged, and the Criminal Law (Second) Amendment Act, 1983[52] introduced Section 498A, 304B and added stringent punishments under Section 306, IPC. These provisions criminalized domestic violence, dowry deaths and abetment to suicide. Simultaneously, Section 113(A) was introduced in the Indian Evidence Act, which states that if a woman commits suicide within seven years of marriage and there is evidence of cruelty prior to her death, her husband and in-laws would be held responsible for her murder unless evidence to the contrary is provided. Also, amendments were made in the Code of Criminal Procedure directing a post-mortem and inquiry in cases of the unnatural death of a woman within seven years of marriage to determine the cause of death. Further, amendments have been made in the Dowry Prohibition Act in 1984 and again in 1986 in order to prescribe stringent punishments to ensure that those who commit violence should not escape the clutches of law. Yet despite these amendments, the practice of dowry has escalated. Today the situation is that families of grooms are making exorbitant demands and are pushing for luxurious wedding arrangements, and the parents of bride are fulfilling these, perhaps because of the social pressure or that society has accepted the devalued status of women.

While such amendments were being made, some lawyers argued that Section 498A created a system of double jeopardy, as it replicates the Section 4 of the Dowry Prohibition Act and the accused is tried for the same crime under two laws, which is legally untenable.[53] However, what is overlooked in this argument is that Section 4 of the Dowry Prohibition Act merely punishes the demand for dowry, whereas 498A deals with aggression, violence and brutalities. This is not to deny that women are tormented for not bringing a dowry, yet besides a dowry, women are abused in their everyday lives routinely for (non)reasons.[54] However, the law implementers portrayed a strong connection between dowry and domestic violence and therefore when a woman approaches them, they advised her to add a dowry component to the complaint to make the 'case strong'. Agnes opined that "the blame also lies with the women's movement which, in the 1980s, gave dowry-related violence greater importance and demanded separate legal provisions to address this issue. This only served to undermine routine domestic violence".[55] Also, law implementers likely see dowry abuse or domestic violence as moral and social evils rather than as crimes that need to be punished.

How 498A failed women survivors of domestic violence

Once the law to criminalize domestic abuse was framed, the onus was on women facing domestic abuse to register their FIRs. However, experience shows that not all women who face abuse come forward to register their complaints. A study conducted in 2005 observed that nearly five crore married women were victims of domestic violence, and merely 0.1 percent (1 out of 1,000) reported their complaints.[56] In fact, women suffered for years before reporting violence. A multitude of factors prevents them from challenging their violent husbands. The lackadaisical attitude of the police and courts and their insensitivities appeared as major barriers.[57] Women have to add vague allegations of dowry demand to the genuine complaint of wife beating because police refuse to register a case under 498A. Corruption, delay in trial, lack of resources, stigma associated with women defying norms and other factors prevented many from seeking justice.[58] Those who reached the court encountered a hostile atmosphere.[59] Husbands harassed women by not appearing in the court. In 40 percent of cases, the accused was acquitted because of inconsistencies in the complainant's testimony or because of lack of sufficient proof to show that violence took place. Witnesses in most cases were relatives of the wife who were not living with her; therefore, their testimonies were dismissed as hearsay.

The experience of over three decades with 498A reveals that though the law provides a platform where a woman facing domestic abuse can raise her concerns, in its implementation, it is limited and has not been able to provide steady solutions to end violence. In other words, as the constitutional guarantee of equality failed to uphold gender parity,[60] similarly, the provisions under 498A could not deter violence within homes. The state reinforces the family ideology, and therefore the law disempowers survivors because it introduced mediation within marriage while linking it to the question of women's survival. Initially, lawyers and women's groups used it as a tool to bargain for women's economic rights vis-à-vis violent husbands, thus creating a new legal culture. For instance, when a battered wife complains under 498A, the violent husband is called upon and the counselor or the police negotiate on behalf of the woman. As the victim has no other means to support herself, she is either sent back to the violent situation with no guarantee that she will not be abused again or the case is 'settled' if she stays in her *maika* with little or no recompense.[61] The case is sent to trial only after negotiations fail. It is then that the police may help her in retrieval of her *streedhan*.[62] Punitive action is not taken against the abusive husbands. This is evident by the data available on conviction rates.[63]

Instead of seeing wife beating as a crime against women's body, integrity or dignity, the manner in which 498A is implemented is such that the remedies are linked to the women's economic dependence in marriage, and thus the execution of the law became ambiguous. 498A is used to provide customized solutions to the conventional problem and, in the process, protects abusive husbands while offering no remedy to the battered wife. Rather than empowering women as agents to control their lives, the law took away the privileges complainants have in the criminal justice system. Section 498A has been twisted and molded to create counseling or mediation centers. However, such reshaping granted formal and informal immunity to the abusers, while efficacy of the law is drastically reduced, as it fails to bring social transformation in deterring violence or shaping the concept of equity within marriage.

Also, there exists a gap between theoretical aspects and the manner in which the law is operationalized.[64] Most of the law implementers are men, and in their role as 'protectors' they use laws to enforce more control on women's lives. Conjugality is construed through the prism of family ideology, while emphasis is laid on preserving 'domestic harmony' rather than questioning the hierarchy or abuse of power in the relationship. Women are continuously pressured to defer to authority structures in their affinal homes without agitation despite of facing serious consequences. The conviction rate is low, and this is attributed to the immense pressure created by the police to compromise or to arrive at a settlement between the parties. It their righteous desire to 'save families' – officials offer forced counselling, which is neither the primary role of the judiciary nor the police, and in the process, women are forced to 'adjust' to violent marriages and withdraw their complaints.[65] Serious violence is normalized while negotiating rights of the complainants.[66] Contradictions inherent in the content, structure and process of laws further complicate the matter, as they do not question the fundamental inequality on which the relationship rests.

The operationalization of provisions of Section 498A is problematic, but other related laws that protect the rights of women are also not implemented properly. For instance, while implementing Section 125 CrPC that provides for maintenance to wives and children, the rhetoric of family ideology is utilized. A woman has to prove that she is a dependent and that her marriage is valid, also that she has not remarried and is not adulterous. She has to prove that her husband has the means while she herself could not earn a living. A woman's chastity decides whether she deserves maintenance or not. An 'unchaste woman' disentitles herself from receiving 'protection'. Mukhopadhyay[67] noted that "Section 125 both in its intentions (protecting women from destitution) and in adjudication (protecting the ideal of the 'good and wronged wife') is embedded in a discourse of 'protection". Even in cases where the order is passed, the amount is too low to protect women from destitution. The courts ignore women's contributions or titles to matrimonial property.[68]

Family and polity are seen as separate affairs, and this public-private divide helped the state to evade its accountability and responsibility.[69] Thus, placing a heavy reliance on the state to provide justice to survivors through legal reforms put women's rights at risk. The state promoted the male-dominated hierarchies while the style of control has been impersonal or abstract and bureaucratic. Seeking changes in legislation against domestic violence represents an attempt to obtain state intervention into the family, which for the most part is deemed by the state as 'private' for which traditionally it has no commitment. This presents serious problems both for women being abused within families and for the movement demanding legal reforms. A woman seeking the arrest of abusers is directly demanding state intervention in a private world of the family, which is viewed with suspicion. Similarly, demands relating to strengthening the criminal justice system have been overlooked; rather, the state, without analyzing the data, diluted the provisions of Section 498A while pushing the myth of misuse of law because well-connected male lobbyists made noise.[70]

Family courts uphold family ideologies, not gender justice

Demands were made to establish family courts, and the Family Court Act was enacted in 1984. The law provides for specialized forums to deal with 'matrimonial conflicts' and not domestic violence. These are designed to adjudicate matters such as divorce, custody suits, maintenance, restitution of conjugal rights and connected issues. The goal is to make the courts accessible and less intimidating for women through dispensing with lawyers, legalistic jargon, strict rules of procedures and standard of evidence. These courts depicted mediation as an alternative to the patriarchy-inspired adversary system. This is preferred by many because of its reputation to provide for a better hearing. Yet this system could not aid in reducing violence or enabling justice for women. Studies have shown that the family courts are not free from difficulties like backlogs, the exploitative commercial approach of lawyers, long drawn-out battles, multiple court proceedings and the insensitive approach of officials.

Family courts were created with a view to avoid cumbersome litigation and replace it with *samjhauta*, or 'brokering compromises', in order to achieve efficiency and to shed the burden of the law. These courts mandatorily offer coercive persuasions to forcefully push women back to the violent families, to 'adjust', to 'compromise' to 'preserve marriage', even if it endangers their life and limb. An idea that is constantly being pushed is that the family is equipped to protect women while underplaying violence in it. Perhaps it is easier and more economical to compel women rather than question a man's violent behavior. What is erroneously strengthened is the belief that women prefer to stay within abusive households, and therefore through 'forced compromises' they are compelled to accept the violent situation without any guarantee to their safety or security. No options are offered outside the domain of the 'sacrosanct' family. The rhetoric of 'counselling', 'mediation' or 'settlement' reiterates the regressive family ideology rather than protecting women from violence or providing psycho-social support to victims. The focus on settling 'family disputes' could not deal with the serious violence women face. Family courts negate women's experience of violence rather than providing justice. Theoretically, an adversary system is replaced to resolve the matters expeditiously and harmoniously, but in reality, the criminal justice system is twisted to adjust to the tenor of the patriarchy.

The alternative dispute resolution system diluted the seriousness of domestic violence in various ways. The language itself deliberately lessens the gravity of an offense committed within the *chardiwari* of the household.

The term 'dispute' entails that two parties are equal, as compared to the term 'violence' that implies an abuse of power. The concept of parity among parties on unequal footing is introduced silently by the slyness of the patriarchal forces. No attempts have been made to question the inequality in the relationship. This misconceived approach overlooks the fact that conciliation as a technique poses grave problems, as it overlooks the concept of power within the relation. It expands the state's control over individual behavior within families, and more specifically, it is at times being used to cement the norms of 'good wife', 'good mother' or a 'bad woman'. Further, denial of anger and the command to forget the past and live in the present generate dissatisfaction and give rise to a feeling of injustice. The law has reinforced patriarchal oppression while discriminating against women.

Mediation avoids questions relating to power, property and violence within a relationship.[71] Use of a coercion in a situation when two parties are not on par creates problems rather than resolving issues. This process of 'coercive harmony' as explained by Laura Nader destroys rights by limiting discussion of the past.[72] It prohibits anger, curtails freedom, eliminates choices and removes protection of the law. It ignores a 'victim' status and compels a woman to compromise her health, life or limb. Mediation within marriage does not address the structure of power located within the relationship and ignores the fact that parties in conflict in no way operate within the universe of 'balanced bargaining equity'. It does not satisfy the survivor's need for justice. Rather, it normalizes and trivializes the violence in everyday lives and compels survivors to curtail their emotions and hide the resentments that arise when they face abuse. During the process of mediation, a woman is vulnerable to threats and harassment and is under extreme stress and pressure, yet the reconciliation procedure does not consider these facts. Mediation overlooks legal entitlements and ends up in denying justice to women who have less bargaining power and perhaps lack the capacity to negotiate.

Another choice offered is 'settlement', where a victim is left with no other alternative but to fend for herself and her children in lieu of a meagre amount of money, if any, offered by the violent husband, or she may stay at her *maika* or remarry. Therefore, these so-called 'women-friendly' adjudication spaces failed to address the concerns of the victims of violence.[73] In other word, these courts are 'family-centric'[74] rather than 'victim- or survivor-centric'. This approach rejects the notion of making survivors economically self-sufficient or offer options to lend socio-economic support to victims. The patriarchal imagination failed to provide distributive justice or material relief and support to the abused wives through a single-window mechanism despite the knowledge that a comprehensive rehabilitative package is essential to remedy the situation of violence. The bold notion of challenging male dominance while improving the status of women or providing innovative solutions aiding survivors has not been imagined as an alternative by the state or the society.

The object of PWDVA

The PWDVA was enacted in 2005 to ensure that the concerns that women litigants face once they file a complaint under Section 498A IPC could be addressed. Though Section 498A recognizes the fact that offenses committed within the privacy of the home need to be dealt with on a different plane, it does not restrain a violent husband from indulging in abusive conduct, nor does it offer civil remedies. A complaint under this law can be made only after the crime is committed and the law requires that extreme cruelty must be proved. To seek other remedies such as divorce, custody or maintenance, a woman has to resort to personal laws or civil laws for which an application has to be filed before a civil court to obtain injunctions. Further, for claiming maintenance, a separate application is either filed under Section 125 CrPC or this remedy has to be invoked under the personal laws. Dispossession from the matrimonial home is one of the common complaints reported by women once they register a complaint against their violent husbands. Further, provisions under 498A do not help widows, daughters, women in live-in relationships and other women in a household.

Several women's groups advocated for legislation that would remedy these defects. The demands include a law that would comprehensively define domestic violence. There was also a demand for protection orders that could be immediately passed so a woman would be safeguarded from further violence. Most reliefs that women require in the face of violence are civil in nature as the right to residence, maintenance or custody; the need was therefore felt for a civil law which could offer such remedies. In 1992, a draft of a model law on domestic violence was circulated. This was picked up by the NCW. In 1994, a committee established by the NCW came up with a proposal for the Domestic Violence Bill, where provisions such as the right to reside in the matrimonial home were included for the first time. However, the proponents did not get an opportunity to table this draft in Parliament. In 1998, the Lawyers' Collective, in consultation with various women's groups, proposed an alternative bill in accordance with the UN Framework for Model Legislation on domestic violence.[75] International events such as the UN mandate to address violence against women, CEDAW[76] and the Beijing Conference created sufficient pressure on the government to introduce a bill on the issue.

The Ministry of Human Resources Development proposed a Bill on Protection from Domestic Violence in 2001. It was initially during the NDA regime when the Domestic Violence Bill was first tabled in March 2002. This tabled bill amended the major portions of the draft bill circulated by the women's organizations earlier. For example, the NDA government bill proposed the narrow definition of violence and suggested that husbands can assault their wives in 'self-defense'. This suggestion created outrage, as it gives the right to self-defense to the abuser rather than to the victim. This was a plain case of male bias that is easy to manipulate and allows abusers to obtain acquittal easily. Second, this bill recognized "habitual assault" that could be penalized, which implied that an occasional assault is acceptable and should be forgiven. This idea reflects entrenched patriarchal biases. The definitions, reliefs and remedies were not spelled out clearly on the pretext that it would make the law more flexible and enable the judiciary to provide judgements on a case-to-case basis. However, this bill was not passed and thus the women's movement restarted the campaign. Efforts were made to approach the DWCD for legitimizing earlier claims besides lobbying with the MPs for a favorable law. In response to this concerted pressure, a Parliamentary Standing Committee was set up to re-examine the bill. Its report was laid before Parliament in December 2002.[77] This committee brought back most of the elements that the women's group had demanded. However, progress in the passage of the law was stalled for the next two years when Parliament was dissolved in 2004. The newly elected UPA government referred the bill to the DWCD.

Debate on the PWDVA

In the debates in Parliament before the PWDVA was passed in 2005, the concept of domestic violence was articulated in terms of human rights. Many members spoke on the issue, yet none could question inequalities within the institution of the family. A few raised concerns about the inclusion of different categories of women under the ambit of the law. For instance, Smt Archana Nayak argued,

> Disabled women suffer from a double disadvantage: Apart from their being women, they are also physically or mentally challenged. Such women constitute a special category. Many women, who are physically or mentally challenged, have been sexually abused by close relatives. For example, many of the disabled women in Orissa, who constitute 50 per cent of the 40-lakh disabled population in the State, are increasingly becoming victims of domestic violence. I, therefore, suggest that there should be a special provision in the Bill to award maximum punishment to such perpetrators of violence.[78]

She also suggested that the bill is silent on violence committed on a maidservant who works within the household. Suggestions have also been raised to empower survivors by providing facilities and monetary aid. Smt Krishna Tirath elaborated,

> I suggest that women should be provided free legal aid as when they are going through this trauma, neither natal nor marital family support them. In case, a woman is thrown out, as in situation where grown up children abandon their mothers, they should be provided with shelter and the state must provide them with some stipend and should take care

> of them till they get the justice. For this purpose, rehabilitation centers must be made in line with the working women hostels and these women should be provided with full monetary relief.[79]

Certain members also objected to the application of the law in the context of live-in relationships while pitting the rights of a wife against the woman in a live-in relationship. Smt Kiran Maheshwari opined,

> I cautioned because under the Hindu Marriage Act a woman is granted a status of wife because she comes to her husband's house after completing the rituals. In case, any other relationship is given importance, it will adversely affect the rights of a wife and also would imply promoting modern values where without having valid legal sanction the relationship between two people will be legitimized. Further, I also caution regarding the misuse of this law.[80]
>
> (Translated from Hindi)

The aberrant behavior of men indulging in the act of violence against wives or men involved in bigamous relationships or men abandoning their wives was not raised in these debates. Rhetoric of discomfort with the notions of women's assertion was apparent, as happened during the 1980s while debating and legislating on Section 498A. For instance, Mr. Mitrasen Yadav raised the issue that bringing the law within a relationship may destroy the sanctity of the family and suggested that as per the cultural practice, women are provided protection by the male family members as fathers, brothers, husbands and sons, so there in no need for a separate law. Further, apprehensions have been raised regarding the abuse of the law by women. Ramji Suman suggested that "similar protections should be offered to men".[81] Another member, Shailender Kumar, argued against the bill, citing the culture as a reason and proposed that once a woman within a marriage is empowered, she may attempt to subjugate a man. The misconceived logic of patriarchy blindly asserted male chauvinism rather than examining the vulnerable situation of women in violent relationships. However, despite such deliberations and discussions, the bill was approved in 2005. In September 2005, it received the president's assent and was published in the Gazette of India.[82] It took another year for this act to come into force when the rules and regulations for its implementation could be framed, and it came into force on 26 October 2006.

Salient features of the PWDVA

The PWDVA provides "effective protection of the rights of women guaranteed under the constitution who are victim[s] of violence of any kind occurring within the family". Not only is the PWDVA gender specific; it provides a rationale for having a gender-specific measure, sanctioned in

Article 15(3) of the constitution, which allows special measures to be taken for women and children. It allows women to seek civil injunctions in the form of orders, and breaches of such orders by the respondent are treated as criminal offenses attracting penalties. Even though the law is civil, the access to these provisions is through magistrates' courts, thus aiming to enhance the gravity of orders issued by the courts.[83] Supposedly, it ensures that reliefs are time-bound. The act makes the state responsible for training and awareness, as well as for the coordination among the relevant ministries to implement the law and to periodically review progress. Theoretically, the PWDVA has been appreciated for its compliance with the UN framework for model legislation and is seen as one of the more progressive laws.[84]

Significantly, the act recognizes relationships beyond marriage and broadens the concept of 'domestic relationship' to include "all relationships based on consanguinity, marriage, adoption and even relationships which were 'in the nature of marriage' ". It provides remedies to all women in abusive relationships, including those in fraudulent, bigamous or invalid marriages. It also protects the rights of unmarried women, siblings, widows, mothers and other women living with the abuser.

The PWDVA was deemed to have a universal application above the boundaries of castes and religions. It requires the state to shoulder the responsibility to facilitate access to justice by designating medical facilities and shelter homes to provide immediate relief to the victims of violence. The act departed from the adversarial approach of law. Section 5 of the act places the duty on the police officer, medical facilities, PO, SP and the magistrate to inform the aggrieved person of her rights. However, no onus is mandatorily placed on the state to fulfill its responsibility. Therefore, in cases where medical facilities are insufficient or not working properly or the state fails to create a shelter or similar facilities, making the state accountable becomes difficult when already limited resources are spread among competing sets of beneficiaries such as the old, poor, homeless or disabled persons.

Another important feature is that the act introduced multidisciplinary personnel to assist a woman, such as the Protection Officer (PO) and the Service Provider (SP). The PO is a qualified social worker and is identified as a key person in the implementation of the law. Her role is to assist a woman from the stage of registering her case, taking her case to the court and ensuring that court orders are implemented. Theoretically, a layer of personnel is added to the hierarchical layered structure of the police and court nexus. It intends to provide a woman with a single access point, yet it could not link the wider requirements, such as providing psychological or emotional support or economic skills to enable women to gain self-sufficiency. Even earlier, when the Dowry Prohibition Officers were appointed under the Dowry Prohibition Act 1961, similar problems arose. Experience shows that creating such cadre neither deters nor eliminates the dowry – nor does it reduce dowry abuse.[85] However, this experience has not been relied on, and it is erroneously expected that creating a layer of POs under the PWDVA may eradicate violence.

Definition of domestic violence under the PWDVA

Section 3 of the act define domestic violence as an act of gender-based violence and includes not only physical violence but also verbal, mental, emotional, psychological, sexual and economical abuse. Earlier, the definition of cruelty under Section 498A included mental and physical cruelty, but its scope is evidently limited. Also, it restricts the concept of domestic violence within the ambit of matrimony as compared to civil law, which extends the definition of domestic dispute to include live-in and other relationships. Further, cruelty under Section 498A is inaccurately interpreted in its relation to dowry and does not capture the varied dimensions of violence. In order to register a complaint under 498A, a woman is supposed to prove that the violence she suffered was so severe that she was driven to contemplate suicide or that her life was in danger.[86] This is not required under the PWDVA, but, again, it is left to the interpretation and discretion of the state actors to assess if the particular form of abuse faced by a woman at the hands of her husband or in-laws qualifies as violence under the law. Also, the law, despite the elaborate definition, does not see violence as how Stark proposes: "an ongoing and gender specific pattern of coercive and controlling behaviors that cause a range of harms in addition to injury".[87]

Reliefs available under the act

The PWDVA provides reliefs and remedies which are civil in nature. In view of patrilocal, patrilineal marriages, a woman, by the virtue of her marriage, loses her right to reside in the natal home, or *maika*, after marriage. If she complains about the violence she faces in her matrimonial house, she is often rendered homeless. It is a well-known fact that the husband and in-laws are in a powerful position to throw her out of the *sasural* and she is not welcomed by the *maika* to take up a permanent refuge. This fact itself places women in a vulnerable position. She is frequently forced to face violence once she rejoins her matrimonial home. In order to harass her emotionally, she is deprived of the custody of her children. Hence, in order to deal with such issues, a woman is supposed to either approach the civil courts to obtain injunctions or she may claim relief under the personal laws. The PWDVA is enacted to provide all such remedies at a single instant and therefore, different reliefs such as protection orders, custody orders and residence orders are all provided under the ambit of one law. However, these remedies are temporary in nature and could operate until the case is finally decided. This law, in no manner, offers long-term permanent solutions to alter the situation of women within families.

Remedy for right to residence

The PWDVA provides a woman with the right to stay in her shared matrimonial household. This provision has been rendered as 'revolutionary' because it seemingly protects women from becoming destitute or homeless. The act thus protects a woman's right even when she does not own the house. The fact that a woman lives in a home legally owned by her husband does not alter the legality of ownership. This provision ensures that the woman has a roof above her head. It protects the rights of women who desist legal discourse because of fear of being thrown out of the house. Supporters of this right claim that though the idea of returning to the violent site in close contact with the aggressor is paradoxical, it upholds women's continued access to the children as well as to material resources. The right to residence serves its purpose where there is hope of reconciliation between the spouses, or as a temporary measure where a woman needs time to make a decision regarding her marriage. However, the supporters failed to conceptualize this right in a larger patriarchal context where the favorable laws have not been operationalized effectively, thus negating the concept of the rights of women. Further, the law could not be conceptualized to create a provision for the equal division of matrimonial property as a permanent solution to the situation of dispossession from a woman's marital household in a patrilineal society, where women hardly own any property.

Other reliefs

An aggrieved woman can obtain protection orders, which are chiefly in the nature of 'stop violence' orders by prohibiting the respondent from indulging in further abuse. Nevertheless, in a patriarchal society where the male officials often favor other men, seeking a protection order is not a quick or easy process. The act empowers the magistrate to pass orders to grant monetary relief and compensation or damages to the aggrieved person. However, the act reiterates the provision of providing paltry maintenance to the woman as a temporary measure rather than pressing for the right to matrimonial property. Also, no efforts have been made to recognize the women's visible and invisible contributions, as well as her unpaid labor within household.

Section 21 deals with the temporary custody of children. Though the issues relating to permanent custody is decided in accordance with the provisions of personal law or the Guardianship and Wards Act, per the PWDVA, custody orders may be granted 1) as an urgent measure to ensure that the aggrieved person is not harassed by denying access to the children, 2) to protect the children and 3) to ensure that they are not used as pawns to coerce the woman to stay in a violent domestic relationship. In a system where women's rights are hardly protected, the act seemingly empowers the court rather than the complainants while putting the onus on women to file an application to seek each of the given reliefs.

Section 14 of the act empowers the magistrate to direct either or both parties to counseling at any stage of proceedings to make efforts to arrive at a settlement between the parties, but only if the aggrieved woman so desires. The law states that the aggrieved person should not been coerced into settlement.[88] However, with no other options being made available to a woman except to stay in a violent marriage or be at the mercy of her natal family or to stay on her own and manage herself financially, the law expects her to make choices. Also, it is not the psycho-social support that is provided to women in terms of counselling. Rather tragically, the focus is laid on settlement.

Procedure for obtaining order or reliefs

Under Section 12 of the act any other person on behalf of the aggrieved person may present an application to the magistrate seeking one or more reliefs, who shall fix the first date of hearing of the application ordinarily within 3 days of its receipt and shall dispose of the application within 60 days of the first hearing. The framers of law failed to consider that the courts are already overburdened and disposing the application within the given time frame is difficult. The technicalities and complexities of the legal system were overlooked while framing this provision.

Budgetary provisions

Implementation of the PWDVA requires special systems and structures such as appointment of POs, availability of shelter homes and medical facilities and so on. This requires that the state allocate a sufficient budget. However, the central government has not provided a budget and has put the onus on the states to allocate the money.[89] This situation of lack of resources and awareness hampers the smooth functioning of the law and has a negative impact. Also, different states have allocated different amounts and there is no consistency. The expenditure pattern also varies across the states. For instance, Madhya Pradesh spends the budget allocated on appointment of the POs, while Karnataka spends on infrastructure, computers and travelling of POs, and the allocation in Delhi and Tamil Nadu is utilized on appointing POs, their salaries and in related infrastructure.

Perceptions about the PWDVA

The PWDVA has been welcomed by most but also criticized by some. Some suggested that the PWDVA potentially is a powerful tool, yet it should be implemented properly if it is to serve its purpose.[90] Given the past experiences of operation of the law relating to violence, skepticism is raised about the feasibility of its objectives. For example, it has been argued that too broad a definition of domestic violence may trivialize the serious violence women face.[91] Confusion persisted because a civil law is made applicable through criminal courts. Also, every state has adopted its own procedure to implement the law.[92] Though a piece of central legislation, it is not uniformly applied and is being given different interpretations by different courts. Yet amidst various problems, adverse opinions, growing speculations, hopes and frustrations, the PWDVA has been in operation for more than ten years.

Implementation of the PWDVA

Since the implementation of the PWDVA started in late October 2006 after its rules and regulations were released by the Ministry of WCD, it has been accessed by large numbers of women. In the first nine months of its enactment, 8,000 applications were filed under this law. Data indicate that many women facing violence within the home reported their grievance against their violent family members. According to Right to Information (RTI) applications filed in various High Courts, the number of cases registered under the act in 2013, 2014 and 2015 in Karnataka was 3,332, 3,814 and 4,186; in Maharashtra it was 19,222, 20,465 and 21,165; in West Bengal it was 3,090, 3,979 and 4,253.[93] These statistics highlight the fact that this law has provided a platform for women to air their grievances. The fear or the stigma associated with putting their family members behind bars seems to be eroding as women made applications to seek different reliefs and remedies under this law.

The UN Trust Fund to End Violence against Women released resources for the monitoring and evaluation of this act, and the task was undertaken by the Lawyers Collective which conducted annual assessments from 2007 to 2012 about the performance of this law. It published its reports annually under the title 'Staying Alive'. Analysis of these reports shows that the road to implementation of the law is not easy. Barriers and impediments range from lack of an appropriate physical infrastructure to the lack of training and sensitization of staff, as well as a conservative attitude and mind-set.

The first Monitoring and Evaluation Report in 2007 noted that in the first year after the act came into force, the crucial appointments of POs and SPs were not made. As happened under the Dowry Protection Act, in some states, officers under the Ministry of WCD or other officers were given additional responsibilities, which increased their workload and limited their time, as they could not do justice to their roles. Also, many of those appointed have no prior legal knowledge. In most districts, POs lack facilities such as a vehicle, proper office and other infrastructure required to carry out duties. By 2008, ten states had appointed POs. Maharashtra appointed the largest number of POs: 3,910 for 35 districts. Delhi reported the highest number of cases dealt with by individual PO, with each officer dealing with 203 cases on average per year. Similarly, in Kerala POs dealt with the 103 cases per officer per year.[94] Several states reported that they conduct training and capacity building.

The PWDVA is the only law that recognizes the women's organizations as service providers. By 2010, about 20 states had registered SPs. However, the process is slow, opaque and arbitrary. Besides, within SPs too there is a lack of understanding about the nuances of the law. Moreover, SPs have not been allocated sufficient resources. The fourth report observed that SPs have not been completing the DIRs and instead are sending the aggrieved women to POs or lawyers. In many states, DIRs have not been filed, as these are not considered mandatory by the courts. Ambiguity exists in the operation of law, and uniformity could not be followed. Provision of medical facilities is crucial; however, the public health system is relied on at many places, which has issues in terms of being understaffed, not well equipped and lacking basic medicines or facilities. The capacity and sensitivity of medical staff could not be addressed.[95] Lack of understanding about the law, absence of required infrastructure and ineffective coordination between various functionaries hampered the operation of the law.[96] By 2010, lawyers emerged as the key stakeholders for filing the cases. The fourth report found that in most states *Swadhar* homes have been notified as shelter homes. Nevertheless, there are only 287 such homes across the country, and these are insufficient to cater to the ever-expanding needs of women facing violence.

The fifth report showed that the largest number of cases were filed by married women. It was found that many women were not residing in the 'shared household' after they filed the case. Though in some cases, the provisions have been implemented innovatively. For instance, widows got residence orders and were prevented from being dispossessed from the deceased husband's house. In Rajasthan, activists have used this law to prevent forced marriages. Yet few judges passed ex parte or interim relief orders. Concerns have also been raised about the time frame in which the cases are being disposed of. Often, orders are not executed and women have to run around pillar to post to get relief. Controversy has been generated around the residence orders, as the judiciary is not clear about many of the provisions.

From 2007 to 2012, the police have been found to be the first point of contact for the maximum number of women when they sought help for violence. Yet, in most cases, it has been observed that the police discouraged women from filing complaints. Many opined that the law is being misused by women. More than 80 percent of police officials felt that violence is a family matter that could be resolved through counseling. Also, a majority of policemen felt that the aim of counselling is to get an assurance from the man that he would not be violent and further upheld that compromise must be secured to save the family from disintegrating. Also, it is observed that 50 percent of POs in Delhi and 60 percent of POs in Rajasthan felt that counselling is required before filing the case. By 2010, Delhi made it mandatory for women to undergo counselling before filing a case.

If it were implemented properly, the act could provide short-term relief. However, this is not happening. As observed by the Lawyers Collective in its Monitoring and Evaluation Reports, a variety of critical issues need to be dealt with in relation to training, infrastructure, budget allocations and stakeholder attitudes. Lack of awareness, insensitivity of gender issues, and a conservative mind-set all add up to hinder access to justice by women. Such findings have been corroborated by experts, social organizations and users of the law.

Research studies on the PWDVA

Oxfam[97] observed that not many cases could be timely disposed of by the courts. The main reasons for this were the delay in sending and service of notice and the non-appearance of the respondent in the court. The most common orders sought were maintenance and residence orders. The Centre for Social Justice[98] found that confusion persists about filing DIRs, and only one training program was conducted. Women find the POs non-cooperative. Most of the POs took months to prepare the investigation report. Counselling was a major activity that POs undertook. Mahila Jagran Kendra[99] in Bihar also reached a similar conclusion. Interestingly, 66 percent of respondents did not know that their complaints were registered under the PWDVA. The majority had no information about the existence of a help line in their district, and there is no sufficient allocation of funds for the implementation of law.

These findings have been substantiated in a study conducted in Delhi,[100] where it was found that this law is used mostly by married women. Complainants secured less than 50 percent of the orders that they had asked for. Although most litigants were educated, few had any legal knowledge. TISS[101] in Haryana, Maharashtra, Odisha and Tamil Nadu observed that most of the complaints were related to physical and economic violence. More than 85 percent of complainants were dependent on the respondents. Also, more than half of the women faced violence within a year of their marriage. Further, the courts were reported to act slow in terms of granting relief. Women faced great difficulties in the execution of the orders. Appeals were filed in a few cases.

Thus, in short, it may be said that the PWDVA initially had teething concerns, and the issues continued to remain unresolved even years after the act came into existence. The budget allocated is less, and often the training programs are not undertaken to sensitize those involved in the implementation of the law. POs are deemed as a vital link, yet not much effort has been made to strengthen this link. Further, lack of capacity and differences in knowledge, approach and practices of different stakeholders such as the police and judiciary vary and have an impact on the implementation of the law.

A domestic violence law has been enacted after a long struggle. However, the criminal or civil law provisions have not been able to deter violence or render support to women. There are gaps in the manner in which the law is being implemented. Most of the studies focused on measuring the effectiveness of the law reached to a similar conclusion. Moreover, there is a dearth of data, as not many studies have assessed the situation from the perspectives of survivors or the users of the law or focus on the micro-perspective. Evaluation is more on the infrastructure and implementation of the law from the providers' end, where the voices of women are not considered. The quality of services provided by the different stakeholders is not assessed from the perspective of women complainants.

Fricker[102] conceptualized the term 'epistemic injustice', which describes discrimination when someone is wronged specifically in her capacity as a knower. She explores the idea of 'testimonial injustice' where a speaker receives a prejudicial deflated degree of credibility from the hearer and 'hermeneutical injustice' where due to her relative powerlessness, someone is handicapped to make sense of her social experience. Similarly, in the present study, armed with this idea of epistemic injustice, I propose that the women who face domestic violence provide the live illustration of both testimonial and hermeneutical injustice, because their voice is not given credibility by those who make or implement laws and policies; also, women are at an unfair hermeneutical position in a male-governed system because their interpretive framework is different from that of the law and policy implementers. Besides, their lived experience is rendered intelligible, to others and possibly even to oneself, as they are prevented from making sense of their own violent experiences because of the shame and stigma associated with them. Such a narrow approach pushes women precariously onto the margins. Therefore, both these types of epistemic injustice call for a corrective virtue on the part of the law and policymakers to make sense of experiences women face and to provide solutions accordingly.

The present study takes this philosophical framework of epistemic injustice into account while highlighting the experiences of women survivors and their concerns. It explores the manner in which the law facilitates women to seek justice and explores if the women's voices are given credibility by the police, courts and other actors in the system. It qualitatively explores the women's subjective experiences and the manner in which these are filtered in the legal paradox. This issue merits consideration, as it informs the critical decision relating to law and policymaking and implementing. The relevance of such research is to better attune the responses and frame the policies accordingly. It critically informs the epistemology relating to family violence while exploring the manner in which the law is conceptualized and understood by the women survivors.

Why this research?

Globally as well nationally, a volume of research has been conducted on the issue of violence within homes during the past few decades. These studies define and theorize domestic violence from different perspectives, elaborate on the cause and effect and suggest interventions to deal with it. Many of these are based on the viewpoints of service providers in the domain of health, law or policy. Not much focus has been laid on the perspective of the survivors of violence in India. The present work therefore comprehends violence in daily life of those who are compelled to live with it because either they had no choice to escape or due to socio-economic compulsions are forced to stay within the abusive relationship. This work analyzes the perspective of survivors and their realities as to the manner in which they conceptualize violence, their choice of action against abuse, the acceptable norms according to them and the point at which they draw boundaries against such violence. It analyzes the nuances, nature and pattern of domestic violence and explores the process women use to rebuild their lives that may feed into a broader understanding of the concept of law and policy in terms of the support women need. It brings out the inherent contradictions between 'official' discourses regarding domestic violence while relating it to subjective experiences and realities of women and comprehending the gap between the formal discourse, which is objective and typical, as compared to the participant's perspective, which is subjective and experiential. It underlines the need to develop an understanding of women's oppression in the larger socio-cultural fabric.

Research design

MacKinnon[103] opined that "We who work with law need to be informed about the business of articulating the theory of women's practice-women's resistance, visions, consciousness, injuries, notions of community, experience of inequality. By practical I mean socially lived". Following this approach, in the present work, women's practical experiences in the domain of the state and society have been examined. Women litigants knocking on the doors of the courts seeking justice against their violent family members have been contacted within the premises of the six district courts in Delhi between 2013 and 2015. Primary data include copies of complaints, narratives and testimonies of complainants. Informed consent has been obtained. The initial response was that of suspicion in most of the cases. However, once they felt assured of confidentiality, the response was overwhelming, as many of them eagerly shared their saga of brutalities, pain and sufferings with one who is neutral and an outsider. The personal narrative became a useful research tool to interpret the empirical material gathered and thus build the epistemological knowledge. In addition, interviews have been conducted with the professionals as lawyers, women's organizations, POs and SPs. Also, the orders and judgements passed by the different courts have been analyzed.

The researcher's own experience of working on violence has also been woven into the analysis in what Giddens[104] refers to as 'practical consciousness': "what [the] actor (knows) believe[s] about the social conditions, including the especially the conditions of their own actions, but cannot express discursively; no bar of repression, however, protect practical consciousness as in the case with unconscious". This firsthand experience of the researcher became a useful research tool to relate to the informants and to interpret the empirical material gathered. This means an immediate connection and thus an insight into women's experience of violence and resistance than the micro-level methodologies available to outside researchers. Reflecting on narratives with my personal experiences as a lawyer and as a litigant provide the insider's advantage.

The work maps and documents the legal and social discourse pertaining to violence within 'private and sacred' spaces while drawing its linkages to the journey of women seeking justice. It captures the realities of the women's struggle in legal as well as social terrain. Gathering and analyzing qualitative data is a challenging task, as it involves dealing with the complexities of life which need to be filtered through human subjectivities and sufferings. The women I interacted with have been fighting their lonely battles and are neither trained professionals nor are aware of feminist ideologies; however, it is through their sense of resistance that they created a space within the legal maze while grappling with everyday realities of their lives. For a layperson, understanding legal nuances is not an easy task when the law is androcentric and discriminates against women. Further, for survivors, the path gets complicated because of the stress in coping with the demands, the stigma and the social pressure; additionally, they have to struggle with legal complications and technicalities.

Telling and retelling stories

Black Lives Matter is the civil rights movement that emerged in 2012 after the killing of an American African teen by a neighborhood watch volunteer in the United States.[105] The movement received many contradictory responses, yet one of the significant questions that has been raised is how one should view the life of the 'others' and should the lives of the 'others' truly matter? Similarly, in India, the recent protest 'Not in My Name'[106] against the lynching made one think of the manner in which one should seriously consider the worth of the life of 'others'. In a capitalized, globalized world where an individualistic attitude is increasing, it is essential that such movements remind that the lives of 'others' are significant. While unfolding the stories of life, one may understand the nuances in which power operates and the ways in which one courageously fights through and deals with the challenges.

Benjamin[107] noted that storytelling is a valid form of capturing data that requires no verification and conveys the pure essence of experience in some distilled ways. Through many diffuse occurrences, in this work, too, the storytelling has been used as a tool to paint the imagination in which the legal and the social environment is dealing with the battered women. The narratives of the lives of 'others', women in this case, are being then woven together to comprehend the working of the law. Another issue that requires attention is that, at times, stories may not capture perfectly the meaning that is signified by the words in a language or emotion. Many aspects are lost in translation. Human emotions are located in a cultural context and are multi-layered and complex, which may not be translated into nuances of rigid law. The study through the art of storytelling documents the experience of women who resisted against the norms. It captures the larger picture around the issue of violence while learning from the journeys of survivors where translation served the utilitarian purpose. It builds upon a bubble-up approach in contextualizing violence from the survivor's perspective and raises relevant questions that may be examined while framing laws and policies as compared to a trickle-down perspective. An attempt has been made to look at the systematic subordination of women within the homes, courts or society, while it also examines the resistance and defiance. However, to understand the larger context, there is a need to dig into the socio-economic context in which women are situated.

The urban context: Delhi as a field for research

At the heart of this research is ethnographic field work in settings related to domestic violence and the law. The study was conducted in Delhi NCR, or the National Capital Region, the capital of India. Situated at the bank of the river Yamuna and the foothills of the Aravali range, its area spread around 1,484 square kilometers and has a population density of 11,320 per sq km.[108] The city has a history of resilience, as it been captured, ransacked and rebuilt several times. It is a historically significant place and is known as the legendary capital Indraprastha built by Pandavas in the epic *Mahabharata* and was later conquered and lost by different rulers.

It was during the 1857 rebellion that Delhi was seized by the East India Company and came under the direct control of the British government in 1858 when Britishers made Delhi a provincial town.[109] In 1911, the capital of British-held territories in India was transferred from Calcutta to Delhi, and a separate committee known as the Imperial Delhi Committee was formed on 25 March 1913 to oversee the construction and management of the civic affairs of the new capital. The colonial rulers recognized Delhi as a district legal entity under Proclamation Notification in 1912.[110] The name "New Delhi" was given in 1927, and it was inaugurated on 13 February 1931. New Delhi, also known as Lutyens' Delhi, was officially declared the capital of India after the country gained independence.

The population of Delhi began to increase after it acquired the status of a capital. In 1901, the population was 0.4 million; it swelled to 2.38 million[111] in 1911, and in 2011 it is recorded as 16.8 million.[112] To resolve its day-to-day concerns, Delhi has been accorded the status of a Union Territory and as per the Sixty-Ninth Constitutional Amendment Act, 1991, which confers it a special status.[113]

Delhi is a city where contradictions exist in terms of cosmopolitanism and development, which is in contrast with its fractured nature with poverty and misery amidst a celebration of radical politics through arts, culture and protests in various forms.[114] Delhi is a symbol of growth, yet it is also a home to abject poverty.[115] Uniformity is not a trend. Economic, religious and caste divisions are causing irreparable damage to the social and political fabric of the city. Widening inequalities in terms of power, affluence and values are creating a situation where Delhi consequently is becoming a city of hope as well as despair; it is a city of dreams and desires but also a city of delusions and nightmare, where amidst skyscrapers exist slums and shanty dwellings, and amidst wealth and affluence there subsists poverty and vulnerability, and among the efforts to establish peace and harmony there exists violence and brutality.[116] Delhi is the artifact of the very culture of violence which is endorsed by consumerism and consumption, on one hand, and repression and marginalization, on the other. The city has been recognized as the 'rape capital'.[117] Over the years, the crime rate is increasing, yet, at the same time, Delhi is a witness to protests and agitations.

Social composition of Delhi and the governance structure

In terms of space, Delhi comprises the old buildings of Lutyen's Delhi, as well as fancy mega-malls in addition to private spaces erected haphazardly in narrow lanes. Globalization and a neoliberal economy are transforming the very structure of the city. Lately, the city has witnessed the emergence of high-rise buildings, skyscrapers, plush offices and privileged wealth, which exist in contradiction to the growth of shanty towns and abject scarcity. Each life in the capital has different claims to resources and spaces within the city based on status, which is decided on the principle of exclusion and is determined by the class, religion, caste and property ownership, among others. The sense of belonging is demarcated by the divisive ideology, and the claim on resources and space in the city is determined by the individual's capacity to afford.

Entitlements to the limited public resources are decided on the basis of the individual's background and his or her capacity to pay.[118] Citizenship entitlements are increasingly claimed by those who can afford to acquire materialistic luxuries such as club memberships or the posh pieces of real estate, besides the privileged status that comes with the religion, caste and other such factors. With the extinction of the concept of the welfare state, the onus for being poor now lies on an individual, as the state is completely absolved from any responsibility. Those on the margins are being further being eliminated, ghettoized, demonized and excluded and are pushed to the peripheries. Delhi is hostile to the poor and marginal, while the privileged upper-caste men claim entitlements on manifold resources. Slum demolition is a continuous activity carried out on the pretext of beautification of the city. Local vendors, hawkers, traders, slum dwellers and other marginal groups find no place in selective commercialization.

The category 'women' mostly includes those women who are sisters, daughters, mothers and wives of belongers – the middle-class, upper-caste, Hindu, able heterosexual men – while excluding women who dare to exist independently or even those who are being abandoned, widowed or surviving otherwise.[119] Women, as a category, have been excluded from the public spaces in the cities for generations, and over the last few decades these divisions have been ossified to make their exclusion acceptable. Yet diversity exists in various ways. There are privileged women who may be grounded in an increasing neoliberal conservatism, and there are also those who are struggling hard to venture out and earn a livelihood. Working in corporate offices, teaching in schools, working in beauty parlors, sweating as construction laborers – these women are making their mark while creating a niche.

However, there is increased reports about cases of violence against women. In order to encounter this, the narrative of women being unsafe in public spaces is being floated around that sanctions the restrictions on the mobility of women, rather than questioning the violent behavior of men. The argument of the safety of women is fallaciously framed through the narratives of middle-class women endangered by vagrant poor men from marginal communities and is used to justify the exclusion of both from public spaces. However, the question of women's safety implies that one has to look at the intricate fabric of the layered exclusion and denial of agency to women in a patriarchal context. Safety in public spaces is interconnected and interlinked to the question of safety within homes and is also aligned to the nexus between patriarchal arrangement and its connection with the structural discrimination.

To deal with the enormity of violence, Delhi has developed infrastructure and paraphernalia to implement the laws. Courts, police, counselors, Family Courts and CAW cells all are the part of a huge network. Apart from that, the Parliament and the Supreme Court both are located right at the heart of Delhi, as well as the president's and prime minister's offices. Different ministries and other government offices are situated here. The National Human Rights Commission, NCW and similar such statutory bodies also co-exist. The capital enjoys a special status as it is a hub of political activities where significant decisions are made. Apart from being the 'corridor of power', Delhi also is a place where citizens can demonstrate, protest, dissent and resist, thus adding meaning to democracy though these rights have been threatened recently.

The scale and magnitude of domestic violence in Delhi

In December 2012, when the famous Nirbhaya rape case took place, Delhi was tagged as the crime capital; five years later the situation has not changed much. Crime against women is on rise, and in 2015 it was reported that one rape happens every four hours.[120] Another report indicates that Delhi records 40 cases of crime against women every day – highest among these are rape, molestation and sexual harassment of women.[121] In addition to an increase in crime, statistics on the declining sex ratio (898) indicates that Delhi performs worse in terms of the treatment of women.[122]

As per the NCRB,[123] Delhi accounted for 38.8 percent of total IPC crime reported in the cities followed by Bengaluru and Mumbai. In 2016 Delhi reported 33.0 percent (13,803 out of 41,761 cases) cases of crimes against

Table 2.1 Crime in Delhi in 2016

2016	*Delhi*	*Total UTs*	*All India*
Dowry-Related Deaths	162	166	7,621
Abetment of Suicide (Based on 2015 Crime Report)	20	28	4,446
498A	3,645	4,037	110,378
Dowry Prohibition Act	18	34	9,683
PWDVA	1	1	437

Source: Adapted from Crimes in India, Published by the National Crime Record Bureau, Government of India

women, followed by Mumbai (12.3 percent). Delhi also reported the highest crime rate (182.1) compared to the national average rate of 77.2. Table 2.1 indicates the statistics pertaining to violence women face within homes in the city.

In 2015, the NCW received 1,179 complaints, including domestic violence, dowry harassment, property dispute and rape.[124] Data available with the Police Control Room (PCR) indicate an increase in the number of cases reported, from 95 in December 2012 to 222 calls in January 13 and a total of 1,858 calls in 2013.[125] Dowry is found to be a major reason behind these complaints. Further, the DCW alleged that in 15 districts in the city, a total of 15,698 cases of domestic violence are pending for which FIRs have been registered, whereas a charge sheet has been filed only in 5,573 cases.[126] There is a huge backlog, as 64.5 percent have been pending for more than five years, which validates the fact that police are not prioritizing the domestic violence cases.

Available data indicate that by December 2010, 8,662 complaints had been received in various Mahila Courts in Delhi under the PWDVA.[127] Also, as of 1 July 2013, 9,215 cases were pending under the PWDVA as compared to 95,425 regular criminal cases under the IPC.[128] Also 4,729 cases are pending under Section 125 of the CrPC.[129] Further, the rate of conviction has been steadily falling despite tall claims being made by the state. In 2005, the conviction rate was 31.2 percent; in 2016 it was drastically reduced to a paltry 4.9 percent.[130] The poor conviction rate is due to faulty investigations, delay, hostile witnesses and the long duration of trials, among others.

Delhi district courts

The legal system is a legacy of colonial rule in India, and the Delhi judiciary in 1913 consisted of one district and session judge, one senior subjudge, one registrar and one judge for small-cause court, and three subjudges as a civil court.[131] Two courts of sub-judges were added in 1920. According to the Delhi District Gazetteer (1912), the district magistrate was responsible for the administration of criminal justice, being chief magistrate and supervisor of the police, as far as their duties related to crime. In 1910, there were 19 first-class magistrates, including stipendiary and honorary, 18 second-class magistrates and 4 third-class magistrates, who were deployed to handle criminal cases in Delhi. In 1959, the strength of the sub-judges went up to 21. The district courts of Delhi remained under the administrative control of the Punjab High Court until the Delhi High Court was established in 1966. The judiciary was separated from the executive under the Union Territories (Separation of Judicial and Executive Functions) Act 1969. The act provides for two classes of criminal courts, namely the Courts of Sessions and the Courts of Magistrates. On 1 April 1974 Delhi was declared as the Metropolitan Area by a notification under Section 8(1) of the Criminal Procedure Code 1973.[132] Accordingly, the designation of judicial magistrate first-class or judicial magistrate second-class came to an end. The courts of metropolitan magistrates, chief metropolitan magistrate and additional chief metropolitan magistrates were created under Sections 16 and 17 of the Criminal Procedure Code. Section 18 of the code also provided for special metropolitan magistrates.

Presently, the entire judicial district of Delhi, now the National Capital Territory of Delhi, is composed of one sessions division headed by a sessions judge. It has one chief metropolitan magistrate and four additional chief metropolitan magistrates. At present, there are six district courts. These are the Tis Hazari court complex,[133] catering to the north and west districts; the Patiala House court complex,[134] catering to the New Delhi district; the Saket court,[135] catering to the south and southeast areas; Dwarka court, which came into existence in 2008, catering to the southwest district; Karkardooma court[136] caters to the east and northeast districts; and the Rohini court[137] caters to the western and outer districts.

Other multi-dimensional paraphernalia to assist women survivors of violence

The Department of Women and Child Development, government of Delhi, is the Nodal Department for the implementation of provisions under the PWDVA. Delhi has vibrant women's organizations providing different services and programs.[138] Further, the DCW is running family counselling centers. A community-based model such as *Mahila panchayats*[139] runs in several places. In addition, Delhi has special women's cells, and an initiative to strengthen these cells has been launched by the project 'Save Homes, Save Families' with the collaboration of the NCW and other stakeholders. The Special Unit of Police for Women and Children is also providing services such as mediation, legal aid and self-defense training.[140]

Under the PWDVA medical facilities have to be provided by the state governments.[141] Delhi has recognized 24 public hospital facilities as medical facilities.[142] Further, women victims of violence require psychosocial support and a range of other services besides medical facilities. Delhi has not listed such services separately. In order to obtain these services, a woman has to consult a private practitioner based on her individual capacity to pay. DWCD Delhi has listed 27 counselling centers, three short-stay homes and two shelter institutions for destitute pregnant and lactating mothers.[143] Six shelter homes were listed in 2013,[144] including those run by women's organizations, with total capacity of not more than 500 inmates. These are insufficient keeping in mind the rising number of cases. Also, experience shows that these are overcrowded, and frequently a woman is allowed to stay here for a maximum of two months. Such shortcomings defeat the very purpose of the law. There are omissions in services provided by these homes,[145] as most of the homes are non-functional, shabby, overcrowded and in deplorable condition.[146] Also, there are hardly any schemes which could offer economic assistance or financial support to women in distress.[147]

Under the *Swadhar Greh* scheme launched in 2016 as a centrally sponsored umbrella scheme by the Ministry of WCD, the earlier schemes of *Swadhar* Homes and Short-Stay Homes were merged. Setting up of a home is proposed in each district to provide temporary residential accommodation for women victims of violence besides rendering support to other categories of women in distress.[148] In 550 districts all over India, it may benefit 16,500 inmates where women facing domestic violence can stay up to a period of one year. Also, the One Stop Centre Scheme launched in 2015 was designed to facilitate integrated services, including medical aid, police assistance, legal aid and temporary support services, to assist women affected by violence. So far, 79 centers are operational in 24 states; however, no data are available as to the number of beneficiaries who have been supported by these centers. In a country where a million women are in situations of distress, such schemes appear merely a token effort.

The SPs, POs, legal aid cells, commissions, courts and police stations serve as reminders of the array of contradictions, chaos and turmoil that are present every day, specifically when one is undergoing the trauma of violence within a home. These multiple institutions and agencies are working amid pandemonium to relieve the commotion and mayhem which a woman survivor may face in her daily life. The question of deciding who has responsibility or fixing the accountability of these agencies towards victims and survivors of violence has not been raised as yet.

Budgets and finances for implementing the PWDVA

Over the years, the markers of gender-responsive budgeting indicate that priority is not being given to critical issues like violence, and in 2016, schemes meant for implementation of the PWDVA have not received any allocations.[149] Analysis of budget allocations shows that the money sanctioned for the implementation of the act has not been enhanced over the years despite the fact that the number of cases filed every year are increasing.

Also, there is a huge gap between allocation and actual expenditure.[150] The allocation towards PWDVA increased from Rs. 20 crores to Rs. 67.5 crores in 2012–2013; however, this remains below the recommended outlay for the scheme by the Steering Committee on Women's Agency and Empowerment, as outlined within the Twelfth Five-Year plan. It has further fallen to Rs. 50 crores in the budget year 2014–2015, which is below the recommended outlay. Moreover, funds remain non-utilized. Further reduction in allocation and non-utilization reflects the state's lack of commitment to address violence. Coordination to effectuate a multi-agency response system, monitoring and evaluation has also not taken place due to the budgetary issues.

In 2009–2010, 50 lakhs were allocated to the implementation of the PWDVA in Delhi, which was reduced to 33 lakhs in 2010–2011.[151] In 2011–2012 a total of 40 lakhs were allocated for this purpose.[152] This was increased to Rs. 45 lakhs in 2013–2014, thus bringing the percentage down, even though there was a slight increase in the amount.[153] Delhi reported the maximum expenditure on salaries of the POs and their travel costs. The city has invested a part of the fund in creating awareness through the media. Several posters were put up in metros and on the roads at a few places for a short period. Further, there is no objectivity or rationality in planning budgets or expenditures, and no system of accountability or transparency has been created.[154] Capacity building of key stakeholders has not taken place adequately due to the budgetary constraint.

At a national level, a centrally sponsored scheme in 2013 was finalized to ensure effective implementation of the PWDVA, which requires an estimated annual budget requirement of 1,158 crores. According to this proposal, a PWDVA council will be set up at the national level to monitor and implement schemes under the law. It proposed an advisory body to annually review the state's reports and a coordination committee to ensure inter-departmental convergence. Meanwhile, the same year, the budget of the Ministry of WCD was slashed by 2,000 crores, making the implementation of such schemes difficult. The draft Twelfth Five-Year plan mentioned CSS, it remained silent on the launching of the scheme.[155] Such actions therefore raise questions regarding the commitment of the state. Insufficient budget allocation seriously hampers the intent to implement the law. These facts relating to budget allocation and expenditure, appointment of Protection Officers, difficulties and chaos in recognition of SPs, absence of shelter homes and other such support facilities indicate the apathetic approach of the state.

Protection officers: how much are they protected to protect from the 'protectors'?

In Delhi, the Department of Social Welfare initially appointed 18 POs under the PWDVA.[156] POs are assigned for each area and are attached to the Mahila courts. They are required to operate at the premises of the district courts. POs report to the assistant director of the Women Empowerment Cell of the DWCD Delhi. Delhi has been divided into nine zones.[157] Thus, initially two POs per zone were appointed. Fifteen POs were appointed in 2013[158] despite the fact that the population continues to grow. Further, in comparison to the number of police stations in Delhi, the number of POs appointed are far less than required. The number of police stations in 2013 were 181,[159] with a strength of 84,563 personnel.[160] This implies that one PO is expected to deal with all complaints filed in five police stations. Technically and humanly, it is not possible to handle such a huge workload. Thus, the exercise of appointing POs appears to be merely yet another token effort. Also, the total population of Delhi in 2011 was 16,787,941 of which 7,800,615 are female.[161] Thus, for almost every five lakh women, only one PO has been appointed. This figure is reflective of the gap between the intent and reality.

Apart from the lack of POs, shortage of facilities in terms of adequate office space and staff consisting of data entry operators, counselors and home guards are some of the reasons hindering efficiency. The location of the offices of POs is also problematic. Often, they do not have separate offices, leading to a lack of privacy, which acts as a deterrent when women come to file complaints. About 90 percent of POs claimed that they are often concerned about their own security, as they face 'threats'. A few shared that even when they try visiting the homes to help survivors, they themselves face violence from husbands and in-laws. Many times, they found themselves engaged in resolving aggressions between the parties in dispute. Most of the POs have a large number of women approaching them. Many found themselves involved in counseling, completing DIRs and attending court proceedings. Records reveal no safety plans have been prepared in any of the cases. Further, POs have been appointed on a contract basis, and issues have been raised regarding salaries as well as vacant positions.[162] Though they are qualified social workers, there are issues relating to appointments and non-regularization of services, and the training component is another area that needs to be looked into.

Summary

This chapter looks at the nuances of making a criminal and civil law relating to domestic violence. It focuses on the legal reforms in the context of domestic violence and looks at the making of the law from the perspectives of survivors and victims. It argues that while making the law, the narrow vision of the state has hindered the goal of justice, as the state has not looked into options beyond the family that could be made available to women. The idea of inequality has been engrained in the law, as the legal reforms could not make a dent on the socio-cultural realm or could alter the fundamental power positions within families.

Notes

1 Steinem G (1992) *Revolution from Within: A Book of Self Esteem*, Published by Gloria Steinem USA
2 AIDWA (2003) *Expanding Dimensions of Dowry*, Indian School of Women Studies and Development, Delhi
3 Palriwala R (2009) The Spider's Web: Seeing Dowry, Fighting Dowry, In *Dowry: Bridging the Gap Between Theory and Practice*, edited by Tamsin Bradley, E Tomalin and M Subramaniam, Women Unlimited, New Delhi
4 Jejeebhoy SJ (1998) Wife Beating in Rural India: A Husband's Right? *Economic and Political Weekly*, 33 (15) 855–62
5 Srinivas MN (1984) *Some Reflections on Dowry*, Oxford University Press, New Delhi
6 Nigam S (2001) *Consumerism, Dowry and Marginalization of Women in India*, Kali for Women, Wardlaw, New Delhi pp. 33–39
7 Sangari K (2015) *Solid: Liquid A Transnational Reproductive Formation*, Tulika Books, New Delhi p. 15
8 Lakshmi CS (1989) On Kidneys and Dowries, *Economic and Political Weekly*, January 28
9 Spivak GC (1997) Can the Subalterns Speak? In *Colonial Discourse and Post-Colonial Theory: A Reader*, edited by Patrick Williams and Laura Chrisman, Prentice Hall, Hertfordshire
10 Oldenburg VT (2002) *Dowry Murders: The Imperial Origins of Cultural Crime*, Oxford University Press, New York
11 Oldenburg P (1992) Sex Ratio, Son Preference and Violence in India, *Economic and Political Weekly*, 27, 49–50
12 Chowdhry P (1987) Socio-Economic Dimensions of Certain Customs and Attitudes: Women of Haryana in Colonial Period, *Economic and Political Weekly*, 22 (48)
13 Palriwala R (1989) Reaffirming the Anti Dowry Struggle, *Economic and Political Weekly*, 24 (17) 942–44
14 AIDWA (2003) supra n 2
15 Basu S (2011) Conjugality and Sexual Economies in India, *Feminist Studies*, 37 (1) Spring, 200
16 Agnes F (1992) Protecting Women Against Violence: Review of the Decade of Legislation 1980–89, *Economic and Political Weekly*, 27 (17) WS 24
17 Her mother, Satya Rani Chaddha, became the face of the dowry law campaign. Together with Shahjahan Aapa, she took a step towards building a shelter home later.
18 Agnihotri and Parliwala (Undated) supra
19 Forbes G (1996) *Women in Modern India*, Cambridge University Press, New York
20 Street plays such as *Om Swaha* and *Mein Manjushree* have been used to raise awareness of the manner in which police was dealing with the issue of dowry death in a non-serious manner.
21 Kishwar M (1988) *Rethinking Dowry Boycott*, Manushi, *September–October* p. 10
22 Smt. Pramila Dandvate introduced a bill to amend the dowry law in 1980.
23 Chaired by Smt Krishna Sahi
24 *State vs Lakshman Kumar AIR* 1986 SC 250, Also, Jethmalani Rani and Dey PK (1995) *Dowry Deaths and Access to Justice in Empowerment*, Laws and Dowry Death: Kali's Yug Har-Anand, New Delhi
25 A coalition of women's groups on March 8, 1981, protested the violence. Some of the slogans include "Women are not for burning, Women are human

beings' and 'Let not the marriage fire become a funeral pyre', "*stri par na ho atyachar, ham parosi zimmedar*" (we neighbors are responsible that women are not abused), *Nek gharon ki ye pehchan bahu beti ek samaan* (good homes are those where daughters and daughters-in-law are treated equally) and *Tilak nahi talwaar nahi, shadi koi vyapaar nahi, kharida hua jeevanssathi ab hume swikar nahi* (No to forehead mark, no to dowry, marriage is not a trade, we will not accept purchased partners).

26 Agnihotri I and Mazumdar V (1995) Changing Terms of Political Discourse: Women's Movement in India 1970s-1990s, *Economic and Political Weekly*, 30 (29) 1869–78

27 Palriwala R (2010) *Women Are Not for Burning: The Anti-Dowry Movement in Delhi in Social Movements: Concerns for Equity and Security, Readings in Sociology*, edited by TK Oomen, Oxford University Press, New Delhi

28 Gandhi and Shah (1993) supra

29 Ghosh SV (2004) *Contextualizing Domestic Violence: Family, Community and State in Behind Closed Doors: Domestic Violence in India*, edited by R Bhattacharya, Sage, New Delhi

30 Kapur and Cossman (1996) supra

31 Kishwar M (2005) Strategies of Combating Culture of Dowry and Domestic Violence in India Working Paper, May 17

32 Menon N (1998) Rights, Law and Feminist Politics: Rethinking our Practice, In *In the Name of Justice: Women and Law in Society*, edited by S Mukhopadhyay, Manohar, New Delhi

33 Karat B (2005) *Survival and Emancipation: Notes from Indian Women Struggles*, Three Essays Collective, New Delhi

34 Shariff Abusaleh and Syed Khalid (2017) Abandoned Women Vastly Outnumber Victims of Triple Talaq and Its Time Modi Spoke up for Them, *The Wire*, July 17, https://thewire.in/86335/abandoned-women-triple-talaq/

35 Supra

36 Agnes F and D'Mello A (2015) Protection of Women from Domestic Violence, *Economic and Political Weekly*, L 44, 76–84, 77

37 Iyengar Pushpa (2008) Wound on A Spindle: Will the New Law Help the Girls in Tirupur's Garment Shop? *Outlook*, June 23

38 Singh D (2019) The Arundhati Scheme of Assam: Indulgence in the Cult of Dowry, *The New Leam*, March 9, https://thenewleam.com/2019/03/the-arundhati-scheme-of-assam-indulgence-in-the-cult-of-dowry/

39 *Sify News* (2018) Goa's Laadli Scheme Stoking Dowry System, Study, March 8, https://www.sify.com/news/goa-s-laadli-laxmi-scheme-stoking-dowry-system-study-news-national-ndiuujdfbfjsi.html

40 Bhattacharya R (2018) Is West Bengal Government Encouraging Dowry with Rupashree Scheme? *Daily Hunt*, February 15, https://m.dailyhunt.in/news/india/english/social+post+english-epaper-socposen/is+west+bengal+government+encouraging+dowry+with+rupashree+scheme-newsid-81876135

41 Basu (2011) supra, Vol. 37 (1)

42 Kapur R (2012) Hecklers to Power? The Waning of Liberal Rights and Challenges to Feminism in India, In *South Asia Feminisms*, edited by A Loomba and Ritty A Lukos, Duke University Press, London p. 336

43 From Communist Party of India

44 Smt Geeta Mukherjee 1983d 470–1

45 Lok Sabha Debates 1983 Vol. 42 n. 1 dated 15th July 447

46 Lok Sabha Debates 1982 Vol. 30 n. 1 pp. 305–6

47 Gangoli G (2007) *Indian Feminism: Laws*, Patriarchies and Violence in India, Ashgate, UK

48 Lok Sabha Debates 1984 Vol 45 April 5 279. (Translated from Hindi)
49 Shri N K Shejwalkar, Lok Sabha Debates 1983d 441
50 Shri Ram Lal Rahi 1983d 511 Translated from Hindi
51 Gangoli (2007) supra n 47
52 Forty-six (this numbering refers to the debate of making this law) of 1983 with effect from 25 December 1983 amended the IPC, the CrPC and the Indian Evidence Act.
53 Gangoli (2007) supra n 47
54 Sudhir U (2016) 'Beaten for Leaving Geyser on', Said Hyderabad Techie's Wife Before Death, NDTV, September 13
55 Agnes, Flavia (2015) Section 498A, Marital Rape and Adverse Propaganda, *Economic and Political Weekly*, L 23, 12–15
56 Center for Social Research (2005) *Section 498A IPC: Misused or Abused*, Center for Social Research: New Delhi
57 Human Rights Watch (2009) *Broken System: Dysfunction, Abuse and Impunity in the Indian Police*, New York, https://www.hrw.org/sites/default/files/reports/india0809web.pdf
58 Singh K (2015) *Marital Cruelty and 498A: A Study of Legal Redressal of Victims in Two States*, NCW, New Delhi
59 Palkar, V (2013) Failing Gender Justice in Anti-Dowry Law, *South Asia Research*, 23 (2) 181–200
60 Sarkar Lotika (1995) *Constitutional Guarantees: The Unequal Sexes*, CWDS, New Delhi
61 To obtain maintenance from her violent husband or to obtain a separation of divorce order, applications have to be filed accordingly either under Section 125 CrPC or civil and personal laws.
62 Under Section 406 IPC, *streedhan* can be retrieved with the help of police; however, because of delayed action by the police, women are deprived of this right.
63 Even if the accused husband or in-laws are jailed, it is easier to get bail. Once the accused is out of jail, the criminal case continues, and most end up 'settled' between the parties. Punishment is rarely inflicted.
64 Nigam (2005) supra
65 EKTA Resource Centre for Women (2011) *A Study on 498A in Tamil Nadu*, Tamil Nadu
66 Basu S (2006) Playing Off Courts: The Negotiation of Divorce and Violence in Plural Legal Settings in Kolkata, *Journal of Legal Pluralism*, 52, 41–76
67 Maitrayee M (1994) *Brother, There Are Only Two Jatis – Men and Women*, Construction of Gender Identity: Women, the State and Personal Laws in India, PhD Dissertation
68 Flavia A (2009) Conjugality, Property, Morality and Maintenance, *EPW*, XLIV 44 pp. 58–64
69 Basu A (2008) Legislating on Domestic Violence, *Seminar*, 583, http://www.india-seminar.com/2008/583/583_asmita_basu.htm
70 *The Quint* (2019) Head of NGO for 'Harassed Husbands' Enter LS Poll Fray in Gujarat, April 3, https://www.thequint.com/elections/head-of-ngo-for-harassed-husbands-enters-ls-poll-fray-in-guj
71 Experiences of mediation even otherwise case often is disappointing. For instance, as in in Bhopal Gas Tragedy. Further Details Jaising I (2019) Men of Law, Not Faith, *The Indian Express*, March 11
72 Nader Laura (1994) *Coercive Harmony: The Political Economy of Legal Model*, Presented at the Opening Session of the National Association of Brazilian Anthropologists, March

73 NCW (1992) Family Courts – Report on Working of Family Courts and Model Family Court Rules, NCW, New Delhi
74 'Resolving Disputes Uniting Families' and similar such posters are found hanging in every family court where emphasis is laid on protecting families and not to provide justice to victims of violence
75 As described in Chapter 1.
76 In January 2000, the CEDAW Committee recommended that India should pass a comprehensive legislative framework to promote the human rights of women. Observations on State Report, Committee on the Elimination of All Forms of Discrimination Against Women, CEDAW/C/IND/2–3.
77 124th Report on Protection from Domestic Violence Bill, 2002, Parliament of India
78 Fourteenth Lok Sabha (2005) Debate on Protection of Women from Domestic Violence Bill held on 23.8.05 and 24.8.15, Session 5, Government of India
79 Ibid
80 Ibid
81 Ibid (Translated from Hindi)
82 Gazette of India Extraordinary Part II Section 2 page 22 dated 22nd August 2005
83 Kothari J (2005) Criminal Law on Domestic Violence: Promises and Limits, *Economic Political Weekly*, XL 7 pp. 32–36
84 UN Women (2013) supra
85 In Re: Enforcement and Implementation of Dowry Prohibition Act, 1961 AIR 2005 SC 2375
86 Jaising I (2009) Bringing Rights Home: Review of the Campaign for a Law on Domestic Violence, *Economic and Political Weekly*, XLIV (44) 50–57
87 Stark E (2007) *Coercive Control: How Men Entrap Women in Personal Life*, Oxford University Press, New York pp. 99–100
88 Rule 14(13) & (14)
89 Jhamb B (2011) The Missing Link in the Domestic Violence Act, *Economic Political Weekly*, 46, 45–50
90 Kadam SS and Chaudhari VA (2011) Review Paper: Domestic Violence against Woman: Past, Present, Future, *Journal of Indian Academy of Forensic Medicine*, 33, 261–66
91 Gadkar-Wilcox S (2011) Intersectionality and the Under-Enforcement of Domestic Violence Laws in India, *Journal of Law & Social Change*, 15, 455–74
92 Ghosh B and Choudhuri T (2011) Legal Protection Against Domestic Violence in India: Scope and Limitations, *Journal of Family Violence*, 26, 319–30
93 See Jaising (2016) supra n 86
94 Lawyer's Collective Report 2012
95 Deosthali PB, Ravindran TKS and Vindhya U (2012) Addressing Domestic Violence within Healthcare Settings: The Dilaasa Model, *Economic and Political Weekly*, 68, 66–75
96 Lawyer's Collective Report 2012
97 Civil Society Resource Facility (2010) *A Report on the Status of PWDVA in Orissa, 2010–2011*, Friends' Association for Resource Facility, Bhubaneswar, supported by Oxfam India
98 Centre for Social Justice (2007–2008) *Study on Readiness of State Mechanism to Implement the Domestic Violence Act, 2005*, Sponsored by Oxfam, Gujarat, http://www.centreforsocialjustice.net/wp-content/uploads/2015/12/Study_on_Domestic_Violence_Act.pdf
99 Mahila Jagran Kendra (2016) *An Analysis of Perception of Domestic Violence and Efficacy of Implementation of PWDV Act 2005*, Collaboration with Care India, Bihar

100 Bhatia M (2012) Domestic Violence in India: Cases under the Protection of Women from Domestic Violence Act, 2005, *South Asia Research*, 32 (2) 103–22
101 Sakhrani M and Panchal TJ (2014) *Quest for Justice: A Study of Implementation of Protection of Women from Domestic Violence Act, 2005*, Ministry of Women and Child Development and TISS, Mumbai
102 Fricker Miranda (2007) *Epistemic Injustice: Power and Ethics of Knowing*, Oxford University Press, New York
103 MacKinnon Catharine A (1991) From Practice to Theory, *Yale Journal of Law and Feminism*, 13 (4) 14
104 Giddens Anthony (1984) *The Constitution of Society*, University of California Press, Berkeley
105 Simon Caroline (2018) How Social Media has Shaped Black Live Matter After Five Years, *USA Today*, July 12, https://www.usatoday.com/story/news/2018/07/12/black-lives-matter-movement-and-social-media-after-five-years/778779002/
106 *The Hindu* (2017) What Is 'Not in My Name' All About? July 1, https://www.thehindu.com/news/national/what-is-not-in-my-name-all-about/article19194499.ece
107 Benjamin W (1969) *The Storyteller: Tales Out of Loneliness*, translated and edited by S Dolbear, Esther Leslie and Sebastian Truskolaski, 2016, Verso Books, New York
108 Census 2011 Government of India
109 Government of India (2006) Economic Survey of Delhi 2005–2006, http://delhiplanning.nic.in/Economic%20Survey/ES%202005-06/Chpt/1.pdf
110 Proclamation Notification no. 911 dated 17.09.1912 issued by the Governor General of India whereby Mr. William Malcolm Hailey was appointed first chief commissioner of Delhi. Simultaneously the Delhi Laws Act 1912 was enacted to enforce the existing laws. http://delhicourts.nic.in/History.htm accessed on 23.01.13
111 Kumar Ashok (2012) *Delhi: Growing Problem of Growing Megapolis in Urbanization in South Asia: Focus on Mega Cities*, edited by RP Misra, Foundation Books, New Delhi
112 Census 2011
113 The Constitution Sixty Ninth Amendment Act, 1991
114 Verma R (2018) Why Delhi Isn't Yet a World Heritage City, *The Times of India*, July 1, https://timesofindia.indiatimes.com/city/delhi/why-delhi-isnt-yet-a-world-heritage-city/articleshow/64810418.cms
115 Nigam S (2015) Delhi: A World Class Smart City or an Inclusive, Equitable Capital? *Countercurrents*, February 14, www.countercurrents.org/nigam140215.htm
116 Nigam S (2014) Violence, Protest and Change: A Socio-Legal Analysis of Extraordinary Mobilization After the 2012 Delhi Gang Rape Case, *International Journal of Gender and Women's Studies*, 2 (2) 197–221
117 Alavi AM (2017) NCRB Data Reinforces Delhi's Rape Capital Tag. City Tops in Crime Against Women, *The Hindustan Times*, December 1, https://www.hindustantimes.com/delhi-news/ncrb-data-reinforces-delhi-s-rape-capital-tag-city-tops-in-crimes-against-women/story-APb3zjxQWw3nRkeJlTE8oN.html
118 Phadke S, Khan S and Ranade S (2011) *Why Loiter? Women and Risk on Mumbai Streets*, Penguin, New Delhi
119 Nigam S (2016) The Privileges of Being a Hindu, Upper Caste and Elite Class, Male In India, *Countercurrents*, February 10, www.countercurrents.org/nigam100216.htm
120 Singh SR (2016) Crime Capital: Delhi Reported One Rape Every Four Hours in 2015, *The Hindustan Times*, June 7, https://www.hindustantimes.com/

delhi-news/crime-capital-delhi-reported-one-rape-every-four-hours-in-2015/story-TWF8fODNA5bMx4vydzprVM.html
121 *Firstpost* (2014) Delhi Records 40 Cases of Crime Against Women Every day, Says Police, November 9, www.firstpost.com/india/delhi-records-40-cases-crimes-women-every-day-says-police-1794593.html
122 Dutt A (2016) Low Sex Ratio? Hospitals in Delhi Blame God, Luck, Poverty and Weather, *The Hindustan Times*, August 7, https://www.hindustantimes.com/delhi-newspaper/low-sex-ratio-hospitals-in-delhi-blame-god-luck-poverty-weather/story-DzZhaCTbrz2q6ADfP2V0xK.html
123 NCRB (2017) Crime in India 2016 Government of India
124 *The Indian Express* (2015) Over 9700 Women Rights Violation Cases Registered Since April 2015: Govt, July 31, https://indianexpress.com/article/india/india-others/over-9700-women-rights-violation-cases-registered-since-april-2015/
125 Sharma K (2013) Wife Beating Epidemic Afflicts South Delhi, Cases Gone Up by 10 Times Over Last Year, *India Today*, June 25, https://www.indiatoday.in/india/north/story/domestic-violence-delhi-rural-phenomenon-rising-at-alarming-rate-india-today-167915-2013-06-25
126 *The Indian Express* (2019) Huge Pendency in Domestic Violence Cases: DCW Chief, March 3, http://www.newindianexpress.com/thesundaystandard/2019/mar/03/huge-pendency-in-domestic-violence-cases-says-maliwal-1946065.html
127 Department of Women and Child Development, Delhi Government, www.delhi.gov.in/wps/wcm/connect/58afa7804c0a6fbdbe35bf8696242497/WCD+201_217.pdf?MOD=AJPERES&lmod=-1567516909&CACHEID=58afa7804c0a6fbdbe35bf8696242497 accessed on 02.08.14
128 Delhi District Courts (2013) Statistics pertaining to number of cases registered till 1 July 2013, Government of Delhi, http://delhidistrictcourts.nic.in/Statistics.html accessed on 05.12.13. Later, these statistics were removed from the website.
129 Ibid
130 Sharma A (2018) Conviction Rate in Delhi At All Time Low, *The Indian Express*, January 6
131 Delhi District Courts (2013) History of Courts in Delhi, http://delhicourts.nic.in/History.htm accessed on 02.03.14
132 Notification No. 155 dated 28th March 1974 Ministry of Home Affairs, Gazette of India (Extra) Part II Section 3(ii)
133 Inaugurated in 1958.
134 Shifted from Parliament Street in March 1977.
135 Started functioning in August 2010.
136 Inaugurated in 1993.
137 The Rohini Courts complex, started in 2005, deals with civil, criminal, rent and accident claims cases pertaining to the west and northwest districts.
138 The Central Social Welfare Board in 2012 created a list as per which 25 organizations were marked as SPs.
139 Developed by Action India.
140 Special Police Unit for Women and Children created by Delhi Police http://spuwac.com/other-activities-of-the-spuwc/ accessed on 21.12.13
141 Section 2(j)
142 As mentioned on the website http://wcddel.in/pwdva.html accessed on 01.03.19
143 Department of Women and Child Development created in 2007, Delhi, http://wcddel.in/lfcc.html accessed on 23.12.13 and on 3.1.19
144 The DCW listed these shelter homes – AIWC, Mahila Dakshita Samiti, YWCA, Prayas, Prabhatara and Shakti Shalini (http://dcw.delhigovt.nic.in/Shelter%20Homes.htm accessed on 23.7.13) whereas the Special Police Unit for Women

and Children additionally shows Matritava Chayya, Nirmal Chhaya Complex and Premalya besides four from the above list (http://spuwac.com/shelter-homes-for-women/) accessed on 02.01.15 and on 02.02.19. However, on 02.02.19, the Delhi government website removed the list of shelter homes and list only three short stay homes under PWDVA – Mahila Dakhsita Samiti, AIWC and Shakti Shalini

145 *The Wire* (2018) Nine Girls Go Missing from East Delhi Shelter Homes, December 4

146 Lama P and Bhardwaj A (2016) Homeless Women: Easy Target, *The Hindustan Times*, August 17

147 Delhi has no special scheme to support women in distress similar to Telangana, which launched a pension scheme of Rs. 1000/ per month. It is claimed that this will benefit 36 lakhs unmarried women, *joginis* and divorced women. *The Times of India* (2017) Telangana Launches Single-Women Pension Scheme, First in India, June 5

148 Ministry of Women and Child Development (2016–17) Annual Report 2016–17, Government of India, www.wcd.nic.in/sites/default/files/FINAL%20WCD_AR_English%202016-17.pdf accessed on 28.02.19

149 Tavares RR and Mishra Y (2016) Budget 2016: To Really Transform India, Focus on Women First, *The Times of India*, March 1, https://timesofindia.indiatimes.com/budget-2016/women/Budget-2016-To-really-transform-India-focus-on-women-first/articleshow/51201811.cms

150 Jhamb B (2011) The Missing Link in the Domestic Violence Act, *Economic and Political Weekly*, XLVI (33) 45–50

151 Ministry of Women and Child Development (2010–11) Annual Plan, Government of India, http://wcddel.in/pdf/WCDAnnual%20Plan%202010-11.pdf accessed on 01.12.14

152 Department of Women and Child Development, Government of NCT of Delhi, Planning Branch, Budget Estimates for 2011–12, http://wcddel.in/pdf/Budget_2011-12.pdf

153 Department of Women and Child Development, Government of NCT of Delhi, Planning Branch, Budget Estimates for 2013–14

154 Center for Budget and Accountability (2009) *Gender Budgeting and PDVA in Report on Workshop on Gender Budgeting with Special Reference to Implementation of the PWDV Act*, November 18, Women Power Connect, New Delhi

155 Dhar A (2013) Torment within Four Walls, *The Hindu*, January 29 p. 11

156 Ministry of Women and Child Development About PWDV Act, http://wcddel.in/pwdv.html accessed on 20.11.13

157 North, northwest, west, central, east, northeast, New Delhi, southwest and south.

158 Press Information Bureau (2013) Protection Officers Under PWDVA, 2005 Ministry of Women and Child Development, Government of India, March 1, http://pib.nic.in/newsite/PrintRelease.aspx?relid=92846 accessed on 12.07.14

159 Delhi Government (2013) Police in Delhi, http://delhigovt.nic.in/newdelhi/police.html accessed on 09.08.16

160 Government of NCT of Delhi (2014) *Statistical Abstract of Delhi 2014*, Directorate of Economic and Statistics, New Delhi

161 Census of India (2011) www.census2011.co.in/census/state/delhi.html accessed on 15.07.14

162 In an application filed before the Central Administrative Tribunal, Delhi, OA 2012/12, in Kiran Sharma vs Government of NCT of Delhi decided on 28.1.2014, demands have been made that POs be paid an equivalent salary as

that of Welfare Officers and that the posts of POs be created. The presiding officer partly allowed the application and directed the government to pay POs an equivalent salary as that of Welfare Officer. However, the petition regarding the creation of the post of PO was rejected. In WPC 153 of 2012, it directed that the appointment of a PO should be for a minimum three years and the contractual appointments should be discontinued. However, this has not been followed.

3 Fighting against domestic violence

Weaving stories of pain and courage

In your joint family, I am known as the second daughter-in-law. All these years I have known myself as no more than that. Today, after fifteen years, as I stand alone by the sea, I know that I have another identity, which is my relationship with the universe and its creator. That gives me the courage to write this letter as myself, not as the second daughter-in-law of your family. . . . I am not one to die easily. That is what I want to say in this letter.

– *Rabindranath Tagore, 'Letter from a Wife', 1914*[1]

Scientists claim that the physical world consists of atoms and molecules. However, the emotional world is made up of dreams, aspirations, pain, suffering, struggles, rebellions, hope and courage. Real-life stories consisting of these elements provide a glimpse into the lives of men and women and their interface with the larger world around them. This larger world constitutes family, kinship and others in the surrounding where the relationship between human constituents is governed by rules and law. From birth to death, one often interfaces with the law, more specifically with governmentality, an expression used by Foucault,[2] which denotes the social control or power exerted by the hierarchical state on the everyday conduct of people using means other than rules and laws. The question then arise relating to the manner in which people are being governed and the way they connect and counter the power of the state. Though theoretically, rules or law are inert, rigid and non-malleable, individual stories show their pliability in terms of the impact of the law on real lives.

This chapter looks at women's encounters with the state and their endeavors to fight for justice. Using feminist research praxis, it explores the struggles of complainants around justice within the complex realm of kinship, society and law through the testimonies of complainants. Based on interviews with women, it qualitatively analyzes the data to focus on different facets of abuse. Life story methods enable a broader understanding of power relations using various vulnerabilities axes and intersectionality. An interview lasted for one to three hours and at times, twice or more this amount. While analyzing the narratives of complainants and their experiences when they encounter the state, this chapter concludes that law cannot function in a vacuum. It has to connect to the social context in which it operates. Moreover, epistemic justice operates to ignores the realities and experiences of women, as their voices remain unheard while interpreting and implementing the law.

Domestic violence is pervasive

Domestic violence occurs across the boundaries of age, color, caste, class, religion, education, or employment status, and women are often at the receiving end. Frequently, women face continuous violence for prolong periods and live with the persistent fear that violence could trigger at any moment. There is no escape from such a situation. Veils of privacy shield violence within families. In the present study, though most of the informants are in the age group of 18 to 30 years, there are older women who have been tortured by their families. There are unmarried, divorced or single women or widows who have been harassed as sisters, daughters or mothers besides those being tortured as wives. Koeing et al[3] observed that the risk of spousal violence is higher among younger women who have a lower household income, are less educated, belong to a lower caste, are non-working and are in situations where the male partner drinks or bets. However, contrary to these findings, the present work suggests that women from all ages and from different backgrounds complained against their violent family members. In alignment with several reports, wife battering exists not only among poor or uneducated communities but also has been reported increasingly among the affluent classes.[4] Counter to the popular belief that illiterate or unemployed men indulge in violence, this work reports that these variables make no difference.

Endogamy prevails

Ambedkar[5] saw caste as a complex endogamous institution that has upheld strict rules since ancient times. To maintain stratification, entrenched norms enforce the rule of marrying within one's own caste. A man may enter into a bigamous relationship, but for women, practices such as *sati* and enforced widowhood have been imposed to protect the purity of the bloodline. This notion of caste-, class- or religion-based endogamy is deeply embedded in the general psyche and has continued in the post-colonial nation. Education or affluence has made little impact on the feudal mind-set. It is in conformity to social norms that all of the informants except six in the present research study recounted that their marriage was arranged by parents or larger families. In the cosmopolitan city of Delhi, the culture of marriage by choice is not widely prevalent. Elsewhere, it has been reported that 90 percent of marriages are arranged by parents and family members.[6] The *sanskaars*, which are strongly rooted in patriarchal traditions, restrict women's autonomy in terms of choice relating to marriage. Gendered norms operate where men within natal families act as gatekeepers of women's sexuality. However, there is a growing trend where people are defying conventional norms. Interestingly, love cum arranged marriage, where women chose their partner and sought consent from the natal family, is reported in one-seventh of cases.

Two-fifths of arranged marriages are decided either through newspaper advertisements or matrimonial websites. The rest are arranged through referral by the extended family network or through intermediaries, including well-wishers, friends or other acquaintances. Perhaps the trust in close networks is dwindling or perhaps the ease, availability and anonymity in using digital or print media are increasingly being preferred. Over a decade, matrimonial sites have engineered a social change. They are offering a wide range of services, including 'online matchmaking'. The access to the Internet and mobile phones provides an opportunity to "[m]ix biology and economy in equal measure; add a dash of family values; omit romance; overcook the base of practicality; thicken it with religion and caste; stir in stars and planets – that was always the short and sweet recipe for arranged marriages in India".[7] However, such arrangements have their own pitfalls, as they constrain the bride's family from conducting inquiries about the groom's antecedents. For instance, Disha[8] (32) recounted

> My horoscope says I am a *Manglik*. My parents faced difficulty in finding a match so they went to this matrimonial site. He mentioned that he is an MBA working with a foreign bank earning a six figure salary, but later we found out that he is a diploma holder working with a private company earning meagerly. He used to beat me to get money. I was treated as a maid. He wanted money but my parents are in no position to fulfill his demands.
>
> (2015)

In non-conformity with the rationalist ideas, compatibility in terms of an astrological match is considered significant by many families while arranging marriages. Other factors that put women at a disadvantageous position during marriage negotiations are their age, dark complexion (which is not desirable), multiple daughters in the natal family, socio-economic status of the family, capacity to afford a lavish wedding with a dowry, her education and employment or previous divorce, among others except compatibility among couple of attitude or mindset.

Defining violence from the perspective of women survivors

Domestic violence as a legal problem was framed in 1983 when Section 498A IPC introduced the term 'cruelty within marriage' and made it an offense. Starting with the concern relating to the increasing number of women dying due to 'stove death' because of dowries, it was also acknowledged that women were tortured and abused for various reasons. Yet legislators, police and government are in denial regarding the existence of violence. However, the human rights framework emerged, and with the introduction of the PWDVA, the term 'domestic violence' was defined broadly to include physical, sexual, verbal, emotional and economic abuse. This definition is much more comprehensive than that given under Section 498A. Nonetheless, this work shows that this definition is not yet complete, as it does not consider the everyday reality of women's lives.

Also, the term 'violence' is loaded with subjectivity. Participants shared that they do not undergo merely physical or mental abuse as interpreted in the cruelty paradigm, nor do they categorize violence in its multitude forms as mentioned in the DIR format. From the perspective of women, violence entails multiple forms of continuous abuse. Their lives are circled around violence, and each one is negotiating it in her own way. Violence is not limited to specific incidents as interpreted by the law implementers. Law enforcers imagine domestic violence as a 'dispute', 'quarrel' or 'ego tussle' rather than an act of terror or oppression. This conceptualization incorrectly assumes that women are responsible for violence. It minimizes, trivializes and normalizes violence while ignoring the fact that women are being socialized and patriarchally conditioned to accept it. The complainants' narratives are not limited to receiving slaps occasionally. This work shows that each of the complainants, apart from her varied background or location, has a different experience. Yet certain elements are common and include continuous suffering, a struggle to constantly deal with intense pain and an understanding that the violence needs to be stopped. Analyzing this qualitative data, therefore, is a complex process, as it involves dealing with life complexities and subjectivities that need to be filtered through the lens of legal objectivity. However, an attempt has been made here to broadly describe the complicated multi-faceted violence in simple terms through several case studies.

Domestic violence takes varied forms

This work shows that all participants have experienced continuous, routine, multiple forms of abuse that include verbal, physical, emotional, sexual and economic exploitation for days, months and years. Slapping, beating, pinching, pulling hair, twisting arms, strangulation, kicking, punching, throttling and throwing objects are different forms of daily abuse that women endure. Violence also includes forced sex, denial of basic resources including food, teasing, taunting, demeaning, being thrown out of the house, control over mobility, restrictions in various forms, stalking, suspicion being raised about her character, rape and incest in combined forms in visible or non-visible ways. All participants reported facing mundane to harsher abuses such as belittling, taunts, ridicule, humiliation, insults, scolding, shouting and screaming on a daily basis. Other mistreatments include forcing her to go back to her natal home and using the children as threat. Coercive, controlling behaviors are used to subjugate women, where the perpetrators control their lives using threats, intimidation and other tactics. Thus, domestic violence is a multi-dimensional issue as compared to violence against women in a public space.

Many forms of violence overlap in the narratives such that women themselves find it difficult to distinguish one from the other. Almost all have gone through a prolonged, continuous violence that entails gruesome accounts of unceasing trauma while living in a state of constant fear and an atmosphere of terror, day in and day out. One-seventh reported that they contemplated or tried committing suicide at some point in their life because of severe intolerable violence. Despite going through multiple forms of abuse every day, none of them reported seeking psychological support or treatment for mental distress.

The impact of violence on women is severe, ranging from physical injuries such as cuts, wounds, fractures, broken jaws, miscarriages, multiple abortions or other severe affects. One-third reported extreme physical violence, where one-sixth of these had been hospitalized earlier for injuries ranging from damaged eardrums to serious burns. Only in cases of grave injuries have women been taken to the hospital. Also, two-fifths reported seeking treatment for ailments such as gynecological disorders, internal bleeding and a range of other illnesses. One-sixth of informants claimed that they were badly injured when they left the marital home and required immediate hospitalization; however, only three were admitted to the hospital. One remained under treatment for a month, while another was released after six days. Others reported that they suffered injuries but could not seek medical interventions due to various reasons.

"My parents bestowed my hands to him but he blew fists on me"

I met Ramiya (24) in the Saket court complex. Married to Suresh, a salesman, four years back, she had a child. Her marriage lasted for almost two years during which she faced severe violence. She stated,

> On the first day of the marriage, he punched me in the face, one after the another until the blood oozed out of my mouth. My father drove a rickshaw and my mother worked as a maid. I got married at the age of 19 years. It was an arranged marriage. He (the husband) demanded 50,000/ cash. My father gave 20,000/ and said that he would arrange the rest within a week. My husband did not like it. As soon as I arrived in my matrimonial home, he retaliated. I remained hungry for weeks because he gave me no money. My hand got fractured and I suffered from infections. But when my second child in the womb died because of his furious beating, I walked away.
>
> (2013)

Ramiya was angry. Her mother died a year after her marriage. Her father got cancer. Her brother ran away. She is left with an ill child, a broken body and scarred mind. Within a short period of her marriage, she faced harsh abuse from her mentally sick husband. Her aunt supported her, but poverty cannot be vanished. With her basic education, she took up a job of cleaning an office twice a day in return for a meager salary. For her, marriage is an anathema. She retorted, "Marriage is like a cancer, cancer that is taking the life of my father, will take my life too". Ramiya's experiences are not limited to occasional quarrels, but rather have a serious impact on her life. The intersectionality of class and gender act to deepen the impact of violence.

When protectors become predators

Sonal (29) was waiting for a hearing when I met her in Tees Hazari Court. She is a post-graduate married to a company executive. According to her,

> From the second day of marriage they (husband and in-laws) demanded money for household expenses. When I refused, they assaulted me. During pregnancy also, I was not spared. My daughter is born with Down syndrome. They threw me out. He is living with someone else. For him, life is easy but for me it's a hell. He has extorted money again. I have done everything for him but what I received back is terrible scars, broken trust, dreadful bitterness and a wounded soul. The life of my daughter has been ruined too. It's a heartless world. My parents will not support me for long. What will I do?"
>
> (2014)

Dejected and frustrated, Sonal filed a case under Section 498A, as well as an application under PWDVA for maintenance for herself and her child. At the time of her interview, she was staying with her sister and could not engage in any earning activity, as she can't leave her sick child for long. Her husband has paid only Rs 13000/ as maintenance once and refused to pay further on the pretext that he has lost his job. "He has exploited me when I was staying with him and even now, again I am being victimized running around here and there and not getting justice". Her experience shows that women are being *triply victimized* – within marriage, in her natal family once she is back and further when the legal system cannot offer solutions. And this is not just Ramiya or Sonal – there are others in similar situations who faced extreme violence in their marriage, and with no escape mechanism available, they tolerated brutalities for years. Frequently, getting support from the natal family after marriage is not easy. Also, many are angry, dejected and frustrated because after a long encounter with the legal system, they cannot obtain relief.

Why are men violent?

The discourse around domestic violence relates to the question as to why she stays, or in India, the rhetoric of why she can't tolerate violence for the sake of her family. Less emphasis is placed on the question as to why men choose to abuse women with impunity when violence is legally prohibited. Perhaps in the male-dominated society, violence is sanctioned and legitimized by social norms. A batterer does not act in a vacuum; rather, his actions are legitimized by the hierarchical social order that normalizes and trivializes violence while enabling him to act violently and get away with it. This uneven social order devalues a woman and makes her vulnerable.[9] Such a discriminatory environment is guided by the prejudiced belief that a woman can be denied equal status, safety, security or dignity or be deprived of freedom, a political voice, credibility, the benefits of protection of the laws or, in short, the resources of all kind that enable the self-determination, autonomy and self-esteem of a person. Structural inequalities act to erode female dignity while inflating men's sense of entitlement. The media portrays batterers as innocent, an object of pity and essentially gentle men who are driven to commit violence because of family tensions or a victim's provocative act, or his obsession with alcohol, or the nagging behavior of wife, or because she failed to discharge her marital duties or that she is disloyal or lacks character. Such excuses deflect attention from the fact that men are responsible for violence.

Nevertheless, in the current work, two of three informants felt that their husband was under the influence of his friends or family, who instigated the violence. Two-fifths felt that their husband was of a suspicious and controlling nature, and one-third felt that their husband was having an extramarital affair. The majority felt that the perpetrator was manipulative and was twisting the facts to justify his violent actions. Men's authority is legitimized by social sanctions that reiterate inequalities and favor a display of toxic masculinity. Payal (28), working with an MNC as a sales executive, said, "Often I felt that I am alone, whole world is against me. Nobody questions him. People (neighbors, friends, relatives) point finger at me. He is cleverly manipulating each and every fact to prove that I am wrong" (2014).

A common factor that emerged in this work is that the batterer, in all cases, is a powerful person in comparison to the victim and is better equipped in terms of skills and abilities to manipulate the situation to their own advantage and used cunning tactics such as lies or deceit to demoralize the complainants; they also have the power or resources to hire a battery of lawyers. This factor of better resources – physical, material, emotional, legal and economic – is not considered while adjudicating the domestic violence cases. The privileges the abuser enjoys as a male include disciplining, controlling and violating women's rights, are justified and protected in a male-dominated society. While any individual batterer may imagine that he is operating on his own, he derives his power from the larger social order, which is discriminatory against women.

Why can't women leave the violent situation?

From the perspective of a woman, gruesome violence in the relationship implies not only breaking of trust but also an assault on her dignity. In a marital relationship, a man–woman tie is more than a mere exchange of casual sex or intimacy in lieu of 'bread' or 'protection'. It involves an investment in terms of emotions. Since her birth, frequently, a woman is raised with the hope that her salvation lies in her marriage. Society, religion, the market and such institutions reiterate this message using various modes and paint marriage as a perfect institution. A woman who grows up in such an environment when facing violence feels shocked, betrayed, guilty and fearful and wants that violence to stop somehow.

As a survivor, a woman who faces violence may remain silent about it, may justify it or may take steps to prevent it. Her response is determined by factors that are culture specific, social, economic and based on the availability of resources and support mechanism, besides her notion of violence and justice. In addition, numerous aspects compel women to stay in a violent relationship. These compulsions range from fear of attracting more violence, fear of retaliation, lack of housing and finances, children, stigma, lack of courage or abilities, dearth of legal literacy and resources and secondary status in families. In a male-dominated society, violence remains invisible under the garb of discipline, while the realm of emotions prevents women from walking out of a violent situation. Agnes, in her book titled *My Story . . . Our Story of Rebuilding Broken Lives*,[10] stated that one speaks out only when one has faced 'enough'.

In the current work, initially, all informants have suffered intense pain and endured tremendous cruelty before they raised concerns. Yet none of the informants remained a passive recipient of abuse. Rather, they had done their best to salvage the relationship and despite experiencing gross abuse, they had adjusted, forgiven, forgotten, compromised, sacrificed and reconciled with the perpetrators' behavior multiple times in the hope that the situation might change. The different tactics they used to negotiate the abusive situation include "correcting their own fault", confrontation, "pleading the perpetrator", "being suppliant", "showing defiance", "exerting their agency" or "resisting" in many ways. Most of them wanted violence-free, peaceful lives for themselves and their children.

All informants stated that it was not at the first instance of violence that they sought help. They confided in 'significant others'[11] only when the situation became unbearable, all other strategies failed and they tried to involve other females the within natal or marital family. It is at the later stage that male elderly members in the house intervene. The wider kinship network was consulted later, and influential men in the locality were called upon to mediate. If all these strategies proved futile, then the matter was taken to the local bodies involved in dispute resolution, such as caste councils, community council or religious sect. It is much later that the legal institutions come into the picture. Neha (23), married at the age of 19, revealed

> It was a love marriage. Initially, everything was fine but later he started threatening me. I was not allowed to meet my parents or go out. I tried different ways to make him happy. One day he came in drunk and started beating me with a rod alleging that I was having an affair. I lost a tooth, my wrist got broken and I got six stitches on my right eyebrow. I could not talk to my brother when he called, then my parental family came to know. My parents and relatives intervened but nothing happened. He came at midnight, and created a scene out there. My brother called the police. But they let him off with a warning. I thought about walking out of the hell. But my parents insisted that he would change. Then things got worse. He became more violent. He took my phone and locked me in a room for four days. Somehow, I managed to escape. I have been staying at my parents' house since then. A few days back, I heard that he was with another woman. Then one of our relatives referred us to a lawyer.
>
> (2013)

All participants stated that it is not easy to confront violent family members. Women internalized and accepted domination and tolerated violence for years before they gathered courage to raise a voice against it. The reasons for leaving violent relationships include "could not endure more", "being injured or retaliatory violence", "thrown out of the house", "fear or threat of death", "husband having an affair with another woman", "safety of children", among others. A few put up with violence for more than 10 or 20 years thinking that it may end. Some of them said that they may reconsider going back to the 'violent situation' as 'there is no other option' or 'they will 'forgive and forget' or 'it's man's world where women have no choice'. Many recounted that they left and have gone back again several times before filing the official complaint. However, given the choice, almost half wanted to escape the violence and said that they would not like to go back even if the perpetrator amends his abusive behavior. Two-thirds stated that they do not want to stay with their natal families either because the family refuses or they face violence there too. A few stated that they may focus on study or work and would pursue their professional goals. However, law is governed by uniform sets of rules and regulations and offers different solutions.

Reporting domestic violence is not easy

Reporting is a first step to break the silence around violence. In the present work, married women were found to be the largest users of domestic violence laws. Only a few have filed cases against members of the natal family.

For women who stayed in abusive relationships, the violence continued for years. The length of the relationship is in no way related to the intensity of violence. Two-fifths cases are filed within three to five years of marriage, one-sixth between five to ten years and the rest are filed after ten years of a violent relationship. Three cases are filed after 20 years of marriage. Also, research studies have shown that registering a complaint under 498A is a monumental task.[12] The PWDVA is seen as an extension of Section 498A by the police and lawyers who guide women to take a legal recourse. The Lawyers' Collective in its report[13] arrived at a similar conclusion. Also, though dowry violence and domestic abuse are not connected, in the legal discourse, these are intermeshed in complex ways.

Generally, everyday incidents of violence are considered normal wear and tear of a marriage. The onus is laid on women to adjust, while men are not held accountable for their abusive actions. A culture of silence around violence traps women in abusive relationships. Primarily, the family is considered a closed institution, not be touched or interfered with. Outsiders hesitate to intervene in family matters. Raising a voice against family members in public is considered a disregard of family loyalty and a breach of social values. As per norms, 'good wives' do not complain as it harms the honor, reputation and prestige of the marital as well as natal family, bringing disgrace to both. Regardless of its emotional and physical costs, a woman is expected to bear the torture because 'private' matters cannot be brought into the public domain. The cultural legitimization of violence as both expressive and instrumental in disciplining women and controlling them prevents many from seeking help. I met Ila (54) at Rohini Court. According to her,

> For 22 years, I tolerated everything. My parental family refused to intervene. I am not educated. He tortured me in every way he could. I accepted it as my fate. Two years back, my son, who was 17 then, held back the hand of his father while he was beating me. I realized that at least now my son is with me. I therefore gathered courage to walk out of that hell.
>
> (2015)

Women who face violence are either not aware of the legal provisions or are afraid to confront violent members, or they are too disturbed that they could not think reasonably, or the response of their closer network including natal family or friends keeps them from reporting the matter to 'outside' institutions. Perhaps the economic, emotional and material dependency of women on families enhances their vulnerability. Besides, many lack negotiation skills and the prevalent stereotype of woman as weak and helpless prevents her from negotiating her claims. Those who raise their voice are projected negatively as family breakers. Social norms do not portray violent men negatively or encourage them to discontinue their abusive behavior. For instance, Padma, (41), a homemaker with two kids, clarifies,

> Violence has made my life hell. The first thing I was concerned about is safety of my children. Once he was beating me, my 8-year-old daughter intervened. He hit her hard. She bled a lot. I went to my parents' house. But everyone insisted so I came back. Again, he continued with violence. This time the beating was intense and without any reason. The community pressure, intervention of relatives, all failed. I cajoled, requested and pleaded for him to stop hitting the kids. But he refused to listen. That day he threatened to rape and kill my daughter, then I was compelled to go to police. I have never been to a police station. Neither has anyone from my family. No woman would go to police or court for fun. How will I bring up the kids?
>
> (2014)

Padma's application for maintenance under the PWDVA was pending before the court for one year, along with the future of her marital relationship. In court, her husband has refused to stay with her. Women who were not in marital relations also wanted that abuse in all forms to stop. Amba (53), a single unmarried woman, filed a case against her brother for her right to residence and stated

> [The] house belongs to my father, but he (the brother) thinks that only he has a right over it. We (me and my mother) have nowhere to go. I know I can demand my share. But he is fighting with my mother too. He is doing everything to harass us. We just want to live peacefully. But life is not easy when you are a woman!
>
> (2014)

The legal system does not consider everyday violence and its impact on women. Factors such as power asymmetry in the relationship, embedded inequalities within families, lack of support mechanisms, prejudices and stereotypes are some of the reasons that domestic violence persists and is tolerated and defended. Besides economic constraints, a lack of educational and occupational opportunities among women add up to prevent women from raising their voice against violence. Domestic violence remains invisible because of the false notion of 'protection' being provided within the home. Perhaps this patronizing attitude is used as a tool to socialize family members as to the overall perspective of male dominance and control and therefore give rise to a culture of violence. The atomized view of domestic violence strengthens the norms of privacy that shield the perpetrators from sanctions. The family's sanctity as a normative social ideal therefore needs to be scrutinized.

Domestic violence is multi-oppressive

Wife battering takes place behind closed doors and is a form of a hidden invisible violence. Any intervention by outsiders is considered undesirable. Also, dealing with domestic violence is not an easy task. It involves a range of emotions, subjectivities, sufferings and pain. Further, this becomes complicated in a society in which violence is culturally and social sanctioned with no other support available. Rather, society pressures women to adjust and reconcile to 'save the family', overlooking the discriminatory and inhumane aspects of the relationship. For many women, the family does not represent a safe and protective unit; rather, it reinforces wider patterns of discrimination and legitimizes violence as a method for controlling and subjugating women. However, prevalent social norms glorify families while underplaying the violence women face. Yashasvi (46) alleged

> I left him and then got a job with MNC and booked a flat, however, after 8 years of long proceedings, the judge ordered us to reconcile. I refused but everyone insisted and he pleaded, so I decided to give him an opportunity. But he hasn't changed. Every day he used to pick a fight to put his name on papers for the flat. Then one day, while we had a heated argument, he hit me with a rod, I lost consciousness. I was admitted to the hospital for a month. Since then I am unable to use my arm, as my spine has been injured. I could have died, just because of my wrong decision.
>
> (2013)

Once a woman comes back to a violent situation, she is further prone to facing intense violence due to the culture of impunity in which the perpetrator assumes that he is powerful and that he would not be penalized or that the social sanctions are in his favor. Most of the informants alleged that their natal families forced them back to violent homes, and the perpetrator took advantage of their vulnerability to indulge in more violence; thus, a spiral of violence is created where a woman is trapped in a web from where escape seems impossible.[14] Sofia (41) recollected:

> My family [pressured] me to go back. The house belongs to my brothers. I can't stay there with my kids. He (the husband) realized that and took advantage of this fact and started picking fights over small issues. My mother-in-law didn't help. According to her, it is the duty of a man to control his wife and children.
>
> (2015)

Domestic violence in such cases is embedded in a context of social, economic, cultural and power relationships. Societies organized around gendered, hierarchical relationships legitimize violence while devaluing women. For men, marriage involves enjoying privileges as men extracts women's labor, her worth, her being and her emotions in lieu of providing 'protection', but for the women it entails sacrificing identity, worth and persona, all for the sake of family. A PO shared

> Some cases are horrific. Women suffered burns, multiple miscarriages, injuries, violence during pregnancy, attempted suicide, deprivation, adultery and so on. There are many complications. Sometimes, I feel disgusted. Then there is a huge rush. We have to deal with many cases every day. Sometimes, I feel that I have become insensitive? Therefore, while filing DIRs sometimes I could not think what I should write.
>
> (2013)

In a society where gender discrimination prevails inside the home, in public places, in courtrooms and at workplaces, it becomes difficult for a woman to protest it because the violence is pervasive. Voicing concerns adds to the misery of women rather than bailing them out of the situation. The repressive ideology of saving the family dominates even if the women end up paying the high cost. Men enjoy power, while for women it is an institutionalized nature of second-class citizenship.[15]

The norms of acceptable and unacceptable behavior or femininity and masculinity determine the response to the violence. The cultural construction of perfect wifehood and motherhood entails sacrificing one's worth for the sake of the family and involves a tussle of adopting different roles, leading to mental stress among women.[16] Often, such stereotypes are deeply inherent such that women themselves do not perceive domestic violence as wrong. This situation is further complicated by an entrenched belief that violent acts are an expression of love and merely a desire to help a woman become a 'better' person. Pressure is put on a woman to 'avoid violence' and 'reflect on her own behavior'. India lacks a mandatory reporting system whereby hospitals or other institutions report cases coming to them. NFHS-4 data also show that 52 percent of women and 42 percent of men are of the view that violence is justifiable if the woman does not perform her 'wifely duties'. It shows that 76 percent of women who faced physical and sexual violence never sought help or informed anyone. The WHO[17] reported that between 55 and 95 percent of women who had suffered physical violence in intimate relationships had never sought help from either formal institutions or traditional authorities. Other studies report that a victim endures the abuse for an average of 4.2 years before filing a police complaint against the perpetrator.[18]

Further, women are reluctant to use the law. For many, taking a stand against violence was a tough decision. Rather, all of them used informal venues to negotiate violence before voicing their concerns in the legal domain. Not many are aware of legal technicalities, and the majority never went to the police stations or courts earlier. It is in extreme situations that women decide to use law to claim their entitlements. Widely circulated correct or incorrect stories about corruption, bribery and fear of false accusations, among others, prevented many from approaching the state machinery. Skepticism about the inability of the state to deliver quick justice; the high cost of litigation; the hostile, alienating and intimidating environment in police stations and courts; inaccessible and complicated laws or procedures; and the time-consuming, lengthy process, all prevent informants from getting help from the police and courts.

Any form of support helps to voice the concern

Findings suggest that the availability of any form of support mechanism aids in the recovery and healing of a woman in an abusive situation. However, not many avenues are available to women in distress. The natal family emerged as a pillar to support women in need, despite its tendencies to push women to adjust to the violent situations. Three-fifths of married informants stated that staying away from the perpetrator provided them with immediate respite from violence, though the majority stated that the natal family pushed them back to the violent situation multiple times. Education, financial status, proximity to the natal household, attitude of parents and number of unmarried sisters are some of the factors that shaped the response of the natal family. One-fifth got help from their siblings, friends, neighbors or colleagues. Community support is determined by the subjective worth of women as 'good' wives, mothers or daughters-in-law.

Interestingly, more than education or employment status, it is the availability of the support mechanism that made an impact in terms of voicing concerns. Moreover, in the anonymity of the city, community ties are loosening up while state services and social relations are dwindling, leading to increasing isolation and alienation. A changing socio-economic environment and growing individualist culture all are weakening the available support system.

A miniscule percentage called the helpline or sought the help of NGOs or the women's commission. None of the women directly contacted the POs or SPs as provided under the PWDVA. Many reported that they felt unable to reach out to mechanisms such as helplines or commissions because they either they lack awareness or trust in those agencies. The majority contacted private lawyers through the network of the natal family, friends or colleagues.

Nevertheless, once a woman files a legal complaint, she expects that she will receive justice. However, this is not an easy task. The legal system views complaining wives with suspicion and distrust. Legal institutions strive to protect the family rather than being concerned about the safety of women in their homes. Further, remedies provided under the law are not sufficient or in proportion to the sufferings of women. The law does not aid in removing women from an abusive situation. Any concern raised by the victim is suppressed, and she is stigmatized because of a sense of shame attached to making her personal life public. This narrow approach of the law ignores many nuances of domestic violence.

Domestic violence is more than shedding blood

Law enforcement officials generally presume that domestic violence entails injuries for which medicolegal reports may be filed. However, the present work shows that wife beating entails more than shedding blood or injury to multiple body organs. It includes sexual, mental, financial and emotional cruelty, which cannot be captured by medicolegal examinations, forensic reports or other forms of evidence. Domestic violence involves a pattern of coercive and controlling behavior and cannot be underestimated as an isolated act of aggression. It occurs when one person dominates in a relationship using violence or a fear of violence. It includes emotional abuse through threat and reprisals, exploitation, discrimination and other forms of control and coercion.[19] An abuser may use fear, guilt, insult, humiliation, shame, threat and intimidation to gain power and authority, and his actions have a long-lasting impact on the victim. For instance, Vibha (26) said,

> He (the husband) started beating me the very next day after we got married. His parents wanted 5 lakhs. My parents have already given him a bike and 2 lakh cash. I told them (in-laws) that I will work and earn. But they refused. He threatened me and I was not allowed to go out. We never had sex in four months, I stayed there. And then they (in-laws) blamed me for being an unfertile and characterless woman. They humiliated my parents and insulted them.
>
> (2013)

In these few sentences, the informant shares the myriad forms of abuse she suffered, which are not segregated into different categories. Hence, framing the definition of violence from the survivor's perspective is complicated because their descriptions are perplexing, mired with emotions and pain. To shred subjectivities, emotions and pain into many facets is difficult because violence entails more than shedding blood or fractured bones. It entails a multitude forms of brutality. Besides, many such incidents may take place over a prolonged period. The law considers violence in its episodic forms, ignoring the fact that it is a continuous process. Police, POs or other officials are often not sensitive enough or trained to capture the trauma of these varied forms of violence.

Domestic violence involves living and sleeping with one's enemy

Domestic violence occurs in an intimate relationship that is based on respect, loyalty and trust. Violence destroys all these elements. Even otherwise, the marital relationship involves an investment in terms of emotions, because of which a woman may take steps to salvage the relationship. Violence is woven within the normal day-to-day interactions where the abuser and woman may share moments of affection, hopes, dreams, expectations, obligations and also the abuse. It is endemic to women's experiences of everyday normal lives, because a woman is compelled to live with the perpetrator and is dependent on him, sharing the same household and access to resources. At times, even interactions with the outside world are controlled and determined by the perpetrator. The lives of women are circled and enmeshed around violence.

Further, domestic violence is not an episodic or an incidental form of abuse that may occur once or rarely in a sporadic manner. Rather, it involves a range of continuous, coercive, controlling, threatening and intimidating acts, repeated day in and day out, which create fear and terror to the extent that a victim may feel afraid to seek help.[20] Violence therefore involves repeated victimization by the same perpetrator over time, which makes a deep impact on a woman's psyche. Domestic abuse is much more serious and intense than the violence that occurs in public places where the stranger may have limited control over the victim.

In cases of violence against women within public spaces, the anger, frustration, hatred and similar negative emotions may be expressed and shared openly with others. But in the cases of domestic violence, emotional angst that is produced as a result of the violence needs to be shaped and nurtured into love and care, which is an intricate and a difficult task. As Namita (25) stated, "He beats me, tortures me and yet expects me to love him and sleep with him. I hated him for everything he has done to me. This is insane."

Also, the perpetrator of abuse is person who is deemed as a 'protector'. A husband wields absolute authority over his wife, and because of her dependent status, she is supposed to obey. Thus, domestic violence is different from the violence perpetrated by strangers, where a perpetrator is in no position to control the victim. In case of abuse by strangers, a woman may find safety and security within the confines of the home; however, in case, she is abused at home, she has no other place left to seek comfort, safety and security. She is left isolated, alienated and secluded. The whole specter of family violence threatens the fundamental belief that casts families as a supportive space in which members relate to each other with unselfish and altruistic impulses. Brutalities and the dynamics involved raise skepticism about the fundamental rhetoric of the safe or sweet home.

Violence between strangers is different from wife abuse, because the latter results from an unequal power situation. In domestic violence, control is specific and long term. Each act of violence in a relationship is "embedded in a larger pattern of power and control that permeates the relationship".[21] Violence within homes is shielded from public scrutiny. Misogynist attitudes and restrictive gender norms are at the core of violence. An unequal power relation limits women's choices and reinforces dependency on men. At a deeper level domestic violence relates to the social structure that maintains unequal socio-economic relations between men and women.

Marital rape – violence that is not recognized by the law

Susan Brownmiller,[22] in her famous book titled *Against Our Will*, wrote

> Man's discovery that his genitalia could serve as a weapon to generate fear must rank as one of the most important discoveries of prehistoric times along with the use of fire and the first crude stone axe. From prehistoric times to the present, I believe that rape has played a critical function. It is nothing more or less than a conscious process of intimidation by which all men keep all women in a state of fear.

Thus, rape has been used ubiquitously as a crude weapon by men to exploit, threaten, harass and abuse women since ancient times. More specifically, in the socio-political context, as prevalent in India,[23] the concept of consent is least understood,[24] whether it is rape by strangers or by men in homes.

The majority of women complained of being ravaged against their will. More than half of the informants confided that during pregnancies, periods, before or after childbirth or illness they had been forcefully raped by their partners. Despite the doctor's advice to the contrary or when they had gynecological problems, rape continued. Any resistance on their part hardly matters. Several complained of being threatened, intimidated and tortured if they tried to refuse. One-third lamented that they were forced into coercive unnatural sex, and three said that their husbands allegedly shot their sexual acts as a porn video. Higher socio-economic status offers no protection from sexual violence. This is substantiated by several other studies which reported high incidences of coercive sexual violence during pregnancy, irrespective of education or socio-economic status that adversely affects the mother and fetus.[25] Those participants who complained of sexual violence alleged that they suffered extreme stress, as they find it difficult to share such experiences with anyone else. This is in conformity with other studies which observed that 70 percent of women who faced sexual coercion also suffer from PTSD.[26]

Yet, in a situation of marriage, ongoing rape is a critical issue that has received less attention by the policymakers or law makers in India.[27] Marital rape or incest is considered an impermeable domain wherein both the state and society have refused to intervene though recommendations have been made to legislate against it.[28] The patriarchal ideology construes the man–woman relationship as hierarchical and pushes for men's right over women's bodies. The principle of coverture as propounded by Blackstone[29] continues to guide the legal system. The PWDVA does not provide for specific relief besides protection orders for women who are violated sexually within the household; however, this relief is made available only when specific application is made. But in the majority of cases, women do not openly share details of sexual violence in their complaints, either because they are shy or feel stigmatized. Also, taboos, fear or hostility prevent many from speaking up.

Criminal law maintains dual standards and sanctions this crime within the boundaries of *char-diwari* while creating a hierarchy of violence treating marital rape as non-criminal. Sexual assault by a stranger is treated as a heinous crime, and society desires stringent punishment because a woman is seen as another man's daughter, sister or wife. Marital rape takes place inside the house by one who is known and whom the victim trusts, yet the law negates its gravity. What is ignored in this conceptualization is that marital rape is equivalent to custodial rape where power and authority come into play. Also, it is not a one-time incident; rather, a wife is raped continuously for years, with no escape. No punitive action is taken against a husband for his coercive, non-consensual act, though if he physically abuses his wife, he is penalized theoretically under 498A. For marital rape, what is suggested as a pragmatic approach is 'settlement', 'compromise', or 'adjustment' on the assumption that a 'wife' is the property owned by a man. Such structural contradictions legitimized by law reiterate patriarchal interests and point to a sheer lack of sensitization. What is essential is to inculcate an understanding of the concept of consent, whether in or outside the institution of marriage. Marriage is not a license to rape. The law could be an instrument to spread this message.

Domestic violence entails a denial of sexual and reproductive autonomy

This work shows that newly married brides are denied the power to make choices relating to their own bodies, specifically in terms of pregnancies, use of contraception control methods or when to have babies or the number of births. Because they are dependent economically and socially on their husbands, they are not in a position to negotiate their autonomy or bodily integrity. Threat, humiliation, surveillance, coercion and physical violence are all used to impose strict obedience. For instance, Priya[30] (24) shared:

> I was not ready for marriage. I pleaded but he didn't listen. Instead he said that this is what we are married for. I insisted on using contraceptive, he declined and this is what I got. (Showed the scars of beating) I wanted an abortion, he refused. Then I asked my friend to help. When he came to know, he thrashed me. Since then I became like a machine of producing babies. Now I have three, within five years of marriage, two were still births and one died during her infancy. Doctors told us not to go for more, but this is my destiny.
>
> (2015)

A woman's powerlessness is a critical factor underlying her vulnerability to violence and her exclusion from decisions, including those relating to pregnancy. Women's susceptibility to violence in the social and cultural environment reduces their ability to negotiate sexual relations or to practice safe sex. Other studies also reported that physical violence combined with sexual violence is associated with an increasing risk of HIV infection.[31] Women who face violence are less likely to use contraception and experience an unwanted pregnancy.[32] Yet violence serves as a mechanism to maintain male authority and supremacy. Marriage is construed as an unequal relationship, and men's right over women's bodies is legitimized by social norms leading to abuse such as forced sex, pregnancies, miscarriages, abortions and stillbirths.[33] Inegalitarian gender relations inhibit women from expressing the need for health care, let alone seeking it. When a woman is subjected to violence for transgressing social norms governing sexuality and family roles, violence in that situation is not an individual act; rather, through its punitive and controlling functions, it reinforces prevailing gender norms, thus creating a vicious cycle of subjugation.

Domestic violence involves 'other family members' in the Indian context

In the North Indian belt, violence often involves other family members in the joint or extended family, whether residing under the same roof or separately. This pattern is different from abuse in a dyadic relationship. Around two-thirds of participants shared that their in-laws abused them in various ways, such as emotional abuse (e.g. isolation, social and economic control, domestic servitude, taunting and verbal abuse, among others); economic abuse, which may include deprivation of basic resources; and direct or indirect physical and mental abuse. For instance, Kashi (39) said

> [T]he moment I entered my matrimonial home, my mother-in-law started hurling abuse. She cursed me for not bringing the car. Before marriage they (in-laws) said that they do not want anything. However, on the day of marriage, they demanded a car and 2 lakh cash. She (mother-in-law) took all my jewellery and made me work like hell. She always finds excuses to beat me. My husband never intervened. She never allowed me to talk to anybody. I was given only two *rotis* a day. They made me sleep on the floor in the kitchen without a fan in summers. In winters, I was allowed to use a blanket and spread a mat on floor. I bear everything, thinking that things will change. But there is no end to it.
>
> (2015)

This case reflects that a bride is conferred a subordinate status in her marital home, where she is seen as economically and socially dependent on her in-laws. Her mobility and her access to resources are controlled by in-laws. This exemplifies the operation of the 'classic' patriarchy where violence is inflicted by the mother-in-law as a 'patriarchal bargain',[34] which serves male interests while pitting an older woman against a younger one. Coercion and violence co-exist where an older mother-in-law is entrusted with the task of controlling the new entrant. This authority creates gender hierarchies within families.[35] Also, in such setups, where the male is the bread earner, economic and social security plays a greater role in defining relationships.

Moreover, women's torment and pain cannot be measured with the certainty that the law requires. Satya[36] (33), spoke reluctantly about the way her dignity was violated routinely by her father-in-law.

> He (the father-in-law) often used to enter my room without knocking on the door. That day when no one else was there, he came and held me from behind. . . . I resisted but he used all his might. . . . My husband does not want to listen to anything against his family . . . he slapped me and told me that I should respect his family . . . since then he (the father-in-law) often used to find occasions when no one else is around . . . he knew that nobody believed me . . . I even asked my husband to live separately but that made him more violent. Everyone assumed that I wanted to create a rift in the family.
>
> (2014)

Here, sexual violence is inflicted by the father-in-law, who as a patriarch, exploited the vulnerability and helplessness of a bride, as no one in the family trusted her. Violence therefore needs to be understood in a larger context where power dynamics, domination and submission come into play. Hierarchical role relations are amplified in the context in which realities are construed. The situation is reflective of a male's sense of entitlement to assault a woman's body as property they think 'they own'. In her complaint, Satya has not mentioned this detail, as she found it too embarrassing, though she has mentioned physical violence. She alleged, "Already, they are pointing fingers at my character, if I tell the reality, they will further spoil my reputation". There are similar such cases where women have experienced varied forms of sexual violence but they shied away reporting it. Taboos and stereotypes associated with it prevent women from speaking up. Similarly, Ruby[37] (23) said

> My elder brother-in-law often comes to our floor and when I was alone that day, he tried to molest me. His wife refused to believe me and accused me of being a liar. My husband blamed me of having loose moral character. When his brother came to know, he became more aggressive. He threatened me to keep quiet. I bore it for a while. Then I thought why should I stay in such a relationship where there is no respect. I decided to walk out.
>
> (2013)

The context reflects the vulnerability of a woman within the asymmetrical, hierarchical family arrangement. Power and control in these situations are embodied in everyday practices and legitimize violence by other family members. In this case, Ruby's husband refused to listen to her, as he trusted his brother more than his wife. The sister-in-law, too, accused the victim rather than empathizing with her, probably because in the patriarchal bargain, she may have felt that it is better to favor her husband than trust her sister-in-law, with whom she may share a competitive relationship. Such situations are also substantiated by statistics that point out that sexual abuse within families includes not only rape of wives but also rape of daughters, mothers, sisters, nieces, daughters-in-law, sisters-in-law and similar such 'prohibited' relationships is common.[38]

Domestic violence implies brutality at a broader level

The term domestic violence consists of various situational elements such as relationship, location of offense and type of living arrangement, among others. In the ambit of the PWDVA, violence is visualized in the context of a 'domestic relationship' between victim and offender in a given household. However, 'relationship' also includes ties with the extended family, which may include those connected by blood, marriage or kinship. These relationships do not necessarily require that the victim and offender cohabit. In two-fifths of cases, other family members who are living separately and are not a part of the 'domestic' arrangement inflicted violence either directly or obliquely. Amiya (22) reported

> My married sisters-in-law frequently visit our house. They took away the gifts my parents gave me and treat me like a maid. They told my mother-in-law to keep my plate and glass separate from theirs. I am given just stale rice in morning and leftover food in evening. That day, my food was just left on floor. . . . Am I not a human being?
>
> (2014)

The narrative here reflects that violence has a broader meaning and cannot be categorized literally into the narrow framework of 'domestic household'. In the given cultural context, living in a joint family entails that other family members, who may or may not be sharing the household, 'intervene' in the family affairs. Violence is magnified in this context because of the involvement of 'others' who are not the part of the shared household. For instance, Gauri (24) confides that her husband used to call her friends to 'ravage' her.

> He (husband) used to call his friends at night. When I protested, he beat me black and blue. He put knife to my neck and said he would kill me. Where could I go? Who will trust me? I pleaded and begged, but it is of no use. They used to drink. For him it is free liquor, for me it is terrible

> state of affairs that continued on and on. I resisted in all possible ways and then finally gave it up.
>
> (2013)

The concept of 'violence' thus moved into a situation where violence is inflicted by 'others' who are 'outsiders'. Though violence here occurs with the involvement of her husband within the matrimonial household, the perpetrators were those who were neither the part of household nor are they the part of the joint or extended family. The life-threatening violence stems from deeply rooted patriarchal traditions of men's right to control and own women's bodies. Here, rape becomes an act of dominance. The concept of incest has remained a dark area even today.

Based on their experiences in Western countries, Pence and Paymar[39] have evolved the Duluth Model or Domestic Abuse Intervention Project, which is based on the concept that men use violence within relationships to exercise power and control. This is illustrated by the Power and Control Wheel. It states that men indulge in violence not because of individual pathology; rather, it is because of a socially reinforced sense of entitlement. However, this wheel is based on the dyadic relationship. It does not consider the active role played by the other family members in inflicting violence. While supporting the theory behind the Power and Control Wheel, this work further argues that to apply this model in patriarchal settings, there is a need to examine several factors, such as the unequal relationship between partners and the involvement of one or more perpetrators, which include the husband and other family members who may share the same household or are residing separately and yet could influence the relationship between the abuser and the abused. Further, in the Indian setting, or even in other parts of South Asia, women have no other options outside marriage. Because of a lack of other support mechanisms, the position of women becomes more vulnerable because they are economically and emotionally dependent on the abuser. Pence and Dasgupta[40] have re-examined battering in different situations, including social conditioning of both the victim and the perpetrator; however, in typical North Indian context, certain other factors need to be examined such as a) the belief in a supremacy and hierarchy among men, besides a social approval of battering; b) the role of extended family members and the involvement of more than one perpetrator; c) the dependence of women because of patrilocality and d) absence of support mechanisms outside marriage.

Domestic violence is related to role expectations

In the North Indian context, upon entering her marital family, a young girl is burdened with the responsibility of being a wife as well as a daughter-in-law. If she marries into a joint household, the family plays a crucial role in determining the expectations from the bride. Violence is inflicted if girls neglect their duties or fail to fulfill the responsibilities they are expected to carry out as wives, daughters-in-law or mothers. A woman's powerlessness and her situation of vulnerability is utilized, and she has the least capacity to negotiate or influence her decisions. Violence in such cases is used as an instrument to control and teach her the ways in which she is expected to fulfill her domestic obligations and be a 'good wife'. She is made to feel guilty about 'mistakes' of not performing up to the expectations of her in-laws. The very act of defying the prescribed social role can lead to more violence. I met Anubha (26) in the Karkardooma Court. She said

> I [had] just passed my 12th grade when my husband and father-in-law, (my mother-in-law had died three years back) persuaded my parents to agree to an early marriage and promised that they will allow me to continue my studies. I never learned to cook or do any household chores. But after marriage, they expected me to do everything. Maids were fired and the entire burden fell on me. If I made mistake, they would beat me black and blue. All my calls were monitored. I was not allowed to go out. When I confronted my husband, he thrashed me with *chappals* and belts.
>
> (2014)

Here, a woman's right to make decisions regarding her own life is denied to her. Women are perceived as lesser members within families and are granted limited decision-making authority. Similar results have been reported by a survey conducted by the NCAER, which highlights that only 41 percent of women have a say in marriage. Only one-fifth knew their husbands before marriage, 83 percent observe *purdah* or *ghunghat*, and two-thirds need permission to visit a doctor.[41] The disparate power granted to males is constantly stressed, routinely experienced and daily reproduced in everyday relations. In a male-dominated society, a woman's very existence is created to cater to the rules of the patriarchy, which crafts a social order that upholds feminine virtues such as devotion, subjugation and tolerance, while glorifying oppression through practices and rituals. At times, this form of oppression is glorified using the tools of religion and mythology. In countries as India, Pakistan and Sri Lanka, where arranged marriages are common, the social and familial pressure on a woman to stay in an abusive relationship appears to be one of the factors that increases the risk of suicide.[42]

The brutal dimensions of power operate day in and day out within the marital relationship. In order to punish disobedience and inculcate discipline, family traditions perpetuate everyday violence to intimidate a woman. Threat is commonly used to ensure compliance. Other studies also reported that violence is viewed as a tool to achieve chastisement, where a husband abuses an erring wife as a means to correct her.[43] Batliwala et al.'s[44] study in rural Karnataka similarly observed that violence is triggered by any act of a woman that her husband construes as disrespectful or disobedient or a challenge to his authority.

Domestic violence is an everyday routine, or 'mundane' violence

Domestic violence occurs every day and therefore is often not recognized as a significant or serious issue. It is denied, overlooked or viewed as an individual aberration. It is culturally justified and endorsed as a systemic continuous practice designed to discipline, silence, control and coerce women. For instance, Lavanya (28) pointed out

> He (husband) used to humiliate me over small things and uses terrible language. He said I do not know how to cook. That day he threw the plate at me. He said that I am incapable of satisfying him and said that I am not good looking. He refused to take me to parties saying that I am not worthy to accompany him. I decided to commit suicide one day. Then I thought why should I end my life for such an unworthy person. I took up beauty classes despite his threats. Had I continued staying with him, I would have died.
>
> (2014)

Violence in this case was used to bring down the self-esteem of a woman to the extent that she was on the verge of committing suicide. The continuous portrayal of a woman in a negative light had a major impact on her. Belittling, insulting or humiliating someone may be considered mundane, yet cumulatively, it may have a larger repercussion. Frequently, a perpetrator employs different techniques and tactics to torment a woman. Hema, (32) as coerced into domestic labor and was forced to undergo systematic ongoing humiliation, which eroded her sense of self-worth:

> I was made to work all day and was last to eat, so I have to survive on leftovers. If nothing is left then I have to sleep without food and this happens often. My plate was separate and I was made to sit on the floor while eating and not at the dining table. One day I was feeling uncontrollably hungry so I picked up a banana that was on the table. That day my mother-in-law started beating me and cursed my parents, saying that they have not given enough dowry so I am not entitled to enjoy luxuries of life at the expenses of my husband's earnings.
>
> (2015)

Denying Hema the right to life with dignity on a daily basis was an intentional act to rob her of her self-worth, to exclude her and to otherwise deny her every moment of her existence. Women recounted a myriad of ways they have been degraded, such as not given proper sufficient food, denial of basic daily requirements, not allowed to talk, not allowed to interact with friends or natal families, prohibiting them from using certain items in the house, not allowed to go to social functions and putting restrictions on what they should wear, among many other such degrading acts where they are made to feel inferior. Women spoke of humiliation and distress where the husband and in-laws, in order to assert superiority, utilize every opportunity to demean and exploit their worth.

Domestic violence involves a denial of autonomy and dignity

Violence within homes involves denial of autonomy to women. In many situations, either a woman is not permitted to go out of the house to earn a living, or if she does, her earnings are forcefully taken away. She has no control over her earnings. Violence is frequently used to force her to part with her income, and in the absence of available employment opportunities, skills or support services, a woman may find escaping violence difficult. Controlling mobility and isolating her have an adverse impact on her. Women's wishes, needs and desires have no place in such a biased system.

Everyday abusive practices by husbands and in-laws are both intentional and strategic, where they deploy tactics to control women to exert control over the manner in which she dresses, restrict her autonomy or belittle her parents. Half of the respondents reported that they have been prevented from have contact with their natal families or friends. Controlling a woman's mobility, isolating and alienating her and denying her autonomy are tactics used to mentally and emotionally harass a woman. Two-thirds of participants claimed that their daily lives were being monitored by their husbands. Many reported that their husbands follow them at the workplace, check their purses, almirahs, monitor call logs and messages on their phones, track emails and micromanage their lives. Sapna[45] (31) shared

> He (husband) checks my mobile, mails, purse and almirah almost every day. He never allows me to go out alone. Once I went to see my mother who was unwell, he insulted my parents. He used to scream and shout and would strangle me. I was going mad.
>
> (2013)

The culture of male domination does not allow women to participate in decision making within families. The majority of participants stated that if they have to visit their parents' house or elsewhere, they have to obtain permission from their husbands or in-laws. Employment or education of women and her say is decision making is not correlated. Other studies have reported that women who experience violence are susceptible to a range of mental illnesses, including low self-esteem, anxiety, depression, OCD and PTSD.[46] This continuous pervasive violence clouds their capacity to think clearly and rationally. The cumulative effect of experience becomes more traumatic. Many shared that continuous everyday violence for prolonged periods makes them 'mad' and 'drives them crazy'. However, the law sees violence as an isolated episode, overlooking the fact that violence involves tactics where a woman may feel helpless, and her vulnerability escalates because she is no position to escape.

The law reiterates objectivity and neutrality while excluding the subjective experiences women face in their daily lives. Within the courtroom, violence is defined technically in legal terms rather than considering women's narratives and subjectivities of what constitutes violence. Rashmi, a postgraduate married four years back to Rakesh, explained

> [The] marriage was arranged through a website. He pretended that he was a gold medalist. Later, I found that it was lie. In his home everyone uses abusive language. I was shocked. They demanded money. I refused. He slapped me and said that he wanted to start his own venture. But already my parents have given enough. It was a lavish wedding in a farm house, so much being spent on food, clothes, gifts, honeymoon package. Can I ask more? I want to work. He refused. I insisted. When I went out, he alleged that I was having an affair with my boss. When my son was born, he said that the child was not his. He made me undergo DNA test. I couldn't take more.
>
> (2014)

In the DIR, this case is codified as mental abuse, verbal abuse, physical violence and economic abuse. Other mundane everyday torture was ignored. The law does not consider the nuances of women's agony. Women are abused and tortured in everyday lives routinely, yet the law ignores this, as these are never recorded or documented.

As a researcher, the more I delve deeper, I realize that the system is oppressive. For instance, one of the psychologists in a private hospital shared that

> many of the men have been approaching me where they want a written prescription that their wives suffer from mental ailments even when everything is normal. And they are willing to pay a huge amount of money to do that. It is then I realized that most of them when want to get rid of their wives, they legally declare them as mentally ill to seek divorce on this ground. I was shocked.[47]

For men and their families, it is easier to harass wives to the point of extreme mental stress, and on this basis, they seek prescriptions from specialists to present these in court as evidence that their wives are mentally ill. Perhaps further research on this issue may help to get an in-depth perspective.

Domestic violence relates to a preference for sons

Gender relations are based upon the belief of male supremacy, and thus men are entitled with privileges in the public and private sphere. Within families, the birth of a son is desired, as they are viewed as assets and future providers of economic security. A son ensures continuance of the patrilineage and ascertains that death rituals will be performed by the man, who may take the role of patriarch. It is through the birth of a son that a woman acquires a higher status in a family. Consequently, girls are devalued and discriminated, though simultaneously they have also been treated as repositories of honor and prestige of the families. I met Devi (24) in Patiala House court complex. She recollected

> My in-laws used to take me to astrologers who gave medicines or asked to perform certain rituals as observing fast etc. and if I failed to follow, they would thrash me. When I got pregnant my mother-in-law threatened me that if it was a girl, she would kill her. When my daughter was born, she humiliated and ridiculed me. She forced me to get rid of her but I pleaded. After one year, another daughter was born and since then my life became a hell. They started torturing my daughters too. For them, daughters are a burden.
>
> (2014)

Female children are less desirable and are viewed as economic and social liabilities. Discrimination towards girls is reflected in the religious ceremonies, rituals and customary practices in day-to-day life. I met Reena, (37) a mother of three daughters, in the Rohini court complex. She complained that her in-laws cursed her for giving birth to daughters and forced her to undergo several abortions. Female feticide and infanticide are justified while upholding ideals of a preference for sons. Two informants claimed that they were being tortured because they could not bear children. Laws and policies have failed to make an impact where biases are so deeply entrenched.

Domestic violence relates to skin color or other physical attributes

Historically, skin color has been used as a parameter to accord differential treatment to individuals, both intentionally and inadvertently. And even today, fair skin is considered superior, while those with the darker hues are placed at the lower rung of the social hierarchy. Natasha (29) found her five-year-old marriage in shambles when I met her because of her dark skin color that is not befitting the prevalent norms of beauty. She said

> It was an arranged marriage and we are both from Alwar. Our families know each other. He didn't want to make then unhappy and therefore agreed to marry. He had an obsession with fair skin and used to beat me. His fixation for white skin has spoiled my life. I tried various remedies but nothing worked.

She underwent several phases of counseling. During those sessions, her husband said that "she is not 'civilized' and [does] not know how to behave". This infuriated Natasha. She has appeared for several job interviews; however, because of the 'gap' in her resume, she has been denied a suitable position. Natasha is not the only one who is facing the adverse effect of deep-rooted prejudices; other women too are undergoing a similar ordeal.

Arti (25) got married one and a half year ago. It was an arranged marriage. Her mother-in-law constantly taunted her for her dark color and tortured her to get 1 lakh cash and a bike. The violence continued for several months. She was not allowed to meet her parents. Her husband humiliated her, saying that she "is an evil as she has brought bad luck". Somehow, Arti got a job in a private school at a salary of Rs 12,000/ per month. Her husband used to take away her salary, yet she was relieved that at least she could go out of the violent situation for a while. A few months back, when her brother's marriage was arranged, her husband again raised the demand for cash and a bike. Since then, furious violence started. Several interventions were made by her parents and community members. Then, one day he poured kerosene on Arti and lit fire. With the intervention of neighbors, she was taken to the hospital. She consulted a lawyer, who suggested that she file a criminal case, but her parents refused to do so. Another lawyer suggested she file application under the PWDVA. In court, her husband denied that he attempted to burn her and instead blamed her for being a lazy and characterless woman.

In these situations, morphological differences are ascribed social meanings, where fairness has been culturally constructed to create a false binary. An obsession for lighter skin tone instills prejudices and invokes preferential treatment for those who can fit in the dominant social norms. Skin color as a social construct is a classic example of the normalization and legitimization of structural oppression and involves an array of cultural, institutional and interpersonal dynamics that routinely add to the disadvantages of women while producing persistent, cumulative adverse outcomes. More specifically, this exclusive discrimination widens the hierarchy in a multi-layered society while creating sharp inequalities and places women in disadvantageous situations where they are made to feel incomplete, deficient, marginalized and outcast because of their physical attributes.[48] For an individual, these biases lead to alienation and exclusion. This form of violence remains invisible because it is difficult to articulate it in a legal language, as the situation is more experiential.

Walker called this type of discrimination colorism,[49] as it is characterized by the supremacy of a light skin tone. Both Natasha's and Arti's cases highlight the manner in which the social context operates where women are treated as objects. By combining cultural and traditional values with modernity, a woman's body is commodified to make her a desirable product. The conventional norms shaped by neoliberalism fuel the fantasy of everyday expectations of conjugality and determine the norms of the ideal image of women as wives. And when women fail to fit in this image, they face violence.[50] Natasha's life is an illustration of the powerlessness as well as lack of agency of a woman. Similarly, Arti has been treated violently; however, she chose to resist it. These cases highlight the situation of marginalization, as well as of reclamation, and indicate that women are not ready to bear torture silently. Equipped with a sense of independence, some are negotiating the violence. The views surrounding the weakening of the power relationship within marriage are mirrored through the available statistics too.[51]

Domestic violence involves desertion

Suman (28) was waiting outside the courtroom when I met her. Her lawyer filed an application for maintenance one year ago. However, her husband could not be traced, and she is getting 'dates'. The court has asked her to provide his correct address, but she is unaware of his whereabouts.

> It was a love marriage. I fought with my parents. But later he became jealous and suspicious. He wanted me to accompany him to Manila but I had a job here. We tried to stay in different cities for ten months. Then, for the sake of my child, I left my job to shift along with him. He said he would arrange my travel. But I keep on waiting. But then, I found that he had married someone else there. I was left alone, isolated from my natal family, with no job and none to help. My heart shattered into million pieces, and all for this wretched thing called love.
>
> (2015)

Suman is dejected and frustrated. There has been no physical violence, but according to her, she has been feeling lonely, mentally devastated and emotionally tortured. Her husband has isolated her from her natal family and deprived her of her livelihood. The law could not provide solution to console her. Later, I met several women in similar situations who have been 'abandoned', 'left', 'unilaterally separated', 'deserted wives' with children, waiting for their husbands endlessly, but to no avail. Many have paid huge dowries and have stayed at the matrimonial house for a few days and later were thrown out. They have faced physical and sexual violence too besides dealing with various constraints. However, the state has made no provisions for such women.[52] It was when several NRI women filed a petition[53] before the Supreme Court that the state introduced the bill regarding the same.[54] However, much is required to be done.

Varied forms of economic abuse

Economic abuse is a wide and varied form of violence which includes preventing a woman from taking up a job, forcing her to leave an existing job, taking away her salary, pressuring her to bring money or valuables from her parents and denying her money or resources, among others. It also includes not allowing women to work or study, taking or controlling their earnings, raising suspicion about her character and employment sabotage, among a range of other forms of abuse.

Of those employed at the time of marriage, one-third claimed that they have had to leave their jobs because of violence where their marital families prevented them from working outside the home. Rest shared that their incomes have been either controlled by their husbands or they were compelled to spend it to pay for the daily needs of the entire family, so little is left. The majority complained that questions were raised about their character and integrity by their husbands and in-laws. One-fourth stated that after childbirth they had to leave their jobs to take care of their children.

All participants who reported being economically independent before marriage subsequently had to leave their job once they got married and claimed that they lost value in the job market during the time they were taking care of the family and the household. Men during the same period consolidated their gains in terms of wealth and status, whereas none of the women could get a similar position or salary once they searched for a job after walking out of the abusive relationship. This invisible contribution made by women to a household in terms of sacrificing their career for the sake of the family is not recognized by policymakers. At the time of separation or divorce or while determining maintenance, the courts do not consider this gendered nature of work or invisible loss of income when a woman attempt to re-enter the job market. Manju, (38) who works as an analyst, recalled

> We both worked in the same company. He was one-year senior to me. He got a promotion and I had to leave job after my kid was born two years later. Meanwhile, he found someone else. After huge fights for months, I walked out. I applied for jobs but could not get the salary as I used to get earlier. While taking care of the kid, I could not keep myself updated on the latest technology while he enjoyed trips to foreign countries for training.
>
> (2013)

Women's voices are ignored by the law. The law enforces doubt in women and assigns low credibility to their testimonies, which Fricker[55] has called testimonial injustice. Further, there is a gap in the manner in which the law interprets women's situation and the way women testify. Women are at a disadvantage in the domain of law. Important information conveyed by women is not considered in the legal records.

Domestic violence entails controlling women's earnings

In the neoliberal economy, with the increasing use of technology and rising aspiration levels, deeply entrenched prejudices that disallow women to participate in decision making within the family have not changed, even though they may be participating actively at their workplace. Batterers control all aspects of victims' finances to prevent them from accessing resources, working or maintaining control of their earnings, achieving self-sufficiency and gaining financial independence while depriving a woman of financial resources. This affects her ability to walk out of a violent relationship. For instance, Kamla, (27) working as a manager in an MNC, explained

> they (husband and in-laws) were more concerned about my salary. I was not allowed to go shopping on my own. He took away my credit cards and bank details and changed passwords. Even for daily travel or everyday expenses, I have to beg before him. He makes an issue out of everything . . . as why I got delayed coming home . . . or I must be seeing someone.
>
> (2014)

The situation indicates the manner in which economic violence is perpetrated on a woman who is financially self-sufficient. Also, women are considered an 'outsider' in the matrimonial home, where finances are controlled by men while women are left with no resources. In order to access daily toiletries, clothes or food for children, women are compelled to plead, or they have to depend on their natal families. "For getting [the] baby's instant food, I have to ask my parents as he took all [the] money and wouldn't [give] me a single penny even when I begged", said Rekha (31) hailing from Dwarka. However, in legal records these voices remain unheard.

Domestic violence involves deprivation

Violence in homes occurs in subdued forms and includes control or depriving a woman of her mobility, putting restrictions on her socialization, confinement, abandonment, denial of resources and disapproval of women's interests and inclinations, thus denying her basic human freedoms. Astha[56] (38) recollected:

> I was getting suffocated. But I do not want to take help from parents or relatives. When I insisted on pursuing a job, he prevented me, and when I somehow joined a company, he created a scene there. Now, without any money where should I take my child? I thought of committing suicide, but when I look at my child, I thought, why should we both die for such a man. I realized that he doesn't deserve such worth.
>
> (2015)

The perpetrator here has ensured that the woman is isolated and left with no resources to fight back. Even otherwise, the women in violent relationships do not elicit sympathy from those who implement the law. These people view women as culprits and frequently, the nature of enquiry extends to their 'provoking' behavior. Suggestions are rendered as to the manner in which a woman may salvage her relationship rather than asking a man to amend his violent behavior.

Dowry extortion persists despite legal prohibitions

"Woman starved to death over dowry", reported a news item in March 2019,[57] where 27-year-old Tushara, who got married in 2013 and has two kids, was reduced to a bag of bones with hardly any flesh left, merely weighing 20 kg and died because of prolonged starvation enforced by her husband and mother-in-law. Those who enforce policy and law are living in denial, while dowry system is deeply embedded and is brutally taking the lives of women every day. Despite the fact that dowry is prohibited under the Dowry Prohibition Act 1961 and dowry violence has been criminalized under Section 304B, IPC, dowry demand and abuse are legitimized by socio-cultural norms rooted in the ancient texts and through discriminatory practices such as *kanyadaan* that creates a hierarchical relationship between two families where, strangely, the giver of the daughter and dowry is put on a lower pedestal.

Also, in her natal home, a woman is viewed as an economic liability and dowry as a cultural practice reinforce this belief. Currently, dowry has become a compulsory coercive universal practice that has spread its tentacles across the boundaries of class, caste and religion.[58] The continuance of conjugality is assumingly determined by the material wealth the bride is accompanied with, though in actuality, it devalues the status of a woman.[59] All participants in the present study, except two, reported that a dowry was given at the time of marriage and even later demands were made by their marital families. Seemingly, dowry enables a woman to secure a place in her husband's home.

The commodification of marriage has led to a rise in incidences of coercion, extortion and violence. In fact, many families look for brides who earn handsomely, yet they also demand a dowry and yearn that the bride should be 'homely' too.[60] Satisfying lust to acquire wealth quickly to upgrade economic status by receiving large transfers through dowry is an easy available option, and, if this does not happen, men subject their wives to violence. Disha (32) explained,

> When I got married, I was earning well. His family demanded a dowry. I protested. But my parents insisted that it was a common practice. They gave everything, including a flat, huge feast, yet he asked me to give my salary to his parents. I refused. He became adamant and violence started since then. They want me to work like a maid at home and work outside to earn and give them money. I wanted to leave, but everybody told me

> to be patient. He then left his job and demanded money to start his own business . . . and these demands keep on increasing day by day.
>
> (2014)

The amount of dowry and the manner of wedding celebrations are determined by the patriarchs from the two families at the time of marriage. Girls having little role in the decision making, though elder women in families do play either an invisible or visible role in deciding on gifts, gold or wedding expenses.

Demands expand to celebrate lavish weddings

The majority of informants reported coercive demands being made by the groom and his family for lavish wedding arrangements. A large part of the expenses allocated for marriage are on celebrations, including giving gifts and cash to relatives, friends and others. Perhaps such a celebration is seen as an indicator of social status.[61] One-third of informants conveyed that such specific coercive demands were made just a day or two days prior to the wedding. Arushi (34), an eye specialist, reported

> It is a form of an extortion. They (husband and in-laws) cunningly made demands when everything was finalized, invitations have gone and we have paid advance to caterers, decorators, etc. Terminating the marriage at that point would have cost us a fortune, stigmatized us and would have destroyed our family.
>
> (2015)

Similarly, Nandini (26), residing in South Delhi, shared that

> Even the expensive farm house wedding could not make them (husband and in-laws) happy. They keep on taunting me that other families were offering destination parties in foreign locations, huge list of VIP guests and honeymoon abroad . . . just for the sake of pretension, they (in-laws) created a mess in my life. And he (the husband) did not take a stand, though we were in a relationship for three and a half year. My parents have invested their entire savings but their greed is never ending. For them it is like child's play, they don't take it seriously.

In fact, in many cases this aspect of spending a huge amount of money on celebrations has been highlighted, which is different from the dowry. Huge expenditures are incurred in organizing the feast and arranging gifts during the marriage, which in no way could aid the bride or constitute her *streedhan*. Marriage in the neoliberal globalized economy has become an indecent display of the culture of conspicuous consumption.[62] Gender discrimination has taken a new turn as women are being treated as a commodity in a marriage market.

Domestic violence involves dowry coercion and abuse

Dowry violence includes coercive demands made at the time of marriage and after marriage when the husband and in-laws systematically abuse brides to extort and extract wealth transfers. Dowry harassment has been found in two-thirds of cases. Violence or the threat of violence is used as a means to acquire resources from the bride's family. Cash is the common demand, and it ranged from 50,000 to 75 lakhs rupees. In two cases, demands were made for more than one crore rupees. A car was demanded in several cases, besides flats, furniture, jewelry and other expensive items. One in three reported that their natal families took out loans to arrange for the dowry and marriage expenses. A large number of complainants said that dowry harassment began within a few days after they arrived in their matrimonial homes. Many complained of being assaulted during the initial days of the marriage, and coercive demands continued until they stayed in their marital homes, where the husband and in-laws demanded a dowry during festivals or the birth of children. Dissatisfaction with the dowry received is directly related to the gravity of abuse. For example, Aruna (29), a teacher in a private school, got married to Mukesh, who went abroad, leaving her behind with his parents within 33 days of marriage. She said

> Since he left, his parents tortured me and forced me to leave the house. They took all my jewellery. Initially, he said he will call me but now he is not picking his phone. Today, his family is torturing me, tomorrow he will remarry and will harass somebody else for money. It is an extortion racket. They demand a dowry and after enjoying all the lavish food, expensive gifts, they then throw the girls out thinking that on remarriage, they will get more money, more dowry. For them marriage is like a game. Such people should get jailed.
>
> (2015)

Coercive demands for dowry have also been confirmed by several other studies. A study of 1,330 allegations made in the FIRs between January and June 2017 reveals the manner in which the 'dowry bazaar' is working openly.[63] Persistence in the dowry system has led to a situation where brides have been harassed to the extent that they have committed suicide.[64]

Streedhan: do women own or control assets?

Though dowry and *streedhan* are not related yet, in common parlance, it has been adduced that valuable gifts given to the bride at the time of her marriage are returned in cases of separation or divorce as *streedhan*. However, almost all informants shared that much of the amount earmarked for the marriage had been spent on organizing a lavish celebration and a large amount of money has been spent on giving cash, gold and gifts to the husband and his relatives. Further, *streedhan* has not been returned in 88 percent of cases. Two-fifths of informants claimed that old, useless items are returned in the name of *streedhan*. Jewelry, ornaments and expensive gifts or clothes were already taken on one pretext or another by the husband or in-laws, or had been removed from the marital house when women went to claim their *streedhan*. Half of the participants reported that the police did not help to recover *streedhan*. In case of Muslim women, *meher* has been paid partly only in two cases—the money given has been spent either in taking care of children or oneself. Therefore, most of the women have been dispossessed of the assets on their separation or divorce.

No house in my name: an unresolved quandary for women

The UN Report[65] (2010) states,

> Although women's literacy rates are rising, they still make up nearly two-thirds of the world's illiterate and continue to be two-thirds of world's poor, perform two-thirds of world's work, and produce 50 percent of the food, while earning only ten percent of the income and owning one percent of the property.

Thus, gender biases and inequalities are inherent and are persistent the world over while negating the paradigm of equality and social justice as promised within the legal codes or the human rights instruments.

In India, property is acquired primarily through inheritance, adjudication by the state or purchase. However, all these institutions are discriminatory and deprive women of resources to acquire property. Though amendments made in the Hindu Succession Act in 2005 grant equal rights to daughters as coparceners in the HUF, yet women as wives still remain deprived of their rights to marital property despite their visible or invisible contribution and paid or unpaid work in the matrimonial household. In situations of violence, women are deprived of their right to shelter, and at the time of separation or divorce, they are entitled only to meager alimony as per the laws. This nonrecognition of entitlements enhances women's vulnerability and threatens their existence.

For instance, Bobby (46) filed an application under the PWDVA against her brother. The property belonged to her parents, but after their death, her brother forced his two sisters to move out of the house. She confided that her brother is using various tactics to harass them. The question of women's property rights is interlinked with violence and reflects that though the law on paper has empowered women, the reality is quite different. With no assets or ownership, women are facing varied problems and the law offers little redress. The present study shows that the vested interests of men as brothers have also prevented a few women from leaving a violent marital relationship because often the brothers state that once their married sisters come back, they may demand their share in the property.

Most of the married participants shared that they began facing harassment as soon as they entered into the marital relationship, yet they filed complaints once they were thrown out of the house and are compelled to face the situation of destitution, or they left the marital home fearing imminent danger to their life. Two-fifths of women were not living in a shared household at the time they were interviewed. One-third were living with their parents, and one-sixth have been sharing accommodations with siblings, friends or relatives. Those living in shared households confided that they were pressured to vacate the house, as their in-laws had filed an injunction suit against them.

In one-third of cases women reported that they do not know who owns the marital house. Others stated that the marital house is in the name of the parents-in-law. Around two-fifths of informants stated that once the trouble started, the husbands cleverly gave up their assets in favor of their parents or siblings. Discussions with lawyers and activists show similar results. The provision relating to the 'right to reside in a shared household' is confused with the right to share in property, and thus the accused husbands give up their inheritance right in favor of other family members while depriving women access to it. Rani (32), residing in a joint family post-marriage, recalled

> [O]nce the complaint had been filed at the Crime Against Women Cell, my parents-in-law moved out of the house. They declared that they (parents-in-law) had no relationship with their son or myself. Then after two months my mother-in-law filed a suit against us asking us to vacate the house declaring that the house is in her name. I consulted a lawyer who told me not to do so. Even earlier, my husband used tactics as making my mother-in-law a nominee in all his bank and other accounts.

Many informants such as Rani shared similar stories of a denial of their right to reside in the shared household, where different tactics were deployed by the marital family to oust women from the matrimonial house. Civil injunctions are being filed by parents-in-law in several cases. Thus, the law is manipulated in different ways to deny women their rightful claims.

In one-third of cases, the marital home was a rented accommodation, and women reported that their husbands and in-laws moved somewhere else, leaving them with no other option but to move out of the house because they had no money to pay rent. Sangita (40), a homemaker, alleged that for 13 years she stayed with her in-laws, moving from one rented place to another, but then she came to know that her husband had a relationship with another woman. He moved out of the rented accommodation on the pretext of finding job and relocating in Allahabad. Later, within two months, her -in-laws also went to Kanpur to their native place. She was left alone with her 11-year-old daughter. Initially, her husband paid rent for two months, but later he stopped. She filed a case for right to residence under the PWDVA; however, despite the court's orders, her husband is not paying her money. Sunanda (54), reported, "I made that home with my money and my labour and he conveniently asked me to leave that house". The law does not take into account the fact that marital violence is not a simple case of ego tussles or separation; rather, it relates to women's survival and shelter.

The children are the worst sufferers

Research studies conducted the world over show that domestic violence has a severe impact on children. Amidst violence, children are deprived of love, care and the affection of their parents. Children in violent situations may become aggressive, withdrawn, maladaptive and may become intimidated.[66] Also, children who witness violence may be abused in the process.[67] They may show signs of trauma and may get angry, anxious and fearful. They may show signs of grief as well as PTSD.[68] Children blame themselves for violence.[69] It impedes their ability to develop a trusting relationship and secure bonds with the caregiver.[70] A child may develop low self-esteem, and this may affect her cognitive and emotional development and may lead to other conduct disorders.

Many women reported that children are victimized and tortured by the perpetrator, who used them as an emotional tool to oppress women. The aim of harming children is to dominate mothers, thus perpetrating the continuum of coercive control. In the majority of cases, women reported that their children show signs of anxiety, fear and stress and often fall behind in their studies when they witnessed violence. Many women explained that during an episode of violence, when their husbands beat them up, children tremble with fear or hide in a corner. Even simple actions such as screaming and shouting can affect children, as these induce fear and threat. Half of the informants reported children being harmed more than once because of violence. Farzana (36) testified that her child was badly injured.

> It was a cold winter night. He (the husband) came back drunk and kicked the four-year-old who had a high fever, then furiously beat me as I refused to serve food at midnight. The child started bleeding profusely. He became unconscious. I tied dupatta on his bleeding skull and ran out to my sister's place. Her family took the child to the hospital. He wouldn't have been alive had those people not helped. My elder daughter is afraid of him . . . I want to take my children away, but where will I go? I am not educated.
>
> (2014)

In a marital relationship, children suffer the most not only in terms of physical health but also in terms of emotional and mental health. Sulbha (33) recounted, "My two daughters became so scared seeing ever day beating that they stopped going out to play or to school. I have to forcefully take them out otherwise they would cry in one corner". When granting custody orders or visitation rights, the courts ignore these realities. The common perception is that both parents are required to protect the 'best interests of the child'. What is ignored in this conceptualization is that a violent situation cannot promote the best interests of the child. A child witnessing horror may develop fear, trauma and emotional scars. Family violence may produce a long-term intergenerational cycle of abuse.[71] A battered mother has to prioritize her own safety, as well as the security of her children, because often batterers use children to coercively control the mothers.[72]

For women, survival with dignity is a major issue

For women who faced violence in the homes and resisted it, the major challenge they face is survival with dignity. Violence has an adverse impact on their physical, mental and economic being. Aparna (44), who has a PhD in biology with two kids, explains,

> Though my parents are supportive, yet my whole life is destroyed. My major concern is how will I survive. Continuous violence has incapacitated my thinking ability. With so much of gap in my career, I lag behind and compelled to take up this low paying job so that I could earn bread and butter for my kids. But that is frustrating.
>
> (2014)

Thus, the talent of women is in jeopardy, and the contribution that they could have made to their development as citizens cannot be made. Similarly, Mala (32) recalled,

> I was working as a Manager with an IT Company. He came to my office and talked all negative against me with my manager and colleagues. He sent them mails and as a repercussion, my boss asked me to leave the office. I was about to get promotion but now I have to accept a job in a lower position with a supply company.
>
> (2013)

Employment sabotage by her husband in this situation has not allowed Mala to continue with her high-paying job with a big company. Kiran (38), the mother of three children and a home maker, reported

> I am not educated. My parents are taking care of my kids. But for how long they will do that. My father is not keeping well. My brother got married and my sister-in-law wish that I should not stay in their house. I don't know how we will survive. It is like moving from one hell to another. Am I not entitled to lead a life with dignity?
>
> (2015)

Other women in jobs recounted that their careers were sabotaged, and for those who do not have jobs, ambiguity regarding survival takes a different form. Anju (32) pointed out

> I am not educated enough. I do not know what to do. My two children are not keeping well. Where should I live them if I go out to work? My sister has helped me but I cannot ask her for more.
>
> (2014)

Thus, questions relating to survival and uncertainty regarding the present and the future emerged as a major issue. According to the majority of women, the support network which is aiding them currently may not continue in the long run. However, the state has not provided any solutions for women in distress.

Reclaiming lives: these women are not helpless victims; they are the agents of change

Maya Angelou noted, "Each time a woman stands up for herself, without knowing it possibly, without claiming it, she stands up for all women".[73] When I met the complainants, I realized that when they took a stand against violence in matrimony, they made a dent on a rigid and rabid patriarchy. They refused to accept what is presented as 'normal' and engaged with the authority in a given situation. What they demanded is not pity or sympathy, but their right to lead a violence-free dignified life. The general perception is that those who face domestic abuse are either 'helpless victims' (*bechari*) or are shrewd 'disgruntled women' who file cases as a personal vendetta. However, in this work, none of the informants could fit into these categories. When women confronted private violence in the public domain, they questioned the conventional stereotypes. This resistance by women challenged the image of 'always and already' victims that has been painted in the general discourse.[74] Gordon opposed the paradigm of the 'woman as a victim'[75] and stated that it is false to assume that women are powerless. In perilous life situations, with no resources and with little support, the women I met exhibited agency and portrayed extraordinary courage to boldly defy traditional norms. As agents of change, they negotiated the patriarchal strictures and even in the most restricted environment made efforts to resist violence. Though for many, the struggle was difficult and long, yet they persisted.

Omvedt[76] argued that the struggle of women is located in the cultural traditions. She aptly used the term "*virangana*", or heroic, courageous women, portrayed in the local folklores and cultural material as the source of bravery, valor, strength and ingenuity. Historically, women have played a significant role in nationalist struggles, participated in the freedom movement and have contributed in the making of the constitution.[77] In the postcolonial period too, women actively participated in the *Chipko*, *Telangana* and *Tebhaga* movements; the anti–price-rise movement;[78] and the *Narmada Bachao Andolan*, protest by *Naga* mothers, among others, where they collectively addressed a plethora of issues ranging from work, violence, wages, sati, dowry, rape, health, alcohol and others. Mass movements of rural poor women have used several mechanisms to challenge the oppression.

Even individually women have shown defiance, as in the cases of Bhanwari Devi,[79] Irom Sharmila and other known[80] or unknown women. Women are courageously fighting against an oppressive culture in courtrooms and may gain a small triumph because of their persistence.[81] Similarly, in the present research work, I met women who are challenging the patriarchy, defying the norms, resisting the cultural boundaries, asserting their claims and striving for justice with their sheer resilience while challenging the status quo. Their journey to justice is a quest for survival with dignity. Struggling against multiple discrimination at various levels is challenging and requires huge effort and courage. With little knowledge about the law, scant resources and a lack of material or economic support, women are challenging the patriarchy in their own way, despite the fact that they have been conditioned to accept and believe that marriage is a compulsion, whether violent or not, or that marriage is an undisputed institution and any existence of women apart from marriage is stigmatized. It is not that the courtrooms are sympathetic to women's concerns; rather, it is the grit of women who persist and are challenging the hegemonic constructions of gender identities in the courts which are male bastions.

Summary

The analysis of the experience of complainants shows that domestic violence is a multi-dimensional issue that is having an adverse impact in terms of health and cost. Also, women are at an unfairly hermeneutical disadvantage situation in a male governed socio-legal system because their interpretive framework is different from that of those who implement the law. Besides, their lived experience is rendered intelligible to others, and possibly even to oneself, as they are prevented from making sense of their own violent experiences because of the shame and stigma associated with it. Therefore, it is suggested that the law should be interpreted while considering women's situations and their quest for dignified survival. Also, in order to challenge the differential power equation that exists in the marital relationship, many aspects need to be considered, such as influencing the public consciousness through education and sensitization, questioning the cult of masculinity and challenging the entrenched patriarchy.

Notes

1 As quoted by Nussbaum Martha (2000) Women's Capabilities and Social justice, *Journal of Human Development*, 1 (2) 219–47

2 Foucault M (2007) *Security, Territory, Population: Lectures at the Collège de France 1977–1978*, edited by M Senellart and translated by G Burchell, Palgrave Macmillan, Basingstoke p. 88
3 Koenig MA, Stephenson R, Ahmed S et al. (2006) Individual and Contextual Determinants of Domestic Violence in North India, *American Journal of Public Health*, 96 (1) 132–38
4 Sharma K (2013) Wife Beating Epidemic Afflicts South Delhi, Cases Gone Up by 10 Times Over Last Year, *India Today*, June 25
5 Ambedkar BR (1916) *Caste in India: Their Mechanism, Genesis and Development*, Paper Presented at an Anthropology Seminar at Columbia University 9th May, www.columbia.edu/itc/mealac/pritchett/00ambedkar/txt_ambedkar_castes.html accessed on 01.11.18
6 Toledo M (2009) First Comes Marriage Then Comes Love, *ABC News*, January 30, https://abcnews.go.com/2020/story?id=6762309&page=1
7 Datta D (2008) Netrimony: The New Dating Game, *India Today*, March 24, https://www.indiatoday.in/magazine/cover-story/story/20080324-netrimony-the-new-mating-game-735716-2008-03-13
8 All names and places are changed to protect identities and maintain confidentiality.
9 McIntyre S, Boyle C, Lakeman LF et al. (2000) Tracking and Resisting Backlash Against Equality Gains in Sexual Offence Law, *Canadian Woman Studies*, 20 (3) 72–83
10 Agnes F (1988) *My Story . . . Our Story of Rebuilding Broken Lives*, Forum for Oppression Against Women, Bombay
11 Andersen SM, Glassman NS and Gold DA (1998) Mental Representation of Self, Significant Others and Non-significant Others: Structures and Processing of Private and Public Aspects, *Journal of Personality and Social Psychology*, 75, 845–61
12 Palkar V (2013) Failing Gender Justice in Anti-Dowry Law, *South Asia Research*, 23 (2) 181–200, 041121
13 Lawyers Collective (2013) Staying Alive: Evaluating Court Orders, Sixth Monitoring and Evaluation Report on the Protection of Women Against Domestic Violence Act, New Delhi
14 MASUM (2010) *Chakrabedh*: Coils of Violence and Redressal Solution (In Hindi) Pune. During my discussion with the director of MASUM, Mr. Ramesh Awasthi, in a meeting held in 2019, the factor which came to light is not only the natal family's refusal to accept women back but also the violence continues at both natal and marital homes in rural as well as urban areas.
15 Heise LL, Raikes A, Watts CH et al. (1994) Violence Against Women: A Neglected Public Health Issue in Less Developed Countries, *Social Science Medicine*, 30 (3) 1165–79
16 Nambi S (2005) Marriage, Mental Health and the Indian Legislation: Presidential Address, *Indian Journal of Psychiatry*, 47 (3) 3–14
17 World Health Organization (2005) *Multi-Country Study on Women's Health and Domestic Violence Against Women: Initial Results on Prevalence*, Health Outcomes and Women's Responses, Geneva
18 *The Hindu* (2007) Delhi Wives Wait for 4 Years Before Reporting Abuse: A Study, August 15 p. 8
19 Kelkar G (1992) Stopping the Violence Against Women: Fifteen Years of Activism in India, In *Freedom from Violence: Women's Strategies from Around the World*, edited by M Schuler, OEF International, Washington, DC pp. 75–99
20 Nigam Shalu (2002) Violence Against Women: Silent Enemy in the Home, *Social Welfare*, 49 (4) 12–16

21 Johnson MP (1998) *A Typology of Domestic Violence: Intimate Terrorism, Violent Resistance and Situational Couple Violence*, Northeastern University Press, Lebanon, NH p. 6
22 Brownmiller Susan (1975) *Against Our Will: Men, Women and Rape*, The Ballantine Publishing Group, New York pp. 14–15
23 Nigam S (2019) A Year After Brutal Gang-Rape and Murder in Kathua: Apathetic State Agenda, Regressive Policies and Escalating Violence Continued, *Countercurrents*, February 4
24 Nigam S (2017) From Mathura to Farooqui Rape Case: The Regressive Patriarchy Found Its Way Back, *Countercurrents*, October 9
25 Koenig MA, Stephenson R, Ahmed R et al. (2006) Individual and Contextual Determinants of Domestic Violence in North India, *American Journal of Public Health*, 96 (1) 132–38, Also, Chhabra S (2008) Sexual Violence Among Pregnant Women in India, *Journal of Obstetric and Gynecological Research*, 34 (2) 238–41
26 Chandra PS, Satyanaryana VA and Carey MP (2009) Women Reporting Intimate Partner Violence in India: Associations with PTSD And Depressive Symptoms, *Archives on Women Mental Health*, 2 (4) 203–9
27 Nigam S (2015) The Social and Legal Paradox Relating to Marital Rape in India: Addressing Structural Inequalities, *Countercurrents*, June 3, www.countercurrents.org/nigam030615.htm
28 Justice Verma Committee Report 2013 recommended a law against marital rape; however, this was not done.
29 Blackstone (1765) supra, Vol. 1 pp. 442–45
30 She has studied up to class 10 and has been working with a private hospital as an assistant after her separation.
31 Silverman JG, Michele R, Decker N Saggurti et al. (2008) Intimate Partner Violence and HIV Infection among Married Indian Women, *JAMA*, 300 (6) 703–10 Also, Go VF, Sethulaksmi CJ and Bentley ME et al. (2003) When HIV-Prevention Messages and Gender Norms Clash: The Impact of Domestic Violence on Women's HIV Risk in Slums of Chennai, India, *AIDS and Behaviour*, 7 (3) 263–72
32 Stephenson Rob, Koenig MA, Acharya R et al. (2008) Domestic Violence, Contraceptive Use and Unwanted Pregnancy in Rural India, *Studies in Family Planning*, 39 (3) 177–86
33 Madhok Sumi, Unnithan M and Heitmeyer C (2014) On Reproductive Justice: 'Domestic Violence', Rights and the Law in India Culture, *Health & Sexuality*, 16 (10) 1231–44
34 Kandiyoti D (1988) Bargaining with Patriarchy, *Gender and Society*, 2 (3) 274–90
35 Fernandez M (1997) Domestic Violence by Extended Family Members in India: Interplay of Gender and Generation, *Journal of Interpersonal Violence*, 12 (3) 433–55
36 Married three years ago to an executive engineer, she has an MBA and has two years' work experience
37 She has a BA in Economics and is staying at her parents' house. She got married to a businessman.
38 NCRB (2014) Crimes in India, 2014, Government of India
39 Pence E and Paymar M (1993) *Education Groups for Men Who Batter: The Duluth Model*, Springer, New York
40 Pence E and Dasgupta S (2006) *Re-examining Battering: Are All Acts of Violence Against the Intimate Partner the Same?* Praxis International, USA, www.ncdsv.org/images/Praxis_ReexaminingBattering_June2006.pdf

41 Desai SB, Dubey A, Joshi BL et al. (2010) *Human Development in India: Challenges for Society in Transition*, Oxford University Press, New Delhi pp. 173–95
42 Gururaj G, Issac MK, Subbakrishna DK and Ranjani R (2004) Risk Factors for Completed Suicide: A Case Control Study from Bangalore, India, *Injury Control and Safety Promotion*, 11 (3) 183–91
43 Jejeebhoy SJ (1998) Wife Beating in Rural India: A Husband's Right? *Economic and Political Weekly*, 23 (15) 588–628
44 Batliwala S, Anitha BK, Gurumurthy A et al. (1998) *Status of Rural Women in Karnataka*, National Institute of Advanced Studies, Bangalore
45 She has completed a fashion designing course and got married four years ago to a man working in a private company.
46 Kumar S, Jayseelan L, Suresh L and Ahuja R (2005) Domestic Violence and Its Mental Health Correlates in Indian Women, *British Journal of Psychiatry*, 187, 62–67
47 Personal discussion conducted on 12.2.18.
48 Nigam S (2014) When Beauty Is Only Skin Deep: Intensifying Social Inequalities Through Rangbedh or Colour Discrimination, *Countercurrents*, November 25, www.countercurrents.org/nigam251114.htm accessed on 31.03.17
49 Colorism is a term coined by Alice Walker in 1983 in *Search for Our Mother's Garden: Womanist Prose*, USA Harcourt Brace Jovanovich.
50 Jeddy GM (2018) Woman Allegedly Poisons Guests at Feast, Say She Was Tortured Over Her Complexion and Cooking, *The Hindustan Times*, June 24
51 *India Today* (2011) On the Rise: Divorces Under 25, December 29 Also, Reddy H (2013) Made in Heaven Broken on Whim, *The Hindustan Times*, March 21 Also, Dummett Mark (2011) Not So Happily Ever After as Indian Divorce Rate Double Up, *BBC New*, January 1
52 Shariff A and Khalid S (2017) Abandoned Women Vastly Outnumbered Victims of Triple Talaq and It's Time Modi Spoke Up for Them, *The Wire*, April 17
53 Mishra PN (2018) Wives Abandoned by NRI Husbands Petition SC for Protecting Their Rights, *Live Law*, November 13
54 *The Economic Times* (2018) Government to Bring Bill to Stop NRI Husbands from Abandoning Wives, November 30, https://economictimes.indiatimes.com/news/politics-and-nation/bill-against-nri-husbands-deserting-wives-in-next-session-sushma-swaraj/articleshow/66848313.cms
55 Supra
56 She got married 10 years ago and is a mother of seven-year-old child. She managed to get a job with a BPO after she was separated. Her husband is working as an accountant with a public-sector company.
57 *The Hindustan Times* (2019) Woman Starved to Death Over Dowry, March 31, https://www.hindustantimes.com/india-news/woman-starved-to-death-for-dowry-in-kerala-husband-mother-in-law-held/story-Jc1PY3Dq8PZDj60qzylABN.html
58 Bradley T, Tomalin E and Subramaniam M (2009) *Dowry: Bridging Gap Between Theory and Practice*, Zed Books, London
59 Menski W (Ed) (1998) *South Asians and the Dowry Problem*, Trentham Books, London
60 An analysis of matrimonial advertisements reflects that men prefer brides who are earning yet who are 'homely'.
61 Akundi Sweta (2019) #gettingmarried in 2019, The Hindu January 23, https://www.thehindu.com/life-and-style/gettingmarried-in-2019/article26069516.ece
62 Nigam S (2001) *Consumerism, Dowry and Marginalization of Women in India*, Kali's Yug, Warlaw, March pp. 33–39
63 Lama P and Sharma M (2017) Buffaloes to Audis: This Is What Sells in the Delhi Dowry Market, Where Harassment Cases Have Doubled Over 5 Years,

The Hindustan Times, August 14, https://www.hindustantimes.com/delhi-news/dowry-harassment-cases-in-delhi-double-in-5-years-gold-jewellery-refrigerator-top-demand-list/story-3yGU4JzcwLOymuelIkhbhL.html
64 Kumar V (2004) Poisoning Deaths in Married Women, *Journal of Clinical and Forensic Medicine*, 11 (1) 2–5
65 United Nations (2010) UN Chronicles 2010: Empowering Women, Progress or Not? *UN Chronicles*, XLVII (1) *United Nations Department of Public Information*, New York p. 59
66 Meltzer H, Doos L, Vostanis P et al. (2009) The Mental Health of Children Who Witness Domestic Violence, *Child and Family Social Work*, 14, 491–501
67 Edleson J (1999) Children's Witnessing of Adult Domestic Violence, *Journal of Interpersonal Violence*, 14 (8) 839–70
68 Dutton D (2000) Witnessing Parental Violence as a Traumatic Experience Shaping the Abusive Personality, *Journal of Aggression*, 3, 59–67
69 Nicholas Bala (1996) Spousal Abuse and Children of Divorce: A Differentiated Approach, *Canadian Journal of Family Law*, 13 (215) 335–37
70 Hungerford A, Ogle R and Clements C (2010) Children's Exposure to Intimate Partner Violence: Relations Between Parent-Child Concordance and Children's Adjustment, *Violence and Victims*, 25 (2) 185–201
71 Payne B, Triplett R and Higgins G (2011) The Relationship Between Self-Control, Witnessing Domestic Violence, and Subsequent Violence, *Deviant Behavior*, 32, 769–89
72 Stark E (2017) A Battered Mother's Dilemma, www.youtube.com/watch?v=TcQjbg8PNmI accessed on 30.03.2018
73 Jones J (2007) When It Comes to Politics, Friendship Has Its Limits, *The New York Times*, July 23
74 Mohanty-Talpade C (1984) Under Western Eyes, *Boundaries*, 12 (3) 333–46
75 Gordon Linda (1991) What's New in the Women's History? In *A Reader in Feminist Knowledge*, edited by Sneja Gunew, Routledge, London
76 Omvedt G (1990) *Violence Against Women: New Movements and New Theories*, Kali for Women, New Delhi p. 42
77 Scaria M and Nigam S (2016) *The Founding Mothers: 15 Women Architects of the Indian Constitution*, Media House, New Delhi
78 Gandhi N (1990) Anti-Price Rise Movement, In *Space Within the Struggle*, edited by I Sen, Kali for Women, New Delhi
79 Pandey Geeta (2017) Bhanwari Devi: The Rape That Led to India's Sexual Harassment Law, *BBC News*, March 17
80 Scroll (2017) Watch: Rupen Deol Bajaj Talks About Sexual Harassment Case She Won Against KPS Gill, June 5, https://video.scroll.in/839715/watch-rupan-deol-bajaj-talks-about-the-sexual-harassment-case-she-won-against-kps-gill Sharma MG (2017) Breaking Barriers: How DJ Varnika Kundu Stood Up to VIP Stalkers in Chandigarh, *The Hindustan Times*, August 13
81 In Ram Rahim's case, the Godman backed by politicians made an attempt to suppress the voice of women Sadhvis who filed the case against him. *India Times* (2017) Fearless Efforts of These Five People Made Sure That Influential Ram Rahim Gets Convicted, August 26, https://www.indiatimes.com/news/india/fearless-efforts-of-these-five-people-made-sure-that-influential-ram-rahim-gets-convicted-328571.html

4 Women's experiences with the law and the legal system

"No woman had a voice in the design of the legal institutions that rule the social order under which women, as well as men, live".[1]

The law provides for criminal as well as civil remedies against domestic violence, which theoretically seems to empower women survivors. Civil law requires lower standards of proof, and women may exert their autonomy while choosing actions rather than becoming the object of legal proceedings, as is done in criminal law. The PWDVA thus seemingly fills in the gaps left by the criminal law. For such reasons, initially, women's groups were enthusiastic about this, whereas others criticized it, arguing that an excessive focus on law implies increasing control of the state. This chapter, while considering these debates, examines the challenges women face during implementation of the domestic violence law in the courts. It examines the microprocesses involved during the process and points out the gaps that exist in the legal framework. It concludes that although the law has helped provide a platform for women to obtain short-term remedies, it has failed to make a dent in the prevailing patriarchal culture. Those who enforce the law see wife beating as a prerogative of the husband. Other barriers and impediments range from a lack of appropriate infrastructure to the insensitivity of staff, as well as a widespread conservative attitude and mind-set within the system. The law is enmeshed in a complex social framework, rather than protecting the rights and dignity of women as citizens. It argues that the reliance of the women's movement on the law has not helped address systemic and structural inequities, though the law may have enabled short-term gains.

Women's encounter with the legal system

The courts play a significant role in translating rights into actions and establishing constitutional values.[2] Ideally, courtrooms are spaces where justice is facilitated as per the rule of law and oppression is challenged. Courtrooms essentially are enablers as well as facilitators of justice to the victims. The courtrooms, preferably and mandatorily, should be democratic, egalitarian, transparent and participatory. However, in practice, this is not happening.

Also, ideally, while interpreting the criminal law on domestic violence, the gender-sensitive courts may consider the plight of the victims and, while adjudicating, may address the accountability of perpetrators, whereas while construing the provisions under the PWDVA, the courts can enhance judicial responsiveness by utilizing innovative strategies to protect the rights of survivors. Theoretically, with the availability of sensitized and dedicated human resources such as POs and SPs to handle the cases, the courts are in a position to provide efficient and effective justice to the victims of violence. Courts are also in a position to send the clear message that violence will not be tolerated by ensuring that the batterer is held liable for his violent actions. However, this work shows that reality is different. Violence by husbands is readily condoned by those who enforce the law.

Also, frequently, laws are written in a vague and ambiguous manner to keep them open to interpretation so as to leave space for official discretion.[3] These provisions may be interpreted judiciously by the courts in a sensitive manner to deter violence and promote the rights of victims. Yet the police and courts are highly resistant to putting these provisions into practice. The prevalent legal culture[4] is limiting the scope of the law because the focus is laid on blaming the women rather than on questioning the man for his unlawful behavior. Male superiority and privileges operate in the court, while the concept of family privacy is being upheld. A chastisement doctrine is being endorsed by the courts, which grants the prerogative to husbands to beat their wives.

There is also a disjuncture between the manner in which the women's movement defines and shapes the law and the way in which it is implemented by those who enforce the law.[5] This work observes that complete reliance of the women's movement on the law-centric approach has not helped address the structural issues in a patriarchal society or the inequalities and power imbalance within the marriages in which violence is embedded. In fact, currently, the patriarchy is operating in a harsh manner and women have to struggle hard to overcome the male-dominated, conservative, regressive notions both inside and outside the courtrooms.

The exploitative patriarchal agenda

The police are the first line of contact in most of the cases should a woman decide to file a criminal complaint. They act as the gatekeepers of the criminal justice system. Their sensitivity, attitude and understanding towards domestic violence cases are important. However, this work shows that police often work against women in such cases. Many feel reluctant to go to a police station to register their complaints. The police attach a low priority to domestic abuse incidents.[6] Similar to courts, the image of police stations as hostile is deeply embedded in the common psyche. An FIR is not registered at the first instance. Cases are mandatorily being send to CAW cells for mediation. Many of those who enforce the law stated that provisions under Section 498A should be used a last resort, as there is 'no scope for reconciliation' after filing a criminal case. Also, the police often refuse to register a complaint if the component of dowry demand is not added to it. The majority of complainants reported making repeated trips to the police station. The police do not arrest the violent husbands or in-laws easily after the guidelines pertaining to arrest have been issued in several cases.[7]

Those who enforce the law use patriarchal morality to decide the rights and wrongs within a marriage, thus forcing a reconciliation to maintain family integrity.[8] They uphold the prerogative of men to beat women and do not act against family members involved in this crime. Complainants reported being dissuaded by police from registering their complaints while invoking family values. Copies of FIRs were not made available in one-tenth of cases, and several reported financial exploitation when attempting to get basic legal information. Many were made to wait for hours in police stations while pressure was exerted to compromise the case. Agnihotri and Parliwala[9] explained that the

> Stereotypes of the 'Indian family' cast it as a haven from the travails of a materialist and modern world, an arena in which women – mothers, sisters and daughters – were respected and honoured. Family is seen as an epitome and the crucible for the love and spirituality on which Indian civilisation rested. These stereotypes played an important part in raising the apathy of the neighbours and the government, and guide the attitude of the police and the in-laws to cover up the crimes.

The predominant presumption is that matrimonial discord is the key for filing cases, and in the process, violence is negated.[10]

Investigations are not done properly and evidence is not gathered; therefore, many cases are dismissed on technical grounds. Medical evidence, such as lacerations, wounds, injuries, burns or scars, play a significant role in proving the crime, yet in none of the cases were medicolegal or forensic evidence collected. Statements of complainants and other crucial witnesses are not recorded, and in few cases where this was done, it took months and years. Often, the abuse is perpetrated behind closed doors. Those family members who witness the brutality are apprehensive about or shy away from testifying because of fear or their loyalties to the accused. Courts do not take these factors into account. Also, many participants complained that police do not support them in their attempts to recover the *streedhan* in a timely manner. Mandira (32) recounted the horror as she said,

> My in-laws already were informed that I will be reaching to collect my *samaan* (dowry items) they therefore removed all expensive items and jewelry from my matrimonial house. What was left was empty boxes and then my father-in-law threatened '*Mein tumhe ek tinka nahi le jaane*

> *doonga*'. (I will not let you take even a straw) Police men didn't questioned them and even during *supardari*[11] my husband and his brother unashamedly mocked me down and made fun of me when he counted the broken toys of my kid, spoons and *katoris* (bowls), petticoats and my undergarments as a list of *streedhan* items returned in front of all male policemen there.
>
> (2014)

Many informants complained about the rude behavior of policemen and alleged that instead of helping them, the "police sided with abusive husbands and in-laws". Others said that some policemen made offensive comments, while a few reported that policemen demanded money. Also, the police, in its zeal to prove its efficiency, register fewer cases and, in the process, deliberately ignore domestic violence complaints. Police apathy is a major reason that fewer cases are reported or, if reported, result in few convictions. Intervention in domestic situations is not perceived as 'real' police work. Often, domestic abuse cases are viewed as unglamorous and unrewarding, and therefore few personnel are interested in dealing with the same.

Numerous studies have reported that police hardly support women survivors of violence. Even in the present study, none of the informants claimed that they received any form of support from the police. Often, the IO does not complete the investigation in a timely manner or properly or accurately. The courts in several cases, while writing their decisions, have pointed out the gaps in the police investigation. For instance, the court noted that,

> If the complaint of domestic violence made by women against a member of family, the police without proper verification and investigation cannot submit report that no case is made out. Investigating agency is required to make proper inquiry not only from the members of the family but also from neighbours, friends and others. After such inquiry, the investigating agency may from a definite opinion and file report. It is for the Court to decide finally whether to take cognizance of offence under any provisions of the D.V. Act.[12]

The biased wrong attitude that 'the domestic violence law is misused and abused by women' is so deeply entrenched that the police in many cases do not even listen to the women's complaints with an open mind or may not record the complaint properly. Arrests are often not made, and the delay in the recovery of *streedhan* by the police harms women's economic interests.

Interaction of survivors with the protection officers and service providers

In comparison to the operation of Section 498A, where a woman is supposed to register her FIR, the PWDVA created a cadre of POs to assist the courts as well as complainants in preparing the DIRs, writing applications on behalf of women, ensuring that aggrieved persons get legal aid, maintaining a list of service providers and shelter homes, getting the aggrieved person medically examined and ensuring that orders issued by the court are executed. Different from the role of police officers, POs need to devise a strategy for every case. Equally, it is essential that POs develop a gendered understanding of the nature of violence and empathetically handle the complaints. However, the analysis reveals that there is a lack of understanding of the act among POs themselves. Frequently, POs are involved in counseling. Moreover, to ensure that the POs 'handhold' women in distress, they first needed 'handholding' themselves. However, training or sensitization of POs is rarely carried out.

Also, the rights of the complainants are compromised at every step. Women are not made aware of their rights or the legal process, and therefore they reported experiencing confusion and uncertainty about the procedure and its outcome. A lack of legal orientation created enormous anxiety among participants. Commonly, POs, just like the police, are not familiar with the dynamic nature of intimate violence, nor are they aware of the nuances behind the victim either mobilizing the system or dropping her complaint. For instance, Vimmi, (33) a post-graduate in commerce, recalled,

> I was exhausted by everyday verbal abuse and beating. When I told her (counsellor) that I do not want to go to natal house, she suggested that I can stay at my matrimonial home, he cannot throw me out of the house. But I am just looking for peace. If I go back to natal home, they will push me back to marital home. I just want to think of what's going on in my life. I need some solace. What should I do?
>
> (2013)

The complainant here requires services such as a short-stay home. However, the counsellor has not offered the same, perhaps due to the unavailability of such homes or those which are there have limited space. A complainant requires emotional and psychological support, but the PO is too overburdened to look into these details. The complainant wants the violence to stop, but the counsellor suggests that she go back to a violent situation to assert her right to reside in the shared household. In other cases where women interacted with the POs or counsellors, the majority reported dissatisfaction. Also, POs have their own issues, such as increasing workload, contractual positions, safety, lack of facilities, overcrowded offices and salaries not paid on time, among others. POs, such as dowry prohibition officers are not given proper resources, training, facilities and sufficient time to deal with each case. They are routinely filling out DIRs rather than assisting victims. Adding another bureaucratic layer to an already overcrowded system of police and courts has not helped resolve the issues complainants are facing.

The PWDVA introduced Service Providers, which recognize the role of community organizations and women's groups in mediating between women and the formal system. Their presence reveals that laws legislated for the protection of women produce different practices, distinct from the courtrooms. These forums are known for their inimitable style of speedy and flexible disposal of cases in a chaotic way, which may or may not be marked by arbitrariness and spontaneity. The state selectively allows for an informal devolution for implementing the law. Such delegation not only results in the formal and informal critically impinging on each other's constitution and jurisdiction but also affects the very definition of rules and legality. There is a deep suspicion regarding the abilities of the local and customary fora for dispute resolution. Some are opportunistic and keen on money making and follow violent or authoritarian practices. Many acts against women who are renegotiating the traditional authority structures. These relatively new disciplines of legal pluralism work in complex ways in which local practices and formal laws compete, coexist with and incorporate each other. For instance, institutions such as caste panchayats, *khap* panchayats and *jati* panchayats are violating the legal norms by controlling women's sexuality and honoring the traditional codes relating to marital alliances.

Lawyers and legal aid service authorities

Lawyers occupy a significant position when implementing the law. They act as mediators and translators of law while acting as a bridge between the litigants and the courts. Lawyers translate the subjective sufferings of women into legally recognized categories of violence and play a crucial role in shaping the trial. As mentioned earlier, a few women went to legal aid lawyers, while others went to private lawyers. Those who went to legal aid lawyers reported delay and dissatisfaction. Those who contacted private lawyers through the network of their natal family, relatives, friends or acquaintances complained that they have been paying fees and running around in the courts, but the process is slow. Complainants expect immediate relief. However, the procedure followed by the court is complex and has its own nuances. This creates discontent.

Half of the informants reported that the lawyer rarely appears on time or barely explains what has transpired in the courts. Padma (41) stated that, "The lawyer was not appearing in the court. He was not telling me what was going on. He has no time. What help will he provide? I went to his office and sat for hours yet I have received no reply to my queries". Only two informants expressed their satisfaction with the services of their lawyers, others were ambivalent. The gap in communication between the state actors, lawyers and complainants adds to the misery of women. Lisa (25) got married two years ago and shared,

> It was a love marriage. The problems started within a month of marriage when my husband got a job in Chennai. He never took me there

> on some pretext or the other and I also never insisted as I had a job then. Earlier, he used to visit every week. Slowly, the number of visits reduced and he didn't even pick up his phone despite of repeated calls. For more than six months when no contact could be established, I visited Chennai and found that he has been living with someone else and has changed his job too. I contacted a lawyer who charged a hefty fee. However, later he said that notice could not be served. Eight months have gone and nothing has happened. My husband has not appeared once, though on her mobile he has been sending all kinds of messages to harass me. The lawyer has not told me this earlier. I thought that it is the duty of police to locate him.
>
> (2015)

Also, almost all informants were neither aware of the provisions of law, nor they were aware of the types of reliefs they can claim. None of the litigants reported that the police or POs helped them understanding the procedure or told them about their rights under the PWDVA. It is on the advice of lawyers that applications were filed. The majority of participants stated that they were made to sign the application and affidavits – their lawyers had not told them what was written there. Thus, the process of operationalizing the civil law through the criminal courts is not assisting women. The purpose of enacting the special law is lost behind the technicalities and procedures in implementing it.

FIRs and DIRs: a significant process being overlooked

FIRs and DIRs are significant statutory documents that must be done correctly in a timely manner. The police and the POs are dutybound to file these documents. Technically, both the FIR and DIR provide an account of the violence the aggrieved person has faced. However, the present work observed that DIRs were not filed in one-third of cases, as initially the POs were filing the DIR only after the court ordered them to do so. Delay was reported in several cases. All participants claimed that they were not aware of the content of the DIR. Also, complainants neither have control over the content of applications filed under PWDVA, nor can they understand the technicalities of the process.

Litigants frequently make oral claims in their native language, which is then filtered, translated and recorded into the language of the court by the police, POs or lawyers. The process of writing DIRs or FIRs thus involves the complicated task of transferring the verbal grievances of women into formal legal documents while fitting individual experiences into legal categories, on the basis of which legal claims are contested within the courtrooms. Legal language is objective, direct and neutral, whereas the individual situations are subjective and grounded in emotions. Thus, writing FIRs and DIRs involves translating complex emotive pain and subjectivities into technical legal language, which is a tough task that requires intricate skills and sensitivity. While recording the real-life experiences into formal documents, many aspects are lost, as the discourse of law and its objectivity underscore the difficulties women face. The law emphasizes coherency, and in order to achieve that, the emotional aspects of narratives are erased and the women's sense of injury is rendered invisible in the legal documentation.

The content of FIR or DIR further must be confirmed within the courtrooms by the verbal testimonies of the complainants, and it also must be established during their cross-examination. Any gaps in interpretation or translation are interpreted against the complainants. The mismatch between the DIRs or FIRs, petitions and oral deposition is contested within the courtrooms. Defense lawyers try hard to gain an advantage when FIRs or DIRs are not reported correctly or are improperly written. They technically twist and manipulate the shortcomings in the legal records to the advantage of accused. For instance, in the matter of *Sanjay vs State*,[13] the survivor was married in 2007. She had one daughter who was three-and-half years old at the time of filing the complaint. Her husband died in 2011. Her complaint was that after the death of her husband, the respondents (in-laws) harassed her and worked to throw her out of the marital house. She was not allowed to use her phone or talk to her parents. She succeeded in saving her life with the help of the police. While filing the DIR, the PO marked off a few items, such as sexual abuse by her *Jeth*, demeaning and humiliating remarks, ridicule and name-calling and any other verbal abuse, and in the economic violence column she marked 'not providing money for maintaining you and your children, not providing foods and clothes for you and your children'. The trial court took the view that "there is no absolute or specific allegation or incidents of domestic violence averred in this petition the respondents, allowing the present proceedings to continue against the respondents would be sheer abuse of the process of law". The appellate court held that the appellant had marked all types of violence under different categories. She did not specify in the DIR that she is facing verbal or emotional abuse and confined her claim to maintenance and *streedhan*; therefore, the appellant had failed to show that she has been subjected to violence. Her application was dismissed on these grounds. Thus, the victim was denied justice because of gaps in technicalities in reporting the DIR. While adjudicating the matter, the court has not considered the pain of the victim. In this matter, the woman has suffered a range of abuses. The severity and multiplicity of violence, when compounded together, bring out narratives that are too unfathomable to be translated into objective legal rhetoric, yet the court failed to consider these nuances. The law codified the violence into a set of objective incidents from where it draws its interpretation. It expected the victim to transform her experiences of violence into legal language while overlooking the fact that there is a strong disjuncture between the subjectivities of sufferings and the objective vocabulary of the law.[14] The 'wrongs' in this matter could not be fixed, because the language of the law could not capture the certainty of violence despite the evidence produced that the damage has been done.

Further, many lawyers contacted for this work suggested that "POs are not aware of legal technicalities. DIR frequently fails to mention the facts significant to decide the case". Whereas one of the POs remarked, "Courts generally consider the pleadings, evidences or the arguments and the way lawyers present their case. Relief is not granted as per what is suggested in the DIRs". Similarly, police, while filing FIRs, dilute the cases and do not report the incident properly, and gaps have been reported in conducting investigations. The prosecution, too, acts to grant formal and informal immunity to the men who beat their wives. Thus, adding layers of personnel to the justice delivery mechanism has not helped to enhance the efficiency.

Can a woman control what to write in her DIR/FIR or application?

Only a few informants confided that the police, POs or lawyers while filing the DIR, FIR or application under the PWDVA explained to them what it is and how it will be used. The majority of participants were not aware as to what is implied by DIR or FIR and how it would be used in their case. However, in the courtrooms, decisions are made on the basis of the pleadings and content in these documents. Discrepancies may arise in DIRs, FIRs and complaint or petitions in the courts because of the differences in the perceptions of lawyers, police and POs and their sensitivities to the women's concerns. This fact is not being considered while deciding matters. For instance, Nirmala (52), working in a government job, got remarried to a man who works with a private organization. She stated

> It was a love marriage. We have been staying together for past 15 years. My daughter is now 11-year-old. We purchased a small flat a few years back. I am paying EMIs from my salary. He said he will use his money for paying household expenses. Then three years back he asked me for my savings and jewellery to buy a bigger flat. Initially, I was reluctant, then I thought that it is our future security. When I asked him for the papers of the flat, he made the excuse that the builder is delaying. He then left his job and went to his native place in Jamshedpur saying that his father is not well. I can't go leaving my job also my daughter was having her exams. Since then, he used to visit us occasionally. But then many people from bank and finance companies started knocking my doors every other day saying that he has taken huge loan and has given my name as a surety, so I have to repay. I tried to contact him but he re-located somewhere else. I cannot find his whereabouts. Now, bank goons are after me to re-pay his loan. I am already paying EMI for this house; from where will I get more money? I then contacted a lawyer

> because I also want my daughter to be safe from those goons who are knocking my door for loan repayment.
>
> (2015)

The complainant in this case requires specific orders for protection and monetary relief. Specific directions are required to protect the daughter of the complainant from the goons of the finance companies, but no such provisions are available under the domestic violence law. The DIR mentioned only the maintenance order for the child. There is a mismatch between the needs of the complainant and recommendations made in the DIR. On her FIR also, no action has been taken because the police evaded their responsibilities on the pretext that the whereabouts of the accused are not known. Also, the sections pertaining to cheating or fraud in the IPC have not been evoked because those who enforce the law do not see that her husband has exploited her. Hence, a vast gap exists between the manner in which women tell their stories and the way in which those who enforce the law interpret the violence. The objectivity and the rationality of the law does not consider the basic nuances relating to the sensitivities of her sufferings. The law fragments the continuous life experiences of women into several pieces to derive legal meaning, but in the process fails to capture their trauma. At the time of pronouncing verdicts, the courts overlook fine nuances, and therefore, justice becomes an elusive concept for women who are already in distress.

The law does not scrutinize the continuous history of violence women face

All participants claimed that the police and the courts have trivialized their cases. This claim has been verified through the DIRs, pleadings, documents and records. A huge discrepancy could be observed between the women's testimony and the available material record. The subjectivity of the women's claims has not been captured by the legal documents, and the narratives that women shared orally have not been reflected on paper. Smita (29), a manager with a private firm, reported

> After a few days of marriage, he insisted that I should leave my job. When I refused, he slapped. Since then, every day, he used to insult me in front of relatives, friends, maids and drivers and made negative remarks about my work or appearance. He keeps a tab of my salary account and would not allow me to spend the money. The day I got promotion and announced that news, he stopped talking to me. After a few days, he told me to take leave to take care of his parents and when I refused, he threw me out of the house. His lawyer claims that I am an ambitious woman not willing to make sacrifices.
>
> (2014)

According to Smita, the police emphasized the act of physical beating and refused to acknowledge the narratives of everyday insults she was facing. The IO remarked, "These are common adjustment problems. Why are you insisting on such petty things?" The biases of those who implement the law frequently creep in. The definition of domestic violence is narrowly interpreted here by the police. Subjective complexities are ignored in the legal discourse. Smita felt verbally and emotionally humiliated; however, those who enforce the law do not think that way. For them, it is a normal routine issue. The emotional scars of women are rendered as private and out of the purview of the law. These layered sensitivities and differences in the manner violence is experienced by women and is comprehended by those who implement the law frequently creep in. In his petition for divorce that her husband filed later, Smita was portrayed negatively as too "ambitious" and "career minded" who has refused to act as a "dutiful wife". Her husband pleaded that she is having extramarital affairs in the office and is reluctant to leave her job. She is portrayed as a "bad woman and a terrible wife". Her case depicts the manner in which stereotypes operate within the legal system that view women complaining against their husbands with distrust and reinforce prejudices.

The role of the law is to resolve crises and fix the 'broken family', and this is done while preserving the authority of the husband to control his wife. The layered definition of violence as stated in the PWDVA has not helped, because it cannot weave in sensitivities relating to women's pain. Bacchi,[15] too, holds that the domestic violence is seen as a 'social breakdown' issue, and therefore the resolution seemingly lies in tighter social control by men. Domestic violence is seen as an issue relating to a 'power struggle', and it may be addressed by empowering and liberating women. However, the tendency is to label it a 'social problem', and this attracts a response that cannot address the underlying causes.

Further, under the PWDVA one of the significant reliefs made available is the right to residence in the shared household. However, Smita could not obtain this relief, because once the matter was filed, her husband moved out of the house and she was forced to move into a separate cheaper rented accommodation. The court has asked him to pay the rent, but he has been evading it on the pretext that his income is less and he could not afford to do so. His lawyer made the case that she is earning and therefore is not entitled to claim maintenance. Besides, there are other cases where different sets of arguments are raised to deny women the reliefs provided under the law, thus defeating the whole purpose of it. The law thus has enabled new ways of engagement with the state, yet it has failed to make a dent in the entrenched notion of women's vulnerabilities and could not imagine women as active agents.

The torment women undergo cannot be measured with the certainty that the law requires. Further, the scope of violence is limited to address the abuse inflicted by those who are not in a domestic relationship or are not part of a shared household yet play a significant role in inflicting violence. The law systematically excludes experiences of women because the gaps in the interpretive framework of the law put women in a hermeneutically disadvantaged position. The Delhi High Court[16] has captured this paradox of filtering subjectivities through the rationality of law. It states,

> Human relations are built on feelings. Not on reasons or logic. Feeling is not an exact science. It has vagueness around it. Law and justice is built on reasons and logic – not feelings. Therefore, the process of judicial decision making in matrimonial affairs is riddled with complications. To a person who is weathered by time and circumstances and whose emotions have been overcome by vagaries of time, a hard word spoken may be inconsequential. To a soft minded person, where feelings matter more, even most trivial word would be cruel. More the love – more the affection. But the danger would be that a slightest dent would break the edifice. The situation is indeed paradoxical.
>
> (2016)

Safety plans rendered meaningless

Under the Rule 8(1)(iv), it is the duty of the PO to prepare a safety plan that may include measures to prevent further violence to the aggrieved person after assessing the dangers involved in the situation. However, in none of the cases I interviewed have safety plans been prepared. This fact is substantiated by the response to an application under the RTI that revealed the courts in Delhi have not sought the assistance of welfare experts, nor have POs prepared safety plans for the victims in any case.[17] A PO explained that

> Many of the provisions of the Act cannot be implemented because it is a time-consuming process. In order to prepare a safety plan, one needs to conduct the home visits, interact with the complainant, her family, document, follow up and assist women in all possible ways. It is humanly impossible keeping in mind the number of cases which are earmarked to us.

Thus, the overburdened POs, lack of time or will and administrative hurdles all combine to make the significant provisions of the law ineffective and redundant.

Also, the act dictates that the magistrate may secure the services of a suitable person engaged in promoting family welfare for the purposes of assisting the court in the discharge of its functions. However, the present work found that nowhere is such a list of experts made available, and neither the POs nor the magistrates are securing services of experienced professionals, except counsellors. Also, no uniform procedure is being followed by SPs, and SPs barely are linked to the police station or the POs. The judiciary is not aware of the services provided by SPs, and none of the cases have been referred to shelter homes or other such services, though in the majority of cases such services are required.

Burdened courtrooms

India has a low judge-to-population ratio. There are 17.8 judges per 10 lakhs of the population as compared to the 50 judges that is recommended by the Law Commission.[18] For Delhi, this figure is 47.33, as compared to UP, where only 10.54 judges are available per 10 lakh people. For Mizoram, this figure is 57.7.[19] A huge gap exists in the sanctioned strength and positions filled.[20] In the subordinate courts, there is a shortage of more than 4,000 judges all over India, while many posts are lying vacant in the higher courts. More than 2 crores cases are pending before the subordinate courts. Around 70,000 more judges are required to clear the backlog.[21] Given the extent of the burden, it seems impractical to expect courts to deliver efficient, effective and quick justice unless additional staff is appointed and steps are taken to reduce the workload. Nevertheless, the litigants expect quicker justice. Therefore, there is quite a mismatch between the expectations of litigants and the actual process of delivering justice.

Also, situations such as domestic violence warrant effective, efficient and speedy justice. Delayed justice in cases of violence sends a message of impunity to the perpetrator, which may escalate his violent tendencies. For the victim, it implies a denial of fairness and deprivation of relief. Considering the overall gaps in the system and the fact that a low priority is accorded in such cases, the complainants are not receiving quick justice. Matrimonial cases are seen as an additional burden on already overburdened courts because these involve dealing with complex human emotions. These issues are seen as time-consuming cases as compared to other branches of litigation. Said one lawyer:

> Most of the time of the judges is being spent on conducting counseling and resolving their dispute amicably. Also, people often start fighting within the courtrooms. Most of them do not understand the professionalism and behave as if they are fighting within their homes. Sometimes, judges have to interrupt and shout at them.

Male-dominated courtrooms

As per law, courtrooms must operate neutrally without any biases; however, the reality is different. The unfairness is clearly visible in terms of the number of men and women who occupy these spaces. Court premises are full of men – as judges, court clerks, lawyers, litigants and accused. A small number of women judges can be found in the courtrooms, and their number reduces further as one moves from the lower judiciary to the higher courts. The courtrooms are hence not the 'neutral' or the 'equal' spaces and instead perpetuate a masculine ideology.[22] Sexism manifests in both overt and covert forms. Though in some places, efforts are being made to reduce disparities,[23] sexism is still deeply embedded. The Supreme Court has 3 female judges in comparison to 24 male judges.[24] Of the 229 judges appointed at the level of the Supreme Court as of 2015, only 6 were women. Representation of women among High Court judges is merely 10.86 percent.[25] The Delhi High Court has 7 female judges in comparison to 30 males, the Bombay High Court has 9 female and 62 male judges and Madras has 10 female and 58 male judges. The Supreme Court has designated 17 women senior counsel as compared to 403 men, whereas this ratio is 8 women for 229 men in the Delhi High Court. Several cases of sexual harassment in the court premises have been reported.[26] Also, as per the data[27] available, only 10.36 percent women file cases in the courts as compared to the number of men who may be accessing the legal system. Thus, merely in terms of numbers, far fewer women have physical access to the courts.

In a petition[28] filed by the Supreme Court Women Lawyers Association to include more women in the High Court and Supreme Court as judges, arguments raised by petitioners were not taken seriously by the apex court.[29] The glass ceiling is too strong to be broken. Margaret and Jardim, while highlighting the prevalence of the glass ceiling in business, commented, "The ceiling isn't glass. It's a very dense layer of men".[30] Similarly, for the Indian courts, it may be said that men occupy the significant portion of the system, making it inaccessible to women not only in terms of physical access but also through establishing and propagating an androcentric culture that operates within the courtrooms. For instance, a biased attitude is reflected in the five-judge constitutional bench created to adjudicate on the matter of the validity of the *triple talaq* where the men from different religions have gathered to rule on the significant issue that is related to women's rights rather than choosing a woman judge to adjudicate on the matter relating to the 'dignity of women' and 'gender equality'.[31]

Not only does discrimination exist in terms of the number of men and women who get to rule in the higher echelon of the judiciary, but patriarchy also exist in various forms in the everyday practice in the courtrooms. In this work, the majority of participants found the courtrooms hostile territories. The stereotypical, biased attitude of society prevents a large number of women from reaching the court premises. Not many women said that they easily could get justice in the courts. "It was full and crowded and I was surrounded by many people, mostly men. I felt nervous", shared Lekha (24), who had attended her first court hearing when I met her. Two-thirds stated that in the court when the judge asked them any questions, they felt nervous and anxious. The behavior of the judge influences the courtroom culture. Manju, (26) a shy woman, who had attended two court proceedings said,

> There were too many men in the courtroom – male lawyers, police men and other men. And the judge is asking me about my personal life. Can

> I share such information in front of so many men? Then she questioned if I want to stay with him. If I would have then why I would be here? His mother was shouting. I felt nervous. Then the judge screamed at me. She said "you are grown up and married. You need to speak up". Tears rolled down my eyes.
>
> (2015)

Thus, according to survivors, courts are insensitive. Even though Manju shared that the judge scolded her mother-in-law, this could not console her. A woman judge may be conducting the proceedings, yet factors such as an overcrowded room, the presence of males, the style of functioning and an authoritative approach all add up to create an intimidating culture in the courtroom for litigants who may not have exposure or the experience of moving around in public spaces. Also, the emotions, desires and anxieties associated with the conjugality add up to create an unruly atmosphere in the courtrooms. Emotional breakdowns in the courtrooms are considered extraneous. Women reach courtrooms facing much resistance from the family and the community. Therefore, they have high expectations from the courts, as they consider that the judge holds authority and is in a position to provide them fair justice. Small gestures, sensitivity or a token of appreciation favoring women goes a long way in boosting the morale of the complainants. However, the overburdened courts have little patience to dwell on the tedious, time-consuming details.

Elite justice marginalizes women's issues

The attitude of the judge, his sensitivity to women's issues, the time spent in each case and the nature of the remedies provided to the complainant all shape the outcome of the litigation. Judges play a crucial role in determining the respondent's behavior and his compliance and execution of the order. However, judges have their own biases, prejudices and stereotypes. For instance, Saira (30), working as a journalist, said, "The judge appointed earlier here was good. She used to ask a lot of questions and would shout at my husband whenever he used to tell lie. She never allowed the lawyers to intervene. But this judge is horrible. He doesn't listen". Besides, the infrastructure, building, premises, facilities, overall space, record maintenance and services provided by the support staff contribute to determine the quality of justice being delivered. Certain courtrooms performed better than others in relative comparison because of differences in services being provided to the complainants.

Moreover, the judge has to listen to the litigant in their native language and then translate it to record it in legal language. The process therefore has a fundamental gap because of the inability to translate emotions and the colloquial language into the official record. This becomes prominent in situations relating to taboo or intimate topics, such as those relating to consummation of marriage or sexual violence. Sunita, (28) shared,

> The judge is very rude. She asked me openly several questions which I cannot answer in front of everyone. In the other court (where her application for maintenance is tried) the judge is very patient she called me once in her chamber and then asked details. I have requested my lawyer to get this case transferred before another judge.

For a woman, speaking in court equates to agency, and for the judge it implies interpreting silence, translating emotions, comprehending resistance and deducing pain into legal language. The sensitivities of judges therefore become crucial while dealing with cases of violence. For instance, during a proceeding, the magistrate asked a litigant, "Why after 12 years [do] you want to leave your matrimonial home? Why can't you adjust? At least for your children you can do so". The woman replied, "For 12 years I have been staying, putting up with physical violence doing every possible 'adjustment' but he has not changed. Why nobody asks him to mend his behavior?" This conversation reflects on the prejudices of the courts, which blindly pressure women to adjust without considering the relevant details of the matter. Experience shows that often the courtrooms situated in a deeply embedded, layered, hierarchical, patriarchal society regularly reinforce masculine values and androcentric morals while ignoring the fact that their prime concern is to disburse justice as per legal provisions. Rather than using the legal tenets to approach the legal problems, the courtrooms use the subjective, rudimentary, patriarchal lens to address matters. An analysis of everyday proceedings in the courtrooms reveals the manner in which sexism operates while the hegemony of the court is reinforced in daily decisions, orders, conversations, jest, reasoning and assumptions based on an ideology that subjugates women.

Are courtrooms litigant friendly?

This work shows that courtrooms are not litigant friendly. In reality, the courtrooms work in a typical bureaucratic, hegemonic and stereotypical manner. Further, the strict discipline enforced in the courtrooms and the procedural tenacity maintained by the court staff combined with the complexities of an adversarial system act to intimidate the complainants seeking justice. Also, the adversarial system is not victim-centric and does not compulsorily provide for rehabilitation or recompense to the victims.[32] Winning or losing a case is the prime motive in the adversarial system, and in the process the wrongs women face are ignored. Courtrooms act as valiant guardians of the hierarchical family while ignoring the rights of victims. More specifically, in the criminal law, the culprits are granted several rights ranging from ensuring a fair trial, to the right to engage a lawyer, to the right against self-incrimination, to the right to seek bail and a range of other protections. However, for victims, no such remedies exist. The system is complicated and is blindly built around technicalities rather than providing justice.

Additionally, courts are places where ego clashes take place on a continuous basis between various stakeholders – judges, advocates and litigants. The judge, being on a higher level, shows his authority in various ways, while the lawyers consider themselves professional experts. It is the litigant in the adversarial system who lacks power once she sets the wheel rolling by making a complaint. Probably, a litigant lacks awareness of the law and its technicalities. Though courtrooms are created for the purpose of delivering justice, the complainants remain at the receiving end with little participation in the process. In Foucauldian language, the process, approach and environment of the courtrooms are marred with governmentality. The nitty-gritty, bureaucratic procedures and technicalities observed in the courtrooms create trouble for litigants and hamper the efficiency of the law.

Also, courtrooms are not neutral spaces in a true sense have their own subjectivities. As an organic dynamic entity, the courtroom has its own persona. Courtrooms are not free from biases,[33] corruption, nepotism and other forms of various problems.[34] Rather, class, gender, caste and other biases operate in a hidden manner. Often, the courtrooms use the prism of a rigid official bureaucratic lens while adjudicating, and in the process of providing socio-legal solutions to the complainants, become the autocratic upholders of rudimentary traditions. More specifically, when the concern relates to women, courtrooms act as moral guardians and the custodians of patriarchal values rather than as upholders of the rule of law or defenders of women's rights. Frequently, the rule of law is not followed in cases where a woman is a complainant because courts do not see women as neutral citizens. Women's claims are viewed through the prism of relationships as someone's daughter, wife or mother, which does not happen with male complainants.

The multiplicity of litigation continues

The majority of the informants reported that once the complaint has been filed, the opposite party files multiple cases relating to divorce, restitution of conjugal rights, custody and similar applications in different courts to counter women's claims and to pressure and deter the complainants, thus creating a spate of litigation where women are compelled to run around in different courts. In one-sixth of cases, the husband or his family members have filed eviction suits against complainants who chose to exercise their right to reside in the shared household.

The PWDVA, similar to provisions under the Family Court Act, is enacted to provide a single-window system to women in need. However, multiple litigation continues, and survivors are compelled to attend several proceedings in different courts on different dates, thus negating this aspect of the single window system. For the survivors who are struggling with many issues such as taking care of the children, handling their own lives and earning to survive besides running around in courts attending different proceedings or chasing lawyers, it becomes difficult to keep up. And all this happens when the recovery from the adverse impact of violence is not yet complete. In the majority of cases, with no psycho-social support or economic aid being made available to women, they are struggling somehow to pick up the pieces of their lives. For instance, Tanya, (30) shared,

> My child is not keeping well. I have a private job. Taking leave every other day is difficult. Though my lawyer is cooperative, yet I have to mark my presence in each proceeding. I have to run around in different courts. I feel depressed and stressed. Sometimes, I wonder if asking for justice is a crime.

In many countries, laws have been made to rectify the situation of anti–strategic lawsuits against public participation (SLAPP), which imply that the law takes care of situation where defense in many cases intimidates, censors and silences critics or complainants by filing frivolous lawsuits.[35] Many governments across the world have enacted laws to provide early termination of an invalid abusive suit or impose penalties on those who file frivolous lawsuits with ulterior motives. In India, too, abusive husbands retaliate against litigating wives by filing counter-claims; for instance, to counter the petition for maintenance, the husbands file application under Section 9 of the HMA or custody suits or similar such applications to defeat women's claims and intimidate them. However, not much is done to rectify the situation. For instance, in *Anupriya Pal vs State of UP*[36] the apex court said that, "This is a classic case of taking revenge by the husband against the wife since he was aggrieved by the action of wife moving an application seeking maintenance". But in many cases, the courts could not recognize the situation where husbands abuse the process of law. Often, women with limited resources hardly are in a position to run around and pay lawyers' fees. Hence there is a dire need to initiate a debate on the issue of frivolous litigation filed to thwart and silence or intimidate parties who are already at the receiving end of abuse.

Compounding the non-compoundable: trivializing the legal process

According to the law, under Section 498A, a crime that is committed against the state is a cognizable, non-bailable and non-compoundable offence. Therefore, the police are duty bound to investigate, and the prosecution is obliged to support the victim. However, charges under 498A are not tried in a similar manner as is done for any other crime listed in the Penal Code.

When dealing with all other crimes, the law follows a strict legal course to punish the guilty. Even in the case of a dispute between neighbors or violence by a stranger, a standard procedure is adopted because all such offenses are considered crimes against the state. Conversely, when a woman reports a case of cruelty, legal procedures are slyly twisted. While framing the charges under 498A, other provisions such as those relating to hurt, grievous hurt, conspiracy, wrongful restraint or confinement, criminal force or aggravated assault causing miscarriage so on and so forth are not invoked. Even in cases when women approach a police station with serious injuries, broken bones, bleeding, bruised, crippled or scarred bodies, no other penal provisions are invoked while registering her complaint. The violation of the bodily integrity of victims is not prioritized, and no law enforcement agency seriously considers this issue. Perhaps crimes against women's bodies are not recognized as worthy enough to be penalized. Confusion and perplexity are created around domestic violence. 'Cruelty' goes unnoticed and unpunished while this crime is rendered invisible. Counseling is being forced, and the irony is that neither the police nor the judicial officials are competent to provide the same.[37]

Enormous pressure is being put on woman to settle the matter – either to go back to a violent situation with little assurance that the violence will not be repeated or to take her *streedhan*, withdraw the case, apply to quash the criminal proceedings and 'move on'. The focus is on saving the institution of marriage per se, rather than providing a violence-free environment to the survivor or to meet the ends of justice by penalizing those who commit the crime of violating a woman's mind, body and soul. Provisions under 498A are twisted to reinforce the family ideology, rather than addressing an iniquitous social structure. The culpability of a crime is reduced by pushing the alternative dispute redressal mechanism. Arguments are raised as 'pursuing the criminal case will not help as it may only satisfy woman's vengeance' or that '498A is a hindrance in life of both the parties'. However, these flawed assumptions overlook the fact that it is essential to maintain law and order and to prevent the crime from recurring. The aim of criminal law is deterrence, and the same is applicable to wife battering cases. The element of deterrence works when perpetrators are held accountable, convicted and penalized, irrespective of the repercussions on the relationship between the victim and the accused. Trial or sentencing based on economic dependence of the victim is biased and does not meet the ends of justice.

In the bulk of cases, the resolution hinges on negotiations and settlements rather than on providing rights-based justice to the complainants. The terms 'counseling', 'settlement' or 'compromise' replace 'decrees', 'orders' and 'awards' in the formal legal system. However, this vocabulary is problematic and deviates from the rights-based approach. The way these are instrumentalized is skeptical because the content of settlements is never discussed in its complexity. The legality of such a settlement and its enforceability is questionable. Often, women end up paying the huge cost because of a twist in the legal syntax. Also, during mediations, the ability to counter allegations and to strike a hard bargain comes into play. Here, litigation extends beyond the scope of statute to spill over into the domain of human relationships. Fine-tuning of rights and balancing the claims of contesting parties become crucial within the emotionally charged arena. Winning or losing the case hardly matters in such a situation, as it always places women at the receiving end.

Yet with the help of counselors and other personnel, judges make attempts to negotiate a settlement within the ambit of the matrimonial law. A 'mutual agreement' is considered the most suitable way to protect the interests of all. However, these processes are counterproductive for the survivor in various ways. It delays the matter and discourages survivors. It does not satisfy survivors' need for safety or justice. In fact, through this process, the system tries its best to convince victims to forget about the violence inflicted upon them and reconcile with the perpetrator. Thus, most mutual agreements are tactics employed by the accused party to escape criminal liabilities. Victims who withdraw their case lose their hard-earned legal ground.

In the present work, the process of mediation is either ongoing or has failed in all cases. Says one lawyer:

> Many a times, women compromise in such cases because of lengthy procedures with no relief available. In many cases, even when the maintenance or residence orders have been passed by the courts, they are not executed on timely basis. We file execution applications but that takes time. Husbands refuse to pay maintenance or pay it partly or come with number of excuses to deny women of their rights. Most of the women are dependent on their natal families and pressure is strong on them to compromise the case or settle it somehow.

A sense of cynicism prevails when a survivor interacts with a system that results in shattering her belief in the rule of law. Instead of supporting the survivor, the system enhances her vulnerability and disempowers the one who is already dispossessed of her rights while granting impunity to the perpetrator.

Personal law provisions relating to the restitution of conjugal rights, fake custody battles, denial of maintenance and divorce applications are all strategically deployed as tactics to harass the complainant by the oppressors who are powerful and can exploit resources. Applications are filed to delay the matter with the sole aim of pressuring woman to give up the litigation. Implicating the complainant and her family in false cases is also one of the techniques deployed besides blaming the victim. The purpose is to forcefully negotiate the non-compoundable. Proceedings are quashed whereby the complainant is compelled to make a statement that all her grievances are resolved or amicably settled, and acquittal is sought on the grounds that the complainant has turned 'hostile', thus the case should be closed. The courts, police and society all compel women to give up the path of litigation and discourage their attempts to seek justice.

The state sanctions the violence by focusing on settlement

Bargaining and compromise as the amicable resolution of disputes are not unique processes that are applied to cases in the domain of family law; rather, mediation is considered a process by which litigants may negotiate their claims. Overburdened courts are constantly finding ways to weave the notion of bargaining into the formal court structures to the extent that the formal increasingly resembles the informal. Yet under no other branch of law does the process of bargaining become an integral part of statutory law itself as it does in family law. It is assumed that mediation may "offer a way around the oppressive trials, interminable delays, and fuzzy legal language, setting up women as empowered agents in control of their narratives, and transforming legal authority".[38] Therefore, while adjudicating the so-called 'family matters', stress is laid on 'saving the family' as an institution, rather than ensuring justice for the victims or penalizing the perpetrator of the crime. The state thus grants immunity to the perpetrator of violence while legitimizing and sanctioning violence under the guise of settlement.

"Matrimonial dispute" treatment of domestic violence assumes that both accused and victims are on an equal footing; thus, this approach overlooks the structural factors surrounding an inegalitarian marital relationship while also undermining the seriousness of the violence. Equating the dynamics involved in 'dispute' with that of 'violence' in itself is an injustice to survivors. In a society where gender discrimination prevails everywhere, inside the home, in public places, inside the courtrooms and at workplaces, it is difficult for a woman to raise her voice. Hence, voicing the concerns adds to the misery of women rather than bailing them out. As mentioned earlier, Laura Nader[39] has used the phrase "coercive harmony" to describe the use of mediation in a marriage that is fraught with the predominant question of power, property and violence.

As the *Khap Panchayats* issue *diktats*, similarly, the formal, informal or quasi-judicial fora force women to see a violent marriage as a lovable zone and compel them to adjust to it. At each subsequent stage of the criminal justice system – from pre-litigation to trial – the pressure is put on women to settle the case. In cases where the trial continues, the complainant is compelled to give up the battle because of reasons like paucity of funds, delay and complications in the system, lack of support and so on.

These procedures of pressuring the complainants using undue force and coercion to intimate them against pursuing their cases is unlawful. Often, women end up paying the high cost of such repressive notions. Mohini (35) revealed the manner in which she was pressured to compromise.

> My parents refused to support me. They insisted that marriage is the destiny for any woman. My mother herself has faced violence on daily

> basis. For them, violence is regular wear and tears of the relationship and I should learn to adjust. Even when I showed them my scars, they said that things will settle gradually. My parents-in-law suggested that once the child will be born then it will be ok. I tolerated everything, then my daughter was born. He abused me more. Then, the court forced me to give him a chance. And then when I took up a job, he assaulted me more. He wanted my salary but accused me of being a woman of loose character. Nobody has ever told him to stop beating me. I thought that at least the court will understand my situation; however, even the judge asked me to "settle the matter".
>
> (2014)

Here, the barbaric history of serious assault is overlooked by the court, family and other institutions while pushing the women to adjust. Within the patriarchal society, the pressure to save a marriage does not operate upon the husband in same way as it does upon the wife. What is ignored in this presumption is that the purpose of law is to correct the 'wrong' and to 'fix' whatever is not befitting the definition of 'normal' in the matrimonial relationship.

Negotiations occupy a central space within the laws dealing with the 'dispute' within the family. During these negotiations, what is negotiated is not the facts or the law, but rather intense social and emotional pressure is being laid on women to ignore the violence. Conciliation is encouraged more in matters where children are involved, without recognizing the fact that batterers use children as pawns in domestic violence cases. Also, the argument of the economic needs of the survivor and her children is deployed to coerce the complainant to give up the legal battle. Utilizing the fact of economic dependency of a woman to deny the seriousness of an offense amounts to a mockery of the law. The idea of 'protection' within marriage erases the concept of justice and ignores the oppressive aspects and structural vulnerabilities within the relationship. The reason relating to the 'needs' of the survivors cannot be used to detract from the course of litigation merely because the crime happened inside a household.

The majority of participants who opted to go back to the violent situation after counseling reported that it proves to be a futile decision. Instead, the violence further escalated and the perpetrator became more aggressive. I met Jyoti (32) in Patiala House Court complex. She is educated up to class 10 and is a homemaker. She was compelled to go back to the violent situation and was waiting to sign her mutual agreement. According to her,

> Even earlier, I went back to my marital house as per the directions of the court. The judge assured that my case will remain open and I can come back if required. On her assurance and for the sake of children, I went back. For three days things were ok, but that night he becomes more violent, he threatened me that if I go out, he will kill me. He beat me blue and black and this time more on my neck and head, and repeatedly

> told me that 'go now, what proof you had that I had hit you?' Nobody intervened thinking that it is a usual story. He is supposed to provide me money, and if the court put him inside the jail who will give me food? Once the court has fixed maintenance, but he has not paid me single penny then. My brothers have refused to take me and my kids back. Running around in the court is difficult. So, I thought, even if he beats, at least my kids will have a roof over their head. They will not die of hunger.

It is not only the fear, threat or intimidation by her violent husband that prevented Jyoti from raising her voice again, it is the fear of losing economic security. After a year and a half since filing the complaint and after numerous counseling sessions, she understood that to feed her children, she needs financial support, which is not available outside marriage. Thus, counseling acted like a double-edged sword in this case. First, it prevented her from raising her voice and second, she understood that nobody will rescue her multiple times, as no one will take on the burden of feeding her and her children. In the absence of any economic support being assured, Jyoti realized that there is no fallback or any other viable option to rely on, and therefore according to her, "it is better to 'compromise' and accept violence". In fact, for many women like Jyoti, family does not represent a safe and protective unit. Rather, it reinforces wider patterns of gender discrimination and legitimizes violence as a method of subjugating women. Women negotiated their right to safety for their economic necessity because no other options are made available outside the institution of marriage. For those who are struggling to merely survive, their decisions are centered around managing their lives in material terms. It is not that the state lacks the resources to help women in need; rather, it is through sheer lack of will that women are denied resources, support or facilities; perhaps enabling women who raise their voices implies strengthening the struggle against patriarchy.

Legal remedies are inadequate

Violence is ruthless, but remedies in law are limited in scope. Courts further interpret these reliefs in a constricted manner and are reluctant to support complainants. Women who engage with the legal system confront stubborn patriarchy yet the tedious bureaucratic apparatus does not lend them support. Rather, it adds insult to the injury. Yet "people bargain in the shadow of the law, shaping it to their end and building new legal cultures".[40] This is because of their sheer grit and resistance that these women challenged their violent husbands in the courts. The efficacy of the law is determined because of the persistence of litigants to go through the obstacles put forward by the system and not on the benevolence of those who created it or are implementing the laws.

These women challenged the patriarchy, expecting that they may get justice and seeking different legal remedies. Not all have filed criminal complaints. The majority just wished for the violence to stop. Therefore, they sought protection orders. Maintenance orders were sought in two-thirds of cases, compensation orders in two-fifths of cases and residence orders in one-sixth of cases. Custody orders were sought in one-fifth of cases. In almost all cases, more than one relief has been sought. Even to reside in a shared household in a situation of domestic violence, one requires multiple forms of protection to lead a violence-free life. Therefore, in cases where a woman files application for a residence order, she may also apply simultaneously for the protection order in case she stays in the shared household where the perpetrator of violence is also staying. Interim relief is sought in three-fifth of cases, but only rarely have applicants received a favorable order. Rather, these applications have been pending for more than six months in two-fifths of cases. At times, the interim application took years, thus making a mockery of the intent of the term 'interim'. This delay in adjudication of interim relief applications indicates the apathetic and insensitive approach of the courts. In cases where women have sought multiple reliefs, this does not imply that she has been granted any of them. It is deduced that not many have been able to get the reliefs they have demanded.

Legal remedies for domestic violence are short term

Under the PWDVA, a complainant may file an application to obtain several orders depending on her facts and circumstances. However, orders passed under this law are short term until the case is settled. Even in those cases where the orders have been passed, execution is often not carried out easily. For instance, in the case of Vandana (37), the residence order and protection order were both passed in her favor after a long battle of eight years. However, the house is in the name of her mother-in-law, who is doing "every possible thing" to evict her such as "not allowing her to enter the kitchen to cook food, not allowing her to do her laundry, abusing her verbally, locking the door of the house thus restricting her mobility", and it is becoming difficult to execute the orders passed by the court. Her husband reportedly has shown that he had incurred loss in his business and is dependent on his parents. Vandana confided that her parents are in Kanpur residing with her brother and therefore she has decided to not go back. Similarly, Kalpana (41) recalled

> It was a love marriage. We were in same college. But later I realized that it was a huge blunder. Problems started within three months after marriage. I tolerated for years to save our relationship and underwent three miscarriages and two abortions. A son born after three years of marriage died within two months because he had congenital abnormality

> and they blamed me. It was the third day after my son has died, my mother-in-law taunted me for the ills. It is not that this has happened the first time. But I was under depression and argued back. He slapped me in front of everyone and asked me to leave his house. . . . 'His house' . . . I have given my everything and this is the reward I got. I went to my sister's place and applied for a job. I got an offer to work as a teacher but I am not in mental state where I can focus after all that is happening. (2014)

The court has ordered Rs 6000/ per month as maintenance, but her husband has filed an appeal against this order. "It took years to get those orders and still I am struggling. Every time the judge asked me that I should settle but I don't know what to do? I have filed FIR too, but nothing much has happened there. He got bail the same day". Also, her husband, in this case, has filed an application for divorce, and she is running around in different courts. "This stress of litigation is killing. Mediation happened many times at the instance of courts but failed", she added. The domestic violence law provides for short-term relief. But in this case, the complainant is looking for long-term possible solutions. The law is not helping this complainant, perhaps because neither the criminal nor the civil law pertaining to domestic violence provide long-lasting solutions for the survivors.

Are protection orders sufficient enough to protect women?

Protection orders are prohibitory in nature where the purpose is to protect women or their children from further acts of violence. It is not retrospective and does not penalize the perpetrator for his past actions. Yet the execution or monitoring of protection orders is rarely done, as is evident from Jyoti's case mentioned earlier. The practical difficulties in protecting women include not only the survivor's situation but also the approach and attitude of law enforcement agencies, including the police as well as POs. In the present work it is observed that first, obtaining such orders is a difficult and a time-consuming process and second, these orders are frequently breached. Complaining to police has not helped in any manner, reported the majority of informants. Sadhna (33) shared

> I went back to the matrimonial house again thinking that there will be no violence. However, this time he (the husband) intimidated me and threatened me and that night he put a knife on my child's throat and said that he would kill him if I raise my voice. Every day I cannot go to the court. The day when I went to the PO's office, she told me that I can live separately from him. But we are living on rent here. Who will pay the rent for the separate house? My brother gave me some money so I manage to run the household. Will this drunkard pay anything then if he is not paying for the food for his kids now?

The protection order passed in this case becomes irrelevant, as the informant has not been able to protect herself and her kids. The police didn't help her. In Sushila's (39) case, she applied for a protection order as the case involves serious allegations of assault. She submitted the medical report and alleged that her left hand was fractured and she got several stitches in her lower abdomen. The applicant has a long history of physical assaults in seven years of marriage but alleged that over the last few months the violence had intensified in frequency as well as in its seriousness. She complained of strangulation, threats to kill and hitting their son. Sushila stated that she could no longer cope with his behavior and alleged that her son had become fearful of his father. The respondent denied these allegations in the court. The magistrate hearing the case said that 'you two need counselling and help with your marriage'. Thus, the court upheld the husband's right of chastisement while the serious problem of violence is condensed and the man is easily allowed to escape his liability. The husband is treated as the master, the lord, while the victim is compelled to adjust by the court.

Hence, it may be inferred that the courts are not issuing protection orders easily and second, in cases where such orders have been issued, these are not helping the women because of various reasons. The courts do not take the issue of providing protection to women seriously. Even in cases where women do submit the required evidence in the form of medical records, the courts ignore the gravity of the crime. In another courtroom, a magistrate shouted at a survivor who was vocal about her safety during mediation proceedings in the courtroom, "You are saying that he has physically assaulted you and he is refusing. How can the court believe you without any evidence?" A woman accompanying the survivor retorted, "But she was assaulted badly, therefore she complained. Should she wait till he breaks her body? Her soul will come to ask for justice then (In whispering tone)". The lawyer tried to intervene, but the magistrate didn't pay heed and scolded the woman for being disrespectful. These incidences show the insensitivity of the courts towards the survivors of violence.

Right to reside in the shared household

Section 17 of the PWDVA provides for the right to reside in a shared household. The right to residence does not create any substantive rights, but merely protects the right of the survivor to stay in her matrimonial home without any fear of eviction unless warranted by the law. However, the present study shows that except for a few, not many survivors could obtain the benefits under this provision.

Seema (26), a home maker married four years ago to a businessman, stayed in a joint family along with her parents-in-laws and his siblings. After her abortion within 11 months of marriage, she put on weight and felt that since then his behavior changed. Even her parents-in-law started behaving differently. Her mother-in-law is now encouraging her husband to marry someone else. She has been thrown out of the house several times and went to her brother's house. Her three brothers are married and are not interested in her painful life. The intervention of community leaders failed; then her brother helped her to contact a lawyer. Meanwhile, guided by the fear that she may file a case under Section 498A, her parents-in-law started living separately two lanes over while asserting that they have no connection with their son or his wife. Although in lieu of monthly maintenance of Rs 6000/ fixed by the court, her husband has paid a total of Rs 20,000/ once only in two years since the case has been registered, all has been spent on bills and repairs. Her monthly ration and grocery bill are being paid by her brother. Her mother-in-law has filed an eviction suit against Seema, asking her to vacate the house. After numerous counseling sessions, the judge suggested her to go to a rented accommodation where her husband may pay the rent. But Seema is apprehensive, as he is not paying maintenance, so he will not pay for the rent too, and then she will be left with no home. The right to reside has helped her for the past two years, as she is staying alone in her matrimonial home. She is afraid that this will not continue for long, as the eviction suit may be decided against her. Meanwhile, her husband has also filed an appeal against the maintenance order passed by the court. The judge in the appellate court has called both the parties for counselling and urged them to settle the matter. Her husband remained adamant that he will not stay with her, while she persisted that she is not ready for divorce. However, when this interview was conducted, she was running around in courts attending several proceedings in various courts where cases have been filed for maintenance, appeal against the maintenance order, her eviction from the shared household and the one filed under Section 498A.

For the survivor of violence, the right to reside in the shared household leads to the situation where she is compelled to stay under the same roof with the abuser. Astha (25), a graduate who got married three years ago, is now regretting her decision.

> He started physical abuse within three months of marriage. I do not want to involve my parents as they are living in Bangalore and my father is a cancer patient. I tolerated. He then started bringing another woman to our house. He introduced her as one of his colleagues. Initially, she stayed for few days in our house, then she became an unwanted guest, after two months or so, they both connive together and forced me to leave the house. In desperation, I requested a friend of mine to help me who took me to a lawyer. After, four years, the court ordered that I have a right to stay in that house. He has filed an appeal against that order. Now, even I don't want to get into that house, even if she (the other woman) is not there. What is a guarantee that he will not repeat the same thing again? That house haunts me.

The law acted as a 'subversive site' where the concept of the 'right to reside' fails to consider the broader framework of gender inequality within the realm of marital entitlements. Technicalities within the system often work against women, and at times, even the verdicts in their favor are not implemented because of biases inherent within the system. For instance, Nimmi (26) said,

> I was thrown out of the house. It is a joint family. My mother-in-law does not want me to stay because she wanted my husband to marry another girl. She used to beat me with a rod. The other day she threw a hot utensil on me and I got burned (showed a burn mark on her face). The court said that I should go back. How can I? He is mama's boy. Who will save me if she [encourages] him?

In the absence of quality welfare services, compelling a woman to stay in an abusive household is not a feasible means of protecting the victim from violence. This provision therefore accords a dubious status to the law, and a cursory reading of the 'right to reside' appears anachronistic. The PWDVA does not offer any viable long-term solution. The law does not provide any substantial right to a married woman. It narrowly focuses on women's rights within the matrix of *maika* and *sasural* network and does not challenge the oppression of women within marriage. The law does not mandate the provision of shelter homes though most of the POs and activists interviewed reinforced that shelter homes are urgently required.

Section 19 of the PWDVA states that the magistrate is empowered to restrain the respondent from dispossessing or disturbing the possessions of the aggrieved person or directing him to remove himself and restraining him from entering the shared household or directing the respondent to secure alternative arrangements for the aggrieved person. However, in practice, this is not happening. Laxmi (29), a graduate hailing from Kanpur, married Abhay (32), an insurance agent from Meerut, and they settled in Delhi for the past three years. It was a love marriage. Within a year, Abhay started beating her on one pretext or the other. She wanted to go back to her parents' house but they refused to accept her back. Abhay started drinking daily and left his job. He stopped paying rent or bills and stopped coming home for days at a time. The torture was becoming worse day by day. A neighbor took her to an NGO. However, it demanded money. Meanwhile Laxmi got a job as a private teacher but the salary was not enough. After running around for three years, the court ordered maintenance and directed Abhay to pay rent. Initially, with reluctance and under pressure, he paid money for three months. But later, when he stopped paying rent, the owner asked Laxmi to vacate the house. According to her,

> In spite of running around in the court I have got nothing. The court said he will pay rent. But now it is not taking any action against him. I repent for marrying him. For loving him, I was terribly abused, (showed scars of burns) for trusting him, I lost the support from my natal family and

> became lonely, for sacrificing all for him, I am now on the streets. So much price to pay for just one mistake called love.
>
> (2014)

For Laxmi, 'love is a mistake' she has committed. Orders under Section 19 could not work in this case, as the respondent has stopped paying rent and the landlord is not allowing her to stay. The law does not consider situations where, despite hassles, the system of an alternative arrangement cannot work. There are multiple other similar cases where the right to reside is not working for women despite obtaining favorable court orders. The law overlooks the social realities and dynamics of situations of domestic violence. In terms of the right to residence, often the provision is defeated because there are various difficulties that the litigants have to undergo, even including the execution of the orders.

Munni (36) has a husband who had a clothes shop in Narela. He is alcoholic and used to beat her routinely. Her two daughters died at the early ages of seven and ten, and her son got pneumonia when he was eight. She asked money from her husband for the son's treatment. He refused. She borrowed money from her neighbors. Her husband got angry and beat her black and blue and accused her of having an affair. Meanwhile, the son died, and Munni went into a depression. But this did not prevent her husband from inflicting violence. He tried to throttle her neck. Her husband accused Munni of "killing her son as she was spending more time making friends". Fed up, she decided to take action as "he was becoming more violent day by day". She filed an FIR and also an application under the PWDVA for maintenance. Her husband, in order to counter her complaint, filed a divorce application alleging that "she is a characterless" woman. She took a job as a sweeper in a private school. The matter continued in the courts for eight years, during which time a 'settlement' was worked out. After interventions by the court, her husband submitted papers saying that she can sell the house. Now, Munni has shown the papers to various property dealers, who are saying that papers are incomplete and fake so nothing can be done. In the court, when she raised this issue, the magistrate asked her if she is willing to take money in lieu of her share of the house. She refused. According to her, "why don't he leave that house. It belongs to my children. I fought the long battle because it is their memory which gave me strength". The law does not address these fine nuances; rather, it provides for rigid solutions. The court has failed to see her drunkard husband as a vile man who has been creating troubles for her. Rather than penalizing the troublemaker, the court is pushing the woman to accept whatever is being offered.

Monetary orders: are they really helping women?

Maintenance orders protect survivors from destitution and vagaries. It is a pressing economic necessity for a woman who walks out of a violent relationship. The law imposes a duty on a man to pay maintenance. A husband sees this as a burden and resents paying alimony to an estranged wife. The experiences of women reveal that once a complaint is filed, the property, if it is in the name of the husband, is transferred to the name of his relatives, the valuables are taken away and any bank accounts or nominations in any financial matters are reassigned to deprive women of their rights. Even the children are not spared; their school fees or related expenses are denied. Violent husbands, if in private jobs, business or are self-employed, deploy all possible tactics to hide their real incomes and suddenly become 'unemployed' with no or little earning to avoid paying any maintenance. The courts frequently turn a blind eye to such manipulative strategies while deciding the amount of maintenance and ask complainants to provide evidence of income of their self and their husband. Women are frequently in no position to provide proof of a husband's income or assets he is holding. More specifically, if he is in private job or is self-employed, the veracity of his income certificate cannot be verified. For instance, Dipti (32), a graduate and a mother of a 13-year-old son, claimed that

> My husband is an IT professional having his own business. He is earning more than a lakh per month. After marriage, I resigned because the office was far and my mother-in-law was not keeping well. Now, the advocate asked me to get the proof of his income. It is difficult to get details of his actual earnings. The court has asked him to pay 6000/ for my son. He has not paid a single penny. For me, it is not easy to get another job.
>
> (2013)

The courts ignored the situational context while adjudicating the application for maintenance. Here, Dipti had to leave her job to take care of her family. Now, after years of being out of the job market, finding another job is tough for her. The husband in this case has not submitted the correct details of his actual income and pleaded that Dipti has not taken care of the family and is not a "good mother" and that she is an educated woman and is capable of earning on her own. The court has not considered all these details while calculating the amount. Alimony settlements are frequently made under conditions of compliance to social norms of being a 'good' wife.[41] Often, the lawyers invoke the stereotype of bad wives and construe women who demand maintenance as a 'parasite living on the expenses incurred by decent men', without realizing the fact that the state does not offer any real economic or material alternative.[42] Further, maintenance is not paid for years despite the court's order. "He is into business. He often visits Dubai and other places and earning a lot but does not want to give a single penny for his kid. When the court ordered him to pay 6000 Rs, he said that he is not earning", shared Huma (28), who has a three-year-old daughter. Many women who have got maintenance orders complained that it is not easier to get money despite this. The law ignores the structural and gendered division of labor between a man and a woman within a family and overlooks the fact that women are at disadvantageous position in the labor market, particularly when they have spent a portion of their life caring for children, managing the household and looking after the family.

Custody orders: children are not pawns

The issue of child custody is a double-edged sword. The operation of matrimonial law reveals that often children are used as an instrument to harass woman. When abusers find that they no longer can control the victim through physical violence or emotional control, they use the legal system to harass the victim. Depriving a woman of the custody of her children is a usual practice deployed to emotionally abuse her. Even if women obtain immediate custody, they are made to run around the courts under laws such as the Guardianship Act, or the lawyers on the behalf of the husband file the application for visitation.

Women and children are put at risk because of visitation rights being imposed without arranging for safety. Abusive men often use visitation as an opportunity to intimidate and threaten women. Frequently, it is not for the love or the interest of the children that they want visitation; rather, the abuser utilizes the custody provisions as a pawn in the battle to coercively control, pressure and harass the mothers. Fathers who abuse their wives also commit violence against children. The courts ignore this aspect while adjudicating the custody applications. The court also utilizes the parameters of mothers being 'good' or 'bad'; however, the same lens is not applied to fathers while adjudicating the applications. The law uses the 'welfare principle' narrowly when deciding custody applications.[43]

Economic security or the needs of the child or the woman are intermeshed while the system focuses simultaneously on marriage, parenthood and maintenance while ignoring the welfare and protection of the mother and the child. Asha (29) married Raju a year and half ago. Asha has graduated, and Raju is a government employee. The couple lives in Najafgarh in a joint family arrangement. Initially, Asha reported that she had two abortions because her mother-in-law insisted that "it should be the boy". She has been taken to astrologers and has been forced to observe various rituals. She said

> My mother-in-law and sister-in-law have created many problems in my life. They used to beat me and forcefully and took away my twins. My mother-in-law initially took away my son and insisted that it should be given to my sister-in-law in adoption. When I refused a big fight took place immediately after delivery. My husband obeyed his mother blindly and took both babies from the hospital without the permission of the doctor and threatened me not to enter the house. I therefore contacted the lawyer. During mediation, he claimed that I am not taking care of

> the children because 'I wanted to enjoy freedom'. Even in the appeal, the matter couldn't be sorted out. If I am interested in my freedom as he claimed than why would I have gone through the pain of childbirth? My mother-in-law is feeding '*dabbe ka doodh*'[44] to the kids. It is all because of their ego and their greed, me and my kids are suffering.

The custody battle is deployed to use children as a pawn to uphold the ego of the powerful party. When Asha went to her matrimonial house to claim her babies, they threw her out of the house. Her parents pleaded with her in-laws but in turn were humiliated. It was then that the FIR was filed and both the families were called to the police station. However, no agreement could be worked out. Her parents then hired a lawyer, who filed a custody application under the PWDVA. The magistrate, after counseling, ordered that custody of the twins to be given to Asha, but her husband filed an appeal before the High Court. Her role as a mother and a wife was questioned in the court. She was portrayed as a bad mother unwilling to take care of her kids. The court, without looking into the veracity of the claim made by the husband, admonished her. The cruelty committed by the husband and his family was not considered while adjudicating her claim. The role of the man as a father and as a husband was not highlighted during the process, and the question of coercive demand remained hidden under the guise of the women's role as a mother. When the interview was conducted, Asha said that the judge in the High Court, after listening to both the parties in her chamber, has ordered in her favor; however, her husband has again filed another application for revision in the High Court. Asha was worried about her babies.

Relationship between the nature of violence and relief available

Domestic violence is a complex and multidimensional issue and involves different elements. The PWDVA categorizes domestic violence as physical abuse, sexual abuse, verbal and emotional abuse and economic abuse. Relief provided under PWDVA is limited to protection orders, monetary orders, residence orders, custody orders, compensation orders, interim relief and ex parte orders. These remedies are of temporary nature until a woman decides what to do with her life. The law does not offer long-term solutions to survivors. No action is taken against the perpetrator for the violence he has committed in case a woman decides to not to file a criminal complaint. Also, punishment or reliefs ordered are not in proportion to the injury women suffer for years.

Further, women face multitude forms of violence, and for many forms of violence no remedy has been made available under the law. For instance, for verbal and emotional violence such as name calling, threatening, insulting, demeaning or humiliating repeatedly, there is no proportionate relief that is available. Most of these acts are considered routine mundane violence, while the cumulative results of such continuous day-to-day violence is not considered by the law. Marital rape is another issue that needs to be examined. Also, for violence such as putting restrictions on the mobility of women; not allowing her to meet her parents; asking her to do too much work; denial of reproductive rights or situations where a woman is forced to undergo abortions, miscarriages or other forms of violence that deprive her of her dignity, no remedy has been made available under the domestic violence law. The law tends to minimize and trivialize the violence.

The law does not see domestic abuse as a continuous form of violence. It ignores the terror, control and fear of the threat of violence that is being created in between the episodes of abuses. It also ignores the role played by other family members in inflicting violence on women. In light of the continuity of intense violence, it is suggested that the battered woman syndrome model conceptualized and applied in West may be re-examined and reframed in the Indian context, where women undergo continuous torture over a long period, where the relationship between the parties is iniquitous and where escape from violence seems impossible because no other form of support is made available outside the relationship.[45]

Non-compliance of orders

The lengthy and expensive court process creates problems for women who are already facing problems in their lives ranging from managing the kids, to finding a job, to worrying about the expenses and keeping a roof over one's head while going through the recovery phase. Moreover, despite positive verdicts, the implementation of the verdict appears to be a tremendously complicated process. Two-thirds of informants claimed that favorable directions have been pronounced by the courts but were challenged by the other party. Also, the maintenance orders are mostly not complied with, and often women have to run around and seek alimony for themselves and their children. Three-fourths of participants recalled that years have passed since the maintenance orders were issued by the courts, yet they have not been complied with. Says one lawyer:

> For women recovering maintenance is difficult. Firstly, they have to bring proofs of husband's income and then later in execution it is difficult to attach property because meanwhile the long process adopted by the courts, husbands strategically maneuver all their assets in the name of other family members.

Also, women hardly have the resources to run around. In cases where they manage to get favorable custody orders, their husbands file applications under the personal laws to delay the claim. Compliance with the residence order often becomes difficult due to various reasons. Bina (27), living in shared household, said,

> My mother-in-law has filed a case saying that this house belongs to her. The court asked me to live separately as he (the husband) will pay the rent, but he is not paying maintenance even after the court' order, will he pay rent? Why the court is not putting him behind the bar for not obeying the orders? I will be on street. The court is asking for compromise and when he refused to stay with me, the judge said that you take some money and settle. How can I do that? Who will marry me?
>
> (2014)

Execution applications made by the complainant's lawyers to execute the court orders do not yield quick positive results. A decision on an execution application takes time. For many survivors, the sluggish implementation of court orders and long battles are discouraging. Data on the numbers of appeals and execution applications filed in the lower courts are not available separately, which could have provided insight into the cases in which executions are pending and appeals have been filed against these orders.

Delay in adjudicating the cases

A woman who faced violence knocks on the door of the court, expecting that her complaint will be resolved quickly. Speedy relief is important in these cases because women are in dire need of support. However, the reality is different. The system follows its own pace and is marred with technicalities. In the cases filed under 498A, once the FIR is registered, years go into recording statements, cross-examination of parties and witnesses, examining evidence and delivering orders. The formal law gets stymied if the complainant does not come with the requisite proof. Accused persons are either not arrested or are released instantly on bail. Besides counseling, multiple litigation, combined with the number of applications being filed, play a significant role in deferring the proceedings. Delay tactics are being deployed by the parties who possess power in terms of money and resources to file appeals against orders passed by the lower courts. This delay compels complainants to withdraw the case or compromise with the perpetrator of the violence. Elsewhere, Schulhofer[46] noted, "Criminal law is – and has been for centuries – a system of rules conceived and enforced by men, for men and against men". This holds true here too. Criminal law does not support battered wives.

Similarly, the PWDVA is structured around timelines. Timelines are important because complainants in violent situations require immediate help. However, none of the informants contacted could get relief within the prescribed period of 60 days. Many cases have been pending for years. "Often notices are returned un-served, correct address or whereabouts of respondents could not be located, and this happens in number of cases", reported a PO. "Delay happens because courts are overburdened, a court has to hear 50 to 60 matters or sometimes more, in a day. Uncertainty is a part of the system", explained a lawyer. In one-tenth of cases, either the notice has not been served or cases have been pending for more than a year where the respondent has not even turned up and the aggrieved person is getting 'dates'. Anjana (26) stated, "It 'is frustrating. I took up a job but then every other day I have to take leave to come to the court. It is not an easy task . . . leaving my 3-year-old child." In another case, the litigant said that her husband went to his native place and died there before the notice could be served. She has been waiting for the court to help her to get his death certificate.

Many lawyers shared that the time taken is too long even to get interim reliefs. In Munni's case described earlier, the 'settlement' agreed to after eight long years of litigation stated that the matrimonial house be sold and the amount received to be equally shared between the parties; however, clever tactics have been used by her husband, as he produced papers that are not in order. Munni claims that she has been running around showing papers to property dealers, but they stated that those are incomplete. Her husband cunningly deprived her of her share of the house, and after creating much commotion she was offered a 'pittance' in lieu of this.

Other challenges women face in the courts

About two-thirds of women said that they could not follow the court proceedings. Miscommunication or non-communication between the lawyer, court and complainant are also issues that have been raised. Sunita (31), who has been coming to the court for past five months, finds it difficult to follow the proceedings. She shared that "what is happening around I don't know, whatever the lawyer says I do that. My brother talks to the lawyer. If he asks me to sign, I put my thumb print". The non-availability of shelter homes as well as earning opportunities are the gaps within the system. Some women may have achieved small gains by stumbling upon a compromise or a settlement. The process of litigation is not only protracted and expensive but it is also unpredictable in terms of.

Further, the false narratives of the law being misused by women is propagated. Such opinions are not substantiated by research, fact or data, yet they guide the process of implementing the law. Such myths of false complaints make access to justice tough for survivors. Women claiming action against the perpetrator are projected as 'bad' and vengeful who use law to settle the score. Such fables are projected without considering the realities. This perceived notion of women making false claims has resulted in legal requirements for the corroboration of women's accounts of violence. Relatives of the husband who are allegedly the party to the crime are not served notice because they are not residing in the shared household and because of widespread incorrect notions that women falsely rope in the relatives of husbands. For instance, Aanchal (31) alleged that

> the aunt of my husband used to come every day to my matrimonial house and used to make negative comments about me. She also used to instigate my mother-in-law saying that I am not good looking and I have got less dowry and that she could find a better match for my husband. But the judge said that as she was not residing in the shared household she should not be implicated and the court has refused to serve her notice.

Therefore, even before the trial takes place, those relatives of the husbands who may have a role in the crime are painted as innocent by the courts. Domestic violence law was enacted for the purpose of providing protection to women who have been facing abuse. Nevertheless, the manner in which these provisions have been interpreted and implemented by the courts indicates that the courts are not protecting the 'rights of women'; rather, they work on the premise to 'save the family' while negating the intent of the law. Therefore, there is a need to re-examine the technicalities, procedures and interpretation of law with the gender lens.

Impact of litigation on women

The majority of women claimed that their life has become worse after marriage and consequent litigation. They felt disappointed by the delay in the court proceedings. For a large number of women, their socio-economic position has become worse. An inability to get maintenance orders executed has pushed many into poverty. Many reported difficulties in managing their self and children, paying lawyers' fees, litigation cost, etc. Problems multiply when a woman herself is not earning, because in most of the maintenance cases, husbands evade the court's directions. She therefore has to depend on her natal family. Two-thirds of married women are dependent on their parents or siblings for their daily sustenance. Those who have jobs claimed that it is becoming difficult for them to continue because handling court cases, children and stress together without support is difficult. Further, for the survivors, the path to resistance becomes complicated because of the stress of surviving within the given social realities, coping with the demands and the pressure to compromise the case and struggling with the legal complications besides facing financial difficulties.

Almost all participants felt that they have been fighting lonely battles. The culture of shame is used to socially pressure women while stigmatizing them. Women are compelled to deals with compulsions to remarry; dealing with gossip and rumors within extended families is taking a toll, according to many survivors. The culture of violence is deeply entrenched such that society, instead of blaming the perpetrators of violence, victimize women.

Those who are compelled to stay on their own shared that it is not easy for them to get an accommodation because society denounces lone women who live independently. Four out of five claim that they are in a state where they cannot think clearly of their present or future. They expressed feelings of anger, helplessness, loss, despair, injustice and fear; nonetheless, they manage to carve a niche while negotiating for violence.

For a layperson, understanding legal nuances is not an easy task – even more so when the law is operated by male ideology and discriminates against women. On the chance to rethink the decision, two-thirds of women said that they would have filed the case even if they were facing difficulties or financial hardships and other problems. One of the complainants, while expressing her anger and frustration, said, "I have been running from pillar to post in the courts for years, I got frustrated. But Karma is cyclic. He (the husband) was unfair to me but now he got cancer a few days back" (2015).

Grouped with the ordeal of social apathy, discrimination and neglect, the chronicles of women's sufferings weave a rich tapestry of patriarchy, violence and abuse of power, yet each woman is negotiating in her unique way to collect the pieces of her life. Experiences show that there is a huge gap and mismatch of expectations between what women want and what the state offers and in the manner in which the law is operationalized. Various other studies have substantiated this fact.[47] Thus, there is a need to reform the arena of martial regulation along with the response of its stakeholders.

It may be concluded that law, in itself, could not alter structural inequalities. The shift in the attitude, approach and style of the functioning of the courts is essential. There is a huge gap between the manner in which those who enforce the law implement the law and the way in which women experience violence. Traditional myths guide the legal culture. Women's narratives of violence are filtered through the lens of an entrenched patriarchy. The courtrooms, as a symbol of authority, defend the values of male supremacy, legitimate inequalities and reinforce regressive norms while shielding the resourceful perpetrators, rather than assisting the oppressed women. These widespread, deeply embedded stereotypes and biased attitudes, in addition to narrow, cynical interpretations of law, result in underuse of domestic law. This needs to be addressed while dealing with larger structural issues. Skepticism persists because those who enforce the law pay lip services to the women's questions without really shaking the core of the patriarchy.[48]

However, those on the margins with their conviction in the values of democracy, justice and the rule of law, have been persistently shaking the system. Through individual actions, the marginalized are challenging the power structure and are compelling the state to make a social and political transformation at a larger level. Women, with their sheer will and conviction, are marching ahead to claim their right to lead a violence-free life. They are challenging the powerful institutions to assert their rights while claiming that the constitution, the law and the courtrooms do not belong to a handful of judges or lawyers, but belong to the people – the women, poor and marginalized. The system is powerful, but people are more powerful than the system. The courts in several cases have handed down positive decisions because of the sheer will power of those who persisted and fought relentlessly, shaking the rigid system. Women are being victimized and discriminated against, yet they are contesting their claims and fighting hard battles inside and outside the courtrooms to carve a path to justice for themselves and for others. What is required is the radical interpretation and implementation of constitutional values to support the claims of those who are contesting from the position of marginality.

Summary

This chapter examines the operation of the law through the experiences of women as complainants and litigants. It observes that although the law tries to bring order in the family, it itself has been mediated by and enmeshed in a complex cultural framework of saving families rather than protecting the rights and dignity of women as citizens. The constitution guarantees equality; however, the norms of sexual equality are not internalized by those who enforce the law.

Notes

1 MacKinnon Catherine A (1991) Reflections on Sex Equality Under Law, *Yale Law Journal*, 100 (5) 1281–321
2 Robinson Nick (2013) The Indian Supreme Court and Its Benches, *The Seminar*, 642, http://india-seminar.com/2013/642/642_nick_robinson.htm
3 Stanko Elizabeth A (1985) *Intimate Intrusions: Women's Experience of Male Violence*, Routledge, London
4 Friedman Lawrence (1994) Is There a Modern Legal Culture? *Ratio Juris* 7 (117) 130
5 Hunter Rosemary (2006) Narratives of Domestic Violence, *Sydney Law Review*, 28 (4) 733 has also arrived at a similar conclusion.
6 Karlekar M (1998) Domestic Violence, *Economic and Political Weekly*, XXXIII (27)
7 Arnesh Kumar vs State of Bihar supra
8 Karlekar M (1995) *No Safe Spaces, Report of a Workshop on Violence Against Women*, March 27–28, CWDS, New Delhi
9 Supra
10 Trivedi PK and Singh S (2014) Fallacies of a Supreme Court Judgement: Section 498A and Dynamics of Acquittal, *EPW*, XLIX (52) 90–97
11 Items are kept in the custody of police and are returned to the owner after verification and other procedures.
12 Santosh Bakshi vs State of Punjab AIR 2014 SC 2966
13 Cri App. No. 06/14 Delhi District Court, Karkardooma
14 Sen Rukmini (2010) Women's Subjectivities of Suffering and Legal Rhetoric on Domestic Violence: Fissure in Two Discourses, *Indian Journal of Gender Studies*, 17 (3) 375–401
15 Bacchi, CL (2006) *Women, Policy, and Politics: The Construction of Policy Problems*, Sage, London

16 Rajdeep vs Gurmeet Singh Mat App FC 4/2013 decided on 19.2.2016, p. 2
17 Madhukalya Amrita (2015) Domestic Violence Act: Ten Years on, Women Yet to See the Promised Legal Redressal, October 26, *DNA India*, www.dnaindia.com/india/report-domestic-violence-act-ten-years-on-women-yet-to-see-promised-legal-redressal-2138781 .
18 Law Commission 245th Report July 2014 Arrears and Backlog: Creating Additional judicial (wo)manpower, The Government of India
19 The Press Trust of India (2017) District Courts: 2.81 Crores Cases Pending, 5000 Judges Short Across India, *The Indian Express*, January 15, https://indianexpress.com/article/india/district-courts-2-81-crore-cases-pending-5000-judges-short-across-india-4475043/
20 Law Commission 245th Report op. cit.
21 Prakash S, Sinha B and Singh SR (2016) Waiting for Justice: 27 Million Cases Pending in Courts, 4500 Benches Empty, *The Hindustan Times*, November 15, https://www.hindustantimes.com/india-news/waiting-for-justice-27-million-cases-pending-in-courts-4500-benches-empty/story-H0EsAx4gW2EHPRtl1ddzIN.html
22 Nigam S (2017) Fighting for Justice in Patriarchal Courts, *Countercurrents*, August 30, https://countercurrents.org/2017/08/30/fighting-for-justice-in-the-patriarchal-courts/
23 In Kerala's merit list for selection of Munsif Magistrates women outnumbered men. *Live Law* (2017) Women Outnumber Men in Kerala Munsif Magistrate Selection, August 7, www.livelaw.in/women-outnumber-men-kerala-munsiff-magistrate-selection/ accessed on 17.09.17
24 Nigam Shalu (2015) Hail Patriarchy! Of Supreme Law and Elite Judges, *Countercurrents*, November 7, www.countercurrents.org/nigam071115.htm accessed on 11.06.16
25 Lok Sabha (2017) Response to the Unstarred Question No. 5218 answered on 5.4.17 Ministry of Law and Justice, http://164.100.47.190/loksabhaquestions/annex/11/AU5218.pdf accessed on 11.06.16
26 Mishra S (2016) I Was Sexually harassed in the Corridors of Supreme Court: Interview with Indira Jaising, November 13, *The Week*, www.theweek.in/theweek/cover/interview-indira-jaising-senior-lawyer.html Also, *India Today* (2013) Justice Ganguly Kissed My Arm . . . Ask Me to Share Room, Said Law Intern in Supreme Court Affidavit, December 16
27 National Judicial Data (2017) http://njdg.ecourts.gov.in/njdg_public/main.php On July 5, 2018, the total pending cases filed by women are 2,843,488 as compared to the overall total pending cases of 27,440,116 which amounts to 10.36 percent.
28 WPC 13/2015 on behalf of Supreme Court Women Lawyers Association for Consideration of Meritorious Women for Adequate Representation in Appointment as High Court Judges/ Supreme Court Judges
29 *Live Law* (2016) After Complaint of Gender Bias, SC Promises More Women Judges in Apex Court and High Courts, November 10, www.livelaw.in/after-complaint-of-gender-bias-sc-promises-more-women-judges-in-apex-court-high-courts/
30 Henning Margaret and Jardim Anne (1977) *The Managerial Women*, Doubleday Press, Garden City
31 Venkatesan J (2017) SC Begin Hearing on Validity of Triple Talaq with 5 Judges from Different Religions, *The Asian Age*, May 11, https://www.asianage.com/india/all-india/110517/triple-talaq-in-sc-today-judges-from-5-religions.html
32 Provisions of Section 357A of the CrPC are rarely utilized to provide compensation. Some states have formulated policies to compensate victims of crimes, yet many are denied relief.

33 Shukla Rakesh (2017) To Remove Caste Bias from the Judicial System, Judges Need to Self-Correct, *The Wire*, March 23, https://thewire.in/118065/caste-bias-judicial-system/
34 Bhushan Prashant (2009) Misplaced Priorities and Class Bias of the Judiciary, *Economic and Political Weekly*, 44 (14) 32–37
35 Sheldrick B (2014) *Blocking Public Participation: The Use of Strategic Litigation to Silence Political Expression*, Wilfrid Laurier University Press, Canada
36 2018 SCC OnLine SC 1316
37 Ekta Resource Center for Women (2011) *A Study of 498A in Tamil Nadu*, Madurai
38 Basu S (2015) *Trouble with Marriage: Feminist Confront Law and Violence in India*, University of California Press, Oakland, CA p. 4
39 Nader Laura (1994) supra
40 Basu (2015) supra p. 4
41 Mukhopadhaya M (1988) *Legally Dispossessed: Gender, Identity and Process of Law*, Stree, Kolkata
42 Smart Carol (1984) *The Ties That Bind: Law, Marriage and the Reproduction of Patriarchal Relations*, Routledge and Kegan Paul, London
43 Cain M (1979) The General Practice Lawyer and the Client: Towards a Radical Conception, *International Journal of Sociology* (7) 333
44 Milk powder substitutes are available for infants.
45 Nigam S (2016) Battered Women Syndrome: Applying this Legal Doctrine in the Indian Context, *Countercurrents*, August 6
46 Schulhofer SJ (1995) The Feminist Challenge in Criminal Law, *University of Pennsylvania Law Review*, 143, 2151–207, 2154
47 Suneetha A and Nagraj V (2006) A Difficult Match: Women's Actions and Legal Institutions in the Face of Domestic Violence, *Economic Political Weekly*, 41, 4355–62
48 Rautray S (2013) Naina Sahni Judgment: The Perverse Patriarchy of the Highest Court, *The Economic Times*, October 31, https://economictimes.indiatimes.com/opinion/et-commentary/naina-sahni-judgment-the-perverse-patriarchy-of-the-highest-court/articleshow/24961394.cms?from=mdr

5 The economics of love

Women's rights within families and a changing economic paradigm

"*Women's domesticity is a circle of learnt deprivation and induced subjugation: a circle decisively centered on family life*".[1]

The neoliberal economy has changed the manner in which labor, love and relationships have been organized, recognized, appreciated and structured in a hierarchical society. In the West, the industrial revolution disrupted the old discriminatory structures, paving the way for a new society, whereas in societies such as India, capitalism has refueled the embedded feudal Brahmanical patriarchy, thus creating a worse situation where multiple patriarchies act in a combined fashion to create a culture of violence and impunity. Further, in the wake of the economic crisis that has cropped up in recent years, when employment is shrinking, the economy is dwindling, and the state is rolling back from its welfare character, uncertainty looms, and common people are left with little options to earn their livelihoods. The consumer paradigm in the neoliberal economy put the onus on an individual to seek services such as health, education or employment in the market, rather than making the state accountable to provide for these services. This has a significant impact on social relations. This paradigm is deeply affecting women on the margins.

Economic changes are having an adverse impact on the social institution of the family, which is weakening and being threatened in the neoliberal environment where money is replacing love, commercialization is substituting for the social and emotional bonds, civic relations are waning away and community support is becoming extinct while community strictures on women are tightening. Economic violence is taking new forms. In the affluent families, women are facing violence in terms of control, both economic and sexual, whereas for women in marginal families, access to resources becomes more difficult. Marriage as an institution is being commodified. Dowry demands and dowry violence have escalated, women are denied their basic needs while at the same time, those with jobs face *multiple victimization*, where their incomes are controlled by men. Women are forced to work more vigorously and for longer times at home, and at the workplace, men are trying to sabotage women's employment and workplace harassment continues to grow. In the age of digitalization, new forms of controls are imposed upon women. Controlling women's bank balances, monitoring their mobile phones and social media activities, forcefully using women's hard-earned money to make purchases and forcing women to repay loans are different forms of violence that are affecting women's lives in the neoliberal economy.

More importantly, in the poor or middle-class families, when because of severe violence women are compelled to walk out of the marital relation, with no support from the state, community or extended family, their situation becomes even more challenging. In the absence of matrimonial property rights, women who are abandoned, separated or divorced are denied their right to survival with dignity. Women from upper-caste or affluent families too face the double crisis, as neither the law nor society recognizes their paid and unpaid contributions to the household. Denial of material or economic support or substantial rights to women who are compelled to walk away from the marital relationship has a deep impact on their survival.

This chapter suggests that the state neither constructively supports women when they face violence in homes nor does it make any arrangements to assist women when they attempt to escape an abusive situation. It concludes that despite the legal provisions relating to maintenance or other relief made available under the PWDVA, women whether poor or otherwise, are compelled to struggle in their daily lives in the absence of any form of social or economic support. The law cannot imagine situations outside the paradox of the family, nor has the state enacted policies that could offer alternatives to lead a dignified life. Trapped in the web of legal technicalities and the complexities created by the market norms, women are facing increasing vulnerabilities, where the state has refused to bail them out in any manner. It is therefore suggested that the law relating to separation and divorce needs to be re-examined. The concept of the division of matrimonial property among the separating parties needs be looked into. Giving women equal rights in the marital property is not only a moral imperative but is also an economic necessity. More specifically, in cases of domestic violence, several interventions are required to specifically provide economic support and assistance to victims and survivors. Innovative solutions may be imagined outside the domain of the family. It is also recommended that provisions relating to social security and welfare measures need to strengthened and, wherever required, special interventions be made to support women and children in distress.

Atomized economic man in a free market economy is becoming the norm

A neoliberal economy has replaced the concept of the human as a social being with *homo economicus,* or an 'economic man', who is consistently rational and is working solely to maximize profit. The term 'economic man' was initially used by John Stuart Mill when he explained that

> [Political economy] does not treat the whole of man's nature as modified by the social state, nor of the whole conduct of man in society. It is concerned with him solely as a being who desires to possess wealth, and who is capable of judging the comparative efficacy of means for obtaining that end.[2]

This model does not consider the human element or social dimensions that motivate an individual to attain higher social goals relating to altruism, solidarity or the need to forge social bonds without expectations of material wealth or economic exchange. Adam Smith, in his famous work *The Wealth of Nations*, explained

> It is not from the benevolence of the butcher, the brewer, or the baker that we expect our dinner, but from their regard to their own interest. We address ourselves not to their humanity but to their self-love, and never talk to them of their necessities but of their advantages.[3]

Sen[4] has criticized this model, arguing that there are pitfalls in limiting rationality to selfish rationality while adding dimensions relating to sympathy and commitment in this model. He elaborated that human behavior is a complex phenomenon driven by multiple motivations, including socialization. However, despite its criticism and its limitations, the *homo economicus* model dominates and is enforcing disparities, resulting in a situation where consumerism has replaced the human element. Market forces are driving individuals to behave in a self-centered manner, leading to individualization, alienation, isolation and atomization.[5]

In this market-driven paradigm, the state is relieved from its obligation to provide basic services to its citizens, while inequalities have become acceptable. An individual is perceived as a consumer of welfare services, and therefore the onus is placed on a person to avail themselves of basic services such as health, education or employment.[6] Privatization construes individuals as self-sufficient entities not dependent on the state machinery and thus stigmatizes those who avail themselves of public assistance. In the market-regulated economy, the state is abdicating its social obligation and is becoming subordinate to the market forces.[7] This is affecting the social fabric of the communities. More specifically, in growing economies such as India, where the social security support system already lags behind, an increasing focus on marketization is distressing individuals, destroying social relations, devastating neighborhoods, fragmenting communities, rupturing solidarities and reinforcing the patriarchy in its worst form. Emergence of a free market has eliminated different forms of social protections where now everything can be bought and sold irrespective of its ethical, social, moral or human consequences. Further, the free market has abolished restrictions on the buying and selling of land or labor previously restricted by the customary rights and community, social and moral norms; structures of family and kin; or the mercantile policies of the state. These economic transformations are having an adverse impact and hit hardest those on the peripheries, leading to the 'marginalization of the marginal'. With no social support, those who have been oppressed are further subjugated. The market economy is altering the concept of justice, welfare state or democracy with anarchy, autocracy and oligarchy. The role of the welfare state is shrinking as inequality is widening and further intensifying the domination of those already in powerful positions while marginalizing those at the receiving end.[8]

In the market economy, relationship is reduced to a commodity

The conceptualization that individuals are driven by economic needs has also altered social relationships. With the process of marketization, the value placed on the quality of social relations is diminished.[9] The qualitative social relations are reduced to numbers where every element of human emotions, such as love and care, can be measured in terms of parameters such as output, productivity, cost, time span or money. Becker[10] has applied the principles of market economy to the social question relating to marriage and argued that people operate as rational agents in family life too. He propounded that in a market, human beings could be considered a social capital, and monetary values could be allocated to prestige, love and affection "by applying elegant sets of mathematical formulas".[11] In his *Treatise on the Family*,[12] Becker analyzed the household as a sort of factory producing goods and services such as meals, child care and shelter. The proponents of commodification argue that "anything that some people are willing to sell and others are willing to buy in principle can and should be subjected free market (*laissez faire*) exchange and everything people need or desire is to be conceived of as commodity".[13] Thus,

> everything that is desired or valued is an object that can be possessed, that can be thought of as equivalent to a sum of money, and that can be alienated. The person is conceived of and spoken of as the possessor and trader of these goods, and hence all human interactions are sales.[14]

Nevertheless, the use of the market model to analyze the family has been criticized because it does not take non-monetary variables into consideration. For instance, personal attributes such as bodily integrity cannot be considered an object. Also, this argument ignores the fact that this system is created by men who command force, prestige and wealth in all societies and therefore put women on a lower level.[15] Commodification construes freedom as a negative liberty and monetizes personal attributes, relationships, philosophical and moral commitments besides alienating the self. A few scholars, on the basis of the concept of market inalienability, argued that market rhetoric cannot and should not be applied to every situation. Radin[16] argued that

> Universal commodification undermines personal identity by conceiving of personal attributes, relationships, and philosophical and moral commitments as monetized and alienable form of self. A better view of market should understand many kinds of particulars – one's politics, work, religion, family, love, sexuality, friendships, altruism, experiences, wisdom, moral commitments, character, and personal attributes – as integral to the self.

Further, in an unideal world of ignorance, greed and violence where poverty, racism and sexism prevail, commodification harms the individual as well as society by powerfully legitimizing and reinforcing class or caste division besides perpetuating gender oppression. The opponents of commodification state that in situations of inequality and disempowerment, commodification exacerbate oppression and powerlessness while perpetuating subjugation.

However, despite these criticisms, the commercialization of social relations continued. The imperialism of economics[17] is shaping the world today in numerous ways and is harming the social order. Marketization is having an adverse impact on society while reducing human interactions to a commodity. Love and care are outsourced, and the relationship within the family and marriage is being altered with the emergence of new players in the markets.[18] This is weakening the emotional bonds while shattering the social ties that bind the family. Also, the support provided by the extended families and the community is waning away because the market is altering the household arrangements. In the process, community strictures are becoming stronger, while women are facing a crisis because of the virulent patriarchy that has been intensified and affecting women in harsh ways.

The market economy has intensified the patriarchy in India

It is not that women were not oppressed before the advent of capitalism, but globalization has reorganized economies worldwide, and in the zeal to earn profits, this arrangement is altering gender relations while intensifying the hierarchical divisions in societies such as India where the patriarchy has been deeply embedded.[19] Engels's work on '*The Origin of Family, Private Property and the State*' has shown that women's oppression is rooted in the advent of private property and class division. Capitalism has reorganized male domination and women subordination in a new way through heterosexual monogamous arrangements promoting gendered division of labor while controlling women's sexuality and perpetuating their servile status.

Capitalism reinforced patriarchal ideologies while strictly defining feminine duties, while utilizing the notion of good or bad women to justify the hierarchy and violence within the family.[20] It has paved the way for women to enter into the labor markets, yet this could not lead to their liberation from feudal oppression.

In India, colonialism combined with capitalism has created havoc. Patnaik,[21] while analyzing differences in patterns of gender oppression in advanced countries in comparison to India, argued that in advanced capitalist countries, the old pre-capitalist structures were destroyed to establish the new world order while disintegrating the patriarchy. However, in India, the stubborn feudal structures such as caste and patriarchy are retained even after the economic liberalization, leading to multiple forms of patriarchal oppression. He argued that continuation of the old feudal structure combined with elements of 'lumpen-proletariats' has created a difficult situation where women are compelled to deal with an entrenched patriarchy in a newer form. Elsewhere, with migration, the patriarchy has been dismantled, but here, the migrant population consisting of uprooted, alienated individuals could not acquire moral moorings. Therefore, the lumpen-proletariats could not unite or adapt themselves to a new 'community' or 'morality' and this breeds criminal behavior, especially toward women who defy patriarchy and chose to be independent. Hence, the advent of a market economy has worsened the situation for women who already have been under feudal oppression. Capitalism refueled the embedded feudal Brahmanical patriarchy, thus creating a worse situation where multiple patriarchies act in combination to create a culture of violence and impunity.

Women are facing a harsh burden of increasing inequalities

> "I will never forgive my husband for what he has done, but I am worried over future of my six children who are now being forced to fend for themselves as my husband is in jail".[22]
>
> (2019)

The 36-year-old tribal woman who was allegedly brutalized by a piece of metal by her husband gave this statement while she was hospitalized in critical condition in an intensive care unit at a hospital in Indore. A team of doctors removed a 20-cm-long grip of a motorcycle handle from her uterus which damaged her bladder and bowel. She has been suffering intense pain for several months, but her husband did not allow her to see the doctor, fearing arrest. When her pain became unbearable, she went to the police station to lodge a complaint and fell unconscious there. Her husband is a laborer, and the alleged assault occurred eight months ago when she confronted him over his relationship with another woman. The hospital told her to undergo an operation a few months back, but she could not afford it. This case shows that the apathy of the state, the indifference of the market economy are increasingly forcing harsher forms of violence within families are affecting women and children the most. Marginalized and brutalized within homes, communities and markets, with no legal or social protection, women are being forced to survive in appalling conditions.

The neoliberal model has widened inequalities and is harming the poor and vulnerable. A recent report by Oxfam shows that world's 26 richest people own the same wealth as the 3.8 billion poorest half of humanity.[23] Such massive wealth disparity is threatening the idea of democracy and equality. Women are hit hardest by such inequalities. "Economically unequal countries are countries where men and women are more unequal too", noted the report.[24] Most of the rich people are men, as they own more wealth. Globally, women earn 23 percent less than men. This is despite the fact that women are continuously engaged in visible and invisible work.

A report by Mckinsey[25] suggests that 75 percent of unpaid work done by women, if valued, could be equivalent to $10 trillion of output per year, or 13 percent of global GDP. Women cook; clean; do laundry jobs; take care of the family's health; care for the sick, elderly and children; act as mediator, teacher, counselor and secretary; baby sit; get household supplies; gather firewood; or fetch water, walking for miles, and do loads of other work besides bearing and raising children quietly and therefore could not take up paid employment. This work steals time from women and leaves them unable to take advantage of social, economic or political opportunities.

An OECD report[26] estimates that women are investing 351.9 minutes in a day doing domestic unpaid work such as caring for family members as compared to men, who are investing 51.8 minutes in unpaid work. Women as wives and mothers spend most of the time taking care of the children and looking after houses, which is an exhaustive, dull, toiling, stressful and tedious job, and yet this continuous work remains unrecognized and invisible. India Spend,[27] in a survey of 3,177 mothers with children in the age group one to six years in Rajasthan, found that, on average, women spend 9.4 hours each day doing unpaid work as against 17 minutes doing some form of paid work. Unpaid work includes cooking, tending to animals and working on family-owned fields, and 2.5 hours is spent caring for the children and elderly in the family.

In the press release titled 'Inequality Has a Female Face in India',[28] it has been acknowledged that women are less likely to have paid work than men. Those women who are in paid work receive less wages and, therefore houses which rely only on female earnings are poorer. The gender pay gap is 34 percent, and often women's ability to undertake paid work is determined not only by economic considerations but also by social norms. Also, according to the World Bank Report 2016, the female work force participation rate in India is 24 percent – well below the world average of 39 percent. In fact, India is ranked 172th out of 185 countries in terms of female labor force participation.[29] The Global Gender Gap Index by the World Forum placed India at 108th out of 144 countries for the year 2017. The country was ranked 87th position for the year 2016 for gender parity across four dimensions – economic participation and opportunity, educational attainment, health and survival and political empowerment.[30] Thus, despite taking care of households and doing unpaid and paid work, women have been discriminated against not only in terms of wages but also in terms of social, economic and political engagement with the world around them. From a gender perspective, the situation is worsening, as the patriarchy is being reinforced in its virulent form in the market-driven economy, where women who already have been placed on a lower level are denied their basic right to live a dignified life in a feudal capitalist environment.

The commercialization of marriage is intensifying the patriarchy

Today, the marriage relationship in India is delicately poised between the complex realm of market, religion and law. Once a traditional institution governed by religious scriptures and socio-cultural norms, today, marriage has become more of a commercialized practice where men and women may approach the marriage bazaar through thousands of match-making, matrimonial advertisements and Internet sites.[31] The market for online matrimony business is 1,500 crores, with a compound annual growth rate of 65 percent.[32] Though the online matrimony profile is skewed towards 18- to 35-year-old working-class male users, the market is growing, with 95 percent revenue in matching alliances and dating services targeting "30 percent of population between 15–30 age group eligible for marriage in next five years".[33] The Capitalist-Brahmanical patriarchy provides an ideological framework for such market-driven marriage relationships. The language of the market operates to describe the qualities of brides and grooms to seek a perfect match that could fit in the concept of purity of blood line while maintaining the caste hierarchy and also the exchange value of an individual is highlighted, depending on his or her socio-economic background while maintaining the hierarchical relationship between the bride and the groom. The rates for a dowry are fixed depending on the groom's qualities such as his superior status, caste, salary, wealth, power and his earning potential.[34] For brides, the qualities that are sought include her perfection in terms of looks and beauty, skills and abilities to perform household work, her earning potential, the status of her parents, capacity of her family to pay for the dowry, wealth and number of unmarried daughters in the family, in addition to factors such as her caste or class. The marriage market treats men and women as commodities to be bought and sold. The state hardly intervenes during such negotiations or transactions. It is only at the later stage that regulations come into play.[35] Also, when the law intervenes, it completely ignores the impact of socio-economic transformations on the social relations. The law has failed to keep pace with the changing economic realities.

The dowry and wedding celebration are resynthesized in the market economy

Historically, payments between families at the time of marriage existed in many societies across the world and are determined by economic conditions, social structure and family characteristics.[36] These are seen as a way of distributing wealth, as well as ensuring the welfare of women arranged by the parents of respective spouses as a dowry or bride price. However, commercialization changed the way in which payments around marriages are organized, where elements of care or affection are replaced with the lust, greed and insatiability. In the commodified world, frequently marriages are organized not on the basis of social or emotional compatibility between the parties, but often on the basis of volume of transfers and the parameters of social and economic status of the parties.

The concept of dowry existed before the advent of capitalism, but with the changing economy, its forms have also been evolving. It has become more a symbol of socio-economic status. Coercive demands today are not only restricted to expensive items or cash payments but also on the basis of affordability of lavish arrangements to be made for the weddings. A dowry is not construed as the inheritance rights of daughters in parental property or as *streedhan*; rather, it has been converted to the groom's price, which is demanded coercively. If the bride's family cannot afford to pay, then either the daughter cannot get married or she is easily abandoned – or murdered if the demands are not fulfilled. The fine line between *streedhan*, spending on lavish wedding celebration and coercive demand is completely blurred.

Further, the marriage market is expanding. Huge expenses are incurred on 'big fat lavish Indian weddings' which is taking a toll on many families.[37] It is estimated that a wedding costs between 5 lakhs and 5 crores in today's scenario, with a person spending one-fifth of the accumulated wealth in a lifetime on the occasion. In fact, the marriage market is booming and is flourishing as a recession-proof business. Estimates put the wedding industry as a $50 billion market growing at 25 to 30 percent annually.[38] The wedding industry includes range of services from catering, decoration, invitations, wedding planners, photographers, theme weddings, makeup, gold and gifts sellers, designer dresses, dance choreographers and honeymoon planners, among other services.[39] And as per the social and cultural norms, this cost is born by the brides and their families. From arranging expensive clothes and ornaments to be given as 'gifts', to organizing the extravagant feasts for the guests, to organizing 'destination weddings', money is spent on items including cars, flats and other luxuries, depending on the socio-economic status of the families.[40] Special malls have been created to cater to the needs of those who can afford luxuries items for weddings.[41]

Conspicuous consumption is the sole aim of this form of commercialization, where pleasure, morality, imagination and fear of failure are exploited by the market forces.

Though a risky business for the parents of brides, with no guarantee that the marriage will last, in many cases, families of brides take out loans to organize marriage functions,[42] knowing that this cost may not be shared by the groom or his family and that it cannot be recovered in any manner later if the marriage fails; yet the bride's family spends a huge amount of money due to societal pressure to maintain and preserve their status.[43] A household survey on India's Citizen Environment and Consumer Economy, covering 61,000 households conducted between April 2015 and March 2016, shows that more than a quarter of households are indebted and the majority of them borrowed from informal sources rather than banks or other financial institutions.[44] Nearly a third of those reported taking out loans to pay for wedding feasts. The proportion of such households is higher at the bottom of the pyramid than at the top. The status of a girl in a patriarchal society thus is further devalued because the market has converted an ordinary marriage custom into a stylish, glamorous, pretentious, superficial ritual.

The traditional mode of giving gold to women as *streedhan* in lieu of economic entitlement to property or a bank balance is not a benchmark for economic rights in modern India. Research has shown a link between the rising gold price that enhances the cost of the dowry with the low spending on girls, leading to their neglect and even abortion of girl children.[45] A woman thus became more prone to facing violence in her natal home as well as in the matrimonial home in case expectations relating to wedding celebrations or the dowry are not fulfilled.

However, law makers and policymakers seemingly are turning their eyes blind to these social realities. The regulation of social relations built around the transfer of money is not being done by the state or the market, even when coercive demands are being made and women are maltreated or murdered in case demands are not fulfilled. In cases pertaining to the Dowry Prohibition Act, the conviction rate was merely 15.6 in 2016, and in the cases relating to dowry deaths, the conviction rate was 30.5. In a free market economy, the law has failed to keep pace with social realities. The state probably has shut its eyes while giving in to the reign of the free market; thus, in a way, it is legitimizing dowry.

Newer forms of violence are being inflicted

Women in India are facing a harsh burden of increasing inequalities, while marketization has refueled the old forms of violence while intensifying gender hierarchies within families. Women are denied paid employment or property ownership in various ways. Moreover, with a changing economic scenario, as women are acquiring economic assets and are participating in paid employment, this has introduced tensions and struggles within a household. Perhaps the increased economic strength of women leads to more violence because it threatens the image of the male bread winner and challenges the status quo. Globalization has unleashed new ways to repress women through reinforcing the notions of production and reproduction, where women are essentially seen not only as a factor for producing or rearing children or managing household work within families, but also are exploited as they entered the wage market, where marketization has reduced them to a commodity.

Bhattacharya,[46] while analyzing the NFHS-3 data, observed that married women who are financially self-reliant experienced spousal violence. They are more likely to be employed year-round and also are more likely to work for cash remuneration and yet have less say in the vital decision on how to spend their earnings and thus are susceptible to financial exploitation. Luke and Munshi[47] observed that when women in the tea plantations in South India earn a higher share of the household income, the probability of marital violence increases. Female employment threatens men's authority in relationship dynamics; therefore, women are abused.[48] Increasing female property rights increased conflict within households, and this resulted in more suicides among both men and women.[49] Paul[50] reported a positive association between women's workforce participation and physical as well and emotional abuse by husbands. According to this study, employed women are more exposed to intimate partner violence. The study argued that the emotional cost may become higher for men when household decision-making power diverges from traditional gender norms; therefore, men may turn more violent to assert their domestic dominance.

The family is a site where violence can remain hidden under the guise of women's chastisement. The family teaches men to assert their entitlement over women's labor, sexuality and reproduction. The state and capitalist forces want more women to be drawn into labor forces, but at the same time they do not want women to acquire autonomy, mobility or greater control over their lives because the family provides them an alternative where women provide unpaid care and perform work without demanding wages.[51] What benefits the state and society is a docile, disciplined worker who cannot revolt. The state therefore has not shown its interest in challenging the systematic denial of women's autonomy or freedom from domestic violence.[52]

In an age of globalization, with the emergence of technology, women are facing newer forms of violence. Economic abuse is taking new forms in all families above the spectrum of class, caste or any other parameter and occurs as a repeated pattern of abuse. Capitalism has compelled women to take up low-paid jobs in informal working conditions, but at same time when they venture out to earn, they are subjected to violence both at home and at the workplace. Coercive social, sexual and economic control is being imposed within private and public spheres. In the guise of safety, women's mobility is controlled. As discussed elsewhere in this book, many are not allowed to take up educational opportunities or jobs to fulfill their aspirations before or after marriage. Those who dare to go out are stigmatized, as questions are raised about their character. Men make attempts to sabotage women's employment. Dowry demands and dowry violence have escalated, while at the same time, women face denials and deprivations in different forms. For women in marginal families, access to resources becomes more difficult. Women lack say in decision making as to how money should be spent. Women's jewelry is being sold on one pretext or another or is acquired by the husband or in-laws. Many women are kept unaware of information regarding family finances.

Those women in jobs are compelled to face *multiple victimization*, where incomes of women are controlled by men, women are forced to work vigorously for longer times at home and at the workplace and hostility at the workplace continues to grow. In all of the cases I came across, men, as abusive husbands, controlled all aspects of financial resources. In the majority of cases, the women's bank account is controlled by abusers, who take money from women's purses, leaving them with no resources to meet the needs of themselves or their children. Often women who earn have been given inadequate allowances for their daily transportation or toiletries. Men used women's credit or debit cards to buy products and make women liable for the bills. In several cases, this happens either coercively, fraudulently or through deception. Withholding child support after separation is evident in most of the cases (as discussed elsewhere in detail in this book).

In the age of digitalization, new forms of controls are being imposed upon women. Controlling women's bank balances by accessing their password or PIN number is a new form of exploitation that is different from the traditional forms of abuse,[53] taking out loans in the names of women or giving their names as surety, monitoring their mobile phones and social media activities and forcefully using women's hard-earned money to make purchases when women are forced to repay loans are different forms of violence that are affecting women's lives in the neoliberal economy. A survey shows that 83 percent of women are compelled to leave their matrimonial home because of domestic violence.[54] Research in developed countries over the years has shown numerous ways where the abusers have inflicted financial violence[55]; however, in India, more research needs to be done.

Economic violence as interpreted by the courts

As mentioned in earlier chapters, in a family court, in the situation of violence between the parties, mediation is enforced, which reduces the marital relationship to a tangible product that can be measured in quantifiable parameters. Individuals, both men and women, are seen as factors of production, while the family is seen as a unit where the husband is supposed to provide financially and the wife is supposed to be relegated to her role of being a *carer* and a nurturer. Relationships are described in terms of the earning capacity of the husband; similarly, a wife is supposed to be 'adjusting', loving' 'devoting', 'loyal' and a 'silent diligent worker' who would sacrifice for the sake of family. As per the law, a husband is liable for maintaining his wife, provided she remains dutiful and chaste. But at the same time, while quantifying maintenance, alimony or settlement, the law could not acknowledge or quantify the paid or unpaid work women do at home in terms of producing or rearing the children, caring for the sick or elderly or the work involved in maintaining the household. Market norms are not applied to quantifying a woman's labor involved in production or reproduction. Her visible as well as invisible contribution within a household is ignored. The fact that she has given up her well-paying job to 'adjust' in marriage or to do household work is not considered, while quantifying what she brings to the table at the time of separation or divorce. Rather, women who take up employment after separation or dissolution of the marriage, even if the employment is very low-paying, get less sympathy from the courts in terms of maintenance or alimony.

Moreover, divorce is considered an anomaly as per social norms, while the law of the division of matrimonial property is not applied; therefore, women cannot demand the massive contribution they make to the household. In addition, the personal laws relating to marriage, divorce, custody and maintenance are governed by religious norms and cannot keep pace with the socio-economic transformations. The result is that women are suffering because of such intricate arrangements. There is a huge lag between the conceptualization of entitlements for men and for women and their obligations as per personal laws with that of the quickly changing economy of social relations. The socio-cultural and religious practices as prevalent in North India do not accept divorce easily; therefore, bargaining for rights at the time of separation or divorce becomes difficult from this perspective. The discourse on rights within relationships in the market-dominated discourse requires reconsideration.

Second, in a society where the economic and employment situation is worsening day by day because of policies adopted by successive governments over the years, both men and women are denied suitable work opportunities.[56] In the absence of employment, families and the households are suffering immensely. Increasing precariat working conditions have an adverse impact on survival as well as social relations.[57] In such precarious situations, disintegration of the family creates additional demands. For the poor and marginals, the situation has become more intense. The rollback of welfare measures by the state is creating havoc. For women and children, the situation becomes even more difficult when the violent culture, repressive religious norms and regressive social culture combine with such precarious economic situations. The narratives described next portray the manner in which economic dimensions are adding insult to the injuries of women who knock on the doors of court seeking redress against injustices they faced in their family lives.

A quest for dignity: Kamla's ordeal with the law

I met Kamla (42) in Patiala House Court in the hot summer of 2014, where she was looking for a lawyer to seek advice. She is compelled to shuttle between Kanpur and Delhi to make both ends meet. At the age of 23, she got married to Kanwarlal, an engineer working in Meerut, and went to live in his house. Her parents provided a large dowry, including jewelry. The couple moved to Delhi, as her husband got a job in a private company. It was an arranged marriage, and a son was born. The marriage survived for seven years, during which the husband bought a new house while taking out a loan and selling the ornaments given to Kamla at the time of her marriage. Her husband later left her for another woman, and she has been thrown out and is dispossessed of the house she has been staying in. Later, she filed a case for divorce in Kanpur. The case went on for 11 years, and the lawyer took a lot of money. Yet she could not receive maintenance for herself or her son. "My lawyer has not told me to file criminal complaint. Every time I used to travel from Delhi to Kanpur on 'dates' the lawyer would say things are proceedings. I am not a learned person and I believed whatever he said", she added.

According to her, only once has she received 25,000 Rs, and this is all he has paid in lieu of her *streedhan* and maintenance for herself and her son. "I have paid more than that to my lawyer plus so much money is going into travelling on each court 'date' ", she stated. After a long struggle she obtained a divorce but was made to sign a document stating that in the future, she has no right to claim anything from her husband or his family. Meanwhile, she came to Delhi to stay with her sister and her family. She trained herself as a beautician, and while staying in Delhi she claimed she could earn a bit. "Kanpur is not an expensive city as Delhi. Not many people pay for the beauty enhancement job", she asserted. Initially, she worked in a beauty parlor in Delhi, but since the shift is longer and her son requires her attention, she left the job and started working independently.

> But now my son has grown old and the schools in Delhi are charging high fees and this house is too small to accommodate my sister's family and myself. My sister's kids are also growing and then my son and her two kids fight all the time. So, I took my son to my parent's house in Kanpur. I have been shuttling on and off since then.

According to Kamla, her parents are taking care of her son, and she is paying for his educational fee besides daily expenses.

> But how long will they take care of him. My brother's family is also growing. I have to make some other arrangement. Without any support, life becomes difficult. Both my brother and sister are doing their best

> to help me, but they have their own families. In order to survive, I am looking for solution. I do not see re-marriage as a viable option. Already life is in a mess.

Violence thwarts women's economic agency and empowerment. For Kamla and for many others in similar situations, struggling as abandoned, separated or divorced women is tough. Neither the law nor the society could provide any solution. Divorce has not helped her to get enough money even to take care of the educational needs or daily expenses of her child.[58] She has tried to acquire skills as a beautician, but this has further added to her woes, as she could not find suitable income opportunities in the town where her parents stay. She is compelled to stay in the city to earn her living and is moving routinely between two geographical areas to take care of her son. The capitalist economy has severed her two-member family and separated her from her only son who could have provided her emotional security in a time of distress. Between the necessity to earn her livelihood and to rear the child, a woman's life is torn into pieces. She could not obtain any rights in the matrimonial property, as the law could not recognize her unpaid contribution in the household. She could not even claim the price in lieu of her gold ornaments or *streedhan*, which was sold by her husband to buy a house from where she has been dispossessed. While twisting and manipulating the law, her husband has denied paying maintenance to her or to their son and has cleverly deprived her of any settlement amount so she can start her life afresh with her son. The law could not help Kamla to claim her rights as a wife or as a citizen.

Law is blind: Reena's saga of pain

Similarly, Reena (33), working in a private firm in Noida as a receptionist, earns 25,000/ per month. She has a son who is six and staying with her. She got separated from her husband five years ago. "He never liked me and his family demanded dowry. I did my best to save our relationship but he used to physically beat me on and off without any reason. I could not take it beyond a point, so I walked out", shared Reena. At that point she was unemployed. She filed the application under Section 12 of the PWDVA claiming for maintenance. After ten years of marriage she came back to her parents' house, where her married brother is also staying with his wife and two kids. Her father died a year later. According to her,

> For five years, I paid hefty fee to the lawyer every year but nothing could materialize. My husband paid 10,000/ twice as maintenance and nothing else is given. Not even my gold jewellery or expensive gifts have been returned. I have just been running around in the courts. Now, my brother has asked me to end this litigation. He said that I should move to our parental home in Ambala with my mother. I have to file for

> second motion for mutual divorce now. My husband was not willing to settle. He is earning well in his business and is living with another woman and has a child from her so for him settlement does not matter. My lawyer negotiated with him on the condition that I would not demand any compensation or settlement amount or even my jewelry. My brother wants me to move quickly so I have to agree. What's the purpose of continuing litigation for years? I know I will not get justice. Courts are for rich and resourceful men like my husband. I will stay at our parental home with my mother and will look for a job there.
>
> (2013)

Reena has to give up her right to claim maintenance as well as *streedhan* because her brother compelled her to end the litigation and move to their native place. The prolonged litigation with no results has led to frustration and tiredness. She claimed that during the five years of her legal battle, the lawyer has not suggested she file the criminal complaint under Section 498A or 406 IPC, though he took a lot of money. Her husband took advantage of her vulnerable situation and refused to part with money for maintenance of the child. The law has turned a blind eye to the compelling reasons for which Reena decided to end the protracted litigation and ignores the fact that her husband, with all resources at his command, is in a powerful position, whereas Reena, with her limited resources and scant support, is in dire need of social, financial and emotional support. Though her brother provided her little assistance, he also has not supported her claim to her natal house property in Delhi and forced her to move to Ambala despite the fact that she has been pursuing her job in Delhi. What is overlooked in the process is that for ten years she has made visible and invisible contributions to her marital home, yet her husband denied all her lawful entitlements. The law could not protect her monetary entitlements, including her *streedhan*; therefore, looking at the questions of her contribution to the matrimonial home is too high an expectation a woman can make from the legal system. From the perspective of the court, as the matter is settled between the parties, there is no need to spend time on it to pursue it. What is ignored here is that after years of struggle for justice, the woman has been compelled to give up her rights and entitlements in favor of her husband. The violence inflicted by her husband is ignored in the process. Providing justice to the woman as a citizen is not the concern of the court; here, the focus is to end the litigation. This approach is disastrous as well as discriminatory, yet in the official record, the matter has ended.

My Lord, the time is not with me: the case of Jhumri

I met Hansram and his wife Jhumri in Dwarka Court in 2015. He belongs to a Dalit family from Jharkhand and has been living in Delhi for more than 18 years. His father used to work as a postman but died of tuberculosis

25 years ago. His mother died a few days later. The three brothers who survived have no source of earnings left. The elder one took the small piece of land his father left and threw both the younger ones out. Hansram came to Delhi and since then never bothered to go back to his village. He survived while taking up odd jobs in the city. Ten years ago, he married Jhumri, the second youngest daughter of Sardar Singh, now 65, who owns a small shop in Rohini. His two sons are managing the shop. Jhumri studied up to the ninth grade, while his elder brother completed his graduation and the younger brother did a diploma course in mechanics. Jhumri and Hansram have two kids ages six and eight. One of them is crippled since birth because of infection. Hansram could not provide for his wife and kids. Often, the couple used to fight. Jhumri has been staying with her parents for the past three years and has filed a case under the PWDVA. The court has fixed a total of 3000/ Rs maintenance per month for Jhumri and her two kids, but Hansram has not paid a single penny for the past 15 months. According to him, for past three years the market situation is getting worse. Even the odd jobs he has been doing earlier are not available now. Therefore, he finds it difficult to earn his livelihood and couldn't pay maintenance as ordered by the court. The magistrate firmly asked Hansram to make a payment. He asked for more time.

The magistrate got angry and said, "But you have not paid a single penny for [the] past 15 months, how will she survive? If she would have been living with you, won't you feed her?"

Hansram replied in a shaky voice, "*Huzur*, I was putting up the book stall in the market, but this time they (the local municipality) raided the market and took away my books. I will pay within a week".

Meanwhile Jhumri's lawyer intervened, "He has been saying this for [the] past 15 months but has not paid [a] single penny. The child is ill and needs medicines which are expensive, from where should she meet the expenses"? She showed medical papers of the child.

The judge became concerned, "Why you are not paying for the treatment of the child?"

Hansram meekly replied, "*Huzur*, I am trying my best. I felt ill last year and therefore, I could not earn"

"Where is your lawyer?" further enquired the judge.

Hansram in a low voice replied, "*Huzur*, no money left to pay to vakil *saheb*".

"But aren't you feeding yourself, it is your job to provide for your wife and kid, when you can eat yourself, you should also feed them. If she has been staying with you, wouldn't you be feeding them. Give her something", directed the magistrate.

Hansram pleaded, "*Huzur*, presently I don't have anything. Give me some time . . . I will pay".

The magistrate said in an angry tone, "But why not now? You have not paid her a single penny in 15 months. Pay her now or I will send you to jail".

Hansram said, "*Huzur*, the book fair is starting on [the] 1st, I will put up a stall there and whatever I earn I will pay. The municipality took all my books. I am left with nothing. Time is not with me. Else, I would have arranged for the money".

The magistrate continued, "Why next month, why not now? This is your kid and your wife . . . why should her parents feed them? If you are not paying now, I will send you to jail". To the policeman he said, "take him and put him behind the bars". The policeman came forward and held the hand of Hansram.

Hansram, with teary eyes and shaky legs, said, "*Huzur* give me some time. I will arrange the money. If you put me in the jail how will I do that".

"You people thought that we are sitting here to listen to your lame excuses . . . you can fool us and get away easily. . . . Pay right now or go to jail", retorted the magistrate.

Hansram whimpered, "Give me ten days, I will do something. Don't send me to the jail, how will I get the money? Nobody will help me." He said this with tearful eyes and his entire body trembling with fear.

The magistrate later adopted a softer tone and said, "Ok, I [am] leaving you this time and giving you a week. You have to pay money. If you make some lame excuse, I will put you behind the bars".

Seemingly, a simple case of non-payment of maintenance has complex socio-economic intricate layers, with its roots in the market-driven economy. In this situation, the man's ability to pay is controlled by his politico-economic situation, whereby the local municipality took away his source of livelihood on the pretext of removing illegal vendors from the city. Being low skilled, he is left with not many options to survive, but in the court these aspects could not be factored in. The fact that the dwindling economy is making a devastating impact on the livelihood of many daily wage earners in the city such as Hansram is out of the purview of the court. On the one hand, the state is taking steps to beautify cities, yet on the other hand, no steps are being taken to secure the life of the people surviving on the margins.[59] Rather, the livelihoods of many are being destroyed by the state in its urge to embellish the city, which offers them nothing in return. The state in nexus with the market is demonizing everyone – not just the poor and homeless.[60]

Caught in the vicious circle of poverty and trapped in the intricate web of law, many people are finding it difficult to make both ends meet and to provide for their families. Jhumri hardly has the skills to survive in the competitive market. Because of the secondary position being accorded to women, her parents have not bothered to ensure that she should complete her education or acquire skills to survive. Additionally, she is burdened with taking care of a sick child.

The courts as the implementers of law cannot help men and women entrapped in a vicious economic circle of poverty because the law has a narrow and limited approach.[61] The magistrate, being aware of the fact that Hansram, with his unstable economic situation is not in a position to arrange money, still used imprisonment as a threat to pressure him to arrange for the treatment of the child. The rule of law which sees men as 'providers' fails to consider the inability of men to provide for families in a market-driven economy where men are poor or illiterate or for any other reason could not earn sufficiently. The state has not devised social support programs or policies that could help men and women in precarious economic situations. The law cannot imagine the situations where in case, men fail to 'provide for' the family, any other alternatives could be devised to protect the women and children. The law ignores the social, political or economic circumstances and visualizes solutions only in the narrow construct of the marriage and the family. The World Bank in its report[62] also stated that for men, laws work in a straightforward manner; however, for women, laws work more like a maze[63] – more so in patriarchal societies, where the situation is much worse.

The weakening of social relations and community bonds in the capitalist economy has further affected those who are on the margins. In the case of Kamla and Reena, their natal families could only provide limited support. However, many women, with no social support from natal families are marginalized, as they could not escape easily from a violent marital situation. Instead of eliminating poverty or reducing inequalities, the state is taking all steps to get rid of the marginalized themselves. Men, women and children in such circumstances are denied their right to earn livelihoods or to survive with dignity. The free market economy is giving rise to the culture of violence where the subalterns are being mistreated and neglected. In the market economy, the poor are already marginalized because of the crisis in terms of the rollback of social security provisions, rising unemployment and growing inequalities, single women and their children are further relegated to the margins because of their inability to cope up in competitive world. The constitution guarantees the right to life with dignity, yet the state has not evolved any mechanism to ensure that citizens assuredly could live a dignified life. The personal laws guided by the religious philosophy are not sufficient to consider the changing socio-economic realities.

Indian law and the economic rights of women

The criminal or civil law on domestic violence provides temporary relief. Either the woman could go back to her marital home, or the provisions relating to long-term remedies such as separation or divorce are available under the domain of personal laws. However, personal laws, too, are limited in their approach and construe women's rights from a narrow perspective. For instance, as per legal provisions, at the time of the separation or dissolution of a marriage, a Hindu woman can claim the assets which she acquired either before her marriage or at the time of marriage by the way of gifts or inheritance as *streedhan*. However, as is evident from the cases of Kamla and Reena, frequently, those are denied in the long, tedious, one-sided process of litigation. Also, often, after years of staying in a marriage, these gifts are often utilized and therefore could not support a woman at the time when she may need them most.

Also, as per the law, if a woman separates from her abusive husband, she is deprived of her right to stay in her matrimonial home, is deprived of material assets and is alienated from the joint family.[64] She can claim for her maintenance or alimony, but that, too, is conditional and is provided to prevent her falling into 'destitution or vagrancy'[65] and is available as long as she remains chaste. If she files for divorce, she is deprived of the economic security which she enjoyed within the institution of marriage.[66] A Hindu wife becomes a part of her husband's joint family upon marriage, and he is duty bound to maintain her. Upon his death, the family in which a woman marries is responsible for supporting her. However, she cannot become a coparcener in the matrimonial property. The family in which she marries can provide her only with a minimum amount of security and shelter upon the death of her husband.[67] The concept of joint matrimonial property is not recognized under Hindu law. The colonial rulers interpreted the then existing traditions and customs through the prism of the Victorian lens, and those in post-colonial India also could not bring in major transformations, despite the fact that this situation contradicts the goal of equality and justice enshrined in the constitutional framework.

The inegalitarian status of women remain engrained in the Hindu family despite several attempts to make amendments in the law. The Hindu Women Right to Property Act of 1937 provided for a 'limited estate' to Hindu women; however, this was undone by the Hindu Succession Act of 1956. The Hindu Code Bill introduced by Ambedkar, though accepted, underwent several changes, so the inequity still persists. Kishwar[68] stated that the Hindu Succession Act remained the most controversial and key part during the debate on the codification of Hindu law, as no other right could be effectively claimed by women unless they enjoy their basic economic rights as daughters, as wives and as mothers in the family. The situation that exists today is that the law does not recognize the rights of divorced women to matrimonial property. A married woman cannot lay claim on her right over the matrimonial property to which she may have contributed through her visible or invisible labor and which may include not only what she has earned if she takes up employment but also the contribution which she makes as a homemaker, nurturer and carer within the households. Sivaramayya[69] referred to such system as one based on the 'separation of property' model under which the 'corpus of matrimonial property' is not recognized over which both spouses can make a claim. Each spouse leaves the marriage with the property to which he or she holds the title. The courts are not empowered to distribute assets while considering financial or non-financial contributions.

To cope with such a discriminatory regime, Section 27 of the Hindu Marriage Act provides that the courts can make provisions about the property 'which may belong jointly to both the husband and the wife'. The expression 'jointly' demarcates the limit of the jurisdiction of the court to the property which has been given to the spouses at or about the time of marriage, and second such property must be given to them directly while living out the significant portion of the property that the parties may have acquired before or after the marriage or during the period of matrimony for meeting the common needs of the family.[70] The Madhya Pradesh High Court, in *Rajendra Singh vs Tulsa Bai*,[71] said that a petition under Section 27 of the Hindu Marriage Act is maintainable if it is about the joint property of the couple and not their exclusive property. In *Surinder Kumar vs Madan Gopal Singh*[72] the court opined that the word 'belong' does not, necessarily reflect title to the property in the sense of ownership and elaborated that

> Properties and articles presented from any source and to any one of them which by very nature of the present, or by intention of the donor, or by agreement of spouses, has come to be jointly in use by both the husband and the wife, can well be said to belong jointly to both the them.

The courts, therefore, are vested with power to interpret the law in a gender-sensitive manner; however, accessing courts and getting favorable orders is a tedious process.

The Special Marriage Act of 1954 includes no provisions to address the settlement of property upon divorce. The Muslim law made a provision that upon divorce, the wife shall receive the property given to her and an amount equal to the sum of *meher* as agreed. Thus, the personal laws relating to the post-divorce property division are totally inadequate to address the needs of women and children. Equality or the concept of partnership in marriage is not recognized by the law when it comes to the division of assets, as the courts could not see the invisible labor or contribution of women which has resulted in an accumulation of wealth jointly to benefit the family as one unit.[73] The law ignores the invisible contribution made by women in the matrimonial homes when it comes to the division of property upon divorce or separation.

For men, divorce makes little impact on their income or lifestyle, but for women, it implies social and economic damages besides the loss of economic support. Therefore, women cling to abusive marriages, no matter the extent of destruction it may cause to their life or limb. Also, the economic situation plays a crucial role at the time of the dissolution of marriage.[74] Post-separation and after divorce, it is the women who face difficult economic circumstances despite their increased work participation rates. Not only do women have fewer assets but also their access to income declines and they are forced to face poverty. In patriarchal societies where women are deprived of any property or assets and where women's participation in formal paid work is less, most of them find it difficult to leave an abusive marriage. Therefore, in the majority of cases, divorce proceedings are initiated by men.[75] In fact, many women are abandoned by the informal process where neither any legal claims or entitlements are provided to women nor their basic rights protected. Often, males who abandon the women ignore all their material and social responsibilities toward their children. The approach of the court in decisions in cases such as *SR Batra vs Taruna Batra* need to be re-examined and women may be permitted to claim the rights to the share of the husband in the joint family's property which he is entitled to at the time of marriage. Public policy, too, has failed to provide basic essentials to women who experience marital violence by not ensuring economic security or social stability. Policymakers have failed to grasp the realities of women's lives, or the patriarchal attitude prohibits them from acknowledge the reality.

The majority of women are forced to find support and residence with their natal family. But not all are supportive or are in a situation to help their married daughters. In a country where women have no economic assets and a lower work participation rate, staying in a marriage seems the only option available for ensuring social and economic security. Ghosh[76] notes that even in urban India, in a mega-metropolis like Mumbai, "being employed does not necessarily translate to having capacities to leave an abusive marriage because of the informality and poor pay of women's work in slums and the lack of alternative shelters". Most of women, post-separation, are dependent on their parents or brothers, and though some are involved in paid work, their earning is too less to survive on their own independently or to manage their children; thus, they live in extreme deprivation, creating an inter-generational cycle of poverty. The majority of women are burdened with the responsibility of taking care of children singlehandedly with no economic or material support from their husband, resulting in accentuated inequalities between the earnings of women and the men. The legal system has failed to see the situation where women face the loss of income or cannot enter the workforce during marriage. Also, for the single, separated, divorced or abandoned women, neither the law nor the society can imagine possible alternatives outside the institution of marriage.[77] The conservative neoliberal society has failed to imagine possibilities for women who exist independently outside the institution of marriage. In societies ridden with patriarchy, casteism, feudalism and other such hierarchies, the neoliberal world order is further fueling the divide and is intensifying hierarchies.[78] In cases of female-headed households where a woman is single, abandoned, divorced, widowed or otherwise for various reasons the main bread earner, she is not supported by the state or the community in any manner.

Though the Portuguese Civil Code, 1867, as applicable in Goa has certain fair provisions and it recognize the concept of joint matrimonial property, a systematic study on the division matrimonial property law on separation or divorce is essential. The Indian courts in several cases have taken initiatives such as pushing the concept of the registration of marriage;[79] however, in case of matrimonial property division, much more is required to be done.

Indian laws need to elaborate on the concept of the matrimonial property, and suitable provisions need to be made to ensure that separating spouse should be treated with equity and fairness. The amendments to the Hindu Succession Act to provide daughters an equal share in the property is a laudable provision. However, it may be noted that the parents of the girl spent considerable resources in her upbringing and education and later she is transferred to her husband's house, where she contributes her visible and invisible labor in taking care of the matrimonial household, and yet she is deprived of a share in the matrimonial property. The concept of giving and taking dowry, or coercive dowry demands, adds to the property of the matrimonial house in which girl marries. Yet at the time of separation or divorce, this contribution is not counted. This is an incongruity in social and legal terms that needs to be addressed by introducing the concept of matrimonial property, where property could be equitably distributed among the spouses. As per the law, the concept of matrimonial property needs to be clearly defined, and the rights of each spouse need to be elaborated to protect women from victimization while recognizing the contribution in terms of the productive work women make in their matrimonial home. This may also assist women in providing material and financial security. The Maharashtra government has taken a step in this direction and introduced a bill[80] titled Matrimonial Property (Rights of Women upon Marriage) Bill-2012, which attempts to formulate the rights of women in marriage. However, at a broader level, steps must be taken to recognize women's contribution to matrimonial relationships and to protect women's rights in the event of separation or divorce.

Evolving jurisprudence regarding recognizing the contributions of women

The general recommendation on Article 16 of the CEDAW[81] noted that

> the State parties should provide both spouses equal access to marital property and equal legal capacity to manage it. They should ensure that the right of women to own, acquire, manage, administer and enjoy separate or non-marital property is equal to that of men.[82]

It further elaborated that the state parties must provide equal formal and de facto legal capacity to own and manage property to achieve formal and substantive equality with respect to property rights during the dissolution of marriage. Substantive equality could be achieved when the states examine the application of the effects of laws and policies while accounting for women's disadvantages and exclusion. Duty is cast upon the state to provide information on the economic consequences to individuals entering into a marriage of its potential dissolution by divorce or death.

Across, the world, countries have recognized the fact that women suffer the most when a marriage ends. Therefore, when defining matrimonial property, they consider the fact that assets that both the husband and wife accumulate during the marriage, both visible and non-visible contributions, be included. The laws provide for an equal division of matrimonial property, and the courts are empowered to order its division between the spouses at the time of divorce or separation. In case the spouses were married without any provision concerning matrimonial property law, the default statutory system of limited community property is applied.[83] As per this provision, the property acquired during the marriage is held in common, although gifts and inheritances acquired during the marriage are the separate property of each spouse. In the UK, United States, Europe, Singapore and Tanzania there are specific laws that deal with the distribution of marital property. Under the provisions of the Matrimonial Proceedings and Property Act, 1970, of the UK, the courts can order either spouse to make financial provisions or can transfer the property or can issue an order regarding a settlement to ensure that married women's right to property is protected besides protecting the rights of children. The laws in the United States recognize that women are in a disadvantageous position in a marriage, and therefore provisions have been made to protect the right to the matrimonial property of wives. The Australian Family Law provides that the courts assess the non-financial contribution made by wives to the welfare of the family through unpaid work at home and in the care of children. In Ireland, a wife's domestic duties are recognized under the law, and the community property ownership model applies. Both spouses are joint and equal owners of the properties, irrespective of the fact that the title of the property belongs to one of them.[84] The Canadian law governing the division of matrimonial property stipulates that childcare, house management and providing finances is a joint responsibility that brings joint rights over property. Kenya enacted the Matrimonial Property Act in 2013 to provide for the rights and responsibilities of spouses in relation to matrimonial property.

In England, while recognizing the principle of equality in terms of the division of property at the time of the dissolution of the marriage, the court in the case of *White vs White*[85] ensured that both the parties, upon divorce, receive their rightful share of the matrimonial property. Lord Nicholls stated that "there should be no bias in favour of the money-earner and against the home-maker and child-carer". This is not automatically translated to an 'absolute' equal split of property. The court as well as the legislature recognizes that in a number of cases such a yardstick may bring an unfair burden to one of the parties. The House of Lords in *Miller vs Miller*[86] articulated that the rationale for the redistribution of resources from one party to another may be based on three dimensions which include need, compensation and sharing for redistribution. In other countries, too, women's right to matrimonial property has been interpreted widely to recognize women's paid and unpaid contributions to the household.

However, in India, there are no specific laws that recognize joint ownership or that acknowledge women's invaluable invisible contribution to the family. The courts in India, have made scattered attempts to quantify women's work within the household, mostly in cases related to insurance. For instance, it has been noted by the court that

> For compensating a husband for loss of a wife, therefore courts consider the loss of income to the family. It may not be difficult when she had been earning. Even otherwise a wife's contribution to the family in terms of money can always be worked out. Every housewife makes a contribution to her family. It is capable of measuring in monetary terms although the emotional aspect of it cannot be.[87]

Further, in *Lata Wadhwa vs State of Bihar*,[88] while awarding compensation to a family injured in a fire, attempted to estimate the value of services rendered by the housewife and fixed Rs 3500/ as the monthly income. In *National Insurance Company vs Deepika*[89] it was noted that

> The role of a housewife includes managing budgets, coordinating activities, balancing accounts, helping children with education, managing help at home, nursing care etc. One formula that has been arrived at determines the value of the housewife as, Value of housewife = husband's income + wife's income + value of husband's household services, which means the wife's value will increase inversely proportionate to the extent of participation by the husband in the household duties.

Thus, the Indian courts have utilized the principle of calculating the homemaker's income in the insurance compensation–related cases, but have not applied this to women who file complaints against their abusive partners.

Reforming the law in India to formulate the right to matrimonial property

The goal of equality proclaimed in the constitution remains a dream for many, despite the fact that India attained independence decades ago. Though many laws have been enacted to even out the disparity in the social and economic structure, the social reality has remained unchanged for many. The majority of Indian women are working as homemakers toiling hard; caring for the children, sick and elderly; fetching water; collecting wood; taking care of animals; cooking; cleaning; and doing all forms of visible and invisible work at home silently, without being paid or being acknowledged for their contribution. Those who work in the informal sector remain highly underpaid. A large number of women hold no property in their name. They only can inherit property either as daughters or as widows. In matrimonial homes, women are in a vulnerable position because most of them are dependent economically and socially on their husbands and in-laws. In case of violence in marriage, a woman is left with no choice because there are no support systems or alternatives available beyond the institution of the family. Post-divorce, too, alternatives available for women are limited. She may remarry and choose to reenter into another risk or remain at the natal home and thus be dependent on the parents or siblings, or be on her own and sink into deeper poverty because the market paradigm does not offer any other options. The state has not created any support mechanisms for women in vulnerable situations.

The Law Commission, in its Consultation Paper on Reform of Family Law,[90] noted that the legislature should first consider guaranteeing equality within communities between men and women rather than 'equality between communities'. It further recommended recognizing the community of all self-acquired property after marriage of either spouse to be treated as a unit between the couple. While recognizing women's unpaid contribution, it recommends that

> it is the women who compromise on careers in order to support the families, they also contribute in in most households in India to a major share of housework which is never calculated in monetary terms. The society inadequately values the housework and further for working women, childbearing results in career break which affect their employment in a way that it does not affect their husband's career. Therefore, it is important that regardless of whether the wife financially or monetarily contributes to the family income, her contribution to a household in terms of household labour, home management, and child bearing and care should entitle her to an equal share in a marriage and thus all property for income gained after marriage should be divided equally upon divorce. This does not mean that inherited property will also be included in this division but its value can be taken into account by the court for determining maintenance and alimony.[91]

However, in order to acknowledge the contribution of women and their right to matrimonial property, and to economically empower them, what is required is amendments in the laws relating to marriage and divorce, and more importantly, the will on the part of law makers and those who enforce the law to recognize the concept of equality and democracy within the family as a basic unit of the society.

Women's access to economic resources enhances bargaining power

Several studies in India have shown that women's bargaining power may increase within a household in case she is employed or is in a position to control assets. Female ownership and control over property enhance a woman's economic security, reduce her willingness to tolerate violence and deter spousal violence. A systematic review of 22 studies conducted in low- and middle-income countries found that women's access to paid employment protected them against violence in some contexts but increased the risk of violence in others.[92] Similarly, both property ownership and access to microfinance had mixed outcomes.[93] In Kerala, it has been noted that women owning immoveable property (land or a house) experience a significantly lower risk of violence than women who may not own any property.[94] In rural Uttar Pradesh[95] it is found that women's engagement in paid work and ownership of property are factors that are associated with a reduction in violence. It has been observed that women in regular wage employment were less likely to be beaten than unemployed women or women in casual, poorly paid jobs.[96] Employed women whose husbands lost their jobs during the period of the study were more likely to suffer from violence than those whose husbands' status had not changed.

Another survey[97] of 256 women in six villages in Karnataka, Telangana and Meghalaya observed that the majority of women felt that land ownership has improved their mobility, enhanced their ability to make decisions about their own lives and ensured a life free of violence. Land ownership has helped them to use their agency and has enabled them to fight back against patriarchal violence. Another multi-site comparative[98] study conducted in West Bengal, Kerala and Sri Lanka in 2006 showed that women's ownership of land deterred violence and improved women's status in different ways. Property ownership enhanced their status in the family, helped them to earn respect in the community and enabled them to participate in decision making while their vulnerability is reduced markedly. Thus, expanding women's right to matrimonial property may help them to escape abuse and may result in their enhanced power to negotiate violence and leave an abusive relationship. Women who own property have a greater voice, have higher self-esteem and have substantial economic independence, and more importantly, an exit option is available to these women.

To strengthen social protections, several studies have explored the potential property ownership and inheritance rights of women as a protective factor against domestic violence. Property ownership may help women to acquire confidence, reduce insecurities, enhance their status and self-worth and empower them to negotiate around violence or walk away from a violent relationship,[99] and therefore, most of these studies have highlighted women's inheritance to property from the natal family or receiving property as a share of the dowry. However, one of the limitations of such an approach is that inheritance or receiving a share of land as dowry is applicable only to the propertied class or those who possess land. Second, it is also dependent on the dynamics of the relationship women may have with their natal families. Third, no arguments have been raised about the women's share in the matrimonial property. Also, these arguments are not applicable to the families which are poor and may not own any form of property or land.

Moving beyond the concept of the law and the free market

Many families are living on the margins in vulnerable conditions and may not own property or any assets. The narratives provided earlier are just a glimpse into the lives and social realities of some men and women. There are many Kamlas, Reenas, Hansrams, Jhumris and their children who are struggling in a worse manner. However, these lived experiences suggest that an inadequate focus on the social laws and policies in the market economy to ameliorate evils such as poverty or gender disparities has failed to yield an effective result. These narratives indicate the wide gaps in the pace of economic transitions with that of changes made in the laws and policies at a socio-political level. The situation has created havoc in the lives of ordinary men and women. Those who are poor and vulnerable are made to suffer in the process. The patriarchy is reinforced, and at the same time those who are poor are demonized and made to suffer. The culture of cruelty that is being enforced because of the policy of imposing a free market economy without any state support mechanism in place is harming ordinary men, women and children. Despite the existence of intricate laws, implementation remains abysmal, and the rights could not be translated into reality because of various hurdles. The discussion therefore suggests that there is a need to imagine innovative solutions outside the realm of existing laws and policies in addition to strengthening social security provisions.

The need is to re-examine the situation and re-think the alternatives beyond the domain of law and economics into the social stream. From the perspective of women who are seeking divorce or are separated or abandoned by their natal as well as marital families, it is essential that special measures be evolved. At a micro level, the provisions of the laws relating to the division of matrimonial property need to be considered, as women's control over marital property could have a positive impact on their economic power and agency. At the macro level, there is a dire need to strengthen the social support and welfare system. Providing financial support, employment security and economic support to women and children is essential to emancipate women with a focus on the fundamental premises of dignity and autonomy.

Strengthening social protection measures

The discourse on social protection in recent decades has gained currency across many developing countries, including South Asia. From proposing simple measures to protect workers, the definition of social protection has been expanded to reduce poverty and target vulnerable groups based on their age, gender, migration and other indicators. Overall, social protection is now viewed as a policy framework that aims to reduce vulnerability and enhance the capacity to manage economic risks while also enhancing human potential and promoting equality in terms of opportunity.[100]

From the perspective of the vulnerable groups who are excluded and marginalized, it is essential to focus on the broad approach of the social protection framework. This is not to say that gender divisions are not applicable to the well-off propertied groups – women's right to property needs to be protected even among those classes who may have access to resources. Formal and informal support mechanisms may be made available by the state or the community. It is essential that focus also be laid on those powerless groups who are becoming more susceptible due to the changing nature of employment and are receiving less and less support from the community networks. Due to intersecting forms of discrimination and disadvantage, those women on the margins are even further excluded from the social protection programs and interventions, though these are women who need more of such support services. Domestic violence among such women who are poor further leads them to destitution unless they have some support mechanism.

It is therefore concluded that women are being compelled to stay in violent relationships because of their economic dependency on men and on the institution of marriage. Therefore, it is essential to provide justice to battered women. The strategies to end violence against women may include strong measures that promote economic security and restitution of survivors.

> Because economic dependence and severe financial stress on abused women can so acutely impact a survivor's choice to stay or leave an abusive relationship and because economic abuse by batterers is often an aspect of the power and control over their lives, stronger legal advocacy for economic safety and restitution is important to the economic empowerment of battered women and the goal of assuring that women may live free of violence and oppression by their intimate partners. Attorneys and advocates, together with their clients, should carefully evaluate the economic costs of past abuse and future survival so that clients' needs are assessed comprehensively and articulated to the court.[101]

Social protection measures may ensure justice to those who cannot afford it rather than relying solely in the courts.

The law alone cannot reform the social situation unless it is accompanied by reforms at a socio-political and economic level. Thus, besides examining the legal framework relating to the rights of women in matrimonial property, short-term solutions such as short-stay homes, shelter homes for abused women, creche facilities, medical services, legal aid and other support mechanisms need to be created, in addition to advocating for long-term solutions like reorienting gender roles toward equality between the sexes and establishing socio-cultural and legal reforms. Sending women back to a violent situation is not an alternative. It is also essential that special interventions be introduced for women and children experiencing domestic violence, which may include special facilities to support children in schools and colleges, provision of employment for women facing violence, entrepreneurship skills and training program, provision of residential facilities, sensitization of officials involved in such programs, transforming the social and cultural environment in terms of masculinity and femininity, engaging young men and boys to bring a shift in the patriarchal mind-set and making larger structural changes to reform the patriarchal environment. Mirchandani[102] has cautioned that the

> welfare state benefits have positioned women and men in gendered ways, fostering men's economic and physical dominance over women in the home. In addition, feminist scholars have found that states can implement policies unequally. In particular, research suggests that in imposing laws, states require women to conform to tightly circumscribed and often moralistic notions of gender imposed in a style that is cumbersome and repeatedly intrusive.

It is essential that affirmative actions be undertaken.

This work suggests that to protect the rights of survivors in vulnerable situations, interventions may be made at various levels:

1 To introduce equal division of marital property by a law on a similar footing as that of the Hindu Succession Amendment Act 2005, besides taking steps to implement the provisions of the Dowry Prohibition Act and a domestic violence law.
2 To create an institutional support mechanism for the non-propertied, vulnerable classes, which may include developing an infrastructure in the form of short-stay homes, shelter homes, crisis centers, medical and health facilities, creche facilities, working women hostels, giving priority to survivors in employment, providing facilities in terms of free education, health, sports, etc., to children of women survivors, providing quality legal aid services.
3 Using Nirbahya funds and other mechanisms to support survivors who are in helpless situations and to introduce schemes such as universal income, cash transfer or pension funds or similar such reliefs to support women.
4 Making policy interventions in terms of addressing gender inequality and structural and institutional biases in other social, cultural and legal interventions.
5 Addressing labor market policies, a gender-aware national employment policy and promoting the employment of survivors in formal and informal sectors through job subsidies and job creation programs while dealing with discrimination and harassment issues against women.
6 Strengthening social safety nets to make an impact on household power dynamics.

7 Evolving measures to include *rozi-roti aur maakan* (employment and housing) with *sammaan* or dignity to survivors and victims of domestic violence.

What is required is interventions beyond the symbolic compliance with the law to direct attention to the asymmetry in power in relationships, as well as challenging barriers to women's rights and equality. There is a need to critically scrutinize the institution of marriage and family with a gender lens. The dominant social arrangement that creates different realities for men and women needs to be questioned. The institution of marriage or family as a picture-perfect institution without any dignity or respect for women is simply an abomination. No society can call itself democratic or just when the so-called basic units of society – 'the families' – become undemocratic and violent – a place of misery and anguish for women. Challenging the social and cultural norms relating to the role of men and women in the family is crucial. At a broader level, the solution may lie in rethinking the situation of women's dependency on marriage, women's value in the labor market and the transmission of property and other resources to women. Employment opportunities need to be generated for men and women while countering the forces that are shrinking the spaces for economic opportunities. Enhancing women's autonomy through education and employment may help, in addition to ensuring women's control over resources. Or as Wendy Brown[103] insisted, that sharing of power and not regulation, freedom not protection, is a true affirmation of democracy which may end the social and legal marginalization of women within families while pursuing the goal of egalitarianism as prescribed by the Indian constitution. 'Another World Is Possible' – the movement that emerged in response to 'There Is No Alternative' – needs to be re-visited as an alternative to the neoliberal capitalist free market economy.

Summary

This chapter examined several cases and concluded that despite the criminal and civil law provisions relating to domestic violence, many women still struggle in their daily lives. The law cannot imagine situations outside the paradox of the family, and the free market approach does not help advocate for social policies that could offer alternatives to leading a life with dignity. Trapped in the web of legal technicalities and the complexities of market norms, some women are facing increasing vulnerabilities, where the state has refused to bail them out in any way. It is recommended that the laws relating to divorce be reconsidered, with matrimonial property being divided equally among the separating parties and the rights of women to marital property be examined. It is also suggested that while considering the ill effects of the capitalist economy, the concept of the provisions of social security and the welfare support measures need to strengthened, and, wherever required, special provisions be made to support the women and children in distress.

Notes

1 Oakley Ann (1974) *Housewife*, Pelican Books, Reprinted by Penguin in 2000 p. 233
2 As quoted by Tittenburn Jacek (2013) The Death of the Economic Man, *International Letters of Social and Humanistic Science*, 11, 10–34, www.scipress.com/ILSHS.11.10.pdf accessed on 23.05.17
3 Smith Adam (1976) *Reprint of An Inquiry into the Nature and Causes of Wealth of Nations*, edited by RH Campbell and AS Skinner, Liberty Classics, IN, http://files.libertyfund.org/files/220/0141-02_Bk.pdf accessed on 15.04.18
4 Sen Amratya (1977) Rational Fools: A Critique of the Behavioral Foundation of Economic Theory, *Philosophy and Public Affairs*, 6 (4) 317–44
5 Kumar Arun (2014) *Has the Quest for Equity Became Irrelevant in India? Yusuf Meherally Lecture*, September 23, Gandhi Peace Foundation, New Delhi
6 I express my gratitude to Prof Arun Kumar for the lectures he delivered at the meeting organized by the PUCL Delhi for elaborating on this concept.
7 Polyani Karl (1944) *The Great Transformation: The Political and Economic Origins of Our Times*, Beacon Press, Boston
8 Nigam Shalu (2018) No Wages for Love: Women's Rights Within Families and Changing Economic Paradigm, *Countercurrents*, March 30, https://countercurrents.org/2018/03/30/no-wages-for-love-womens-rights-within-families-and-changing-economic-paradigm/
9 Nigam S (2014) Outsourcing Love: Globalization, Care Economy and Its Impact on Social Relations Within Families, *Countercurrents*, September 14
10 Becker Gary S (1974) A Theory of Marriage, In *The Economics of the Family: Marriage, Children and Human Capital*, edited by Theodore W Schultz, University of Chicago Press, Chicago
11 Goode William J (1974) Comment: The Economics of Non-Monetary Variables, In *The Economics of the Family: Marriage, Children and Human Capital*, edited by Theodore W Schultz, University of Chicago Press, Chicago pp. 345–51
12 Becker Gary S (1981) *A Treatise on Family*, Harvard University Press, Enlarged Edition 1991
13 Radin Margaret Jane (1987) Market-Inalienability, *Harvard Law Review*, 100, 1850
14 Ibid
15 Bergmann Barbara R (1995) Becker's Theory of the Family: Preposterous Conclusions, *Feminist Economics*, 1 (1) 141–50
16 Radin (1987) supra n 13 pp. 1847–937
17 Lazear Edward P (1999) *Economic Imperialism*, National Bureau of Economic Research, Working Paper 7300, Cambridge, MA
18 Ehrenreich Barbara and Hochschild AR (Eds) (2003) *Global Woman: Nannies, Maids, and Sex Workers in the New Economy*, Metropolitan Books, New York
19 Guenther Julia (2015) Gender and Globalization: Power Relations at India's Margin, *Journal of Developing Society*, 31 (1) 28–42
20 Banerjee N (1999) *Analysing Women's Work Under Patriarchy in from Myths to Markets*, edited by K Sangari and U Chakravarti, Manohar Publications, New Delhi p. 323
21 Patnaik Prabhat (2013) On the Empowerment of Women, *People's Democracy*, XXXVIII (5) February 3, https://archives.peoplesdemocracy.in/2013/0203_pd/02032013_3.html

22 The Hindustan Times (2019) MP woman Assaulted by Husband Critical, May 16. In the same paper, on the same page there is another report which alleged that a 42-year-old woman and her daughter committed suicide in Thiruvananthapuram, and the police recovered a suicide note wherein she blamed her husband and her mother-in-law and other two relatives for getting money from her parents to pay loans her husband has taken out. The note mentions black magic rituals and an attempt by her mother-in-law to poison the duo. The family claimed that it is due to persistent attempts by the bank to repay loans that drove them to commit suicide. Though a further probe may be essential from the legal perspective, such incidents reflect the fact that women are facing harsh violence due to economic imperatives.

23 *Aljazeera* (2019) Oxfam: World's Richest Own Same Wealth as Poorest Half, January 21, https://www.aljazeera.com/news/2019/01/oxfam-world-richest-26-wealth-poorest-190121054249908.html

24 Lawson M, Man-Kwun C, Rhodes F et al. (2019) *Public Good or Private Wealth?* Oxfam, Oxford p. 14

25 Mckinsey Global Institute (2015) The Power of Parity: How Advancing Women's Equality Can Add $12 Trillion To Global Growth, www.mckinsey.com/featured-insights/employment-and-growth/how-advancing-womens-equality-can-add-12-trillion-to-global-growth accessed on 13.04.17

26 Organization for Economic Cooperation and Development as available on the site, https://stats.oecd.org/index.aspx?queryid=54757 accessed on 06.10.18

27 Chandrashekhar A and Agarwal P (2017) More Indian Women Could Opt for Paid Work, if they Found Reliable Caregivers, *India Spend*, August 7, www.indiaspend.com/cover-story/more-indian-women-could-opt-for-paid-work-if-they-found-reliable-caregivers-19547

28 *The Hindu* (2019) Inequality Has a Female Face in India, Women's Unpaid Work is Worth 3.1% of GDP: Oxfam, January 21, https://www.thehindu.com/news/national/inequality-has-female-face-in-india-womens-unpaid-work-worth-31-of-gdp-oxfam/article26048261.ece

29 The World Bank (2019) Labor Force Female (Percentage of total labor force), https://data.worldbank.org/indicator/SL.TLF.TOTL.FE.ZS accessed on 20.03.18

30 Yadavar Swagata (2017) Global Gender Gap Index: India Ranks 108 Of 144 Countries, Down 21 Places From 2016, *Fact Checker*, November 3, http://factchecker.in/global-gender-gap-index-india-ranks-108-of-144-countries-down-21-places-from-2016/ accessed on 18.3.18

31 Sinha S (2015) Reader Tips on Finding a Partner Using Indian Marriage Sites, *The New York Times*, May 9

32 *The Economic Times* (2013) Online Matrimony Business Likely to Touch Rs 1500 Crores by 2017: Survey, December 17, https://m.economictimes.com/news/company/corporate-trends/online-matrimony-business-likely-to-touch-rs-1500-crore-by-2017-survey/articleshow/27529167.cms

33 KPMG and Google (2016) Digital Classifieds in India 2020: A Study by KPMG and Google, https://assets.kpmg/content/dam/kpmg/in/pdf/2016/09/Digital-classifieds-India-2020_new.pdf

34 Chunduri M (2005) Dowry Market: It's Money Honey, *The Times of India*, Hyderabad Edition December 11, https://timesofindia.indiatimes.com/city/hyderabad/Dowry-market-It-is-money-honey/articleshow/1327074.cms

35 Khan LA and Gowhar I (2014) They Eye Money Not Matrimony, *The Hindu*, October 27, https://www.thehindu.com/news/national/karnataka/fraudsters-target-gullible-women-on-matrimonial-websites/article6535615.ece

36 Siwan A (2007) The Economics of Dowry and Bride Price, *Journal of Economic Perspectives*, 21 (4) 151–74

37 Das Usha Rani (2016) The Big Fat Wedding Industry in India: Recap of 2015 and Outlook for 2016, *The Business Insider*, February 16. Currently the industry is 100,000 crores and is growing at 25 to 30 percent annually. It adds over 3 lacs jobs a year during the season.
38 Pandit V (2017) Big Fat Indian Wedding Market Has Foreign Suitor Zankyou Lining Up, *The Hindu Business*, April 7, https://www.thehindubusinessline.com/news/national/big-fat-indian-wedding-market-has-foreign-suitor-zankyou-lining-up/article9622383.ece
39 Bundhun R (2016) India Weddings A Billion Dollar Industry, *The National*, October 22, www.thenational.ae/business/india-weddings-a-billion-dollar-industry-1.162964
40 Das Sohini (2016) Start Ups Target the Big Fat Indian Wedding Industry, *The Business Standard*, May 7, www.business-standard.com/article/companies/start-ups-target-the-big-fat-indian-wedding-industry-116050600818_1.html
41 Saini S (2017) Malls Turn into Destination Centers for Wedding Shopping, *IndiaRetailing.com*, March 14, https://www.indiaretailing.com/2017/03/14/shopping-centre/malls-turn-destination-centres-wedding-shopping/
42 Multiple ceremonies are organized for several days before the final wedding day, and the feast is organized depending on the socio-economic status of the families.
43 Bhattacharya Pramit (2016) India and its Burden for Social Obligations, *Live Mint*, December 19, www.livemint.com/Home-Page/KE02Tqr0Y5Tc5wPe7m6f1N/India-and-its-burden-of-social-obligations.html
44 Ibid
45 Bhalotra S, Chakravarty A and Telim G (2018) *The Price of Gold: Dowry Death in India*, CEPR Discussion Paper 12712
46 Bhattacharya H (2015) Spousal Violence and Women's Employment in India, *Feminist Economists*, 21 (2) 30–52
47 Luke, Nancy and Kaivan Munshi (2011) Women as Agents of Change: Female Income and Mobility in India, *Journal of Development Economics*, 94 (1) 1–17
48 Atkinson MP, Greenstein TN and Lang MM (2005) For Women Breadwinning can be Dangerous: Gendered Resource Theory and Wife Abuse, *Journal of Marriage and Family*, 67, 1137–48
49 Anderson S and Genicot G (2012) Suicide and Property Rights in India, World Bank, www.economics.ubc.ca/files/2013/05/pdf_paper_siwan-anderson-suicide-propety-rights.pdf
50 Paul Sohini (2016) Women Labour Force Participation and Domestic Violence: Evidence from India, *Journal of South Asian Development*, 11 (2) 224–50
51 Molyneux M (2006) Mothers at the Service of the New Poverty Agenda: Progresa/Oportunidades, Mexico's Conditional Transfer Programme, *Social Policy and Administration*, 40 (4) 425–49
52 Batliwala S (2007) Taking the Power Out of Empowerment – An Experiential Account, *Development in Practice*, 17 (4 and 5) 557–65
53 Littwin A (2012) Coerced Debt: The Role of Consumer Credit in Domestic Violence, *California Law Review*, 100, 952–1026
54 Singh K (2013) *Separated and Divorced Women in India: Economic Rights and Entitlements*, Sage Publications, New Delhi
55 Branigan E (2004) *His Money or Our Money? Financial Abuse of Women in Intimate Partner Relationships*, Coburg Brunswick Community Legal and Financial Counselling Centre, Coburg, Victoria, Australia. Also, Sharp-Jeffs N (2015) *A Review of Research and Policy on Financial Abuse Within Intimate Partner Relationships*, Child and Woman Abuse Studies Unit, London; Usta J, Makarem NN and Habib RR (2013) Economic abuse in Lebanon: Experiences and perceptions, *Violence Against Women*, 19, 356–75

56 Mehrotra S (2019) India Does Have a Real Employment Crisis – and It Is Worsening, *The Wire*, February 6
57 Nigam S (2014) Precariats in India: Globalization and Changing Employment Relations, *Countercurrents*, October 30
58 Recently in many cases, the courts, while pronouncing judgements, have stated that women are filing false cases of domestic violence to just get money or to retaliate, as in *Arnesh Kumar vs State of Bihar* or *Rajesh Kumar vs State of UP*. For more details refer to Nigam S (2017) Is Domestic Violence A Lesser Crime: Countering Backlash Against Section 498A IPC, Occasional Paper No. 61, Center for Women Development Studies, New Delhi
59 Nigam S (2015) Delhi: A World Class Smart City or An Inclusive and Equitable Capital, *Countercurrents*, February 14
60 *Times of India* (2018) Following Twitter Outrage, HDFC Bank Remove Metal Spikes Installed Outside Mumbai Branch, March 27, https://timesofindia.indiatimes.com/india/following-twitter-outrage-hdfc-bank-removes-metal-spikes-installed-outside-mumbai-branch/articleshow/63477636.cms
61 Nigam Shalu (2017) Fighting for Justice in Patriarchal Courts, *Countercurrents*, August 30, https://countercurrents.org/2017/08/30/fighting-for-justice-in-the-patriarchal-courts/
62 World Bank (2018) *Women*, Business and the Law, Washington, DC, https://openknowledge.worldbank.org/bitstream/handle/10986/29498/9781464812521.pdf
63 Summers Hannah (2018) No Women, No Growth: Regressive Laws Prevent Economic Inequality Says Study, *The Guardian*, March 30, www.theguardian.com/global-development/2018/mar/30/no-women-no-growth-regressive-laws-prevent-economic-equality-world-bank-study?CMP=twt_gu
64 Unless she chose to file her claim for right to residence under the PWDVA.
65 K Vimla vs Veeraswamy JT 1991 (2)SC 182
66 Sen J (2009) Matrimonial Property Rights: Is India Ready for a Law? *Journal of Indian Law and Society* (1) 129–51
67 She is supposed to file an application under Section 22 of the Hindu Adoption and Maintenance Act for maintenance against her late husband's estate. Also AIR 1986 (P&H) 251.
68 Kishwar M (1994) Codified Hindu Law: Myth and Reality, *Economic and Political Weekly*, 29 (33) 2145–61
69 Sivaramayya B (1999) *Matrimonial Property Law in India*, Oxford University Press, New Delhi
70 Anil Kumar vs Jyoti AIR 1987 Raj 157
71 1(1996) DMC 572 MP
72 1980 HLR. 507 followed in Yudhister Raj vs Sarla Kumari 1981 HLR 37 (P &H)
73 Sen P (1999) Enhancing Women's Choices in Responding to Domestic Violence in Calcutta: A Comparison of Employment and Education, *The European Journal of Development Research*, 11, 65–86
74 De Vaus David, Grey Matthew, Qu Lixia and Stanton David (2015) *The Economic Consequences of Divorce in Six OECD Countries*, Research Report No 31, Australian Institute of Family Studies, Melbourne
75 Palriwala Rajni and Uberoi Patricia (Eds) (2008) *Marriage, Migration and Gender*, Sage, New Delhi
76 Ghosh Sreeparna (2015) The Political Economy of Domestic Violence in a Mumbai Slum: An Ethnographic Analysis, *Journal of Interdisciplinary Economics*, 27 (2) 175–98, 194
77 Nigam S (2017) *Is Domestic Violence a Lesser Crime? Countering the Backlash Against Section 498A IPC*, Occasional Paper No. 61, Center for Women Development Studies, New Delhi

78 Nigam S (2016) The Privileges of Being a Hindu, Upper Caste Elite Male in India, *Countercurrents*, February 10, www.countercurrents.org/nigam100216.htm
79 Seema vs Ashwini Kumar AIR 2006 SC 1158
80 *The Hindu Business Line* (2012) Maharashtra Bill Widens Women's Rights Over Husbands Property, March 11, https://www.thehindubusinessline.com/economy/policy/Maharashtra-Bill-widens-womans-rights-over-husbands-property/article20407546.ece
81 CEDAW (2013) General recommendation on article 16 of the Convention on the Elimination of All Forms of Discrimination against Women, CEDAW/C/GC/29 February 26, http://www2.ohchr.org/english/bodies/cedaw/docs/comments/CEDAW-C-52-WP-1_en.pdf
82 Para 38
83 Hamilton Carolyn and Perry Alison (2002) *Family Law in Europe*, Butterworths, London
84 Frantz Carolyn J and Dagan Hanoch (2004) Properties of Marriage, *Columbia Law Review*, 104 (125) 75–133
85 (2000) UKHL 54
86 (2006) UKHL 24
87 Malay Kumar Ganguly vs Sukumar Mukherjee (2009) (10) SCALE 675
88 AIR 2001 SC 3218
89 MANU/TN/1304/2009
90 Law Commission of India (2018) *Consultation Paper on Reform of Family Law*, August 31, Government of India, New Delhi
91 Ibid pp. 29–30
92 Vyas S and Watts C (2009) "How Does Economic Empowerment Affect Women's Risk of Intimate Partner Violence in Low and Middle-Income Countries? A Systematic Review of Published Evidence, *Journal of International Development*, 21 (5) 577–602
93 Heise LL (2012) *Determinants of Partner Violence in Low and Middle-Income Countries: Exploring Variation in Individual and Population Level Risk*, Doctorate of Philosophy Thesis, London School Of Hygiene and Tropical Medicine, UK
94 Panda P and Agarwal B (2005) Marital Violence, Human Development and Women's Property Status in India, *World Development*, 33 (5) 823–50
95 Bhattacharya M, Bedi AS and Chhachhi A (2009) *Marital Violence and Women's Employment and Property Status: Evidences from North Indian Villages*, Discussion Paper No. 4361 IZA, Germany
96 Sen (1999) supra
97 Kelkar Govind, Gaikwad S and Mandal S (2015) *Women's Asset Ownership and Reduction in Gender-Based Violence*, Landesa, New Delhi
98 International Center for Research on Women (2006) Property Ownership and Inheritance Rights of Women for Social Protection – The South Asia Experience, Synthesis Report of Three Studies, *ICRW*, www.icrw.org/wp-content/uploads/2016/10/Property-Ownership-and-Inheritance-Rights-of-Women-for-Social-Protection-The-South-Asia-Experience.pdf
99 Panda P (2006) *Domestic Violence and Women's Property Ownership: Delving Deeper into the Linkages in Kerala*, In Property Ownership and Inheritance Rights of Women for Social Protection – The South Asia Experience, Synthesis of Report of Three Studies, ICRW, New Delhi
100 ICRW (2006) *Property Ownership and Inheritance Rights of Women for Social Protection – The South Asia Experience*, Synthesis of Report of Three Studies, New Delhi

101 Thomas Christine (2004) Advancing the Economic Rights of Domestic Violence Survivors in Protection Order Proceedings, *Battered Women Justice Project* pp. 8–9
102 Mirchandani R (2006) Hitting Is Not Manly: Domestic Violence Court and the Reimagination of Patriarchal State, *Gender and Society*, 20 (6) 781–804
103 Brown Wendy (1995) *States of Injury: Power and Freedom in Late Modernity*, Princeton University Press, NJ

6 Adjudicating domestic violence in the courts

> "*And yet the wife is the actual bond servant of her husband: so far as the law is concerned, she is as subordinate to him as slaves, commonly so called, are to their masters. She promises life-long obedience to him at the altar, and is legally held to that all through her life. . . . She can do no act whatever without his at least tacit permission. She can acquire no property for herself: the instant something becomes hers, even if by inheritance, it automatically becomes his. In this respect the wife's position under the common law of England is worse than that of slaves in the laws of many countries. . . . The two are called 'one person in law,' for the purpose of inferring that whatever is hers is his, but the parallel inference is never drawn that whatever is his is hers; the maxim is not applied against the man, except to make him responsible to third parties for her acts, as a master is for the acts of his slaves or of his cattle. I'm not claiming that wives are in general no better treated than slaves; but no slave is a slave to the same extent and in a full a sense of the word as a wife is. Hardly any slave . . . is a slave at all hours and all minutes; in general, he has his fixed task, and when it is done he disposes up to a point of his own time and has a family life into which the master rarely intrudes. however brutal a tyrant her husbands lave is – even if she knows that he hates her, and/or it is his daily pleasure to torture her, and/or she finds it impossible not to loathe him – he can claim from her and ·legally· enforce the lowest degradation of a human being, that of being made the instrument of an animal function contrary to her inclinations*".[1]

John Stuart Mill, in 1869 in his thesis on the *Subjection of Women*,[2] while questioning women's subordinate status within marriage, argued that man as a master not only wants a woman's labor but also her sentiments, and he conspires to exploit in order to accomplish this desire for a submissive docile slave over whom he could have an absolute control. Mill rejected the 'cult of domesticity' and wrote that marriage is a form of slavery that confers power to men and "not only to good men or decently respectable men, but to all men, including the most brutal and most criminal" are benefitted by it.[3] Based on such a critique, reforms have been made in the laws in some countries, but in India, laws are still propagating the norms that enslave women.

Though a domestic violence law has been enacted to prohibit, criminalize and condemn any act of abuse which has been socially accepted, normalized and routinized by the social norms by providing legal recourse and remedy against such actions, these laws are construed narrowly in the courtrooms. The purpose of the law is lost in the technicalities and subjectivities involved in translating and interpreting laws.

The object of the law seeks to right the wrongs by equalizing and tilting the power balance in favor of women who are at the receiving end and are socially disempowered and marginalized within their homes. The larger aim is to create a culture that promotes constitutional values and promotes a rule that sternly prohibits violence in all forms within a household. It is expected that through this law the message is being spread that domestic violence is unacceptable and intolerable and that the one who is being victimized is entitled to obtain remedies. The law is therefore created with the goal to attack inequitable and unjust social norms.

Courts, as the custodian of justice, constitutional values and the rule of law, play a significant role in defining and shaping the legal and social norms and ensuring that those who are powerless are rendered justice. In normal parlance, the courts are considered temples of justice by ordinary people. It is expected that the courts, with their progressive and fair attitude, condemn all forms of violence and enforce the law in an innovative manner to provide justice to the women who face abuse. However, analysis of everyday proceedings in the courtrooms reveals the manner in which sexism operates and is reinforced in daily decisions, orders, conversation, jest, reasoning and assumptions based on the ideology that subjugates women despite the fact that the constitution guarantees affirmative provisions in favor of women. Courts often use stiff legal language; are objective, stern and righteous; and are known to instill discipline and authority, and, at times, mirror the society where a frequently benevolent paternalistic and patriarchal attitude is being used to control and fix behavior. Contradictions exist because a litigant approach the court with the expectation of righting the wrong but ends up receiving paternalist sermons. The patriarchy exhibits itself in various forms day in and day out in the courtrooms, while the male-dominated courts often act hostile to women's concerns. Seemingly, what is important is not the voice of a woman, but rather protecting the rule of men.

This chapter looks at the situation in the courts and the manner in which judiciary is interpreting the provisions of domestic violence law to provide relief to women complainants. It concludes that in domestic violence cases, the courts neither provide rights-based justice nor do they offer rehabilitation to the victims of violence. What the courts propose is a network of family ideology and traditional values filtered through the prism of law and subjective biases, an idiosyncratic style and their discretion to decide good or bad, right or wrong. Experience reveals that often, in the layered, hierarchical, patriarchal society, the courts frequently reinforce deeply embedded masculine values and androcentric morals while ignoring the fact that their prime concern is to implement the law and disburse justice as per the constitutional norms. The court in cases of domestic abuse work with the aim of preserving the family, rather than the protecting the rights of an individual woman who has faced hurt. Patriarchal norms are privileged over constitutional or human rights. Morality is redefined and reinterpreted in the courtrooms to deny women their rightful claims. The ideals relating to rights and justice find no space within the private domain of the family, and specifically when the questions relate to the rights of women. Women are discriminated against as wives and daughters in families and as citizens in the courts and other public spaces.

Marriage is not construed as a companionship

> "A wife should be administrator in purpose, slave in duty, Lakshmi in appearance, Earth in patience, Mother in love, Prostitute in bed",[4] wrote the Kerala judge while quoting a Sanskrit *shloka* to interpret the duties of a woman in a matrimonial relationship.
>
> (2018)

Thus, as per the court, a wife should be capable of adopting multiple roles. She must be perfect in work and appearance, should be caring and loving and yet must work as a slave. The role of a wife is painted with high expectations, whereas no such roles are prescribed for husbands by the court. As per this notion, a woman can attain salvation only if she obeys her husband, because for her, her husband is a lord and a master beyond which she cannot have a separate existence. The traditional conservative notions about the 'good woman' who is obedient, compliant, docile and does not question the norms is still prevalent within and outside the courtrooms and prevents many women from seeking justice using the legal system.[5] In fact, the conventional stereotype of an 'ideal uncomplaining wife' is reinforced by the judicial system that reiterates that a devoted and a loyal wife will suffer torture silently. The paternalistic attitude that operates within and outside the courtrooms hinders many women from negotiating for their rights or to obtain justice. In fact, marriage is construed as a sacred relationship and not a tie that is based on companionship. As per this approach, it is a *dharma* or the duty of the wife to look after her family subserviently without questioning. Marriage is considered to be a pious '*Dharmic*' institution[6] which is 'made in heaven but broken on earth'.[7] Much emphasis is laid on the performance of ceremonies such as the *Saptapadi* as per the rituals[8] to accentuate the sacramental nature of the relationship that involves a union of souls that extends not only to one but to seven lives.[9]

Since the colonial era, the courts have been relying on ancient Hindu texts as coded in *Vedas* and *Smritis*. Many of these texts have been interpreted as putting the wife on a lower level, considering a woman to a *dasi* or a slave. The intersection of caste and gender hierarchies is reproduced to arrive at the interpretation of ancient religious literature while construing rights and wrongs within marriage, rather than the constitutional values or legal norms. For instance, the Bombay High Court[10] adduced that as per *Shastras*, in an *anuloma* marriage, marriage between a man from a higher caste to lower-caste woman is valid, and children born out of such a tie are legitimate. However, the children born out of a relationship between Shudra men and a Brahmin mistress or a *pratiloma* marriage, which is declared invalid under the Hindu law, are not *dasiputra* and therefore cannot claim inheritance in their father's property. While using the Brahmanical texts, gender and caste parameters are utilized to deprive a *Brahmin* woman and her children of their rights and penalize her for marrying a lower-caste man.[11] This trend of interpreting rights in marriage narrowly continued in the independent India.[12] Contrary to the constitutional values of equality, justice and liberty, such orthodox ideas and stereotypes are being embedded in personal laws morally, religiously and socially and are evident in the spate of rulings and verdicts pronounced by the courts.

Colonial mind-set operating in post-colonial India

The imperial rulers reinforced the dominant androcentric ideology while also introducing the narrow constricted moral codes of Victorian notions while suppressing women's status. Thomas Babington Macaulay, an officer appointed by the British rulers, when drafting the Indian Penal Code[13] narrowly interpreted the 'Indian culture' and ignored the practices of the majority.[14] He adopted the orthodox Brahmanical understanding while inferring the laws of *Manusmriti* and combined it with the imperial morality to codify the law, and this has been retained and continued to today, propagating the constricted attitude and mind-set that subjugate women. Macaulay and his fellow Englishmen could not recognize the fact that laws propounded by Manu were flawed, as these ingeniously manipulated the values and philosophy of Hinduism.[15] This unreasonably androcentric colonial jurisprudence survived despite unending talks on the modernization of the legal system in free India.[16] Narrow-minded misogynist interpretations of the religious laws deterred the cause of gender equality and gender justice.[17] Currently, the situation is that the penal code as operated in the courts is penalizing the women complainants the most.[18]

The reasoning of the law simply seems to have been stuck in the colonial morality. For example, when deciding the Rukmabai's case, Justice Pinhey evoked the pristine moral past and the logic of native customs to decide a case of a young woman who refused to join the company of her husband, Dadaji, who pleaded for the provision of restitution of conjugal rights.[19] Discourse on law and morality, justice and emancipation, civilization and barbarism, masters and slaves, colonial justice and local customs was raised then to sift justice through the labyrinth of hegemonical interpretations to arrive at a dominant logic to justify the pathological stand while shaping righteousness. Sarkar[20] noted that while adjudicating the matter of Phulmonee, a ten-year-old bride in 1890 who was raped to death by her husband, the English judge exonerated the accused without questioning the husband, who insisted on sleeping with the child, or the barbaric custom which allowed him to do so with impunity because colonial rulers do not want to meddle with the customs of the natives for reasons of political expediency. This approach continues to exist today whereby the state does not wish to interfere with the private violence inflicted within the sanctity of the home.

During the colonial period different standards and scales of justice are utilized by the state to deal with cases pertaining to marriage. In fact, Section 259 and 260 of the Civil Procedure Code of 1877 was revised in 1882 to provide that if a spouse refused to comply with the decree awarded in the suit for restitution of conjugal rights, then he or she should be punished with imprisonment or a fine or both. These decrees were often used against women. Earlier, women could garner the support of extended families in cases of violence by husbands, but the wording of Section 259 was amended to provide that the extended family could not interfere and also Section 260 worked against women who had little property.[21] Thus, colonial rulers "effectively helped Bengali males 'to create a state within a state' by insisting that the household remains a zone of autonomy and self-rule for a Hindu male".[22]

The 'women question' in post-independent India

This trend of neglecting the 'women question' continued in post-colonial India, where the patriarchal structure remained one of the major causes of the oppression of women. The narrow-minded patriarchal interpretations of the religious laws deterred the 'social reforms' that were initiated in the post-colonial period and could not address the realities relating to the persistent discrimination against women. The promise of gender equality as made by the constitution remained on paper only and failed to reach a vast majority. This significant social document failed to create a revolution or achieve a new social order, even though it calls for social justice and democratic governance and is accompanied by a spirit of modernization and development.

The framers of the constitution, departing from the then prevalent norms, introduced the framework of egalitarianism within marriage through Article 42 of the draft constitution[23] that reads:

> The State shall endeavour to secure that marriage shall be based only on the mutual consent of both sexes and shall be maintained through mutual cooperation, with the equal rights of husband and wife as a basis. The State shall also recognise that motherhood has a special claim on its care and protection.

This provision has the potential to address inequalities within heterosexual marriages; however, it was dropped from the final draft of the constitution without a debate. Kannabiran,[24] while analyzing case law, opined that constitutional provisions, laws and facts are intertwined and intermeshed with notional elements of a patriarchal system which 'puts in place an ideological apparatus for juridical understanding of sex-based discrimination'.

In the post-colonial legal discourse too, the 'women' question' was subsumed and merged with the questions of groups and communities. The Hindu Code Bill introduced by Dr B.R. Ambedkar envisaged major changes in the situation of Hindu women and dealt with the questions that particularly affected women's lives such as those relating to succession, maintenance, marriage, divorce, adoption and guardianship.[25] For the first time, the bill suggested that married daughters should get half of what sons are entitled to. It also abolished caste as the basis for marriage and adoption. Most importantly, it recognized the principle of monogamy and granted the right to concubines to claim maintenance. The bill was recognized as a "progressive measure of reform in regard to personal freedom of women".[26] However, protest from the orthodox quarters were loud. The bill was then sent to a committee and while succumbing to pressure from the conservative members, the bill was dropped on the eve of the first general elections. Ambedkar then resigned as the law minister. Explaining his disappointment on the stalling of the Hindu Code Bill which sought to stop the reproduction of the Brahmanical patriarchy, Ambedkar said,

> To leave inequality between the class and class, between sex and sex which is soul of the Hindu Society untouched and go on passing legislation relating to economic problems is to make farce of our Constitution and built a palace on a dung heap. This is the significance I attached to the Hindu Code.[27]

It was only in 1955–1956 that parts of it were pushed as the Hindu Marriage Act, the Hindu Succession Act, the Hindu Minority and Guardianship Act and the Hindu Adoption and Maintenance Act while diluting the provisions given in the earlier bill. These new acts by no means advanced the rights of women. On the contrary, this codification put an end to the diversity of Hindu laws practiced in different regions and in the process destroyed existing, liberal customary provisions. These legal correctives did not go beyond what is phrased as "typecasting women as wombs to bring forth babies, lips to utter sweet nothings, and laps to cuddle infants."[28] The Constituent Assembly Debates maintained the tradition of ignoring women's concerns. Rather, the Indian state infantilized women by giving decision-making powers to the male guardians, taking away women's agency and patronizing them in the guise of providing 'protection'. The woman's body was construed as a marker of male honor and the metaphor of vulnerability and therefore needs to be controlled and protected. What is stressed is the fact that women belong to their families and their communities but not to their own person, which positioned women as wives and mothers and not as independent citizens with the right to autonomy. According to Menon and Bhasin, "Family, community and state emerge as the three mediating and interlocking forces determining women's individual and collective destinies."[29]

This trend continues to dominate, and even today, the courts in general are following the similar regressive approach where the right to equality within families is interpreted parsimoniously by the courts. The courts refuse to apply constitutional values in the domain of the family.[30] The principle to preserve the institution of marriage has been reinforced in several cases,[31] and in *Saroj Rani vs Sudarshan Kumar*[32] while overruling the decision of Andhra Pradesh High Court in *T Sareetha vs T Venkata Subbaiah*,[33] it was determined that the state must refrain from entering the private domain of the home. The public–private dichotomy is thus used to deny women their rightful entitlements under the law. Those who enforce the law discriminate between men and women unconsciously, and this reflects a traditional and rigid attitude toward women.[34]

The state sanctions dowry and domestic violence

The laws relating to dowry or domestic violence have been enacted under pressure; however, the state is not keen to preserve women's rights, as has been indicated in numerous stances where cases have been decided such that a husband is granted immunity to abuse his wife, and therefore the courts promoted domination in the guise of love and discipline. The analysis of decisions pronounced indicate that the rule of men supersedes the rule of law. Regulation of marital violence is covered in the language of husbands' prerogative to justify unequal marital relations. Wife battering is not viewed as criminal conduct by a violent husband; rather, it is justified as an expression of emotions that need to be adjusted and rechanneled into marriage, and the wife is entrusted with the duty of doing so.

For instance, in *Sham Lal vs State of Haryana*,[35] Neelam Rani was set ablaze on 17 June 1987 and died because she could not fulfill the dowry demand. She was facing extreme cruelty in her marital home. The accused persons, including her husband, father-in-law and grandmother, pled that because of frustration that she could not give birth to a child and could not adjust to the village life, she committed suicide. The session court convicted her husband and her father-in-law under Section 302, 304B and 498A IPC. On appeal, the High Court acquitted the father-in-law but convicted her husband on the basis of the findings that she had been doused with kerosene and burned alive. The apex court on appeal in its decision on 20 February 1997 observed that as there was nothing on record to show that she was treated with cruelty or harassed for the demand of dowry, the conviction of her husband was set aside under Section 302 and 304B but he was held guilty under Section 498A. As he has already served three years in prison, he was acquitted. Though Neelam Rani was maliciously burned alive, the insensitive court, unconcerned about the seriousness of the crime, let off the accused with a lighter punishment on technical grounds. Perhaps those guilty of burning her knew that they will be able to escape easily from the clutches of the law. The murder of a woman is not a matter of concern to a male-dominated state. This attitude has led to a culture of impunity.

The criminal law prioritizes the rights of the offenders over the rights of the victim while deciding the case. Technical defects have been pointed out to exonerate the perpetrators of the crime, while the courts turn a blind eye to the suffering of victims. For instance, in the matter of *State of West Bengal vs Orilal Jaiswal*,[36] Usha, a 20-year-old woman, committed suicide within a year of her marriage. Despite giving sufficient dowry as per the demands made by the accused persons, Usha was tortured physically as well as mentally. Her husband used to assault her. She was taunted for bringing a substandard quality of dowry and was also mocked for bringing evil luck to the family. The deceased complained several times to her natal family but later she committed suicide. The postmortem report showed signs of death by hanging. The doctor noted abrasion marks on her body. The session judge noted the lapse on the part of the IO and found the husband and mother-in-law guilty under Section 306, 498A and 34, IPC. On appeal, the High Court set aside the conviction. The Supreme Court convicted both of the accused under Section 498A, but considering the age of the mother-in-law, her sentence was reduced to two years imprisonment. The court acquitted both the accused for the charges under Section 306 while giving them the benefit of the doubt. Thus, no one was held guilty for the torture Usha underwent within ten months of her marriage, and no one could be held accountable for her suicide. No attempts were made to look at the psychological trauma or physical brutalities she underwent, as if her life seems to have no value. The persons who compelled Usha to commit suicide are absolved from their criminal culpability.

In *State of Punjab vs Iqbal Singh*[37] Mohinder Kaur, who was working as a teacher, set herself and her three children ablaze at her matrimonial home on 7 June 1983. Married seven or eight years ago, she was harassed for dowry. She wrote a letter to the DSP complaining of her ill treatment and seeking police protection. Her husband frustrated her efforts to seek a transfer from the school where she was working. Her mother-in-law and sister-in-law encouraged her husband and conspired to kill her by sprinkling kerosene, but their plan misfired. Fed up, Mohinder wrote a letter to her mother sharing her agony and committed suicide the next day. Her mother lodged an FIR. The trial court convicted her husband, mother-in-law and sister-in-law; hence an appeal was made before the High Court, which acquitted all of them on the grounds that the prosecution could not prove the ingredients of Section 306 relating to the abetment of suicide. The Supreme Court, while considering her ill treatment and the atmosphere of terror created for her, restored the conviction of her husband but acquitted his sister. The courts insisted on technicalities and not on the fact that Mohinder Kaur was continuously and brutally tortured to an extent that she committed suicide and killed her three children.

In *Arvind Singh vs State of Bihar*[38] the daughter of Phulmati was burned alive. The deceased disclosed that her husband and other family members forcibly poured kerosene and burned her entire body. The girl was tortured because she was 'ugly looking' and because the demands for dowry for Rs 10,000/ and a gold ring could not be fulfilled. The apex court, during the trial, dwelled on the forms of the burn injuries, the technicalities of the dying declaration, nonexamination of the IO and other evidences and set aside the imprisonment under Section 302 or 304B and 498A because no dowry demands were made prior to the date of the occurrence of crime. Those who murdered Phulmati's daughter with impunity, burned her and then refused to take her body to the hospital knew that the system upholds a mind-set where burning women alive is not considered a deadly crime. Perhaps it is easy to entangle justice in the web of technicalities, nitty-gritty and legal procedures.

Similarly, in *Sher Singh vs State of Haryana*,[39] Harjinder Kaur committed suicide on 7 February 1998 by ingesting aluminum phosphate because she was brutally tortured for not fulfilling the demand for a motorcycle and a fridge. Her husband contested that she was hot-tempered, wanted him to shave his hair and forced him to live separately from his parents. The session judge convicted her husband, father-in-law, mother-in-law and brother-in-law under Section 304B and 498A IPC. The High Court on appeal acquitted all others expect her husband on the grounds that the prosecution failed to establish their role. The Supreme Court acquitted the husband while noting,

> What motivated or compelled her to take this extreme and horrific step will remain a mystery, as we are not satisfied that the prosecution has proved or even shown that she was treated with such cruelty, connected with dowry demands, as led her to commit suicide.

The court could not accept the fact that for a motorcycle and a fridge, a woman was barbarically tortured to an extent that she committed suicide while she was pregnant.

In *Ramesh Kumar vs State of Chhattisgarh*[40] the court undermined the seriousness of the law while holding that a presumption of abetment of suicide by a married woman made under Section 113A of the Indian Evidence Act is not mandatory but permissive. Also, it held that there is a need to establish a cause-and-effect relationship between cruelty and suicide. Even in dowry death cases where Section 304B is applicable and the burden of proof rests on the accused, the courts have demanded that the prosecution prove its case beyond a reasonable doubt. For instance, in *Sanjiv Kumar vs State of Punjab*,[41] the court acquitted the accused while holding that though the deceased was subjected to harassment and cruelty by the appellant and his family members, because the family of the appellant is relatively prosperous compared to the family of deceased, they would not demand petty things such as a TV, refrigerator or cash of Rs 10,000/ and also the deceased had an illicit relationship with her brother-in-law because she went and stayed at his house despite opposition from her husband, leading to incriminating circumstances. This reasoning devalues women where their economic status and character are utilized as grounds for acquittal.

More recently, a court awarded six years' imprisonment to Mohd Abdul Alim who poured boiling water on his wife Noorjahan on 9 March 2013 when she came back from work and was resting. She was taken to Safdarjung Hospital with 50 percent burns on her body, and she died seven days later.[42] In her dying declaration, she accused her husband, as he was suspicious of her character. The court noted that the police failed to establish the fact of her murder and convicted him only for causing grievous hurt. "There in nothing in the postmortem report to show that burns were sufficient in the ordinary course of nature to cause death of the deceased", noted the court. Noorjahan lost her life, yet the accused is not held guilty for causing her death.

There are cases after cases where the courts have upheld the logic of the patriarchy while acquitting the accused persons. Women have died in compelling circumstances. The testimony of witnesses and other material evidence indicates that women have been brutally murdered or were compelled to commit suicide because of unreasonable motives or coercive demands. Yet it does not matter to the state if women are killed brutally – the accused husband and in-laws should not face punishment and therefore in the process, the courts have overlooked material evidence and acquitted the accused person on flimsy grounds, technicalities and an anti-women interpretation of law or while pointing out the fault of women as wives the acquittal of accused persons is upheld. While I was finalizing this work, I came across a news item which states that the world is debating about saving species which may become extinct due to climate change,[43] and here I am pondering murder, suicide and torture of wives and the approach of courts whereby the violent husbands are being let off easily. Perhaps women here are treated as lesser beings than those species on the verge of extinction.

Technical defects are evoked to exonerate violent men

Technical defects have been evoked in domestic violence and dowry death cases to exonerate the violent husbands and in-laws. For instance, in *Satvir Singh vs State of Punjab*[44] the court observed "It is not enough that harassment or cruelty was caused to the woman with a demand for dowry at some time, if Section 304B is to be invoked. But it should have happened 'soon before her death' ". This reasoning has been taken in many other cases.[45]

In another case, a trial court judge, based on technical defects in recording the dying declaration of the victim, exonerated the accused of all charges.[46] This was later set aside by the High Court. In *Narsingh Prasad Singh vs Raj Kumar*,[47] the High Court reduced the sentence of abusers who had mercilessly beaten a victim with a wooden stick and planned to burn her alive to the fine of Rs. 1000 without providing a reason as to why the sentence should be reduced. In *Krishan Lal vs Union of India*[48] it was assumed that "With the passage of time after marriage and birth of children, there are remote chances of treating a married woman with cruelty by her husband or his relatives". In *Mohd Hashim vs State of UP*[49] the accused persons were convicted under Section 498A, 323 IPC and Section 3 and 4, Dowry Prohibition Act; however, the apex court allowed the appeal of the offenders to reduce the sentence under the Probation of Offenders Act. Arguments have not been raised regarding the protection of the rights of the victim, nor have the courts showed concern for substantive justice. In fact, the circumstances have not been considered while pronouncing the decision, and the arguments remained limited to the technical issue around applicability of the law.

In *Mohd Miyan vs State of UP*[50] in a meeting of complainant wife with her husband, mother-in-law and their nine relatives demanded dowry and when she refused, her husband became enraged. It was alleged that her mother-in-law and sisters-in-law caught her hair, and her husband hit her with his fist, breaking one of her teeth. The complainant filed an FIR under Section 498A, 323, 325, 504 and 506 IPC besides invoking Section 3 and 4 of the Dowry Prohibition Act. The accused persons approached the High Court to quash the proceedings, and the court dismissed the petition. In the Supreme Court it was argued that in the FIR, the complainant stated that her divorce took place four years ago. The apex court held that a prosecution is not sustainable under Section 498A IPC or under the Dowry Prohibition Act. The sympathetic court turned a blind eye to the fact that the husband and his relatives were demanding dowry when cruelty was inflicted on the wife. The court could not see the physical cruelty being inflicted on her but instead sympathized with the accused and his relatives. The court did not imagine the manner in which a power structure operates when the nine people surrounded one person to extract dowry from her and forced her physically to concede to the demands.

In several matters,[51] pleas of limitation and territorial jurisdiction have been invoked to exonerate the accused persons. The courts failed to consider that the women have been tortured, brutalized and murdered while allowing the appeal of the accused persons. What is prioritized is technicalities, procedural complexities or the rights of the accused, and what is negated in the process is the sufferings of the victims, the humane element and the object of enacting the law. Justice is denied while twisting and manipulating the law to protect the accused persons and, in the process, the purpose of the law is lost behind the technical maze and complications.[52]

In *Appasaheb vs State of Maharashtra*[53] Bhimabai died because her parents could not fulfill the continuous demands for dowry made by her husband and his mother. The postmortem report showed that the cause of her death was insecticide poisoning. The Supreme Court ruled that a demand for money on the account of financial stringency or for meeting some urgent domestic expenses cannot be termed as a demand for dowry, and therefore the conviction of appellants cannot be sustained. In *Vipin Jaiswal vs State of AP*,[54] the victim received severe burn injuries that she eventually died from. Her husband and in-laws were demanding Rs 50,000/. The trial court convicted the accused under Section 304B and 498A. The Supreme Court on appeal ruled that the demand was made six months after the marriage because the accused husband wanted to purchase a computer to start a business, and therefore this coercion cannot be construed as a dowry-related demand. Thus, the message conveyed is that even if coercive demands are made for any reason after marriage and women were murdered, the same will not be construed as dowry demand and the husband or in-laws could not be held guilty for committing brutal murders.

In cases pertaining to dowry death or suicide, where the accused persons – husbands and in-laws – have tortured women for years and murdered them brutally because their greed is not satiated, they are being let off by the courts on technical grounds such as gaps in the investigation, or not producing crucial witnesses or evidence, or while interpreting the law.[55] In many cases brutal murders were tried as simple cases of suicide. In numerous other cases brides have been burned, murdered, killed, forced to commit suicide or even tortured brutally, but the courts could not hear their painful screams and refuse to see the evidence of serious crime. Rather, the utterly sympathetic courts have protected the men on the grounds of technical gaps, procedural defects or the nitty-gritty of law. The entire machinery is geared to save the 'innocent men' irrespective of the fact that these men have murdered, tortured and burned their wives alive. Though a thorough analysis of the court's decisions is further required, a mere glimpse at many decisions shows that lives of women are considered cheaper than daily household items such as a fridge, TV, cooler, motorcycle, car or cash. Women have been ill treated pitilessly for days, months and years and are murdered because demands were not fulfilled, yet no action is being taken to punish the guilty. Also, apart from not bringing dowry, many of them were subjected continuously to ruthless abuse, humiliation and torture for reasons such as skin color, bringing evil luck, being 'ugly looking' and similar other non-reasons. Yet the learned courts acquit the accused persons on flimsy, technical grounds and in doing so, not only deprive victims of justice but also perpetuate the culture of violence and impunity. The courts do not protect women's rights as wives, but what the courts uphold is men, their might and their privileges. This shows that the logic of patriarchy prevails over the rule of law and reinforces the rule of men.

A woman is painted negatively with suspicion and assigned low credibility in the courts

Courts often do not trust women complainants. A woman's testimony is viewed with suspicion, and she is assigned low credibility as a witness or a litigant. Women who are challenging the patriarchy and questioning the dominant notions relating to marriage or family are viewed with suspicion by the courts. For instance, in *Indrasing Raol vs State of Gujarat*[56] Kailsba got married in February 1986 and committed suicide on 7 March 1987 because she was constantly tortured for dowry. She was reduced to a "bag of bones" and her "miseries know no bound". A few days before she committed suicide, her husband, who employed with the army, after consuming liquor at midnight, beat her indiscriminately, kicking and hitting her because she refused to accompany him. The police therefore registered a FIR under Section 498A and 306 IPC. On appeal, the High Court while acquitting the violent husband argued,

> A woman would prefer to end her life, if continuous, or recurring unabated harassment or cruelty grave in nature, is intolerable or unendurable. Highly sensitive impulsive, reckless, or touchy woman may on one incident end her life, but that exception to the rule is not envisaged by the Section. It should also be stated that after marriage sometimes emotional disorder is created, and that results into frustration and pessimism. A woman sometime becomes psychotic and develops tendency to end her life. A woman being highly sensitive and sentimental, or reckless, or if tired of her life either because her dreamt expectations are not satisfied or found to be the mirage, or for any other reason may become dejected and desperate and may develop suicidal tendency, and end her life.
>
> (para 17, 1999)

The court with one stroke not only generalized the nature of women but also overlooked the fact that the deceased in this case was continuously harassed by her husband. The court contradicts its own statement where initially it stated that because of constant torture, Kailasba was reduced to a bag of bones and an object of misery and later to acquitted her violent husband, thus drawing different conclusions based on a single episode of violence. Her worth is discredited in the process. The subjectivities, biases and prejudices held sway, and the truth is discarded in the process when the court becomes blind to the fact that within a short span of her marriage, Kailasba was tortured so severely that she ended her life. In many cases, it is the woman – her work, her character, her personality – that is being questioned. A man, even if he is a drunkard, vile, criminal or violent, is not viewed with suspicion. Fricker[57] has called this testimonial injustice when a speaker's credibility is defeated by the prejudices of the hearer while blocking the flow of truth. The male-dominated society deems women to have no credibility. Judges subject women to stereotypes and prejudices, because of which women suffer harm, and their concerns are overlooked in the process of delivering justice.

The law questions women, not men

In many cases, the courts have reduced the sentences or acquitted the violent men. Even in cases where women have been burned alive or have been compelled to commit suicide, the courts frequently, while sympathizing with the accused men, ignore the brutalities committed on women. For instance, in the well-known Naina Sahani *Tandoor* Murder case,[58] the apex court commuted the death sentence to life imprisonment "because murder was the outcome of strained personal relationship. It was not an offence against the society". Maxwell Pereira in his book titled *The Tandoor Murder*[59] reconstructed the gruesome crime scene that took place on the night of 2 July 1995 when Constable Kunju, deployed at the Connaught Place police station, discovered that 'a murdered woman's corpse' was being cremated in the middle of night in a secret manner. He went on to describe the turbulent journey from investigation to trial where witnesses turned hostile because the high-profile accused used all his muscle and money power to escape. The trial court handed down a death sentence to the accused, which was confirmed by the High Court. The apex court partly allowed the appeal of the accused and ended up commuting his death sentence while ignoring the ruthless murder.[60] The bench said

> Considering the social status of the deceased, it would be difficult to come to the conclusion that the appellant was in dominant position qua her. The appellant was deeply in love with the deceased. The evidence on record shows that he suspected her fidelity and the murder was the result of this possessiveness.

The apex court revived the history of the relationship and erroneously sent the message that in the case of a 'private' relationship between a man and a woman, if a man loves her, he also has a right to brutally murder her with impunity if he suspects her character. The state will not take such violence seriously, as it is not considered as a crime against society. The legal system took recourse to a conservative myopic vision and reinforced that a man has authority and prerogative to discipline and control a woman if he suspects her character or is possessive.

In *Waghmare vs State of Maharashtra*[61] Sarla Waghmare was emotionally and physically abused by her husband and his family. They regularly beat her and harassed her for a motorcycle, and after two months of marriage, her brother-in-law poured kerosene on her and set her on fire, which resulted in serious injuries. The Bombay High Court held that these incidents of violence were not sufficient to force her to commit suicide and that the demand for a motorcycle was not a dowry demand. The court acquitted the guilty persons because the wife had not acted according to 'conventional' pattern of wifely behavior and was not 'consistent' because "she withdrew the complaint of being burned by her brother-in-law two months after her marriage". The court ignored the fact that there is intense pressure on a woman to withdraw the complaint to preserve the marriage. Courts measure the " 'rightness of women's action by applying stringent rules of wifely behavior and condone violence by men".[62]

Courts uphold conservative notions and not the constitutional values

MacKinnon[63] argued that society as a whole and its constitutive parts, including law, institutions and private relations, are hierarchically organized on the basis of sex and are designed to create and maintain male dominance. This work also suggests that a biased attitude continues to operate within the legal system. In the courts, women are routinely disrespected and infantilized. The relationship matrix is utilized to adjudicate the women's claims. For instance, in *S. Hanumantha Rao vs S. Ramani*,[64] the husband alleged that his wife's unwillingness to wear *mangalsutra* was the evidence of mental cruelty.

Custodial torture within the four walls of the home was neglected for the sake of upholding tradition and culture. The courts construct an image of an ideal stereotype of a good wife who is subservient, submissive and perfect. Any deviation from this norm causes a woman to be considered bad. Such a presumptive culture disregards the fact that men use their abusive power to assault women, create fear and demand compliance as well as authoritative control. In *Arup Hazra vs Manashi Hazra*[65] the husband filed the divorce application on the grounds of cruelty that his wife has "refused to cook food and serve meals to the husband and any members of his family, and used to move out of home without permission". The wife alleged that her husband was harassing her because her family refused to pay Rs. 50,000 as a dowry. The court allowed his application for divorce on the grounds of desertion.

In *Sonia vs Vinod*[66] despite of the report by the PO that the aggrieved woman was in dire need of protection, the Magistrate stated that there was no evidence of violence; rather, the complainant was not cooperating with her husband and harassing him on trivial matters and was not behaving in a traditional manner towards her husband and his family; therefore, the court dismissed the application. In this case, the wife complained that she was harassed and beaten up for the dowry and that her husband used to consume alcohol habitually and mistreated her and therefore she requested a protection order. The magistrate subjectively constructed the image of a 'woman' as a perfect daughter-in-law and a wife who should cooperate with her husband and his family. As the *khap panchayats*, courts uphold the traditional norms rather than upholding constitutional values.

Similarly, in another case, the court held that as "the wife is not performing her pious obligation but she was so much mesmerized by her political thoughts and quiet adamant that she failed to understand the consequences of her negligent attitude".[67] In yet another case, divorce was granted because the wife "taunted the husband for not being able to satiate her sexual desires on account of his [. . .] heavy weight".[68] Patriarchal courtrooms often set boundaries to limit the autonomy, dignity and freedom of a woman and decide her place in society, control her body and mind, regulate her sexual being and control her interactions and her relationships, including controlling her womb and her desires determining each and every step of her life from being an unmarried girl, to a wife, to a mother. The courts opined that in case a wife is forgetful or is "devoid of etiquettes and courtesy", her husband has a right to chastise her.[69] Similarly, if a wife does not have a compromising temperament, this gives the husband the right to get annoyed and angry, and in such a state he could beat his wife. Also, per a ruling by the Supreme Court,

> teasing by the accused-appellant of the deceased, ill treating her for her mistakes which could have been pardonable and turning her out of the house, also once beating her inside the house at the odd hours of night did amount to cruelty within the meaning of Section 498A of IPC.

Courts often presume that violence within marriages occurs due to conflict and stress and that both parties are equally responsible for the dispute. This assumption ignores the reality of the power differential within the relationship in addition to the structural factors that govern the nature, dynamics and social reality of domestic violence. Morality is a part of the legal discourse, and many decisions are couched in a preaching tone while using a patriarchal lexicon and ignoring the impact of violence on women and children. The Bombay High Court, in a public interest litigation,[70] split "violence" down the middle while stipulating that women facing "severe physical" domestic violence must be brought before the court to secure a protection order, but for all other types of violence, pre-litigation "joint counselling" may be conducted by the police and non-governmental organizations to amicably settle the dispute, even while conceding that the "assurances" have no legal binding.

Construing an ideal woman as a perfect wife through a judicial lens

Basu and Jaising[71] observed that often women who approach the courts are viewed with the androcentric moral lens while stereotypes and prejudices operate in the courtroom. While examining Justice J. D. Kapoor's book *Laws and Flaws in Marriage*[72] Basu and Jaising show the manner in which the courts frequently push the gendered norms and reward women who conform to a traditional role of a wife.

High expectations are laid for women as wives by the courts, though no preaching is done on the conduct of a man as a husband. For instance, while dealing with a case of divorce, the division bench of the Bombay High Court observed that the wife should be like the goddess Sita, who should follow her husband, Lord Rama, even during his isolation in a forest, but for a man to be Rama could not be imagined by the misogynist court.[73] "Implicit in a number of judgements is a notion of culture relativism which suggests that Indian women are accustomed to a certain amount of violence and therefore violence against them is not considered as a serious infringement on women's rights",[74] rightly observed a study.

There are many decisions which see women as 'good' wives, mothers or daughters-in-law and uphold a conservative sexual morality. In *Suman Kapur vs Sudhir Kapoor*[75] the court upheld that when women focus on their career, they neglect their household duties. The court failed to appreciate the fact that a woman may seek opportunity to advance her career, and in marriage, being an equal partnership, men should cooperate and actively contribute to the household responsibilities such as managing the household or taking part in the child care rather than misusing the provision of restitution of conjugal rights to force their wives to give up their careers. In *Praveen Mehta vs Inderjit Mehta*[76] it was articulated that the wife's illness could not excuse her lack of cooperation for sex. The court openly upholds the patriarchal logic that the husband could not enjoy the company of his wife because of her ill health. Also, in *Birdichand Sarda vs State of Maharashtra*[77] the wife was visualized as an extremely 'sensitive' person who made unreasonable demands to seek the undivided attention of her busy husband.[78] In *Savitri Pandey vs Prem Chandra Pandey*[79] the court, while strictly interpreting the context of cruelty, held that

> Cruelty, however, has to be distinguished from the ordinary wear and tear of family life. It cannot be decided on the basis of the sensitivity of the petitioner and has to be adjudged on the basis of the course of conduct which would, in general, be dangerous for a spouse to live with the other.

Courts preach on the duties of wives but not about the role of husbands

In a patriarchal society, gendered norms place different social burdens upon men and women. In the specific familial context, expectations are based on the gender of the members such that women are in a disadvantageous position. While propagating the family ideology, in *Narendra vs K Meena*,[80] the court opined that separating a husband from his family amounts to 'cruelty' without recognizing the fact that a girl who is separated from her natal family at the time of marriage also has moral or legal obligations towards her natal family. The Supreme Court stated

> It is not a common practice or desirable culture for a Hindu son in India to get separated from the parents upon getting married at the instance of the wife, especially when the son is the only earning member in the family. A son, brought up and given education by his parents, has a moral and legal obligation to take care and maintain the parents, when they become old and when they have either no income or have a meagre income. . . . As stated hereinabove, in a Hindu society, it is a pious obligation of the son to maintain the parents. If a wife makes an attempt to deviate from the normal practice and customs of the society, she must have some justifiable reason for that and in this case, we do not find any justifiable reason, except monetary consideration of the Respondent wife. In our opinion, normally, no husband would tolerate this and no son would like to be separated from his old parents and other family members, who are also dependent upon his income. The persistent effort of the Respondent wife to constrain the Appellant to be separated from the family would be torturous for the husband and in our opinion, the trial Court was right when it came to the conclusion that this constitutes an act of 'cruelty'.
>
> (2016)

The text points out the manner in which pre-conceived traditional notions, stereotypes, biases and prejudices operate within courtrooms. The term cruelty is interpreted against the backdrop of social norms regarding what constitutes appropriate behavior. The repressive mentality is reflected when the court upholds male supremacy and privilege and reinforces the position of women as second-class citizens. It considers women an appendage to men and the male as an authoritative figure and a breadwinner, while reinforcing the gender and cultural stereotypes. The court upheld conservative notions while reinterpreting the hegemonic understanding of Hinduism.[81] It defined the duties of wives but cast no obligations on the husbands. What is ignored is the fact that in the patrilocal society, a woman is forced to leave her natal home upon marriage and therefore she is isolated. Her parents invest in her education and marriage, and therefore she owes a duty toward them. Moreover, in cases where families only have daughters, it is the duty of daughters to care for their parents. The fact of her marriage cannot take away her responsibility towards them.

Courts on the issue of marital rape

> "I don't think that marital rape should be regarded as an offence in India, because it will create absolute anarchy in families and our country is sustaining itself because of the family platform which upholds family values," Former Chief Justice of India, Justice Dipak Mishra
>
> (2019)[82]

On the issue of marital rape, the state has followed a regressive approach.[83] In a matter before the Supreme Court, the center defended the provisions under Section 375(2) that permits a man to rape his legally wedded wife even if her age is less than 18 years, and the court agreed that marital rape cannot be considered a criminal offense.[84] In consonance with the traditional regressive ideology of glorifying motherhood and preserving the institution of the family, the court failed to see the fact that a person below 18 years of age is a minor and any such attempt to legitimize the rape of such a child for the sake of protecting the institution of marriage will have a detrimental impact on the health of the child. The Child Marriage Prevention and Redressal Act recognizes that marrying a girl below 18 years of age is invalid, yet while ignoring these provisions, the court legitimized the rape of minors while upholding the sanctity of marriage.[85] In other words, the court upheld child marriage which is "actually a 'solemnized invasion' of a girl, her bodily integrity, her sexuality and her mind."[86] The Protection of Children from Sexual Offence Act 2012 contradicts the provisions as laid down under the Penal Code.

Thus, legally, there is no uniformity in defining the age of consent, and different pieces of legislation prescribe different ages. Such an approach systematically pushes back women's rights and liberties while upholding the institution of marriage and undermining women's rights as citizens. The notion of controlling sexuality of women guides such decisions. The issue of consent was not raised while adjudicating, and the court ignored the aspects of women's bodies, mind, agency or autonomy. The bodily integrity and dignity of women are sacrificed at the altar of preserving the institution of marriage and upholding the patriarchal structures of power.

Domestic violence is a continuous offense, not episodic

Domestic violence is a continuous offense, where the victim lives in a state of continuous fear and terror. However, the courts rarely take this fact into account. In *Sujata Mukherjee vs Prashant Mukherjee*[87] the court recognized this fact, and

> that in view of allegations in the complaint that the offence was a continuing one having been committed in more local areas and one of the

> local areas being Raipur, the learned Magistrate at Raipur had jurisdiction to proceed with the criminal case instituted in such court.

In *Jagdish vs State of Rajasthan*,[88] the court held,

> If repeated demand for dowry is made and harassment is meted out to a woman which may be physical or mental is an act of cruelty. It is not necessary that the husband or his relatives must be present at the time when the house wife is subjected to cruelty. If their act or conduct, omission or commission is of such a nature which results in mental and physical harassment it will amount to an act of cruelty to a woman and it is immaterial that the woman is living at that relevant time at her matrimonial home or at her parents' house. The offence under Section 498A is a continuing office and if the act of cruelty continues even while, the woman is living at her parents' house, the offence is triable by both the Courts in whose territorial jurisdiction the act of continuing offence of cruelty has been committed at matrimonial home or the parents' house.

The Supreme Court in several cases[89] dealt with the matter of retrospective operation of the act and held that the past conduct of the parties, even if prior to the act coming into effect, were relevant for passing orders under Sections 18, 19 and 20. However, as discussed previously, not in many cases is cruelty is seen as a continuous offense, and this is problematic.

Standards of cruelty as a matrimonial offense are different from cruelty in criminal law

In *Dastane vs Dastane*,[90] the court held that

> To marry or not to marry and if so whom, may well be a private affair but the freedom to break a matrimonial tie is not. The society has a stake in the institution of marriage and therefore the erring spouse is treated not as a mere defaulter but as an offender. But this social philosophy, though it may have a bearing on the need to have the clearest proof of an allegation before it is accepted as a ground for the dissolution of a marriage, has no bearing on the standard of proof in matrimonial cases.[91]

The court opined that spouse who inflicts cruelty be treated as an offender; however, this presumption is not applied in cases where erring husbands inflict cruelty on wives. Though the law states that the standard of proof in the criminal matter and the matrimonial or civil proceedings are different, the courts maintain dual standards while dealing with cruelty as defined under the matrimonial laws as compared to those elaborated under the criminal law. "In the criminal proceedings, the charges have to be established beyond reasonable doubt whereas standard of proof in matrimonial proceedings is that of preponderance of probabilities".[92] Yet the consequences of two different proceedings have serious implications on the situation of women as these are interpreted by the courts in favor of men.

In *Bhagat vs Bhagat*,[93] it is illustrated that,

> While arriving at such conclusion, regard must be had to the social status, educational level of the parties, the society they move in, the possibility or otherwise of the parties ever living together in case they are already living apart and all other relevant facts and circumstances which it is neither possible nor desirable to set out exhaustively.

Thus, the term 'cruelty' may have different interpretations depending in the facts of the case,[94] yet the courts do not see that the act of cruelty may have deeper implications for women because of the uneven structural implications. But the same courts set different standards while dealing with the criminal liabilities of the deviant husbands who inflict cruelty on their wives. In *Raj Rani vs State*,[95] the court held that the allegations must be of a very grave nature and should be proved beyond a reasonable doubt. In *Girdhar Shankar Tawade vs State of Maharashtra*,[96] it was observed that " 'cruelty' has to be understood having a specific statutory meaning and there should be a case of continuous state of affairs of torture by one to another". Hence, cruelty per se is hardly punished. Rather, it is acknowledged only in serious cases when a woman dies. A perusal of several judgments under this law reveals that there was hardly an instance in which the accused were held guilty under 498A on its own. The judiciary is reluctant to punish or convict men even when there is enough evidence to indicate the guilt of the accused.[97]

The fragile masculinity of the androcentric courts

The courts are composed mostly of men as judges, as lawyers and as court staff, and they use a masculine lens to filter the complaints of women. As in other institutions, in the courts, too, men dominate the higher-level positions. Frequently, human subjectivities pour in while interpreting the facts and circumstances of the case, and any grievance is viewed as man versus a woman's issue. The fragility of masculine courts is often displayed in cases relating to intimate men–women relationships. For instance, in X versus Y,[98] the husband, while challenging one of the orders passed by the family court, filed a defamation suit against the wife because in her pleadings, she used the word 'impotent' toward him. The magistrate found that a prima facie case had been made and issued a process which was challenged by the wife in the High Court. The High Court observed that

> prima facie the word 'impotent' when understood in its plain and grammatical sense, reflects adversely upon the manhood of a person and has

> a tendency to invite derisive opinions about such person from others. Therefore, use of such word and its publication as contemplated under Section 499 of IPC would be sufficient to constitute, in a prima facie manner, the offence of defamation punishable under Section 500 of IPC.

Perhaps a fragile ego got injured because of the use of one word. Despite the clarification provided by the counsel for the wife, the court refused to grant relief to her while focusing on the concept of 'manhood'. The court overlooked the fact that frequently in a country where litigants are hardly aware of the technicalities of the law, lawyers draft the pleading on behalf of the client; therefore, holding a woman guilty would hardly serve any purpose.

Frequently, the discourse on gender-based violence is embedded in the language of the 'protection of women as daughters, wives or mothers'. This discourse seeks to communicate ownership and control of women by men. It perpetuates inequality and strengthens the power imbalance in the relationship and reaffirms discriminatory gender norms and practices. The perpetrator of violence asserts power over the person targeted. Yet the juridical discourse justifies roughness and rationalizes men's control over women rather than recognizing women's independent identity, existence or dignity. Often the courts provide remedies to women who fit into the image of a 'good woman or an ideal victim'. The residential, educational or economic status of women is used to decide whether she is entitled to protection orders or monetary orders. The language of rights is not used, and further the approach is deeply engrained in the patriarchy. This situation calls for re-examining the legal system by making it more gender friendly as well as building more accountability and transparency while adjudicating the matters with a focus on rights-based justice.

Courts penalize woman for giving dowry and not the husbands for demanding dowry

The courts in several cases have pronounced that the bride and her family should be penalized for giving dowry rather than punishing the grooms for making coercive demands and even murdering wives in case their natal families failed to give dowry. In *Neera Singh vs State*[99] the court reasoned

> A perusal of the complaint would show that as per allegations dowry demand was made even before marriage i.e. at the time of engagement and an AC was demanded from her father by her in-laws and her father had assured that AC would be given at the time of marriage. However, she told her father 'You have given car and AC at the demand of in-laws, what will happen if they demand a flat tomorrow?'. Despite her this conversation with her father and despite her knowing that dowry demand had already been made, she married in the same family irrespective of the fact that she was well-educated lady and was an engineer

> and her brother was in police. In fact, these kinds of allegations made after breakdown of the marriage show the mentality of the complainant. I consider where these kinds of allegations are made, the police should simultaneously register a case under Dowry Prohibition Act against the parents of the complainant as well, who married their daughter despite demand of dowry. Section 3 of the Act prohibits giving and taking of dowry. If a woman of grown up age and well educated gets married to a person despite dowry demand, she and her family becomes accomplice in the crime under Dowry Prohibition Act.
>
> (2007)

The flawed logic ignored the fault in the coercive action by the husband and his family members, who demanded dowry and taunted the woman for the same. Further, the judge erroneously reasoned that the practice of dowry is growing because the parents of the bride fulfilled the demands that were made:

> Nowadays, exorbitant claims are made about the amount spent on marriage and other ceremonies and on dowry and gifts. In some cases, claim is made of spending crores of rupees on dowry without disclosing the source of income and how funds flowed. I consider time has come that courts should insist upon disclosing source of such funds and verification of income from tax returns and police should insist upon the compliance of the Rules under Dowry Act and should not entertain any complaint, if the rules have not been complied with. Rule 2 of the Dowry Prohibition (Maintenance of List of Presents to the Bride and Bridegroom) Rules, 1985.

It was added,

> [T]he Metropolitan Magistrates should take cognizance of the offence under the Act in respect of the offence of giving dowry whenever allegations are made that dowry was given as a consideration of marriage, after demand. Courts should also insist upon compliance with the rules framed under the Act and if rules are not complied with, an adverse inference should be drawn. If huge cash amounts are alleged to be given at the time of marriage which are not accounted anywhere, such cash transactions should be brought to the notice of the Income Tax Department by the Court so that source of income is verified and the person is brought to law.

The court finds no fault with the persons who demand dowry and taunt, insult, humiliate, abuse, torture and murder women for dowry but instead recommended strict actions against the givers of dowry. The takers of dowry or the people who demand dowry are nowhere found to be at fault.

No suggestions have been made to level the hierarchical relationship between the bride and the groom's family or to eliminate patriarchal biases.

Courts impose penalties on women for filing false complaints

The PWDVA provides for remedies to the complainants and recommended penalties against the respondents for a breach of orders passed under the law. Nowhere does the law state that the penalty may be imposed on the women complainants in any circumstances. Yet contrary to the legal provisions, in *Sumana Bhasin vs Niraj Bhasin*,[100] the zealous court imposed a penalty on the aggrieved woman for filing a 'false complaint'. In an application under the PWDVA, the trial court ordered for Rs 25,000/ pm maintenance along with Rs 5,00,000/ as compensation which was later stayed by the High Court. The judge, while relying on the technical aspect that the onus of proof lies on the person who makes allegations, dismissed the application of the aggrieved woman while imposing cost of Rs. 1,00,000/ on her. The judge stated that "[t]he imposition of cost is in furtherance of the principle that wrongdoers should not get benefit out of frivolous litigations". It was further held that

> Imposition of actual, realistic cost would go a long way in controlling the tendency of false pleadings and forged and fabricating documents by litigants. It is a fit case which calls for imposition of exemplary cost on the complainant, so that likeminded people are dissuaded from resorting to such malafide practices. . . . The testimony of the complainant throws light on the conduct of the complainant and the extent, to which she has falsified and concocted various allegations and has suppressed important facts in order to harass the respondents and had misused the PWDV Act as a tool to extort unjustified money from the respondent no1 for unjustified personal gain. In such glaring circumstances, the Court cannot be expected to be sit as a mute spectator, where the Law, which is enacted solely for Protection of protect victims of Domestic Violence, is being misused and abused and made a tool of harassment and extortion.

The court therefore, instead of facilitating access to justice to women, created a hindrance while interpreting the affirmative law in an adverse manner. The courts do not penalize a man who delays or avoids paying maintenance or otherwise tries to delay the proceedings. No cost is imposed on men who strategically use tactics to deprive women of their due claims or who intentionally avoid following the orders pronounced by the courts. However, in the case of women, the same courts quickly impose costs or suggest penalties.

An analysis of judgements indicates that a backlash is growing in terms of efforts made to establish women's rights. The lobbying by men's groups to dilute the provisions of the domestic violence law, both civil and criminal, is impeding the process of accessing justice, whereby the state is also blindly repeating the facts without looking at the available data and statistics or without conducting any neutral research. This backlash is a critical and understudied dimension that is working towards the dilution or the complete abolition of vital legal protections for women, and this needs to be looked at from a gender point of view. Utilizing cyber forums, public protests and print media, the anti-women groups are disseminating narratives of women wreaking destruction on the family and weakening family bonds through their alleged misuse of "gender-biased" laws. They conspire to distort reality without any logical facts and jeopardize ongoing any advocacy efforts made by the women's movement. The judiciary, which is influenced by this trend, is dismissing the complaints at the cost of the safety and vulnerability of women, as highlighted in *Arnesh Kumar vs State of Bihar.*[101] The bench, while dropping the charges of cruelty and harassment against a husband, noted, "Petty quarrels cannot be termed as cruelty to attract the provisions of Section 498A, IPC". The order was made without realizing the fact that delays in arresting the accused could jeopardize a woman's life and security in cases where she is a victim of abuse. The court in this matter failed to distinguish the fine line between 'domestic violence' and 'the domestic dispute'. Another disturbing aspect is that this debate continues without any empirical basis. The opinions are not based on in-depth investigations, nor are they informed by theoretical or academic understanding. Dominant stereotypes prevail to form an ill-informed perception of existing laws and dictate the functioning of both the executive and the judiciary.

In *Rajesh Kumar vs State of UP*[102] the Supreme Court, without examining the reality or referring to any research, concluded that the law is misused by "vengeful" women and sees men as victims of this "cruel law". The court took an anti-woman stance where the judges expressed their anguish and pronounced that this law is abused and therefore suggested measures to dilute it. The courts see women through a stereotypical lens and brand them as "disgruntled women" who are "vengeful", "gold diggers" and "liars" while doubting the veracity of their complaints. Courts refuse to look into the data available on dowry death, women's suicide and violence, or the profiles of those lodged in the jails. The courts have not looked into the manner in which this law is implemented at the ground level through the existing paraphernalia consisting of CAW cells, counselling centers, family courts or mahila courts where counselling is done mandatorily and guidelines have been laid down pertaining to the arrest of the accused persons. What is ignored is the fact that the conviction rate is low in such cases because of coercive mandatory compromises or settlements enforced at various levels which start before the registration of the case. Women are discouraged from speaking the truth and are intimidated to remain silent while de-recognizing the historical background of patriarchal structural discrimination. The courts thus mirrored the oppressive culture and uphold orthodox values rather than safeguarding the spirit of the constitution or promoting the rights of women. While closing its eyes to the structural imbalance of power within the relationship, the court reinforces male domination while normalizing violence and coercing women to internalize the subjugation. In one stroke, the court took away the fundamentally guaranteed liberty, dignity and autonomy of a woman. In one stroke, the court breached the sacrosanct, non-negotiable rights of a citizen.

Filing a complaint under Section 498A is construed as cruelty by the wife

In *Christine Lazarus Menezes vs Lazarus Peter Menezes*[103] it was observed that lodging a false case under Section 498A by the wife is cruelty against the husband, and he can seek divorce on this basis. The Gujarat High Court in *Natubhai Somabhai Rohit vs State of Gujarat*[104] quashed the FIR on the ground that it is registered against ten members of the family, and even earlier the complainant filed a complaint under the PWDVA wherein she has roped in all family members, which shows her tendency to indulge in allegations and filing complaints. In another case it was held that women are using the law for the purpose of extorting money from their husbands.[105] The courts deny relief to women[106] while using the lens of morality.[107] Several judgements portray the complainants in a negative light. For instance, in the Batra's case,[108] the complainant was depicted as a woman who has terrorized her in-laws and has been asserting her rights while aggressively utilizing the law in her favor. In Kavita Dass's case,[109] the complainant was seen as a victim who is also a mother and a good woman, as she has been fulfilling all her duties diligently. The judicial reasoning is guided by the moral construct and stereotypes of a 'good woman' and a 'bad woman', and the decisions are informed by the patriarchal assumptions. Kapur,[110] too, has asserted that the legal discourse has the power to create binary assumptions regarding men and women, femininity and masculinity and culture and sexuality. Therefore, the law reinforces the dominant construction of women as weak, biologically inferior, modest and incapable of protecting themselves, on one hand, and evil, bad women as those who do not conform to the traditional norms, on the other.

The doctrine of battered woman syndrome in India

This discussion relating to misuse of the law by women has failed to acknowledge that in the cultural context where women's subordination is a norm and often they are socialized to silently tolerate the oppression, the law does not consider several significant elements. The legal system recognizes cruelty in marriage, yet it still fails to understand the intricate social and psychological complexities of the situation of a woman victim of domestic violence. For example, the history of abuse, pattern of violence and a woman's psychological state or experience are factors in domestic violence cases which may have a major impact on the outcome of the criminal litigation.

The courts in India have hardly dwelt on the same while adjudicating the matters until recently, when the Delhi High Court in one of its landmark decisions, while applying this doctrine, held an accused man guilty of abetting the suicide of his wife. In *State vs Hari Prashad*[111] under Section 306 IPC for abetting the suicide of the victim, the court upheld the doctrine of battered woman syndrome and stated that a victim could defend herself by launching a counter-attack. The court opined that, "Pushpa could not do so because biologically she was weaker. . . . The provocation by Hari Prashad became her compulsion to end the domestic relationship and she did by taking the extreme step of suicide". Though the court portrayed the woman as a docile, obedient wife "who has made every endeavor to stand against torture", they negated the women's agency or autonomy while valorizing her virtues of tolerance and patience, as only "when she was hoaxed" did she take the extreme step of ending her life. Thus, the court utilized the doctrine of battered woman syndrome to understand the situation of a woman in her matrimonial home. In this matter, the court innovatively applied this doctrine to the situation where the victim was already dead, yet it found the accused guilty of abetting the suicide of his wife. Battered woman syndrome is not used here as a defense; however, it has been utilized to establish the guilt of the accused in this particular case based on the reality of the situation.

Can a mother-in-law file a complaint against the daughter-in-law?

The PWDVA has been used to address the situation of women who face domestic violence within their homes. It is common knowledge that once a daughter-in-law asserts her right to reside in the matrimonial home, her husband and in-laws deploy various tactics and strategies to deny her this claim. In most of the cases where the household belongs to a joint family, the usual strategy deployed by the in-laws is to throw out both the woman and her husband of the matrimonial house, as this also helps them to show that they cannot be held liable under Section 498A, and also they can deprive her of her right to reside in the shared household. Often, false claims are made that both the son and daughter-in-law harass the old parents. While implementing the law, the male hegemony slyly deploys the strategy of pitting the rights of the mother-in-law against that of the daughter-in-law while absolving men of their responsibilities. For instance, the Delhi High Court in *Kusumlata vs State*[112] held that the mother-in-law is an aggrieved person and can file a complaint against the daughter-in-law. The court observed,

"This phenomenon of the daughters-in-law harassing their mothers-in-law especially who are dependent is not uncommon in the Indian society". The court generalized the situation and made the daughter-in-law a culprit because she raised her voice against her violent in-laws. This argument ignores the social hierarchies and the power dynamics that operate within the family and feeds into the patriarchy by reinforcing male power. It colludes with the male interest of oppressing women within families.[113]

This argument overlooks the fact that a woman, given no economic or social independence in a patriarchal family, derives her power solely from men – be it as his mother or as his wife. The power struggle between two women in such a structure therefore becomes inevitable. A mother-in-law, by the virtue of her years of marriage or by producing a son, enjoys an authoritative position in comparison to a new entrant. She acts as a carrier of a culture legitimizing and preserving patriarchy while training young women to accept their inferior position within the household.[114] She often feels socially and financially insecure when a new wife enters the household, and because of the internalization of patriarchy, she may abuse her daughter-in-law for a desire for power or to subordinate the weak. Kishwar noted that an ideal family venerates the mother–son relationship, where a woman's status as a mother or a maternal figure is considered more important than that of a wife, who represents a sexualized image of a woman and therefore deserves less respect.[115] This power struggle does not take place in the relationship between a father-in-law and a son-in-law because their spheres of operation are different from each other by the virtue of the fact that they live in separate households.[116] Moreover, in a patriarchal setup, a mother trains her daughter to accept the patriarchy through rigid social and sexual control, yet such authority is accepted as normal and desirable in a misogynist setup, and no voices are raised when women as daughters are abused within the natal family. The courts hardly look into power dynamics or examine the interplay of patriarchal forces within the relationships and act against the interests of women while pronouncing decisions. The courts thus act as mirror and reflect the notions, biases, prejudices and stereotypes that exist in society. Instead of socially transforming the society while pronouncing against the embedded biases, the courts often end up reinforcing the values that are unfair and discriminatory.

The PWDVA: the male is a respondent

Section 2q of the PWDVA clearly defines "respondent" as any male adult person who has been, or is, in a domestic relationship with the aggrieved person. Initially, it was understood that an application can be filed only against a male respondent[117] and a proceeding could not be continued against a female, but the Kerala High Court,[118] MP High Court[119] and the Delhi High Court[120] have held that an aggrieved wife or a female living in a relationship in the nature of marriage may also file a complaint against a relative of the husband or the male partner. It was settled by Supreme Court that in proviso to Section 2(q), a relative of the husband or male partner includes female also and a female relative of husband or male partner may also be seen as a respondent.[121] The court held that the gender-specific nature of the PWDVA was a reasonable classification in view of the act's object and purpose and that the act was therefore constitutional. Nevertheless, in *Hiral P. Harsora vs Kusum Narottamdas Harsora*[122] the Supreme Court struck down the words "adult male" from Section 2(q) of the act, to include women and minors as respondents under the law. This verdict implies that women and minors, and not just men, could be charged for committing acts of domestic violence. The thrust of the judgement is formal equality without looking at the disadvantageous position of women and while ignoring the notion of the substantive equality as guaranteed in the constitution. The court overlooked the fact that the PWDVA has been created specifically to deal with violence against women rather than promoting the notion of formal equality between men and women. The court's logic behind this verdict was based on the fact that the Delhi High Court, in Kusum Lata's case,[123] had already held that a mother-in-law could lodge a complaint against her daughter-in-law under the PWDVA. The SC ruling to change the PWDVA from 'gender specific' to 'gender neutral' has rendered its object invalid and the law regressive, as it provides an adult male an opportunity to have his wife evicted from the shared household by getting other women in the household to file a complaint. It disregarded the need for specific provisions for women and overturned battered women's right to access justice. Any attempt by women to access the PWDVA is already inviting counter-complaints by the female in-laws present in the same household. This gender-neutral provision is further being manipulated and engineered by the men to maneuver the law in their favor. When the court includes children and other female relatives under the ambit of Section 2q, it fails to contextualize the fact that law was originally formulated to create an interim space for a woman "in a domestic relationship" to protect her from violence.[124] This decision was reiterated by the Karnataka court,[125] where it was held that any person, whether male or female, aggrieved and alleging violation of the provisions of the act, can invoke the provisions under the act, though later this order was withdrawn.

A live-in relationship cannot be considered a domestic relationship

The PWDVA specifically provides protection to a woman in a live-in relationship. However, the courts in interpreting the law have constricted the scope of such relationships while upholding the concept of the sanctity of a marital relationship. Without acknowledging the fact that it is the women who suffer in any such relationship, the courts, while emphasizing the technical aspects of the legal definition of live-in relationship, have adversely interpreted the rights of women while negating the object of the law. In Velusamy's case[126] the apex court held that only legally married people and not live-in partners could access the PWDVA, clearly ignoring the fact that according to Section 2(f) of the act, the definition of "domestic relationship" includes a "relationship in the nature of marriage". The court stated that "If a man has a 'keep' whom he maintains financially and uses mainly for sexual purpose and/or as a servant it would not, in our opinion be a relationship in the nature of marriage". While referring to a woman as a 'keep' and implying that a woman could be used for sexual purposes, the court used gendered language and dehumanized women while promoting the unfettered rights of men to indulge in polygamy. The act clearly states that the "relationship in the nature of marriage" fulfills the noted requirements, yet the court negated this aspect while interpreting the law.

In *Aruna Parmod Shah vs Union of India*[127] the court, while referring to the concept of domestic relationship, pronounced that,

> We find no reason why equal treatment should not be accorded to the wife as well as a woman who has been living with a man as his common-law wife or even as a mistress. Like treatment to both does not in any manner, derogate the sanctity of marriage since an assumption can fairly be drawn that a 'live-in relationship' is invariably initiated and perpetuated by [the] male.

Thus, the court made a moral assumption while promoting the sanctity of marriage and assumed that only men can initiate and perpetuate live-in relationships. These assumptions derogate women when courts utilize their own yardstick of defining a woman as a "wife, keep or the mistress". It is indeed worrisome when the courtrooms act as the moral guardians and the custodians of patriarchal values rather than as upholders of the rule of law or justice in cases relating to women. Effort is made to preserve order and morality, and women's rights are sacrificed in the process. Courtrooms do not see women as citizens with autonomy or independence. Rather, the claim of a woman is viewed with reference to her social background and embedded in the web of her relationship as somebody's daughter, wife, mother or sister.

This inhuman logic was reiterated in *Indra Sarma vs VK Sarma*[128] where it held that the "Appellant was aware that the Respondent was a married person even before the commencement of their relationship, hence the status of the applicant is that of a concubine or a mistress, who cannot enter into the relationship in nature of marriage". The court failed to appreciate the fact that the law was enacted to protect women, and it nowhere implies that a person entering into a long-term relationship with a married man cannot seek protection. Relying on the aforesaid principle, the Bombay High Court[129] observed that the lady who knew that the applicant was married and his wife had opposed their relationship cannot say that she was an "aggrieved person" and she was not entitled to any relief under the

PWDVA. In fact, the courts while interpreting the law failed to appreciate the fact that due to the social stigma attached to such relationships, women need more protection. In *Manmohan Attavar vs Neelam*[130] it held that 'domestic relationship' is necessary to permit a party to occupy the shared household. These different interpretations by the court created confusion rather than resolving difficulties. The courts assume that heterosexual marriage as an ideal relationship and any other form of existence is stigmatized while ignoring the fact that women in such relationships are abused and violated. This approach ignores the fact that the term 'relationships in nature of marriage' can convey long term partnership and a woman is thrown out of the household because she is not being recognized by the society as a wife, thus making her situation more vulnerable.

Erasing entitlements: misinterpreting the right to reside in the shared household

The right to reside in the shared household has been considered as a significant right that seeks to prevent a survivor of violence from being dispossessed of the matrimonial home. However, despite the laudable objective of the law in upholding the wife's right to reside in the matrimonial home, it often gets nullified because the courts insist on rules, procedures and evidences besides linking it to the right to property division or the ownership of the household. The act does not create a new right. Earlier, this remedy could be availed under the Civil Procedure Code to apply for injunctions. Yet the courts with their patriarchal mind-set are overreacting in their zeal to save families and property owners rather than looking it as a simple entitlement to stay in the matrimonial home. Rather than providing remedies or relief to the victims of violence, what is being emphasized is the fact that the property of the family should be protected. Frequently, magistrates have been routinely rejecting the petitions for protection orders with respect to the matrimonial home; more specifically, if it is owned by the in-laws, the courts have been bringing in the rights of inheritance against a woman's right to reside in a shared household. The Supreme Court in *SR Batra vs Tarun Batra*[131] refused to grant residency rights to the woman in the house belonging to her mother-in-law. The apex court specified that 'shared household' implies the house belonging to or taken on rent by the husband or house, which belongs to the joint family in which the husband is one of the members. Property exclusively owned by the mother of the husband cannot be called a 'shared household'. The court's decision narrowly interpreted the provisions of the law and defeated the very purpose of the legislation. While there are judgments that reaffirm the wife's right to reside in the shared household by virtue of her marriage, irrespective of whether the property is rented or owned by the husband, the repercussions of the (in)famous *Batra vs Batra* case continue to be felt in the lower echelons of the judiciary.

The case has resonance in other decisions too.[132] In several other cases, the High Courts have held that the daughter-in-law has no right to reside in the house of the parents of the husband against their consent or wishes.[133] Delhi High Court elaborated that an adult son or daughter has no legal right to occupy self-acquired property of the parents against their wishes.[134] In *B Sakunthala vs Vasantha*,[135] the court quashed a complaint filed by the widow against her father-in-law and sister-in-law. In this matter, the house was sold by the father-in-law to the sister-in-law in order to deny the widow her right to reside in the matrimonial home. The sister-in-law initiated the proceedings under the Rent Control Act in order to evict the petitioner. Thus, in many cases, while linking the right to residence to property rights, the courts have denied women their rights to reside in the shared household against the object of the act, thereby rendering women homeless or destitute.

However, there are cases where a different view has been taken. In *Shumita Didi Sandhu vs Sanjay Singh Sandhu*, the marriage was solemnized, yet the wife was not allowed to enter the matrimonial home.[136] She filed a suit, claiming the right to reside in the matrimonial home. The husband argued that she had no such right as she had not "lived" in the house. The court concluded that the woman has no right to reside there, as the house was owned by her mother-in-law, yet she could be dispossessed only with "due process" of the law and cannot be physically thrown out. This judgment makes available to the woman safeguards that are otherwise granted to tenants and trespassers. In *P. Babu Venkatesh vs Rani*,[137] the Madras High Court upheld a residence order application filed on the behalf of a wife. The court found that her husband transferred the house to his mother's name, intending to defeat her right to reside there. The court held that pending divorce proceedings did not affect grants of relief under the PWDVA and directed the police to break open the lock of the house and provide protection to the aggrieved person to reside in the shared household.

Thus in several circumstances, High Courts have held that the aggrieved person has the right to reside in the shared household, such as cases where the property is in the name of the husband and the in-laws[138] or where the husband has a right, title or interest in the property for the purposes of Section 17 of the PWDVA[139]. In *Vandana vs T. Srikant Krishnamachari*,[140] the Madras High Court ruled that where the husband has a right, title or interest in the property for the purposes of Section 17 of the PWDVA, it is shared household and it is immaterial whether the parties have cohabitated in said property. In such cases, by virtue of being a wife, the aggrieved woman has a *dejure* right of residence in the shared household. In *Kavita Choudhury vs Eveneet Singh*[141] and in *Roma Tiwari vs Rajesh Tiwari*,[142] the courts have upheld the aggrieved person's right to reside in the shared household, irrespective of whether she has any right, title or interest in the said household or when the husband has no ownership right in the property. In several cases, High Courts have emphasized the fact that a woman must be provided with a roof over her head.[143] In *Sujoy Sanyal vs Shakuntala*

Sanyal[144] and in *Natasha Kohli vs Manmohan Kohli*[145] it has been held that the wife's right of residence must be respected not only because of the statutory mandate but also on the principles of equity. In *Ishpal Singh Kahai vs Ramanjeet Kahai*, the court,[146] while upholding the injunctions orders by the family court, directed the respondent to remove himself from the shared household and made a specific note on right to residence:

> The human right of a person has little to do with her ownership rights in property. It is therefore immaterial to consider in whose name the matrimonial home stands. In a case of domestic violence, the court has only to appreciate the abuse and protection against such abuse. Section 17 of the PWDVA recognizes right to reside in shared household irrespective of right, title or ownership over, interest over the property.

In *Kavita Dass vs NCT of Delhi*,[147] the Delhi High Court stated that the "court cannot ask the aggrieved person to vacate the house, even though it may be on rent". In this case, the couple was living in a rented accommodation. The husband left the wife and colluded with the landlord to file an eviction suit against her. The wife initiated proceedings under the PWDVA petitioning for the rent and maintenance. She then moved to the husband's rented apartment with the help of a PO under the interim orders. The magistrate observed that the house cannot be held as a shared household and ordered her to evict the house. The wife appealed against it, but her appeal was dismissed. An FIR was also filed against the wife; however, the Delhi High Court reversed the orders while keeping in the spirit of the PWDVA and focused on providing substantive justice to the victim; following the Supreme Court decision in *Kanwal Sood vs Nawal Kishore*[148] this court held that 'shared household' includes any household owned or tenanted by either of the parties in respect of which either the woman or the respondent or both, jointly or singly, have any right. The court held that a wife has a right to live with the respondent, whether he lives in an ancestral house, his own acquired house or a rented house.

In *B.P. Achla Anand vs Appi Reddi*[149] the decision related to tenanted premises where the husband and the wife were staying prior to filing the application under the PWDVA. In this matter, the issue related to the suit for eviction filed by the landlord against the tenant. The question pertained to whether the wife of the tenant can contest the suit when her husband was not interested in contesting the same. The Supreme Court held that "such a wife would be entitled to raise all such pleas and claim trial thereon, as would have been available to the tenant himself and no more." It has been further held that

> a deserted wife continuing in occupation of the premises obtained on lease by her husband, and which was their matrimonial home, and which was their matrimonial home, occupies, a position akin to that

> of an heir of the tenant-husband if the right to residence of such wife has not come to an end. The tenant having lost interest in protecting his tenancy rights as available to him under the law, the same right would devolve upon and inhere in the wife so long as she continues in occupation of the premises. Her rights to obligations shall not be higher or larger than those of the tenant himself.

The court also noted that

> A Hindu wife is entitled to be maintained by her husband. She is entitled to remain under his roof and protection. She is also entitled to separate residence if by reason of the husband's conduct or by his refusal to maintain her in his own place of residence or for other just cause she is compelled to live apart from him. Right to residence is a part and parcel of wife's right to maintenance. The right to maintenance cannot be defeated by the husband executing a Will to defeat such a right. The right has come to be statutorily recognised with the enactment of the Hindu Adoptions and Maintenance Act, 1956.

Thus, while analyzing the many judgements relating to the right of a woman to reside in the shared household, it may be said that there is a lack of clarity about the women's rights secured under the PWDVA. The courts have given mixed interpretations of the law where various factors come into play while deciding the matter.

Quantum of monetary relief

Section 20(2) of the PWDVA provides for monetary relief. However, experiences show that the execution of the maintenance order is difficult. Several matters have reached the Supreme Court where the respondents have deployed tactics and strategies to avoid paying maintenance.[150] In *Francis Cyril Cunha vs Lydia Jane Cunha*[151] an application for the discharge of maintenance was filed, and the trial court summoned the husband for committing an offense under Section 31 of the PWDVA for the breach of the order. The matter went to the High Court, which held that nonpayment of maintenance is not an offense on technical grounds, thus depriving women of their legal rights provided under the law. The Sixth Monitoring and Evaluation Report by the Lawyers Collective in 2013 showed that women are denied rights when they approach the courts under the PWDVA. Thus, interpretation of the provisions of this law is chaotic, inconsistent and marred by confusion. In addition, its implementation was further been problematic, as it is compromised and diluted because of the subjective biases, stereotypes and prejudices of those who enforce this law. Instead of using a proactive approach to expand the provisions of the law, the remedies are denied on excuses based on patriarchal notions, dominant ideologies and traditional ideas about the position and the status of women. This is also made evident by the fact that the state, instead of investing in institutional capacity or the infrastructure, has been shying away from fulfilling its responsibilities.

The basic premise behind domestic violence remains unchallenged

Domestic violence in India is premised on several notions, as follows:

1. The marital relationship is hierarchical and inegalitarian. Women are accorded not legal status within a marriage and the family, where a man is considered the master of the household.
2. The husband and his family have authority to beat the wife in addition to demanding dowry. Chastisement is a prerogative granted to a husband who can commit violence against his wife in the guise of love and discipline.
3. A violent husband is not made accountable even if he brutally murders the woman. The law grants immunity to violent husbands even if the husband is a drunkard, vile or a criminal.
4. The family is a private realm, and no one – not even the law – should interfere with the privacy of such an institution. Domestic harmony is prioritized over safety of a woman.
5. The doctrine of marital unity as propounded by Blackstone persists, which prevents those who frame the law and those who implement it from seeing complainant wives separate people or citizens demanding protection under the law.
6. Courts are expected to uphold constitutional values but instead are enforcing family ideology.
7. The law has been used symbolically and superficially to address violence, but no steps have been taken to address the root cause; for instance, the dowry law has failed to eliminate dowry or address dowry-related violence
8. The legal discourse focused on blaming the victim, stigmatizing her and penalizing women for not 'adjusting' within their families.
9. Due to a backlash, the focus is shifting away from reality, from 'bad men' who are battering or burning their wives, to 'bad or terrible women' who are misusing the law.

   Most of these premises are never questioned even in a court of law. The law does not utilize the principles of rationality while adjudicating the claims of battered or murdered wives. It legitimizes and reiterates social inequalities within the institution of marriage.

Few attempts have been made to change the approach and the attitude of those who implement the law to see women as partners and citizens with equal rights. Legal reforms could not make a dent on the construction of women's 'natural' position within an existing power structure that creates their everyday reality of their life within and outside the family. Additionally, the justice system is part and parcel of a larger patriarchal society where the system is corrupt and inefficient. Courts have used logic relating to the chastisement prerogative and marital privacy while prosecuting men in cases of wife beating. The language of hierarchy, love and discipline is used to protect violent men, and the tropes of both hierarchy and interiority is used to cover bias in the hierarchical marriage arrangements. The regime of immunity is utilized to justify brutal violence while utilizing the dimensions of feelings and domestic space.

The justice system has failed to meet the changing needs of society

Analysis of many judgements shows that women are being tortured, brutalized, burned alive, murdered or forced to commit suicide, yet, tragically, the current judicial discourse focuses on the misuse or abuse of the law by women. The cases relating to dowry deaths, murders of wives, suicide of women in marriage and domestic violence found little space in the media. No sensitivity is being displayed when a wife dies – rather, such cases are normalized and trivialized, and what is prioritized are fake concerns raised by the fragile masculinity, probably because women's concerns are no longer deemed relevant by the patriarchal society. Dowry deaths were highlighted during the 1980s, and the laws have been reformed since then; however, no monitoring or follow-up has been done to ensure that the system of dowry coercion is eliminated. Similarly, domestic violence cases are being reported in increasing numbers, yet no accountability has been fixed to ensure that actions could be taken to monitor the situation. The system has not devised ways to monitor if the police are following the procedures or conducting an investigation seriously. The criminal justice system has failed to respond to the changing situation. Similarly, civil law ignores the realities of women's lives. Perhaps the state is not willing to accept the agency of women challenging and defying patriarchal norms. Yet with the existence of the strong constitutional paradigm in addition to advancements in terms of education, awareness and enhanced aspirations, women are challenging the conventional stereotype and are defying age-old norms. However, once women enter the courtrooms, they face the similar patriarchal restrictions which they have been dealing with outside the court spaces. The courts and investigative agencies dominated by men have failed to transform at the same pace, and this lag in the expectations of women and the working of the state is creating complications. Therefore, there is a need to renovate the mind-set and the attitude of the state towards women's concerns.

Summary

This chapter scrutinizes the operation of law and highlights that though domestic violence was criminalized in India in 1983, the legal system continues to treat wife beating as an offense different from other cases of assault and battery. Also, the authorities intervened only occasionally in cases of marital violence. Men who beat their wives are offered formal and informal immunities, while the courts uphold the concept of 'family harmony' and endorse the chastisement prerogative of the husband. The legal system treats the family as a private space where a public law cannot be applied. It concludes that the law uses the gendered notions of citizenship while adjudicating the cases of violence against women.

Notes

1 Mill John Stuart (1869) The Subjection of Women, www.earlymoderntexts.com/assets/pdfs/mill1869.pdf pp. 17–18 accessed on 20.3.18
2 Mill John Stuart (1869) What Good Reform Would Do? Subjection of Women, www.earlymoderntexts.com/assets/pdfs/mill1869.pdf
3 Ibid p. 47
4 Quoted by the lower court in the matrimonial appeal 360/2013 decided on 1.8.18 in VV. Prabhakaran vs Chandranath AIR 2018 Ker 179
5 Sathe SP (1999) Gender, Constitution and the Courts, In *Engendering Law, Essays in Honour of Lotika Sarkar*, edited by Amita Dhanda and Archana Prashar, Eastern Book Company, Lucknow
6 Prabhubhai Ranchhodbhai Tailor vs Bhartiben Prabhubhai Tailor 004 (3) MhLJ 487, Shiva Mohana Reddy vs Aparna Reddy on 3.9.2004 Andhra HC
7 Bajrang Gangadhar Revdekar vs Pooja Bajrang Revdekar on 18.8.2009 Bombay HC
8 Samit Subhash Agarwal vs Kamlesh Laltaprasad Gupta 27.4.2018 Bombay HC
9 Ajay Lavania vs Shobhna Dubey 28.7.2011 Allahabad HC
10 Ramchandra Doddappa Naik vs Hanamnaik Patil (1935) 37 BOMLR 920
11 This view has been taken in many cases, such as Narain Dhara vs Rakhal Gain (1876) ILR 1 Cal 1, Rahi Wife Of Teja Kurad vs Govinda Valad Teja, ILR 1 Bom 97, Ram Saran Garain vs Tek Chand Garain ILR 28 Cal 194, Sukurmoni vs Kirpal Narain Tewari (1892) ILR 19 Cal 91.
12 Shakuntalabai vs LV Kulkarni, 1989 AIR 1359, Kashibai Jadhav vs Yamunabai Namdeo Jadhav 25.2.2016, Bombay HC, Jairam S More vs Sindhubai I (2001) DMC 407, Yamanaji H. Jadhav vs Nirmala AIR 2002 SC 971
13 Hancher M (2013) Reading and Writing the Law: Macaulay in India, *Law and Language: Current Legal Issues*, 15 (1) 187
14 Chan W, Wright B and Yeo S (2011) *Codification, Macaulay and the Indian Penal Code: The Legacies and Modern Challenges of Criminal Law Reform*, Routledge, London
15 Rege Sharmila (2013) *Against Madness of Manu: BR Ambedkar's Writings on Brahmanical Patriarchy*, Navanyana Publications, Mumbai
16 Kolsky E (2010) The Body Evidencing of Crime: Rape on trial in Colonial India, 1860–1947, *Gender and History*, 22 (1) 109–30
17 Sinha K (2016) Be It Manu, Be It Macaulay: Indian Law and the Problem of Female Body, *Journal of Indian Law and Society*, 5, 61–94
18 Nigam S (2005) *Understanding Justice from the Perspective of Women Litigants as Victims of Domestic Violence in India*, Occasional Paper No. 35, CWDS, New Delhi Also, Nigam S (2017) Fighting for Justice in the Patriarchal Courts, *Countercurrents*, August 30
19 Chandra Sudhir (1998) Enslaved Daughters: Colonialism, Law and Women's Rights, Oxford University Press, New Delhi

20 Sarkar Tanika (2001) *Conjugality and Hindu Nationalism: Resisting Colonial Reason and Death of Child-Wife in Hindu Wife Hindu Nation: Community*, Religion and Cultural Nationalism Permanent Black, New Delhi pp. 119–225
21 Anagol P (2008) Rebellious Wives and Dysfunctional Marriages: Indian Women Discourses and Participation in the Debates Over Restitution of Conjugal Rights and the Child Marriage Controversy in the 1880s and 1890s, In *Women and Social Reform in Modern India, a Reader*, edited by Sumit Sarkar and Tanika Sarkar, Indiana University Press, Bloomington
22 Ibid p. 283
23 Kannabiran K (2009) Judicial Meanderings in Patriarchal Thickets: Litigating Sex Discrimination in India Economic and Political Weekly, *Review of Women's Studies*, XLIV (44) 88–98, 31 Quoted Rao Shiva B (1968) *The Framing of Indian Constitution: A Study*, Indian Institute of Public Administration, New Delhi
24 Ibid
25 Hindu Code (1948) *Constituent Assembly Debates*, Vol. VII (April 9) p. 3628
26 Pattabhi Sitaramayya (1948) *Constituent Assembly Debates*, Vol. VII (9 April) p. 3635
27 Rege S 2013 Against the Madness of Manu
28 Mahanta Aparna (1994) The Indian State and Patriarchy, In *State and Nation in the Context of Social Change*, edited by TV Sathyamurthy, Vol. I, Oxford University Press, New Delhi p. 94
29 Menon Ritu and Bhasin K (1998) *Borders and Boundaries: Women in India's Partition*, Zubaan, New Delhi p. 255
30 AIR 1984 Delhi 66 para 33
31 Rani vs Kumar (1984) 3 SCC. 90
32 1984 AIR 1562
33 AIR 1983 AP 356
34 Gonsalves L (1993) *Women and the Law*, Lancers, New Delhi
35 1997 (9) SCC 579
36 AIR 1994 SC 1418
37 1991 AIR 1532
38 2001(3) SCALE 549
39 Criminal Appeal 1592/2011 decided on 9.1.2015
40 (2001) 9 SCC 618 also State of West Bengal vs Orilal Jaiswal (1994) 1 SCC 73
41 (2009) 16 SCC 487
42 Singh Namita (2019) Man Sentenced to Six Years RI for Injuries Which Led to His Wife's Death, *The Hindustan Times*, April 29
43 *The Hindustan Times* (2019) Million Species at Risk of Wipeout: Draft UN Study, April 24
44 (2001) 8 SCC 633
45 Harjit Singh vs State of Punjab (2006) 1 SCC 463; Thakkan Jha vs State of Bihar (2004) 13 SCC 348
46 Kamalakar Nandram Bhavsar vs State of Maharashtra (2004) 10 SCC 192
47 (2001) 2 SCR 984
48 1994 CrLJ 3472
49 Cri Appeal 1218 of 2016 SLP Cri 6104/14 decided on 28.11.16
50 Cri Appeal 1048 of 2018 SLP Cri 4122/16 decided on 21.8.18
51 Rudrakant Jha vs State of Jharkhand, Jharkhand HC, Cri MP 1204/ 2007 decided on 7.5.12, Sudhir Kapur vs State in Crl.M.A. 799/2009 decided on 10.08.2010, Bimla Rawal vs State (NCT of Delhi) in WP (Crl.) 1541/2007 decided on 03.01.2008; Bhura Ram vs State of Rajasthan (2008) 11 SCC 103; Y Abraham Ajit vs Inspector of Police, Chennai (2004) 8 SCC 100. Onkar Nath Pandey vs State of Jharkhand, Jharkhand HC Cr MP 1100/ 2013

52 Suo Moto vs Ushaben Kishorbhai Mistry Spl Cri Application 5313/ 2015 decided on 27.11.15
53 (2007) 9 SCC 721
54 2013(3) SCALE 525
55 Durga Prasad vs State of MP (2010) 9 SCC 73; Gurdeep Singh vs State of Punjab (2011) 12 SCC 408; Kala Ram vs State of Haryana (2012) 10 SCC 763; Biswajit Haldar vs State of West Bengal (2008) 1 SCC 202; Rajesh Bhatnagar vs State of Uttarakhand AIR 2011 SC 363, Kishori Lal vs State of MP 2007 3 RCR Cri 385, Shailender vs State 169 (2010) DLT 563; Satvir Singh vs State of Punjab (2001) 8 SCC 633, Shanti vs State of Haryana AIR 1991 SCC 1261; Kansraj vs State of Punjab 2000 (5) SCC 207; State of West Bengal vs Orilal Jaiswal 1994 (1) SCC 73; Ramesh Kumar vs State of Chhattisgarh (2001) 9 SCC 618, State of Gujarat vs Avinas Dinkar Joshi, Gujarat High Court Cri App 900 of 2000 decided on 9.4.2013, Indrasing Raol vs State of Gujarat II (2000) DMC 239, State of Maharashtra vs Ashok Shukla AIR 1997 SC 3111 and many others
56 II (2000) DMC 239
57 Fricker M (2008) Epistemic Injustice: Power and Ethics of Knowing, *Theoria*, 61, 69–71
58 Sushil Sharma vs State NCT of Delhi (2014) 4 SCC 317
59 Pereira Maxwell (2018) *The Tandoor Murder: The Crime That Shook the Nation and Brought the Government to Its Knees*, Westland Publications, Chennai
60 It is not that the author is in favor of the death penalty; rather, the arguments given to commute the death sentence are unreasonable.
61 1990 Cri LJ 407
62 Gangoli (2007) supra
63 MacKinnon CA (1987) *Feminism Unmodified: Discourses on Life and Law*, Harvard University Press, London
64 1999 3 SC 620
65 AIR 2009 CAL.135
66 Application No. 1192/1 PS Sultanpuri, MM Rohini Court decided on 15.9.07
67 Usharani Pradhan vs Braj Kishore Pradhan, MAT No. 104 of 2011 High Court of Orissa, order dated 23.9.11
68 SA vs AA MAT Appeal 68/2012 decided on 22.3.2016, Delhi HC
69 Ramesh Kumar vs State of Chhattisgarh supra
70 PIL No 104 of 2015
71 Basu Asmita and Jaising I (2005) *Violence Against Women: A Statistical Overview, and Challenges, Gaps in Data Collection Expert*, Paper presented at Violence Against Women: A Statistical Overview, Challenges and Gaps in Data Collection and Methodology and Approaches for Overcoming UN Division for Advancement of Women, Geneva
72 Justice Kapoor JD (2002) *Laws and Flaws in Marriage: How to Stay Happily Married*, Konark Publishers, New Delhi
73 *The Times of India* (2012) A Wife Should Be Like Goddess Sita: Bombay HC, May 8, https://timesofindia.indiatimes.com/city/mumbai/A-wife-should-be-like-goddess-Sita-Bombay-HC/articleshow/13054421.cms
74 Sandanshiv DN and Jolly Mathew (2005) Legal Reform in Dowry Laws, In *Issues in Contemporary Indian Feminism: Dowry and Inheritance*, edited by Srimati Basu, Zed Books, London & New York p. 73
75 AIR 2009 SC 589
76 AIR 2002 SC 2582 5
77 AIR 1984 SC 622
78 The women's group in Maharashtra initiated a signature campaign and a poster exhibition titled '*Mein Ek Manjushree*'. From Haksar N and Singh A (1986) *Demystification of Laws for Women*, Lancers, New Delhi.

79 (2002) 2 SCC 73
80 SCC OnLine SC 1114
81 Kapur Ratna (2016) Hindu Divorce Case: Retrograde Gender Politics on the Bench, *The Wire*, October 8
82 Kadidal A (2019) Marital Rape Should Not Be a Crime in India: Ex CJI Misra, *Deccan Herald*, April 9
83 *Livelaw Network* (2017) Criminalizing Marital Rape May Destabilize Institution of Marriage: Center Tells Delhi HC, August 29, www.livelaw.in/criminalising-marital-rape-may-destabilise-institution-marriage-centre-tells-delhi-hc/
84 Sinha Badhra (2017) Govt Defends No Action for Legal Exception Allowing Forced Sex with Minor Wife, *The Hindustan Times*, August 10
85 *The Telegraph* (2017) Marriage Defence for Rape, August 10
86 Sinha Shanta (2017) The Centre Has Solemnized the Invasion of Girls' Bodily Integrity, Sexuality and the Mind, *The Wire*, August 14, https://thewire.in/167674/child-marriage-invasion-of-body-mind-sexuality/
87 (1997) 5 SCC 30
88 1998 Cri.LJ. 554
89 VD. Bhanot vs Savita Bhanot (2012) 3 SCC 183 also Saraswathy vs Babu AIR 2014 SC (Cri.) 493
90 AIR 1975 SC 1534
91 Para 27
92 Kajal Roy vs Prasanta Roy (2005) 2 CALLT 567 HC para 26
93 1994 AIR 710
94 Shobha Rani vs Madhukar Reddy 1988 AIR 121
95 AIR 2000 SC 3559
96 AIR 2002 SC 2078
97 Wazir Chand vs State of Haryana, 1989 AIR 382 Also, State of Maharashtra vs Ramesh Damodar More Bombay HC Cri Appeal 12/2003 decided on 11.5.17
98 Criminal Application APL 774 of 2017 Bombay HC, Nagpur Branch decided on 2.11.2018 para 24
99 I (2007) DMC 545
100 Criminal Complaint No. 316/3/2007 PS NFC MM Court Saket Pronounced on 27.5.2015
101 (2014) 8 SCC 273
102 *2017* (8) SCALE 313
103 Bombay HC Family Court Appeal No. 150/2008 decided on 21.4.17
104 Cri Misc Application 20679/2013 decided on 6.4.17
105 Case No. 3/2010, Haryana, Sonepat
106 Crl Appeal 10/2010, Delhi
107 Case No. 3132/2010, Uttarakhand, Kashipur
108 Supra
109 Supra
110 Kapur Ratna (2006) Revisioning the Role of Law in Women's Human Rights Struggles, In *The Legalization of Human Rights: Multidisciplinary Perspectives on Human Rights and Human Rights Law*, edited by Saladin Meckled-Garcia and Başac Çali, Routledge, London & New York p. 105
111 Cri Appeal 333/2000 on 10.2 2016
112 Cri MC No 725 of 2011 decided on 2.9.2011 Delhi HC
113 Gangoli (2007) supra
114 Yuval Davis N (1997) *Gender and Nation*, Sage, London
115 Kishwar M (1997) Women, Sex and Marriage: Restraints as a Feminist Strategy, *Manushi*, 99, 23–36
116 Menon Nivedita (2012) Feminism and the Family – Thoughts on International Women's Day, *Kafila*, March 8

117 Ajay Kant vs Alka Sharma (2008) Crim. LJ. 264 (MP HC.) 7
118 Vijayalekshmi Amma vs Bindu 2010(1) KLT 79
119 Sarita vs Umrao (2008) 1R Cr D Rajasthan HC, Nand Kishore vs Rajasthan (2008) RLW 3432 Rajasthan HC,
120 Varsha Kapoor vs UoI WP (Crl.) 638 of 2010, 3.6.2010 Delhi HC
121 Sandhya Manoj Wankhde vs Manoj Bhimrao Wankhde (2011) 3 SCC 650
122 Civil Appeal 10084/2016, SLP civil 9132/2015 on 6.10.2016
123 Supra
124 Ghose Sanjay (2016) A Gender-Neutral Domestic Violence Law Harms Rather Than Protects Women, *The Wire*, November 3
125 Mohd Zakir vs Shabana Criminal Petition 2351/2017 Karnataka HC decided on 18.4.17
126 Velusamy vs D. Patchaiammal, 2010 AIR SCW 6731
127 WP (Crl.) 425 of 2008
128 AIR 2014 SC 309
129 Deepak vs State of Maharashtra 2015 CRI. LJ 4833
130 Civil Appeal No. 2500 of 2017 Supreme Court decided on 14.7.2017
131 (2007) 8 SCC 2675
132 Raj Kumari vs Preeti Satija IA 500/2011 in CS (OS) 85/2010 Decided on 13.1.2012; Pal Singh vs Priyanka Singh Manu/DE/7325/2011
133 K Rajendran vs Ambikavathy Cri. Rev Case 482/2012 decided on 8.1.13, Madras HC, Also, Neetu Mittal vs Kanta Mittal AIR 2009 Delhi 72
134 Sudha Mishra vs Surya Mishra, RFA. 299/2014, Order 25/7/2014, Delhi HC
135 Crl OP 8503 of 2016 and Crl MP (MD) 4117 and 4118/2016 decided on 7.9.2016 Madras HC
136 MANU/DE/8160/2007
137 MANU/TN/06/12/2008
138 Jyotsana Sharda vs Gaurav Sharda, MANU/DE/3520/2009
139 Rajkumar Pandey vs Sarita Pandey MANU/MH/1295/2008
140 (2007) 6 MLJ 205 (Mad)
141 MANU/DE/3497/2010
142 WPC 10696/ 2017 Bombay HC decided on 12.10.2017
143 Ruma Chakraborty vs Sudha Rani Banerjee (2005) 8 SCC 140, 147
144 MANU/WB/0597/2010
145 MANU/DE/2506/2010
146 MANU/MH/0385/2011
147 2012 ILR 3 Delhi 747
148 (1983) 3 SCC 25
149 2005(3) SC 313
150 Shalu Ojha vs Prashant Ojha 2017 (3) SCC (Cr) 744
151 Criminal Rev Petition No. 758/2015 decided on 18.12.2015, Karnataka HC

7 Conclusion

How easy is access to justice for women?

"In the problem of women was the germ of a solution, not only for their oppression, but for everybody's. The control of women in society was ingeniously effective. It was not done directly by the state. Instead the family was used- men to control women, women to control children, all to be preoccupied with one another, to turn to one another for help, to blame one another for trouble, to do violence to one another when things weren't going right. Why could this not be turned around? Could women liberating themselves, children freeing themselves, men and women beginning to understand one another, find the source of their common oppression outside rather than in one another? Perhaps then they could create nuggets of strength in their own relationships, millions of pockets of insurrection. They could revolutionize thought and behavior in exactly that seclusion of family privacy which the system had counted on to do its work of control and indoctrination. And together, instead of at odds- male, female, parents, children- they could undertake the changing of society itself."[1]

This book has attempted to look at the question of women in the situation of domestic violence while moving back and forth between legislative reforms, courtrooms and women's everyday lives besides understanding their vulnerabilities and their agency in the face of a patriarchal socio-legal culture. By documenting resistance against violence by women in the courts, this work has examined the systemic subjugation, yet at the same time, it also has looked at resistance and dissent to explore new possibilities. This work is built around the lives of women who are trapped in a vicious cycle of violence and yet through their sheer resilience, they resisted and challenged the status quo. Through persuasive ethnographic vignettes as well as on-the-ground realities relating to law, marriage, rights, family, violence, property and the state, this research also reflects on the manner in which the legal reform process is reproducing and reinforcing the profound structural vulnerabilities in an intensely patriarchal society. The findings indicate that the family as a basic institution is a complex, hierarchical, unequal matrix offering support, care and affection to its members, on the one hand, yet also socializes an individual into existing power hierarchies and unequal property relations to justify the use of violence to maintain these inequalities, on the other. Multiple patriarchies operate at a larger level to oppress women. Second, this work shows that domestic violence varies in forms; it is brutal, and yet legal remedies are limited, and these are further narrowly interpreted by those who enforce the law. In domestic violence cases, the law has been twisted to use the dichotomy of public and private, and while articulating the language of feelings and emotions, immunity is being granted to perpetrators while propagating the culture of violence with impunity. Theoretically, the law has provided women a platform to raise their concerns, yet the crucial concern is that the law provides only superficial fixes which often end up working against women. The law does not help women break free from patriarchal chains. The spirit with which the law has been enacted is not backed by a commitment, and the system is being manipulated to serve the logic of the patriarchy as well as the interest of dominant group while reinforcing the prevailing biased social norms. Yet the survivors, who may be powerless and vulnerable, through their sheer grit, are demanding justice and negotiating for their rights, shaking the system and forcing it to respond, so no longer it can remain a subversive site. Rather, the law has become a site of resistance where marginality is being contested.

Domestic violence law, both criminal and civil pieces of legislation, are progressive and provide a platform where battered wives can raise their concerns. Criminal provisions could deter and prevent violence against wives, and civil remedies provided under the PWDVA could aid women in rebuilding their lives. By bringing domestic abuse under the purview of the law, at a theoretical level, the state enforces that citizenship rights cannot be suspended within families. However, at the practical level, there are problems in the implementation of the law. Some of these are technical in nature, but most of these hurdles arise because of an insensitive attitude of the state, a stereotypical approach and biased perceptions of the those who implement the law. Gaps exist because the state, while enforcing the law, has not provided for social and economic security measures for women. The state has not created mechanisms such as livable shelter homes, medical or legal aid facilities, short-stay homes, creche services, employment schemes, monetary aid schemes and other services for victims and survivors. The androcentric approach of the state could not imagine alternatives beyond the '*maika*' and '*sasural*' network to support women who have been struggling hard to manage their lives and yet are brazenly challenging the deeply entrenched biased norms and shaking the patriarchal foundation through pure resilience.

Women are being victimized within natal and marital homes because of the failure of the state to maintain law and order, in addition to the state's inability to protect women's rights in general. Yet instead of supporting the victims, the state further augments their misery by neglecting and negating their concerns, thus creating a vicious circle of violence and victimization. Added to this is the backlash that has emerged lately, wherein the state and other stakeholders wrongly and hypothetically assume that the law is being misused by women. Instead of making a dent in the orthodox culture, the law reinforces the patriarchy. The law, on paper, provides for abstract entitlements considering the situation of women, yet what they receive in actual practice is discriminatory treatment. Therefore, there is a need to critically re-examine this approach of the law which neither can achieve the goal of restoration, nor can it regulate violent behavior; rather, it has become a blunt instrument at the hands of the state to repress women who challenge the patriarchy and defy the boundaries of their homes.

Further, wife battering is shielded behind the garb of affective discipline and is wrapped around the language of love. The law upholds the chastisement prerogatives of husbands and in-laws to abuse and torture wives in the guise of emotions. Wife beating is considered a non-serious issue or is treated as a lesser crime, while the state has failed to alter the inequities within conjugality or to make a dent in the asymmetrical power relationship that exists within the institution of marriage. It could not acknowledge the fact that marriages and families are coercive, inequitable, gendered institutions based on unequal power relations. This work suggests that though visualized as an instrument to 'protect' women's rights, the law has failed to empower the survivors, because those who make the law and those who enforce it could not imagine the possibilities of creating alternative structures within society which question or critically examine the institution of marriage or family, let alone altering the rigid patriarchal order.

The findings recommend that there is a dire need to change the approach with which the law is executed in its present form. The need is to investigate the manner in which the law is being framed and implemented, and the state should ensure that technical and procedural gaps in the law are remedied to focus on a 'women-centric' or 'survivor-centric' approach rather than the 'law-centric' or 'family-centric' approach. Legislative reform could transform the inequities in the social relations by formulating matrimonial property rights for women besides providing socio-economic solutions and comprehensive social protection measures, including priorities in terms of jobs, training or facilities for entrepreneurship; helping children in domestic violence situations by supporting their education; providing for medical and other requirements; housing; and similar such short-term as well as long-term interventions which could facilitate survivors to lead a violence-free life. At a wider level, the need is to challenge the patriarchal culture and counter the regressive ideology by reshaping the discourse on toxic aggressive masculinity and passive femininity, recognizing women as equal citizens and persons within private and public spaces and acknowledging their citizenship rights, engendering the socio-political and the legal institutions, focusing on a rights-based approach to secure social justice and mitigating poverty while emphasizing social welfare provisions and working towards a larger goal of women's liberation. It is also necessary that the backlash against this law be countered and those who enforce the law be constantly sensitized. The system needs to respond positively to eliminate violence against women; unless violence is eliminated, individual survivors through their utter resilience, will keep on shaking up the patriarchal system.

Domestic violence is complex: the legal definition is limited

The PWDVA, in comparison to the definition of 'cruelty' provided under Section 498A IPC, elaborates the concept of domestic violence broadly to include physical, sexual, economic, mental, psychological and emotional violence. However, the present work indicates that the definition needs be expanded to include the situation of continuous varied forms of different violence which occur simultaneously and from which escape is impossible. The PWDVA has created distinct categories of abuse, but in the present work, the informants shared their stories of manifold form of abuse woven together, and their chronicles entail multiple forms of victimization which include economic, sexual, emotional or mental violence, as well as physical beatings, terror, fear, coercion, control, humiliation and other forms of abuses on a daily basis. Their descriptions are interlaced and intertwined with subjectivities and involve members not only from their extended families but also, at times, outsiders. So, the classification of violence as explained under the PWDVA or in the DIR format seems limited. Also, wife abuse, from the perspective of women, entails a history of continuous abuse and is not limited to one or two specific incidents as interpreted by those who enforce the law. An analysis of case law indicates that frequently courts rely on specific episodes while ignoring the continuity of persistent terror and fear in real lived experiences. The concept of battered woman syndrome has been accepted in many countries, yet in India this idea needs to be elaborated on in the wider context of a patriarchal culture.

A common belief held by law enforcement officials is that domestic violence involves 'mostly physical violence' and consists primarily of a 'quarrel' or an occasional argument, bickering or slapping, which could easily be called a 'dispute'. This perception overlooks the fact that violence is far more serious than just a dispute. A dispute occurs between two people on par, whereas violence involves an abuse of power and authority in a relationship. Dispute underpins the argument that women are a party to violence, which is incorrect. Domestic abuse involves long continuous phases of violence that entail a miserable narrative of constant, unceasing pain and suffering that go beyond threatening, insults, coercion, an atmosphere of fear and terror, injuries, coercion, fractured bodies, trauma, agony and probably an environment where one contemplates committing suicide or is murdered. The experience of women is not homogenous. Each one has endured multiple form of violence and has been negotiating around it. Often their lives are circled around oppression. Women in different settings from different backgrounds – each has a unique story, yet common elements include pain and suffering, struggle to constantly deal with abuse, an understanding that violence needs to be stopped and a zeal to fight against it. The law does not consider the comprehensive aspect of this situation.

Based on their experiences in Western countries, Pence and Paymar[2] have evolved the Duluth Model or the Domestic Abuse Intervention Project, which is based on the concept that men use violence within relationships to exercise power and control, which is illustrated by the Power and Control Wheel. It is argued that men commit violence not because of individual pathology, but rather it is because of a socially reinforced sense of entitlement. However, the Power Wheel is based on a dyadic relationship between the two parties. It does not consider the active role played by other family members in inflicting violence. While agreeing to the theory behind inventing the Power and Control Wheel, this work further suggests that to apply this model in the patriarchal settings in India, several factors must be considered, such as the incongruence in the relationship between the partners, as well as the involvement of one or more perpetrators, which include not only their husband but also extended families who may share the same household or are residing separately and yet could influence the relationship between the abuser and the abused. Pence and Dasgupta[3] have re-examined battering in different situations, including social conditioning of both the victim and the perpetrator; however, certain other dimensions need to be re-examined in the Indian context such as a) the belief in supremacy and a hierarchy among men in different cultures and social approval of battering; b) as the role and involvement of more than one perpetrator; c) the emotional, social, financial and material dependence of women on men because of patrilocality and d) the absence of support mechanisms. Perhaps further research may help us grasp the comprehensive situation.

Domestic abuse is narrowly construed to omit sexual violence, incest or marital rape

The definition of cruelty under Section 498A does not include sexual violence; however, this is included in the definition of domestic violence under the PWDVA. But merely defining sexual violence has not helped women who face multiple forms of abuse, including incest, marital rape, denial of reproductive rights or autonomy, forced marriages, multiple abortions and many other forms of violence. Other existing provisions in the criminal law such as those under Section 375 or 376 IPC could not be applied to the situation of marital rape. The present work indicates that women face brutal forms of sexual violence, and the law could not provide any remedy to deal with such situations. The law has failed to address the issue of sexual violence and cannot challenge the traditional asymmetrical relationship. Rather, a regressive view is being taken to deal with this complex phenomenon. Unless such mind-set is transformed to be more accommodative of gender concerns, women will continue to bear brutal forms of violence silently with no remedies being made available to them to even air such grievances.

Women face multiple forms of victimization

For survivors, getting justice is not an easy task. The legal system adds another layer to their victimization instead of offering healing or providing remedial options to aid recovery. Often, a complainant is compelled to run around from pillar to post to seek justice, and in the process, she faces stigma and humiliation, spends money, takes care of the children, earns her livelihood and picks up the pieces of her shattered life. And in return, what she receives is sermons from the paternalist court 'to settle the matter' – which implies 1) going back to violent marriages and 'adjusting' and compromising with the abusive husband; 2) taking a meager compensation in lieu of *streedhan*, maintenance or alimony from her husband and negotiate to settle down back with the natal family or make her own arrangement to stay; 3) remarry and face the risk of entering into another violent situation; or 4) become homeless, without resources, finances, shelter or any other support, fend for herself and her kids and sink deeper into poverty. No other options are made available to rehabilitate women or to ensure restorative justice.

Often women are stigmatized by society if they stay away from violent marriages. Instead of shaming the violent men, society pressures women, demeans them and humiliates them for being too incompetent to survive in a marriage. A victim, left on her own, feels helpless because she loses trust in the system as well as the society. With little or no support available from the natal family or friends or colleagues, in many cases, women often are compelled to 'adjust' to the violent situation and have ended up facing severe violence or are being seriously injured, killed or burned for dowry, or they end up committing suicide. Most of them remain entrapped in the vicious 'coil of violence'[4] or 'cycle of oppression' or '*daman-chakra*', moving back and forth from the natal family to the marital household multiple times and face abuse at both places, leading to unending multiple forms of victimization. In many cases, the natal family refuses to support women, because those separated are considered a burden, and they pressure them to 'go back' to their matrimonial home or to remarry and settle somewhere else. Men, as brothers, feel that she may demand her share in the natal property. Without any resources, aid or facilities, women are being oppressed because multiple patriarchies operate simultaneously all around.

The mechanism to make violent husbands accountable rarely works

Karat,[5] in a public hearing on domestic violence, explained, "The violation of the Line of Control and our territorial integrity brought forth national outrage, as it should have. But every day the LoC that preserves basic humanitarian concerns in interaction between human beings is violated, and we are silent". This work, in conformity with this idea, suggests that domestic violence has been treated as a less serious crime by the state. Violent husbands are not held accountable or even questioned for their brutal actions. The conviction rate is as low as 9.5 percent in cases pertaining to Section 498A and 39 percent in cases of dowry deaths.[6] Perhaps most of the women withdraw their cases when they are pressured by the police and judiciary to 'settle' the case. Therefore, fewer and fewer men are being convicted, even if they break the bones of women, brutally torture them, mentally or emotionally oppress them, deprive them of resources, throw them out of the house or even burn them alive. Instead of seeing wife beating as a crime against women's bodies, integrity or dignity, the law links legal actions to women's economic dependence on men and thus makes the execution of the law ambiguous.

Also, analysis of decisions pronounced by the courts in cases of domestic violence, dowry violence, dowry deaths or suicides by wives shows that men are barely penalized for their barbaric, violent criminal acts. Even in cases where men are punished, most are absolved from their illegal actions as the matter reaches the higher echelons of the judiciary through appeals. Those men who have resources in terms of money or muscle power can easily escape from the clutches of law because the legal system is not victim centric or justice centric. Rather, privileged men abuse the system to further intimidate, coerce and victimize women while also using tactics similar to 'strategic lawsuits against public participation'.[7] The law is implemented in a manner to cater to the demands of patriarchy rather than facilitating justice or supporting survivors in any manner. The rule of men dominates rather than the rule of law.[8]

The law hardly fixes the accountability of violent men when they indulge in committing unlawful acts of violence. The only accountability fixed by the court, if any, is that they are supposed to provide a meager amount of maintenance for their wives and children until the case is settled or alimony in decided in cases of divorce. And men cunningly find ways to escape such responsibility on one pretext or another. For men, life becomes easier, as they have the option to remarry and demand dowry from the new bride and her family.

Domestic violence laws specifically enacted to reshape and challenge the social and power relations in conjugality are twisted to reinforce power imbalances and inequities. A rise in the incidences of the crime of domestic violence could not be controlled because of the insensitivity, bias and negligence on the part of the state actors. The state, through its actions, omissions and commissions legitimizes domestic violence and reinforces prevalent biased social and economic relations. Neither deterrence or retribution could work, nor are arrangements being made to rehabilitate the victim or to provide for restorative justice. What is offered by the state in the name of justice to women is chaos, anarchy and totalitarianism. The state thus perpetuates a culture of violence with impunity.

Domestic violence in India: a case for epistemic injustice

Fricker,[9] in her groundbreaking work, has elaborately described the concept of epistemic injustice and categorized it broadly as testimonial and hermeneutical injustice. The present work suggests that Fricker's conceptualization of epistemic injustice or epistemic dysfunction holds true to the situation of domestic violence in India and adds another layer of victimization of women. Hermeneutical injustice operates because a deeply inherent patriarchy conditions women to accept violence to the point where they cannot see it as a wrong. Structural prejudices operate to prevent women from conceptualizing violence or to understand their own experiences, let alone describe them. There is a gap in the collective understanding of domestic violence that exists because of the relative powerlessness of women in a culturally historical context of a male-dominated society. It is damaging because it puts women at a systematically and structurally disadvantaged position. There are other harms too due to this form of injustice as women encountering violence, dispossessed of their shelter and deprived of their safety, face the risk of death, murder and sinking into poverty.

Testimonial justice operates within courtrooms and in society because women's concerns remain unheard and unaddressed. Neutrality is eroded while prejudices and stereotypes operate within courtrooms and within social setups that put women on a lower level and ignore their voices. Women's experiences of violence are not taken seriously, and low credibility is assigned to complainants. A woman is not treated as a knower, as an informant, as a human or as a citizen within the courtrooms. This harms women, because justice is not being done based on their experiences of violence. Rather, the elite top-down approach prevails. Truth is blocked, and multiple forms of victimization occur in situation when a woman is already facing violence. Deeply entrenched beliefs within the system hinder the process of change and fail to respond to women's concerns. The solution therefore lies in acknowledging the prejudicial approach and taking steps to rectify the situation while providing space to women to resist and to provide justice as per the rule of law.

The law is a site for resistance

Numerous scholars have captured different dimensions relating to law and women's rights in India. Some are of the view that the law has effectively helped citizens to claim their rights,[10] whereas others see it as a subversive site.[11] However, apart from these academic debates, this work shows that the law plays a complex and contradictory role in the life of women facing domestic abuse. The law reinforces subordination, yet at the same time it also provides a space for resistance and change. The law is a subversive site, yet it is a site for resistance against marginality and oppression. The law marginalizes women, yet marginality itself becomes a site of contestation.[12] The law is a site of repression where a regressive family ideology is being used to channel women's claims, yet it has facilitated many mutinies where women have rebelled against oppression, defied patriarchal norms and challenged male hegemony.

The law is a site where marginalization is challenged and resisted by those who are subjugated. On the one hand, the law reinforces the patriarchal discourse, yet on the other hand, it has the authority to set out the social order, and women have used the law to challenge the hierarchy and dominant notions. In domestic violence situations, the law legitimizes the fact that women are not supposed to be victimized within the homes and that women have rights against the perpetrators of violence, yet in contradiction, on the other hand it upholds a husband's right to chastise their wives. The law reproduces, reinforces and perpetuates patriarchal relations as well as gender divisions in the given hierarchical structure, yet women are using the law as a site to challenge hegemonic practices and to foster equality and justice. The law asserts the fact that domestic violence cannot be tolerated, yet it has not created an enabling environment to facilitate violence-free lives for wives as citizens; but women are reclaiming justice. The limiting approach of the law focuses on crime, punishment and fixed remedies, yet women are negotiating their claims and resisting violence. At a symbolic level, the law articulates a shift in social values and norms that could bring a significant transformation in the lives of women, yet, at pragmatic level, it trivializes and normalizes violence within the domestic realm. Because of gaps in the law, the hard-won battles cannot alter the biased social structure, yet women are shaking up the patriarchal system. The law creates public–private dichotomy, yet at the same time, women are using the law to assert their claims and negotiate their entitlements.[13] Foucault, while analyzing socio-political systems, has also focused on the margins, and he saw the margins as "a source of disruption of [the] status quo".[14] Therefore, solutions are required using the domain of law while also paving the way into the realm of the social, economic and political.

This work suggests that women have been fighting tough battles not only against the perpetrators of violence but also against the patriarchy within homes, in society and in the courts. Those who have dared to resist violence and challenged the patriarchy are not feminists, activists or experts. It is the common woman, with her own sense of justice, her grit and with few resources and little support, who is seeking a violence-free life for herself and her children. In order to do so, these women seek support of the natal family, friends or the state. However, the natal family or friends, with their limited capacity or resources or possibly a narrow approach, may not sustain women for long. The legal system in the free market economy, motivated by a family ideology, has not invested resources, and neither it is keen to facilitate survivors who refused to obey the regressive norms. Women, with their persistence and grit, have been negotiating for their rights and contesting their claims and are making a dent in the patriarchy, as well as defining and shaping the legal culture. Therefore, in order to enable women to help them assert their autonomy, it is essential that the state facilitate solutions by providing alternatives.

The stories of women emancipation are not written in abusive homes or violent communities, but these are written in the courage, grit and resilience these women demonstrate while altering the inegalitarian structure within families, in creating democratic spaces with the society and in fighting to seek freedom, or *aazadi*, from patriarchy and violence. It is essential to focus on women's autonomy, as well as on liberation that entails socio-economic self-sufficiency. If it is true that not all women want to walk out of the violent relationship immediately; it is also true that many want to live a violence-free life, and because they lack any other options, they are compelled to stay and bear violence. With the rising aspiration, there is a need to create a support mechanism which could offer women different possibilities in case they wish to lead a violence-free life. Change in the material and social conditions that foster battering should be made.

Legal remedies do not commensurate with the violence women face

Section 498A of the IPC criminalizes domestic violence, where the perpetrator may be imprisoned for a maximum of three years and/or he could be fined. To obtain other remedies under Section 125 of the CrPC for maintenance, or under personal or civil laws, a woman needs to fight a long tedious legal battle. The PWDVA provides for relief which are short term or temporary and superficial in nature. For instance, the protection orders, the custody orders, the monetary relief and the residence orders all provide temporary or short-term solutions until the matter is finally resolved. In case a woman decides to go back to the situation and stay 'amicably' with the violent husband, these orders may become non-operative. In case of separation or divorce, or to arrive at 'settlement', a woman may have to bargain for the terms and conditions, again depending on the facts of the case. Hence, a woman has to negotiate and re-negotiate multiple times, depending on the manner in which the case may be finally disposed of. Thus, both theoretically and pragmatically, the law provides only symptomatic relief but not long-term remedies, rehabilitation or restoration, nor can it address the root cause of violence by addressing the institutionalized patriarchy. Also, there is a disconnect between the manner in which the law is defined and shaped and the way in which it is implemented.

Moreover, on one hand, the domestic violence law targets the institution of marriage as the primary site of violence; yet on the other hand, it prioritizes family integrity over the safety and welfare of women while focusing on coercive counselling. The language of violence is central to the law, yet it fails to grapple with a wider systemic violence, thereby proving an inadequate mechanism to capture the complexity of or the claims for gender justice. The legal lexicon depoliticizes violence while overlooking the larger structure of oppression and inequality. Women's rights require expansive citizenship guarantees and restructuring existing inequalities. The law, whether criminal or civil, is inadequate for this purpose. The law not only fails to challenge the normative gender relations, but it neutralizes the structural oppression that sustains violence by explicitly keeping the state outside the structures of accountability and welfare provisioning. The legal system in fact has become an extension as well as a mirror of the patriarchal family and acts as a moral protector, custodian and guardian rather than a neutral arbiter. The law legitimizes conditions that create an unequal gendered and power relationship, while empowering men over women within families.[15] It accrues privileges to men while reinforcing women's economic dependency and subjugation. Also, the state, being male, opines that empowering women through the law may create havoc and may destroy the traditional family structure.[16] The state thus overlooks the rights of women to lead a violence-free life within homes. The number of cases of violence keeps on increasing, while justice is made less and less available to women.

Need to focus on a survivor-centric or women-centric approach

Currently, the laws and policies, driven by the traditional family ideology, prioritize the 'family-centric' approach where the emphasis is laid on saving the family rather than focusing on the rights-based approach to protect or promote the rights of a woman in a situation of violence. It is the victim who approaches with her complaint before the legal system and rolls the wheels of justice, yet the uncaring, biased, regressive state apparatus cannot resolve her issue or cannot provide her proper remedies. The irony lies in the fact that when women approach the court or other formal or informal setup to seek relief from household violence, these institutions compulsorily counsel them to go back to the very same violent situation without any guarantee of security or safety. The law reinforces conventional stereotypes.[17]

A woman who knocks on the door of the courts to negotiate and bargain for her legal claims and challenge the lopsided social and economic relations thus end up getting re-victimized because the law offers no remedies or support and does not penalize the perpetrator of the crime. Through its language, structure, formalities, technicalities, operations and processes, the law trivializes and normalizes this serious crime while simultaneously suppressing the voices of the complainants and putting their lives in jeopardy. Women's voices remain (un)heard in lawmaking.[18] The law sanctions and legitimizes the social patriarchal norms while favoring the interests of the oppressors. Courts shield violent men in the garb of maintaining 'domestic harmony'. No follow-up mechanism is built into this system to ensure the rights or safety of the victim. The state thus becomes complicit in the crime because it neither punishes the perpetrators, nor does it imagine any other option for women outside a violent marriage. It is because of these gaps on the part of the state that the perpetrator further indulges in more violence with impunity because he knows that he will not be penalized for his wrong-doing.

The state utilizes the domestic violence law to coercively push for 'reconciliation', 'compromise', 'adjustment' and 'settlement' in the garb of '*samjhauta*' while mixing up women's rights to bargain for material and economic support, rather than actually delivering rights-based justice to the complaining citizens. What is prioritized by the state is the goal to 'preserve the family' even if this is done at the cost of the health of women and children. Pushing women back into a violent situation is considered an 'optimal' solution for redressing their woes, without realizing that women cross the boundaries of the homes only in extreme situations and that the purpose of the law is not to 'break' or to 'save' the family but to deter violence and to provide remedies to citizens. An emphasis is laid on the principle of 'forgive and forget' and a 'move-on' approach while overlooking the fact that there is a need to examine the asymmetrical power operation within marriage and its impact on the lives of women. Dubbing domestic brutality cases as a 'domestic dispute or squabble' ignores the hierarchical relationship within families. Thus, the state, while ignoring the fine nuances of domestic violence, dilutes the effect of the law, reduces the gravity of the situation and treats the crime as less serious. It fails to see that violence has its own dynamics and repercussions completely different from the normal dispute.

What is ignored while enforcing the family ideology is that domestic violence is '*daman*' in *dampatya*', or 'oppression in conjugality,' which could be erased by propagating congruency in the conjugal relationship and by dismantling the patriarchy while demolishing the domination of men within families. The formal and informal forums established to deal with domestic violence need to admonish and penalize men for their violent actions rather than compelling women to 'adjust' to an abusive situation created by men. The '*Grihastha*', or the family life, can no longer be based on an uneven relationship where a woman is subjugated. The glorified Indian family can no longer accept the violence under the guise of love and discipline. There is a to recognize the concept of companionship in marriage and democratization of the family.

It may also be interesting to determine the efficiency or effectiveness of the mediation strategies and the manner in which these strategies deter the violent behavior or compel the violent men to mend their behavior. It is recommended that further research be taken up to find out in cases where mediation is compelled and women are forced to accept violent relationships, are they leading a violence-free life or do they 'adjust to' or 'accept' violence silently while losing trust in the legal system? An analogy could also be drawn between 'mediation' and cases where women end up in committing suicide or being murdered. Further, the impact of such situations on children in these relationships also needs to be analyzed. In countries such as India, there is a dearth of research on the issue of the impact of violence on women and children. Much work is required to look into the efficiency or the effectiveness of the counselling or the mediation on the behavior of men and women.

In fact, the biased, lopsided, 'elite urban middle-class' approach of those who implement the law and policy framers fails to see the realities of survivors and therefore does not address the dire instant needs and demands relating to providing socio-economic security that would enable women victims or survivors and their children to sustain in a capitalist patriarchal society. The state does not evoke a law or justice-centric framework to resolve the complex legal and emotive marital issues, so in cases pertaining to adjudication of divorce, the state has not figured out how to protect the interests of women and children who are at the receiving end. While granting divorce decrees, no emphasis is laid on the welfare of children, so it is not that the state promotes a 'family-centric' approach or prioritizes the concern to save the family; rather, the state just tries to escape its responsibilities towards women or children. This approach of the state needs to be re-examined, and specifically in the situation of domestic violence, priority should be given to the women victims and survivors of violence.

Technical shortfalls and operational difficulties

The law bars entry to women in the courts at the admission stage itself. For those who manage to enter the legal system, the process of seeking justice is not free from hurdles. The beginning of a trial is no guarantee that the complainant will receive justice. The law is restrictive, and while dealing with domestic violence, the state upholds the rule of men and not the rule of law. The law has provided a platform to vent grievances but has failed to support battered women to lead a violence-free life. Earlier, many women had to silently bear the misery and suffocate within the four walls of a household because they found it difficult to file a criminal case against their violent family members. Frequently, putting a family member behind bars is considered as a stigma. However, with the advent of civil law, it is expected that slowly an awareness may rise of the fact that wife beating is not tolerable and that criminal as well as civil remedies are available. Yet enactment of a civil law does not address the situation. Problems exist at various levels, ranging from implementation of the law, to the perceptions of those who enforce it, to judicial bias and the backlash that has emerged lately. Contradictions in the civil and criminal laws, together with inconsistencies in the social and legal norms in the given patriarchal structure, have created chaos. These have roots in a capitalist patriarchal society where regressive forces continue to dominate in the face of growing social aspirations for equality, justice and liberty.

As a survivor of violence, women need immediate support. However, this work shows that women are not getting quick relief under the PWDVA, and therefore the purpose of making the law is defeated. The promise of disposing of a case within 60 days from the first date of hearing is not fulfilled. The process of handling the case is also not bereft of trouble. There is a disconnect between the manner in which the women's movement defines and shapes the law and the way in which it is implemented by the those who enforce the law. Often, judges and lawyers are not aware of the fine nuances of the law. Also, the law has failed to clearly distinguish between dowry and domestic violence as two separate issues. Those who enforce the law mistakenly assumed that domestic violence in itself is not a crime unless it is linked with dowry and that violence is a private affair; therefore, they have hesitated to intervene in such cases.

The law does not consider the emotions and sensitivities of a woman who has suffered violence. It codifies violence into set of objective incidents from where it draws its interpretation. Translating women's pain into legal language is not an easy task. The law insists on certainty of violence and proof that damage has been done. It expects the victim to transform her experiences of violence, her pain and sufferings, into legal language, overlooking the fact that there is a strong disconnect between the subjectivities of sufferings and the rigid vocabulary of the law. The range of abuses, severity and multiplicity of violence, when compounded together, bring out narratives that are too unfathomable to be translated into stiff legal rhetoric. DIRs or FIRs therefor need to be interpreted accordingly, but this is not happening. Legal actors translate the provisions on the basis of their own understanding while overlooking the concerns with which the legal reform has been sought. There is a difference in the interpretation of law by those who enforce it and the manner in which it was written. The subjectivity, attitude and personal biases of those who enforce the law hamper the process of justice. Many litigants often give up, as the system does not recognize their sufferings.

The PWDVA is a sharp departure from any other law, yet no provisions have been made to continuously monitor the system for its effectiveness or efficiency. The domestic violence law, which was designed to empower women who sought criminal or civil remedies in a less adversarial environment, has ended up creating new vulnerabilities and paradoxically is reinforcing the oppressive patriarchal culture. More specifically, for women, the challenges increased, as did the complexities.

The majority of women have no control over what is written in their application under the PWDVA or what is written in the DIR or FIR. However, in the courtrooms, decisions are being made on the basis of pleadings and the content of these legal documents. Discrepancies arise in DIRs, FIRs and complaints because of the differences in perceptions of police, lawyers and POs and their sensitivities to women's concerns. This is not considered in the courtroom while deciding on the applications. Also, under Rule 8(1)(iv) of the PWDVA, the PO is duty bound to prepare a safety plan that include measures to prevent further violence to the aggrieved person after assessing the dangers involved in the situation. However, it has been observed that in none of the cases in the present work have safety plans been prepared.

One of the objects of the PWDVA is to avoid multiplicity of proceedings to prevent cumbersome procedures and to make the litigation process women friendly. However, analysis shows that the issue relating to multiple litigation has not been resolved. Many complainants are found to be running around in several courts for different applications filed under various laws, such as those under personal law for divorce, custody or related issues. The contingent of police, CAW cells, POs, SPs and other paraphernalia has not helped much. Often, complainants are made to run from pillar to post to seek small gains. The system is tardy and being worn out by repeated adjournments.

Even when a woman gets an order in her favor, execution is not an easy task. Technicalities within the system often work against women, and frequently, the verdicts in favor of women are not implemented because of the weakness and bias inherent within the system. For instance, the maintenance orders are not complied with. Women have to run around to seek alimony for themselves and their children, or the opposite party files a claim before the other civil courts under the laws such as the Hindu Marriage Act or the Hindu Adoption and Maintenance Act to delay the proceedings.

Also, the quantum of maintenance, or the right to reside in the shared household and interpretations of law, are a matter of serious concern. Moreover, a victim is supposed to hire a 'good' lawyer to defend her case well. As domestic battles are dragged to higher courts and appeals are filed in many cases against the initial orders passed by the lower courts, the picture does not look as rosy as was once expected.

The law has failed to keep pace with changing socio-economic realities. For instance, the dowry could not be curbed despite of the existence of law to prohibit it. And currently dowry has grown to the extent that besides the concept of giving and taking dowry or making coercive dowry demands, a new form of violence has emerged that includes coercive demands for lavish wedding ceremonies. The state has not bothered to address the emerging situations in the market economy where the assets which could help women are no longer available and women are denied any form of economic security in case she stays away from a violent relationship.

The PWDVA made demands on the state to provide for medical facilities and shelter homes, but it could not create any accountability nor fix the responsibility of the state in situations where the state fails to provide for such mechanisms. Nothing is being done to monitor or regulate the provisions relating to medical facilities, shelter homes or other services. The state is not challenged in situations where no POs have been appointed or where the number of officers is inadequate or are not working for whatever reason. Also, shelter homes are far and few between and their services are questionable. The state easily escapes its liability even if it does not allocate an adequate budget for proper implementation of the law. The law has created abstract rights which are not being implemented in practice.

This work indicates that the services within the framework of the act are provided in a fragmented manner. Partly, the onus is placed on the PO, partly the police, and courts are responsible for providing relief to the complainant. This has led to confusion and chaos, where complainants are made to suffer. Lack of clarity about the roles and coordination between these different providers is problematic. The training of POs, generating awareness about the law and sensitizing officials, all require budgetary provisions for which no accountability is fixed. Effective operation of the law requires coordination of several ministries and departments, such as Women and Child Development; Health, Law and Justice; and Social Justice and Empowerment, among others. However, no data are available that could indicate such synchronization is effectively being made.

Domestic violence leads to alienation and dispossession: no provisions for right to shelter or housing

The enactment and the operation of law indicate that the state has failed to imagine alternatives beyond the *sasural* and *maika* network for complainants. Those who enforce the law expect that a woman who is facing violence either stay in the *sasural* where she is facing violence or go back to her natal home. No alternative solutions are offered, such as facilitation in terms of jobs, employment or entrepreneurship to render economic support, or to provide housing or shelter beyond the familial network. A patriarchal society cannot imagine that a woman could survive on her own and can take care of children with little support or social protection measures. In fact, the state has made no alternative arrangements beyond the family for women who are abandoned, divorced, widowed, or stay single for various reasons. The state assumes that women are dependent on their natal or marital families and should remain at the mercy of those social ties until their death. A single woman is considered an aberration, and no long-term solutions have been provided for the survivors of violence.

The PWDVA provides for the right to a residence, yet it does not question the structural arrangements that operate to oppress women within the household. On the contrary, the act upholds the existing power relations and normalizes the patriarchal domestic arrangements. The law in fact is being used against women in many cases while pitting one woman against another; for instance, in many cases the mother-in-law has filed a case against a daughter-in-law to evict her from the matrimonial household once a daughter-in-law raises her voice against the patriarchal authority.

The rule of men dominates: the law has failed to provide justice to battered wives

The androcentric law made several false assumptions while ignoring the on-the-ground realities. It is erroneously assumed that persons within the realm of an inequitable 'private' family are similarly positioned individuals. Further, it is inaccurately presumed that it is easier for a woman to approach the court and to summon the violator of her rights. It is falsely believed that it is easier for the survivors to resist the obstinate patriarchy to seek a remedy. What is overlooked while making these assumptions is that it is difficult for a victim to come out in public and challenge her abusive husband or in-laws. It is also wrongly assumed that courts are fair, quick and neutral in providing justice, whereas in reality, the overburdened patriarchal courts can hardly provide effective rights-based remedies or fair justice. The presumption is mistakenly made that it is easier for a woman who has been victimized for years to continue to share the space within the same household with the perpetrator of the violence. This conjecture overlooks the fact that a woman who is facing continuous abuse needs emotional and material support to mentally recover from trauma in order to fight back against the perpetrator. What a woman facing violence requires instantly is medical services and emotional, social or economic support, which is hardly provided in a patriarchal setup.

Moreover, by making no provisions for the survivors and victims of violence, the neoliberal state is assuming that these women will be able to participate and compete in the market economy and are self-sufficient to take care of themselves and their children. The state assumes that the survivors are self-reliant, entrepreneurial 'private' subjects who suffer harm in 'private spaces' but are capable of asserting their rights within the domain of the law as well as in the realm of market, while ignoring the fact that gender justice is not a private but a public concern. The state atomizes the struggle of survivors while construing them as self-reliant agents who have to institute the proceedings against the perpetrator on their own and, if they choose to walk out of the matrimonial relationship, are able to find for themselves and their children. The law overlooks the difficulties women face in accessing these meager gains while attempting to escape victimization. The state ignores the socio-legal complexities and the reality of women's lives in a situation of violence. The misplaced priorities focus on protecting cows but not women. For instance, the UP government earmarked 816 million rupees for setting up *gaushalas* (cow shelters) in 68 out of 75 districts,[19] while the Himachal Pradesh government proposed to levy Rs 1 cess (to be called *Gau Vansh Vikas* Cess) on the sale of every bottle of liquor to generate revenue for the maintenance of *gaushalas* in the state.[20] The Madhya Pradesh government announced the setting up of a cow welfare ministry,[21] and Rajasthan appointed a cow minister.[22] No such innovative steps have been taken to aid women from the recovery of violence or to build shelters for women in need. This is not to deny the significance of animal rights, but the fact is that women do not have less worth than cows. The state could not hear the screams of women who are being tortured brutally and inhumanely violated day in and day out or are burned alive.

No provisions have been made to provide any support services to women and children in distress or in emergency situations. In situations where a battered woman is raising her children alone, no support is provided by the state to ensure that children should not be made to suffer. In emergency circumstances, if the mother dies because of extreme violence or the father is jailed for brutally murdering the mother, it is assumed that other family members (grandparents or aunts or uncles) will take care of these children. In cases where a family network is not available, it is presumed that these children will grow up on their own somehow and become responsible future citizens. Orphanages are far and few between, and the quality of services provided there again need to be examined. Similarly, the practice of adoption is questionable in such cases. The state accepts no responsibility for children in domestic violence situations. Society has created different labels for such children and takes satisfaction in using terms such as illegitimate or legitimate child; however, no steps are being taken to physically, emotionally or materially support children. In fact, no research has been taken up and no data are available as to how children in violence situations are coping. The elite state cannot imagine alternative solutions for women and children in such circumstances.

Patriarchy rules: the regressive approach of the law

The law recognizes the household as the site of violence, yet it reproduces the normative understanding and fixes only certain categories of gender injustice without treating it as a part of a systemic structure of oppressive gender relations. The PWDVA calls for the 'protection of women' and thus reinforces the 'protectionist approach' rather becomes an empowering tool for women in situations of violence. This protectionist approach in itself is problematic, as it does not address the oppression in marriage or structural inequalities within the patriarchal society. The law has not visualized women as an active agent of change or citizens who contribute equally within society; rather, it sees the women trapped in marriage as victims who are required to be shielded and protected. Theoretically, the law denies agency to women and assumes they are firmly located in the lower level within the relationship. Women are not treated as citizens demanding their rights. Rather, this approach sees women as subjects who need protection and locate them deeper in the web of patriarchy.

DeCrow[23] maintained that

> Women have fared miserably under the law, not only in decisions that went against us, but even in cases that went for us; and we are deluding

> ourselves if we think that women can get justice in the courts. The record of court decisions, statutes, state constitutions and legislative interpretations – all of these are written by men. And until they begin to be written by feminist women and feminist men, women will never achieve equity in our legal system.

The state in India also is male dominated and requires a women friendly approach to achieve the goal of equity, equality and social justice as guaranteed in the constitution. The androcentric state has neither been able to check the growing incidents of violence against women despite enacting numerous laws, nor can it provide protection to women who knock on the doors of the court with the hope of seeking justice. The state as a custodian and preserver of the 'law and order' has failed to fulfill its protective role despite extending its paternalist approach towards women. Women as citizens are denied their equal rights because the state has pursued social discrimination while governing and used a gendered lens to address the 'women's problem'.

The Justice Verma Committee also has observed that the state has failed to implement the provision of a domestic violence law. It states,

> While the enactment of this statute was a welcome measure, it has not led to a reduction in instances of domestic violence. This is primarily because there has been no change of fundamental attitudes towards women. Passing of legislation without adequate dissemination of implementing the spirit of the legislation as a part of normative human conduct is missing in Indian executive governance. The translation of legislation into behavioural attitudes is not simply a matter of psychological skill or acquisition but is indeed a charter of obligations enjoined upon the State. The State, which has the resources of the media, educational institutions, and executive governance, must have full-time long-term advisors who would be able to constantly monitor the condition of women from different standpoints and characteristics. We are unable to see in the Government of India any specialists in the Ministry of Health who are under a full-time employment to be able to ascertain sociologically the condition of women much less their psychological well-being.[24]

Failed laws: blind justice

The legal system, both civil and criminal, failed to provide justice to women because the basic premises behind domestic violence remain unchallenged. Domestic violence continues because it is premised on several notions, such as:

1 The marital relationship is hierarchical and inegalitarian. Women are accorded low status within a family, where a man is considered the

master of the household. Family ideology, and not constitutional values relating to equality or justice, operates to undermine the position of women within marriage.

2 Marriage is construed by the law as a sacrament, and much emphasis is laid on practices that objectify women, such as *kanyadaan* or *karvachauth*. Such derogatory practices have not been questioned.

3 The husband and his family has been granted an authority to beat the wife in addition to demanding dowry. Dowry as an institution that propagates violence and accords a low status to women has not been challenged or eradicated despite the existence of a law. Rather, it has evolved over the years in such a way that in its current form it denies women their right to *streedhan* because much of the part allocated for marriage is consumed in wedding celebrations.

4 Chastisement is a prerogative granted to a husband, who can commit violence against a wife in the guise of love and discipline. Rather than questioning the privileges accorded to men, the law sanctions and legitimizes the act of granting such arbitrary authority. The law grants immunity to the violent husbands even if the husband is a drunkard, vile or a criminal.

5 The family is considered a private realm, and the state is reluctant to interfere when a battered wife complains against a violent husband. However, the same state actors do not hesitate to adjudicate matters such as restitution of conjugal rights where women are forced to join the company of their husband against their wishes, or even in the matter of *love jihad* where the entire state apparatus is utilized to conduct an inquest into a private relationship between two consenting adults.

6 Domestic harmony is prioritized over women's right to bodily integrity or dignity. The state has not created any support mechanisms for battered wives, abandoned or divorced women, widows or destitute women. For women, economic, material and emotional dependence on men is the only option that is being imagined – any deviation from this norm is not tolerated.

7 Victorian notions are perpetuated and the doctrine of marital unity as propounded by Blackstone persists, which prevents those who frame and implement the law from seeing complainant wives as citizens demanding protection under law.

8 The nature of marriage is changing in the neoliberal economy, where violence has taken on a new shape and form, and yet the law has not changed its perception or its response, and this is creating huge gap. Most of these premises remained unchallenged. The law ignores the principles of rationality while adjudicating the claims of battered wives and thus legitimizes and reinforces social inequalities within the institution of marriage, and in the process has created a culture of violence and impunity.

No steps have been taken to counter the backlash

Apathy on the part of policymakers and those who implement the law create further problems. Domestic violence laws[25] have been viewed in a negative light recently by both the boisterous male groups and those who enforce the law – the police, judiciary and lawyers began to state that the domestic violence law has been misused and abused by women.[26] This was not imagined by those who demanded legal reforms. A backlash emerged against gender-sensitive laws to the extent that it began to redefine and reshape the attitude and approach of those who enforce the law. The vocal men's lobby, which has a hold on those who occupy the positions of power within the political and legal domain, began wrongly criticizing and alleging that the women-friendly laws are being misused by women. A group of men under an umbrella network which is cleverly titled Save the Indian Family has protested vociferously against law and are falsely claiming that women are extracting money from husbands and their families, or that the violence has been so broadly construed under the law that women are rushing to report daily domestic squabbles as violence,[27] or that family members of the husband have been falsely implicated, among others. The law against domestic violence is looked at as a weapon misused by educated and elite women to harass husbands and their families to extract money. The law was created to stop violence against women; however, it is erroneously viewed as an instrument to break marriages and destroy the institution of the family.

These lines of thoughts are propagated without looking at the details in terms of evidence or data to substantiate such claims.[28] In fact, the state machinery, comprising men, believing this opinion and exaggerated rumors, took several steps to dilute the legal provisions. Many among the women's movement too have begun to criticize the law for its co-option. Currently, the situation is that neither the civil nor the criminal law can reduce the incidence of domestic violence, and yet, the state actors, based on mythical beliefs and untested opinions, are pushing the idea of the domestic violence law being misused. Jaising countered that

> The truth is that law is empowering and the very use of the law is seen as an act of subversion of the existing social order; hence, "use" of the law becomes an act of "misuse". In short, women are being told: don't use the law or use it on pain of being thrown out of the shared household and being called a "gold digger". It is this that the judges need to see and change in the next decade of the existence of the law and put their own house in order before moralizing about "misuse".[29]

Also, hardly any steps have been taken by the state or the women's movement to actively counter the regressive family ideology propagated by the state. Ideally, the those who enforce the law are bound by the constitution and the law, yet instead of propagating constitutional values or the rule of law, what is enforced is orthodox views regarding the family setup. Despite the existence of a dowry law, dowry demands and dowry violence continue to grow, and no action has been taken against such regressive practices, which demean women. Rather, through market mechanisms, rituals, schemes and practices, the state perpetuates dowry in one form or another.

Contradictions between the patriarchal state and women's rights as citizens

The relationship between women and the state is paradoxical. Over the decades since independence, the state has occupied a central role in mobilizing around the issue of violence and is subsequently held accountable to make interventions through not only laws but also by making policies, development initiatives and programs to facilitate its citizens to lead a violence-free life. Agnihotri and Parliwala[30] have noted that "it was in focusing on the state in terms of law, administration and government responsibility that women's groups came together in a collective effort time and again". However, there are no symmetrical reciprocal interventions made by the state. Whenever the women's movement engage with it, often, the masculine androcentric state recognizes 'women' as the 'problem', and this view is instrumental in shaping the way the state functions or address issues relating to women. In the interest of capital, the state sustains the gendered patriarchal family and its arrangements, including the sexual division of labor.[31]

The General Recommendation on Article 16 of the Convention on Elimination of Discrimination Against Women[32] elaborates on equal rights with marriage and equal formal and de facto legal capacity to own and manage property. It reiterates that the state parties shall take appropriate measures to eliminate discrimination against women in all matters relating to marriage and family. It binds the state parties to create conditions where parties to a marriage enjoy equal rights. India has ratified this convention. However, no steps have been taken by the Indian state to implement these provisions. Inequality within marriage is persistent, despite the constitutional provisions guaranteed under Articles 14, 15 and 21. A woman in a patriarchal family has no right to equal division of matrimonial property at the time of the dissolution of the marriage.

Though the liberal, democratic state has acknowledged the ideal of 'women's equality' and is accountable to create space for 'women's citizens', it has not taken the initiative to overcome religious, capitalist or other forces which pull women 'backward', nor can it resist the feudal or orthodox imperatives that target women as victims.[33] The provision of equality and affirmative steps enshrined in the constitution or under international obligations cannot be achieved because the state has failed to regulate the discrimination and the regressive culture propagated by the misogynist personal laws and the market norms. The laws have failed to create an enabling environment where justice can be assured. Probably the economic, social or political equality of women is perceived as a threat to the patriarchal mind-set of the privileged elite men who occupy powerful positions and dominate in social, legal and political spaces.[34]

The state, by firmly implementing the international provisions and national laws and by formulating progressive policies as per rights-based norms and values could have ascertained the fact that women's safety and bodily integrity are essential and that there should be zero tolerance for domestic violence. Such steps are essential, and it is necessary that the state symbolically as well as actually take the appropriate steps. Yet, today, the interventions made by the state in situations of domestic violence do not reflect such intentions. Patriarchy is pervasive and is an essential part of everyday living. It is ubiquitous and exists everywhere, in homes, in workspaces and in public places. The state and society alike encourage male domination in visible and invisible ways. The trilogy of family, law and society, all interlinked and interconnected, promotes the inegalitarian relationship between men and women and operates to suppress women in both public and private spheres. In fact, the family is construed as a small microcosm of a patriarchal social order that exists in society, while the law mirrors what society portrays. Society epitomizes values similar to an extended family, where hierarchy, violence and subjugation of women become the norm. The patriarchal attitude and conservative mind-set operate at all levels and subjugate women within the homes and in the public sphere. Continuous incidents of violence and discrimination against women within private and public spaces reflect the manner in which the patriarchy operates.

Inconsistencies arise when married women approach a court of law and demand rights as a neutral citizen. Therefore, women knock on the doors of the state with the belief that it may redress their grievance using the citizenship, constitutional and legal matrix, but the state uses the framework of the patriarchal lens and filters their complaints of domestic violence through the web of family ideology. The state does not construe women as independent political citizens vested with rights. Rather, it treats women as secondary beings embedded in their social and cultural framework as wives, mothers and daughters. The state, therefore, in a visible and invisible manner, has propagated the climate of oppression and subjugation of women through laws, policies and bureaucratic interventions. The courts are often reluctant to intervene within the sacred private families, whereas these women assert that the personal is political and the state should protect their rights.

In order to eliminate gender-based violence, what is required is visible and positive changes in gender relations, in general, and specifically, the reduction of violence. The success of gender redistributive policies depends on the perception of those who implement them.[35] This implies that there is a need to transform the way the domestic violence issue is understood and to raise consciousness about the complexity and sensitive nature of it. Domestic violence must be seen as a human rights violation issue rather than as a dispute. A progressive, sensitive approach by those who enforce the law may go a long way to instilling a sense of justice. This work reveals that the state has failed to capture the complexity and multi-dimensionality of the issue of violence within the larger structural power inequalities and injustices and also underplays the struggles around women's rights.

Critically examining the institution of marriage per se

> "It is easy to see the concrete details that trap the suburban housewife, the continual demands on her time. But the chains that bind her in her trap are chains in her own mind and spirit. They are the chains made up of mistaken ideas and misinterpreted facts of incomplete truth and unreal choices. They are not easily seen and not easily shaken off."[36]

The institution of marriage or the family as a picture-perfect institution, without any dignity or respect for women, is simply an abomination. No society can call itself democratic or just when the so-called basic units of society – 'the family' – continues to be undemocratic and perpetuates violence to become a place of misery and anguish for women. The veils of family privacy have shielded it from scrutiny into its intimate and sacrosanct space; however, the judicial arena is a site where it has been exposed and rendered permeable.

Moreover, in the Indian context, contradictions lie in the fact that, on one hand, the concept of marriage and family is glorified, while, on the other, the rights of women within the domain of conjugality are not being appreciated. A married woman is still not seen as an independent entity apart from her existence as a wife, a daughter-in-law or a mother. Also, what is overlooked by the state while implementing the law is the fact that women's vulnerable situation in a marriage and family cannot be transformed without questioning and critiquing the institution of marriage and family per se. The sheer failure to alter the hierarchical power imbalance that exists in the family is one of the reasons that violence against women as a phenomenon is growing and escalating. Safety begins with safe homes. The discourse on safety in public space is hollow without ensuring violence-free homes.

Challenging the notions of masculinity and femininity is crucial. Toxic masculinity needs to be curbed, along with transforming the notion that women are the passive, adaptable, compromising peacemakers with their role restricted to keeping the family together. At a larger level, the solution may lie in rethinking the situation of women's dependency on marriage, women's value in the labor market and norms for the transmission of property and other resources to women. Enhancing women's autonomy through education and employment may help, in addition to ensuring women's control over resources. The idea of marriage as an inegalitarian institution needs to be questioned.

Making the case for the right to matrimonial property

The present work indicates that when a marriage breaks down, a woman is left with no choice because no support systems or alternatives are made available beyond the institution of the family. The legal provisions on divorce allow the wife to escape an unhappy abusive relationship, but she is deprived of the economic security which she enjoys within the institution of marriage. A Hindu wife became a part of her husband's joint family upon marriage, and he is duty bound to maintain her. Upon his death, the joint family is held responsible only to the extent of preventing her from becoming destitute. She cannot become a coparcener but is provided only a minimum amount of economic security and shelter. If she applies for divorce, the only right she can claim is for her *streedhan* or maintenance or alimony, which is conditional, and is provided to prevent her falling into 'destitution or vagrancy'. She could be forced out of the matrimonial home, be deprived of material assets and be alienated from the joint family.

The concept of joint matrimonial property is not recognized under the personal laws. Section 27 of the Hindu Marriage Act provides that the courts make provisions about the property "which may belong jointly to both the husband and the wife". The expression 'jointly' is not interpreted broadly to include contributions made by both the parties before, during and after the marriage or to include visible and invisible contributions made by wives. The Special Marriage Act of 1954 includes no provisions to address the settlement of property upon divorce. The Muslim law made a provision that upon divorcing, the wife shall receive the property given to her and an amount equal to the sum of *meher* as previously agreed. Thus, the law relating to the post-divorce property division is totally inadequate to address the concept of the joint matrimonial property. Equality, or the concept of partnership in marriage, is not recognized by the law when it comes to the division of property or assets. Courts do not consider the invisible contribution of women, which results in an accumulation of wealth jointly to benefit the family as a unit. The courts in several cases have taken initiatives such as pushing the concept of the registration of marriage;[37] however, in the case of matrimonial property division, much more needs to be done.

Several countries have recognized this issue and formulated laws to address the economic violence and financial rights of women in marriage. These laws provide for equal division of matrimonial property, where the courts can order a party to make financial provisions or can transfer the property or issue an order regarding a settlement to ensure that married women's rights to property are protected. However, in India, few efforts have been made in this regard. Amendments to the Hindu Succession Act in 2005 providing relief to women as daughters is a laudable provision; however, women as wives still have no right to the matrimonial property if they separate from their husbands or dared to approach the court to obtain a divorce against their cruel husbands. No other personal law has focused on protecting the rights of property for married women. The concept of matrimonial property needs to be clearly defined, and the rights of each spouse need to be specifically elaborated to protect women from victimization while recognizing their contribution in terms of the unpaid contribution women make in their matrimonial home. This may also assist women in providing material and financial security. The Maharashtra government has introduced a bill[38] titled Matrimonial Property (Rights of Women upon Marriage) Bill-2012, which attempted to formulate rights of women in marriage. However, this bill was allowed to lapse by the proponents of patriarchy. At a broader level, steps need to be taken to recognize women's contributions in their matrimonial relationships and to protect women's rights at the time of separation and divorce.

The Law Commission, in its Consultation Paper on Reform of Family Law,[39] noted that the legislature should consider guaranteeing equality within communities between men and women and recommended recognizing the community of all self-acquired property of either spouse after the marriage to be treated as a unit between the couple. The fact is that it is often the woman who compromise her career in order to support the families and she contributes to a major share of housework in a household. Her work is never calculated in monetary terms. The paper notes that

> The society inadequately values the housework and further for working women, childbearing results in career break which affect their employment in a way that it does not affect their husband's career. Therefore, it is important that regardless of whether the wife financially or monetarily contributes to the family income, her contribution to a household in terms of household labour, home management, and child bearing and care should entitle her to an equal share in a marriage and thus all property for income gained after marriage should be divided equally upon divorce.[40]

Often, arguments are raised that the joint family property may create a hurdle, yet what is overlooked in such arguments is the fact that a man's portion in his joint family could be used to determine the entitlement of his wife. However, this requires an amendment to the laws relating to marriage and divorce and, more importantly, the will on the part of law makers and implementers to recognize the concept of equality and democracy within the family as a basic unit of society. Incongruity in social and legal terms needs to be addressed by introducing the concept of matrimonial property where assets could be equitably distributed between the spouses.

Domestic violence and shelter homes for women survivors in India

Regrettably, the state has not placed much emphasis on the idea of opening shelter homes or other sources of refuge, as the Indian culture of extended families and kinship is glorified here. Also, unlike the West, which comprises mostly resource-rich, advanced capitalist states which have put a strong social security system for their citizens in place, the Indian system, being resource crunched, has relied on the family as the basic support system for its citizens. A report by the CWDS[41] states that in spite of demands made for providing shelter homes and economic security to women, the state has continued to abdicate its responsibilities in terms of providing any substantial support.

Narayan[42] explained that there are contextual reasons as to why some aspects such as organization efforts around domestic violence receive less attention than others. She argued that in the West the demand for shelter homes by women's organizations was built around the availability of the basic infrastructure provided by other welfare schemes, such as unemployment benefits, provisions for public assistance, subsidized housing and free schooling for children. Also, there was no stigma attached to women living on their own. However, in India, welfare services, including education, medical care or legal aid, were virtually absent. All this, grouped with greater unemployment, makes it difficult for the movement to generate structures that would enable women to leave a violent relationship. Further, only a few women are in a position to materially support themselves. Also, the socio-cultural environment in India stigmatizes divorce and separation, and this deters women from leaving a violent relationship. The PWDVA emphasized the 'right to reside' within the shared household. However, no interventions have been made to address the structural inequalities within the social institutions, perhaps because there is a stiff resistance among communities regarding the reform of the personal laws and the issue was politicized after Shahbano's judgement. A severe confrontation took the form of communal riots, controversies and tensions among Hindu and Muslim communities.[43] The women's movement, therefore, while advocating for women's right to reside in the shared household, compromised on the right to housing, and this has adversely affected the rights of women.

Years after independence, when resources are generated, no efforts have been made by the state to support women. The law does not recognize the 'right to shelter' in situations where a woman seeks entry as a matter of choice. A destitute woman, one who is mentally challenged, a prostitute, a vagrant, a beggar woman or an offender woman may be institutionalized; however, in all such cases, she is not making a choice to do so. In all such circumstances, a woman is powerless or 'incapable' of making any decision for herself, and therefore it is not on her initiative that a woman is institutionalized; rather, she may be forcibly admitted there by the police or the family. Nevertheless, where a woman chooses to stay apart from her family, she is in no position to exercise freedom to select an institution, because such shelter homes or institutions hardly exist. Even in cases where women choose to stay separately from their natal as well as matrimonial family, the 'family ideology' prevents them from doing so.[44] Hence, a woman who is forced into institutional confinement is ostensibly released only in the custody of her family member or custodians without recognizing the fact that at times, the family members, perhaps, may be the reason why she requires special treatment or that the family has failed to take care of her and therefore she is being institutionalized.

Also, the shelter homes or the institutions for women which exist are few in number and are marked by stringent regulations. These are recognized as places where women inmates are confined and 'disciplined'. They need to conform to bureaucratic norms and may be punished, 'brutalized and bullied'[45] or face sexual abuse or other forms of violence. The opacity, absence of monitoring and deprivation, combined with dismal material conditions and corruption among functionaries, render these custodial institutions unfit and unwanted places to survive.[46] The ideologies and modalities in these institutions work similar to arrangements found in the patriarchal families and are based on the paradox that women, especially single women, must be confined to 'protect their sexuality' from the real and imagined fear about promiscuity, commercial sex, unregulated fertility and deviant sexuality, and therefore, legal, social, community, religious and state sanctions should be imposed.[47] Other institutions, such as working women hostels or the girls' hostels associated with the educational institutions, also enforce such norms where the 'protection of women's sexuality' is seen as a major concern and therefore stringent norms are administered and restrictions are placed on women's mobility.[48] This approach fails to diagnose the crisis and failure of the modern family to take care of its members. It is the family that neglects, aborts or abandons females or inflicts cruelty and discrimination and deprives them of care and resources. Therefore, the disabled, aged, orphans, widow, and disobedient wives and daughters are treated with cruelty or are left to fend for themselves.

The Justice Verma Committee noted,

> We further express our distress that the State has turned a blind eye to poor and destitute women, and women who are victims of domestic violence and who are unable to provide shelter for themselves. This fundamental lack of empathy, understanding and engagement reflects poorly on the State, which has the constitutional responsibility to provide for those who lack access to justice.[49]

It was further observed,

> Even though Section 6 of Protection of Women against Domestic Violence Act, 2005, provides victims of domestic violence to avail of the facility of shelter, we notice that the State has not made any such provision. We opine that the concept of 'shelter homes' under the said Act may be extended to the protection of destitute women. These homes, which serve as 'safe spaces' for destitute women, should not be confused with protection homes and corrective institutions under other statutes.

We recommend that the State should take the following actions: a) Safe spaces should be completely accessible to persons with disabilities in architectural design, management and provision of services. b) Residents of Safe Spaces to be trained and these institutions ought to be managed in a manner where the residents have a participatory role. c) Where destitute women have children, concrete linkages to child rights services. d) Institutional access to comprehensive health care services. e) Physical location of Safe Spaces should be centrally located with public services in close proximity and connected by public transport. f) Destitute women should not be institutionalized and sent to protective homes or beggar homes. They should also not to be sent to jails for their safe keeping. If necessary, steps are not taken by the State to provide basic amenities and guarantees in line with the Constitutional mandate, the State runs the risk of alienating its own citizens. We are phrasing this note of caution consciously."

Evolving rights of victims from a gender perspective

The rights of a victim under the criminal justice system as a subject has not received much attention from the judiciary or Parliament. The Supreme Court, in several of its decisions, has recognized the fact that victims and their families face a range of difficulties in getting the FIR registered.[50] Considering the ordeal of the victims during investigation and trial, the court has laid down several guidelines to protect the rights of victims,[51] including the protection of witnesses[52] as well as vulnerable witness,[53] discouraging the practice of obtaining adjournments,[54] the right of the victim to file an appeal in cases of acquittal and highlighting the importance of a victim's impact statement.[55] The Law Commission in its 154th Report in 1996 also dealt with the rights of victims and established a Victim Assistance Fund. The Nirbhaya Fund also was created in wake of the rape of Jyoti Singh in a moving bus in Delhi in December 2012. In its 221st Report, the Law Commission recommended for the right of a victim to file an appeal against an order or acquittal by the magistrate. However, the courts and the Parliament or the Law Commission have yet to focus on the rights of wives and children as victims of domestic violence. More specifically, in cases where women and children are in situations where no one else is there to support them the rights of victims need to be clearly spelled out.

Looking beyond the law and legal discourse

Currently, the law has a limited misogynist vision. It provides symptomatic relief and does not deal with the preventive aspects relating to the culture of violence. Both the law and society hardly can imagine the possibility of restructuring social relations that are egalitarian or uphold dignity and respect. What is celebrated is the sociopathic, narcissist, toxic, masculine culture which neither preserves the human element in a relationship nor does it trigger compassion.[56] The narratives of consumerist cultures that fuel fear, superstitions, conservatism and violence are frequently proliferated through the media and other social institutions. A fundamentally hostile culture is being reproduced by the obnoxious mix of religion and culture which reinforces hate – against minorities, against marginal communities and against women.[57]

To deal with such noxious discourse, it is essential to imagine an alternative rhetoric which is premised on the narrative of peace, justice, dignity, solidarity, compassion and rights. The pursuit of justice has been at the heart of feminist theory and practice. The aim is to examine the processes of material exploitation and epistemic violence from the gender perspective, as well as to outline strategies that may enable the climate of gender equality and encourage the participation of disenfranchised individuals in the access to and control over resources, thereby recognizing them as agents of change. Efforts may be made to enable the involvement of female citizens in social and political processes and institutions which are accountable to them. Contemporary discourses on gender justice are multi-dimensional and include discussions on agency, autonomy and the capabilities of women as political subjects and citizens with equal rights. The political context consists of questions relating to equal participation, rights, democratization and citizenship. Other questions relate to economic policies about access to and control over resources, issues of cultural politics and representation, discussions about judicial reform and practical matters of access to redress. Debates on justice are increasingly employing the model of intersectionality, which outlines how different forms of discrimination co-constitute each other, thereby producing particular conjunctures of vulnerability and inequality. Furthermore, the production of injustice is located in a range of interconnected socio-political institutions like the heteronormative family, the community, the market and the state. At the pragmatic level, therefore, there is a dire need to create support structures beyond the law.

Spivak[58] cautioned that law is an introductory strategy rather than a solution and that societal changes and legal reforms are mutually linked and together constitute a continuous, ongoing process of social and political negotiation. Haksar[59] points out the conflict with the tribal movements and argued, "I strongly feel that we should resort to the law only when the movement is strong enough to carry the law reform forward. In almost all such cases a legal battle should only supplement the political battle outside the courts". Thus, any legal struggle has to be strengthened by making political, economic and social interventions simultaneously. Law reform, in a regressive patriarchal society, in itself is not sufficient. An alliance between the dominant structures and the state has to be countered by a social movement where the law is just one component, and it has to be augmented by other necessary interventions.

There is an urgent need to create shelter homes where qualitative services are provided in terms of medical facilities, psychological and emotional support and legal aid. Providing financial support, employment security and economic support to survivors becomes essential to emancipate women, with a focus on the fundamental premises of dignity and autonomy. Short-term solutions such as short-stay homes to house abused women need to be created in addition to advocating for long-term solutions like reorienting gender roles and establishing socio-cultural and legal reforms, such as examining housing rights and the division of matrimonial property. In addition, there is a need to direct attention to the asymmetry and power in relationships besides challenging barriers to women's rights and equality. There is a need to critically scrutinize the institution of marriage with a gender lens. The dominant social arrangement that creates different realities for men and women needs to be questioned.

Against all odds: women's journey in the socio-legal realm

Women as citizens who approach the court with their individual struggles seeking legal interventions are not seen by the state as individual subjects who are demanding or claiming their rights. In fact, the state in cases of domestic violence views women with suspicion rather than as victims or the 'traditionally underprivileged' or 'naturally disadvantaged' category of persons being victimized in the power dynamics in the 'patriarchal' household. The state does not consider the fact that a woman files a complaint against her violent husband because 'circumstances are beyond her control'. Rather, the state construes a woman in a domestic violence situation as a person who is to be 'blamed', because all other women are deemed competent to handle the situation which these complainants could not. Or in extreme cases, victims are blamed for their misfortune. This approach of 'blaming the victim' fails to take a compassionate, humane approach, and instead women are frequently treated as mindless bodies incapable of making decisions and are to be used as vessels for producing and rearing children rather than as citizens or the holders of rights. Further, as complainants are defying the familial boundaries and are moving out to challenge the male hegemony, they are subjected to exploitation when already they are in a vulnerable situation leading to their marginalization and segmentation. Exclusive rights cannot be granted because they do not fit into the patriarchal category of being 'good' women. The constitutional commitments of equality and justice therefore do not translate easily into 'rights' or 'entitlements', and women's entitlements are betrayed because the law puts them into the category of 'bad', 'incompetent', 'shrewd' or 'defiant' women who have dared to challenge the patriarchy. They are treated as lesser beings when compared to the normative, tax-paying, able-bodied citizen and even less when compared to those women who go along with the patriarchal norms and comply with the dictates of patriarchy, thus leading to further discrimination and eventually to an endless cycle of vulnerability.

The general social perception guided by this approach, therefore, is that those who face violence within their homes and seek justice through the court are either 'helpless women victims' (*bechari*) or are shrewd 'disgruntled women' who file cases against their husbands and in-laws as part of a personal vendetta. However, this work indicates that women who dare to challenge the patriarchal norms do not fit into any of these categories. Women are not the silent victims of patriarchy; rather, they operate in their different capacities to negotiate within the given social order. Even in the most restricted environment, they make efforts to reduce violence and use the various informal and formal resources available within their immediate environment. These different forms of resistance by women challenge the image of 'always and already' victims that has been painted in the general rhetoric.[60] In the present work, I met women who are fighting their lonely battles, utilizing the legal platform to challenge the abusers. They are playing an active role in resisting violence, on one hand, and challenging the patriarchal hierarchical rigid social structures, on the other hand. They are defying norms and as agents of change are striving for justice with their resilience and grit. With little knowledge about the law or legal rights; few resources; and lack of physical, material or economic support, women have developed their own ideas pertaining to rights and justice within family relationships and are attempting to grapple with the patriarchy in their own unique way in spite of the fact that they have been culturally conditioned to believe that marriage is a sacred compulsion, whether violent or not, or that marriage is an undisputed institution that cannot be challenged or changed and that the existence of women apart from marriage is stigmatized and is unacceptable. Women in perilous life situations, after facing extreme situations of violence, are persistently negotiating around the deeply embedded patriarchal norms while exhibiting extraordinary courage and are marching ahead on their own. While engaging with the law, women are challenging the hegemonic constructions of gender identities in the courts, which are the male bastions and maintain patriarchal order. There is a need to reconsider the dynamics and to expand the options available for the survivors of abuse. Women are pushing to gain space using their constitutional and legal rights, thus making the constitution a living reality. They are asserting that values enshrined in the constitution are not based on the textual contents or academic ideas, but these are related to and affect their daily lives. Women, through sheer grit, are persisting and pushing the state to make their violent husbands accountable and to claim entitlements for self and children. The purpose of the law is to facilitate this autonomy, and those who implement the law need to connect to the realities of these women's lives.

The law should address the broader concerns of the patriarchal society

Domestic violence is not a personal problem or an individual issue. An act of violence, control or subjugation of women reinforces sexual inequalities in a larger social context. Wife battering therefore involves a complex situation which is surely more than a man-versus-woman issue. The law is not against men. Rather, it is against the oppressive system that subjugates men and women. Pitting women against men or women against women is not the agenda of the law. The purpose of the law is to act against the oppression women face within the four walls of their home and to transform the behavior of the perpetrators. The statement that the domestic violence law is misused ignores the fact that it has been formulated to protect women from violence and to transform the structural, systemic, historical and cultural roots of family violence. Domestic violence is a social phenomenon that needs to be dealt with from multi-dimensional perspectives with a focus on the hegemonic regressive culture that induces and allows such abuse. "To see domestic violence in terms of man woman relationship would be to miss the essence of the problem, which is the institutionalized nature of female second-class citizenship".[61] The law is enacted to deal with the systemic abuse of power against the powerless. At a broader level, the aim of the law is to contest the patriarchy within homes, eliminate violence and create democratic family structures where women's autonomy is enhanced.

The way forward

> "The law should not be seen to sit by limply, while those who defy it go free, and those who seek its protection lose hope".[62]

It is crucial that the voices of women who have been oppressed within families be heard and the law against domestic violence, both criminal and civil, provide a platform to raise and to effectively address such concerns. However, this has not been happening. Though the PWDVA, despite its limitations, has been used creatively and imaginatively at several places by maneuvering women's rights within the patriarchal framework, at most of the places and in most of the cases it has failed to support the egalitarian domestic framework. While the law tries to bring order to the family, the law itself has been mediated by and enmeshed in a complex cultural framework of saving the institution of family rather than protecting the dignity of women within the families. The legislative framework fulfills most of the requirements as prescribed by the international human rights standards, yet loopholes exist at various levels. Due to technical and other reasons, many survivors cannot receive proper remedies under the law, and above all, this law itself provides for temporary relief until a woman 'compromises' or 'reconciles' with her violent husband or until she ends her marital relation through divorce – the law may help her, but not beyond that. The domestic violence law has neither offered permanent solutions to the battered wives nor it has deterred violence. Also, essential provisions relating to economic or material support for women by the state are not provided. The law has failed to look imaginatively beyond the *sasural* and *maika* network into the reality of the women's lives who decided to speak against the violence.

This work highlights the fact that the coordination between the survivors and the service providers is confounded because of reasons such as lack of awareness and sensitization among different stakeholders, subjectivities involved or their approach and attitude. An overburdened system and limited resources have added to the chaos. Institutional and cultural barriers hinder the effective functioning of the legislative framework. The freedom available to an individual woman to write her own future after leaving the site of violence is not available, which often compels her to stay within a violent home. The family perpetuates unequal gender roles; therefore, to fight violence implies a restructuring of the family as an institution and the democratization of familial relations. The solutions therefore are required to be sought within the social fabric to balance the unequal power equation.

Further, it is also recommended that the mechanism created under law needs to be strengthened. Recruitment, training, facilities and support to police and POs is just one aspect that needs to be examined besides increasing their numbers. Gender sensitization programs are crucial. The infrastructure as provided under the act that includes medical facilities, shelter homes and childcare facilities, among other components, needs to be strengthened to provide safety and security to women in vulnerable situations. Making and implementing safety plans and the rehabilitation of survivors require special attention. Preventive interventions with regard to the safety and security of women and children in at-risk situations is essential. Special schemes and facilities such as finding jobs for survivors, special fee concessions and support during school or college admissions to the children surviving situations of violence are some of the decisions that could be made at the policy level. There is a need to build in a principle of accountability to ensure that laws are properly implemented by the agencies who are entrusted with the task. Addressing the gap in the institutional processes and mechanism is required while creating an enabling environment to ensure that the rights of the women and children are protected. A monitoring mechanism, as well as periodic review of the implementation, is essential. The cases of violence should be taken up on a priority basis without any delay in a time-sensitive manner.

The state is responsible for protecting the rights of women and children and is under a constitutional obligation to uphold women's rights as equal citizens. It is also necessary to root out and check discriminatory practices against women within private and public spaces. Further, it is also recommended that providing matrimonial property rights is essential so that women can claim their entitlements in a marriage. Merely providing the right to maintenance or *streedhan* is insufficient. The majority of women work hard, doing all forms of visible and invisible work, without being paid or acknowledged for their contribution. Those who work in the informal sector remain highly underpaid. A large number of women hold almost no property in their name. In matrimonial homes, women are in a vulnerable position because of their economic and social dependence on their husbands and in-laws. The goal of equality proclaimed in the constitution remains a dream for many, despite decades of independence. Though laws have been enacted to even out the socio-economic disparity, the social reality has remained unchanged. It is suggested that effective social protection measures be carved out to ensure that women's right to a life with dignity is recognized legally and social measures may be evolved include *rozi-roti aur maakan* (employment and housing) with *sammaan* or dignity to survivors and victims of domestic violence.

This work recommends that there is a need to push the idea of the 'personal is political' and create a space where abused women within families are not seen as moral subjects but as citizens vested with rights. The idea is to demand for rights-based justice in order to support women who are defying the orthodox norms. The potential of the law has to be strengthened by the accompanying socio-political struggle at a broader level. Challenging the dominant discourse that reinforces women's subjugation is essential, and the limitations of law need to be questioned. There is a need to draw linkages between the law reform and the broader social movement towards women's liberation. Or as Wendy Brown[63] said, that sharing of power and not regulation, freedom not protection, is a true affirmation of democracy which may end the marginalization of women within families. In other words, justice is a major concern of law and society, and women cannot be deprived of this. Women's groups have demanded that the domestic violence law be reformed. Currently, there is a backlash and the state, under pressure, is diluting the law through its decisions and orders, yet survivors who are wronged have been challenging their violent husbands and are determined to seek justice. They are knocking on the doors of the courts, forcing the system to respond. And until violence is eliminated, those oppressed will keep on challenging oppression and will keep on reclaiming justice while shaking the roots of the patriarchy. When those in power argue 'There Is No Alternative' to justify capitalism,[64] there are voices which say 'Another World Is Possible'.

Notes

1 Zinn Howard (1999) *A People's History of the United States*, Harper-perennial Modern Classics, New York
2 Pence E and Paymar M (1993) *Education Groups for Men Who Batter: The Duluth Model*, Springer, New York
3 Pence E and Dasgupta S (2006) *Re-examining Battering: Are All Acts of Violence Against the Intimate Partner the Same?* Praxis International, USA, www.ncdsv.org/images/Praxis_ReexaminingBattering_June2006.pdf accessed on 20.02.13
4 Gupte M and More A (2010) *Chakrabedh: Coil of Domestic Violence and Safety Measures* (Hindi) MASUM, Pune
5 As reported by Menon Parvathi (1999) Focus on Domestic Violence, *The Frontline*, 16 (18)

6 National Crime Record Bureau (2016) *Crimes in India*, Government of India
7 This is a term used in several Western countries, which shows how the system has been exploited by those who are powerful to gag the voices of those who speak against wrongs.
8 In the recent matter of the harassment of an ex-employee by the chief justice of India, women's organizations protesting have raised this issue with slogans as 'Due Process not Dude Process'.
9 Supra
10 Parashar A (1997) Family Law as a Means for Ensuring Gender Justice for Indian Women, *Indian Journal for Gender Studies*, 4 (2) 199–229 Also De Rohit (2018) *The People's Constitution: The Everyday Life of Law in The Indian Republic*, Princeton University Press, Princeton, NJ
11 Kapur and Cossman (1996) supra
12 Bell hooks (1990) Marginality as a Site of Resistance, http://pzacad.pitzer.edu/~mma/teaching/MS80/readings/hooks.pdf accessed on 03.07.14
13 Nigam S (2014) From the Margins, Revisiting the Concept of Marginalized Women, *Countercurrents*, September 3
14 Cole D (1984) Strategies of Differences: Litigating for Women's Rights in a Man's World, *Law and Inequality: A Journal of Theory and Practice*, 2 (1) 33–96
15 Smart Carol (1984) *The Ties That Bind: Law, Marriage and the Reproduction of Patriarchal Relations*, Routledge and Kegan Paul, London
16 Nigam S (2008) Legal Literacy: A Tool for Empowerment, *Social Action*, 2 (3) 82–91
17 Schneider EM (1986) Describing and Changing: Women's Self-Defense Work and the Problem of Expert Testimony on Battering, *Law Reporter*, 9 (195) 214
18 Gilligan Carol (1982) *In a Different Voice: Psychological Theory and Women's Development*, Harvard University Press, Cambridge
19 Rawat VS (2018) UP's Cow Protection Agenda: Yogi Govt Allocates 816 million for Gaushalas, *The Business Standard*, July 5, https://www.business-standard.com/article/economy-policy/up-s-cow-protection-agenda-yogi-govt-allocates-rs-816-mn-for-gaushalas-118070500760_1.html
20 Bisht G (2018) Himachal Pradesh Levies Cess On Liquor to Run Gaushala, *The Hindustan Times*, March 10, https://www.hindustantimes.com/india-news/hp-to-levy-cess-on-liquor-funds-to-go-towards-maintenance-of-cow-sheds/story-LZgBBJV9ZFyveXsmMF1tsO.html
21 Dwary A (2018) Shivraj Chouhan Announces ow Ministry for Madhya Pradesh Ahead of Polls, *The Times of India*, September 30, https://timesofindia.indiatimes.com/india/ahead-of-polls-shivraj-singh-chouhan-announces-to-set-up-cow-ministry-in-mp/articleshow/66019099.cms
22 *India Today* (2018) India's First Cow Minister Otaram Dewasi Loses Sirohi Seat in Rajasthan, December 11
23 DeCrow K (1975) *Sexist Justice*, Vintage, New York p. 3
24 Justice Verma Committee Report Page 63
25 Often those in power allege that most of the people-friendly laws have been misused. So not only the domestic violence laws but also those relating to rape or sexual harassment, or even the SC/ST Atrocities Prevention Act or the RTI, have all been alleged to be abused. Laws which are actually misused, such as those relating to sedition, UAPA, AFPSA and several others, against which civil society has been raising its voice, have not been considered for amendments by the state as yet.
26 Nigam Shalu (2017) *Is Domestic Violence a Lesser Crime? Countering Backlash Against Section 498A*, Occasional Paper CWDS, New Delhi
27 Ghosh Biswajit and Choudhuri T (2011) Legal Protection Against Domestic Violence in India: Scope and Limitations, *Journal of Family Violence*, 26, 319, 323

28 Sumana Bhasin vs Niraj Bhasin Cri. Complaint No. 316/3/2007 PS NFC MM Court Saket Pronounced on 27.5.2015
29 Jaising Indira (2016) Domestic Violence Victims Now Have Access to Justice, *The Livemint*, October 28, https://www.livemint.com/Opinion/g27TCzrZfM8Y8kSZ8Fxu2L/Domestic-violence-victims-now-have-access-to-justice.html
30 Agnihotri I and R Parliwala (1993) *Traditions, the Family and the State: Politics of Contemporary Women's Movement*, Mimeograph, Centre for Contemporary Studies, Nehru Memorial and Museum Library, New Delhi p. 3
31 McIntosh Mary (1978) *The State and the Oppression of Women in Feminism and Materialism*, edited by A Kuhn and A Wolpe, Routledge and Kegan Paul, London
32 CEDAW (2013) General recommendation on article 16 of the Convention on the Elimination of All Forms of Discrimination against Women, CEDAW /C/GC/29 February 26, http://www2.ohchr.org/english/bodies/cedaw/docs/comments/CEDAW-C-52-WP-1_en.pdf accessed on 29.04.16
33 Rajan (2003) supra
34 This was evident when a dismissed female employee alleged sexual harassment by the chief justice of the Supreme Court, and in the aftermath many judges asked for male staff at their residential offices. *Latestlaw.com* (2019) Effect of Allegation Against CJI: Many Supreme Court Judges Asked for Male Staff at the Residential Office, April 23
35 Kabeer N and Subrahmanian R (1996) *Institutions, Relations and Outcomes: Framework and Tools for Gender Aware Planning*, IDS Discussion Paper, UK
36 Friedan B (1963) *The Feminine Mystique*, WW Norton Company Inc, New York p. 31
37 Seema vs Ashwini Kumar AIR 2006 SC 1158
38 *The Hindu Business Line* (2012) Maharashtra Bill Widens Women's Rights Over Husbands Property, March 11
39 Law Commission of India (2018) *Consultation Paper on Reform of Family Law*, August 31, Government of India, New Delhi
40 Ibid pp. 29–30
41 Sharma K (2010) *Changing the Terms of Discourse: Gender Equality and the Indian State*, General Editor V Mazumdar, Pearson, New Delhi
42 Narayan Uma (1997) *Dislocating Cultures: Identities, Traditions and the Third World Feminism*, Routledge New York
43 Rajan S (2004) Rethinking Law and Violence: The Domestic Violence (Prevention) Bill in India, 2002, *Gender and History*, 16, 769–93
44 Arora S (2017) No Room for Single Women, *The Asian Age*, February 5, https://www.asianage.com/life/more-features/050217/no-room-for-single-women.html
45 Joint Women Programme (1991) Women Towards Beijing, *Lokayan Bulletin*, 12 (1–2) 67–73
46 *The Telegraph* (2019) Criminal Apathy in Shelter Homes for Women and Children, February 11, https://www.telegraphindia.com/opinion/criminal-apathy-in-shelter-homes-for-women-and-children/cid/1684159
47 Narayan (1997) supra n 42
48 *Newsclick* (2018) Pinjra Tod Activists Protest Against Hostel Curfews in Delhi University, October 9, https://www.newsclick.in/pinjra-tod-activists-protest-against-hostel-curfews-delhi-university
49 Justice Verma Committee Report (2013) Report of the Committee on Amendments to Criminal Law, Government of India, pp. 270–71
50 Lalita Kumari vs Government of Uttar Pradesh (2014) 2 SCC 1
51 Sakshi vs Union of India (2004) 5 SCC 518

52 State vs Sanjeev Nanda (2012) 8 SCC 450; Mahendar Chawla vs Union of India 2018 (15) SCALE 497
53 Sampurna Behura vs Union of India (2018) 4 SCC 433
54 State of UP vs Shambhu Nath Singh (2001) 4 SCC 667
55 Mallikarjun Kodagali vs State of Karnataka 2019 2 SCC 752
56 Nigam S (2018) The Cult of 56 Inches and Toxic Masculinity, *Countercurrents*, June 23
57 Naqvi F (2019) For the BJP, 'Women's Rights' Are Really All About Men, *The Wire*, April 24
58 Spivak Gayatri C (2010) *Situating Feminism, Beatrice Bain Research Group Annual Key Note Lecture*, Program In Critical Theory, University Of California At Berkeley, 26 February
59 Haksar Nandita (1999) Human Rights Lawyering: A Feminist Perspective, In *Engendering Law: Essays in Honour of Lotika Sarkar*, edited by Amita Dhanda and Archana Prashar, Eastern Book Company, Lucknow pp. 86–87
60 Mohanty-Talpade C (1984) Under Western Eyes, *Boundaries*, 12 (3) 333–46
61 Women Speak: United Voices Against Globalization, Poverty and Violence in India
62 Jennison vs Baker (1972) 1 All ER 997
63 Brown Wendy (1995) *States of Injury: Power and Freedom in Late Modernity*, Princeton University Press, NJ
64 Flanders Laura (2013) At Thatcher's Funeral, Bury TINA Too, *The Nation*, April 12

Glossary

Bechari: A vulnerable or powerless woman in a helpless situation.
Brahmin: The topmost rank as per the Hindu varna system.
Chappals: Kind of footwear.
Char-diwari: Four walls of the house.
Daman: Oppression.
Dampatya: Conjugal life.
Dasi: Enslaved women.
Dharma: Moral and spiritual duty.
Dharamshastras: Ancient legal text from where many of the Hindu laws are derived.
Ghristha: Family life.
Huzur: Formally addressing men of honor.
Kanyadaan: The practice where the father donates a daughter, along with the gifts and money or *dakshina* (donation), to a man. Gifts cannot be taken back; similarly, the daughter, once gone, cannot be accepted back in her natal family.
Karta: Coparcener in the Hindu undivided family who is responsible for managing its affairs and assets.
Karvachauth: A cultural practice in the Hindu tradition which is celebrated with much hype where a woman observes a fast for the long life of her husband, which is glamourized by television serials and Bollywood.
Khap Panchayat: Community organization representing a clan or a group of clans in North India that may exert significant social influence despite of the fact that it is not legally recognized.
Maika: Natal house.
Mangalsutra: An auspicious thread or necklace tied by the groom around the neck of the wife which identifies her as a married woman.
Manglik: Superstition based on Hindu traditions where someone born under the influence of the planet Mars is considered as having Mangal dosh, or Mars defects, which is inauspicious, and his or her marriage with a person who is non-*Manglik* is perceived as disastrous.

Manusmriti: Ancient legal text among many of the Hindu religion used to formulate Hindu laws by the colonial rulers.

Meher: Also known as dower or bride wealth and refers to a payment specified at the time of marriage from the husband or his family to his wife to support her in the event of separation, divorce or his death.

Roti: Popular bread in North India that is round in shape.

Samjhauta: Compromise.

Sanskaar: Social and moral values.

Sasural: Matrimonial house.

Saptapadi: As per Hindu marriage rituals, the bride and groom take seven steps around the sacred fire accompanied by seven resolutions.

Streedhan: The exclusive and absolute property of a married woman under the Hindu law mainly consisting of gold and other valuables given to a woman at the time of her marriage. Under Section 406 IPC, a woman can file a complaint for the criminal breach of trust and can demand the return of her *streedhan*.

Index

For Product Safety Concerns and Information please contact our EU representative GPSR@taylorandfrancis.com
Taylor & Francis Verlag GmbH, Kaufingerstraße 24, 80331 München, Germany

www.ingramcontent.com/pod-product-compliance
Ingram Content Group UK Ltd.
Pitfield, Milton Keynes, MK11 3LW, UK
UKHW020017200926
475702UK00014B/1935

* 9 7 8 0 3 6 7 7 7 7 7 1 5 *